PENGUIN AFRICAN LIBRARY AP8

Editor: Ronald Segal

South Africa's Hostages

JACK HALPERN

South Africa's Hostages

Basutoland, Bechuanaland and Swaziland

Penguin Books

Penguin Books Ltd, Harmondsworth, Middlesex, England
Penguin Books Inc., 3300 Clipper Mill Road, Baltimore 11, Md, U.S.A.
Penguin Books Pty Ltd, Ringwood, Victoria, Australia

First published 1965
Copyright © Jack Halpern, 1965

Made and printed in Great Britain by
Cox & Wyman Ltd, London, Reading and Fakenham
Set in Monotype Plantin

N 106

FOR SOPHIE

Contents

Abbreviations

A.N.C.	African National Congress
B.A.C.T.U.	Basutoland Congress of Trade Unions
B.A.D.	Department of Bantu Administration and Development
B.C.P.	Basutoland Congress Party
B.D.A.	Bamangwato Development Association
B.D.P.	Bechuanaland Democratic Party
B.F.L.	Basutoland Federation of Labour
B.N.P.	Basutoland National Party
B.P.P.	Bechuanaland People's Party
C.D.C.	Commonwealth (Colonial) Development Corporation
C.D. & W.F.	Colonial Development and Welfare Fund
C.P.L.	Communist Party of Lesotho (Basutoland)
F.M.P.	Freedom-Marema Tlou Party
N.N.L.C.	Ngwane National Liberatory Congress
P.A.C.	Pan-African Congress
S.D.P.	Swaziland Democratic Party

ABBREVIATIONS

S.N.C.	Swazi National Council
S.P.P.	Swaziland Progressive Party
U.B.B.S.	University of Basutoland, Bechuanaland and Swaziland
U.S.A.	United Swaziland Association

Acknowledgements

The attempt to write a comprehensive book on modern Basutoland, Bechuanaland, and Swaziland, either singly or collectively,
has not as far as I know, been made before. In rashly undertaking
it, I soon discovered why. Not only is there a dearth even of
specialized writing on the Territories; there is an almost total lack
of reliable statistics. Officials struggling with reports and development 'plans' have been only too ready to tell me that their figures
are for the most part really 'guestimates'. They now have my
fullest sympathy, as well as my warm thanks for the ready
assistance which they have given me during a 12,000-mile trip,
lasting five months, through the Territories, in Cape Town,
Pretoria, and in London.

In particular, I would like to record my thanks to Sir John
Maud, formerly High Commissioner for Basutoland, the
Bechuanaland Protectorate, and Swaziland; Mr C. R. Lattimer,
chief secretary of the High Commissioner's Office; Sir Peter
Fawcus, Queen's Commissioner for the Bechuanaland Protectorate, and, amongst his staff, particularly Major Alan Donald, Mr
Masubula Sinombe, and Mr Phil Steenkamp; Sir Brian Marwick,
who recently retired as Queen's Commissioner for Swaziland,
and Mr Athel Long, Swaziland Government Secretary; Mr
A. G. T. Chaplin, formerly Resident Commissioner of Basutoland, Mr Gordon Hector, Basutoland Government Secretary and
some-time Acting Resident Commissioner, and, amongst their
staff, particularly Mr Bert Youngjohns and Mr Peter Stutley, and
Mr Percy Selwyn, Senior Economic Advisor at the Colonial
Office. To Mrs Peggy Donald, who nursed me through tick-bite
fever contracted in Bechuanaland, I remain deeply grateful.

In the Territories, too, I was privileged to draw heavily on the
time and invaluable knowledge of the leaders of all political

ACKNOWLEDGEMENTS

parties; His Highness Moeshoeshoe II of Basutoland; The Ngwenyama, Sobhuza II of Swaziland; Chief Bathoen and other Senior chiefs in Bechuanaland; members of the Legislative and Advisory Councils; educationalists, doctors, trade unionists, churchmen, traders, peasants, workers, and a host of others. My very warm thanks go to them all; if they think this book useful I shall feel well satisfied.

To Professor Julius Lewin of the University of the Witwatersrand, who was responsible for my undertaking the writing of this book, I have long owed a special debt which is now further increased. Mr T. R. Betts of Oxfam, Miss Mary Benson, and Mr John Lang have all been generous with their time and knowledge, and Professor J. F. Holleman kindly allowed me to draw on the Social Survey of Swaziland which he directed.

In tracking down such material on the Territories as does exist, I was greatly helped by Mr Philip Laundy, formerly Librarian of the Southern Rhodesia Legislative Assembly; Mrs Betty Lunn of the Library of the University of the Witwatersrand; Miss Jane Symonds and the staff of the Africa Bureau; Mr R. M. Bostock of Edinburgh University; and the staff of the Colonial Office Library. Mrs Bobby Vanderwaal and Mrs Margaret Moore of Salisbury, Southern Rhodesia, and Mrs Bessie White and Miss Margot Light of London were most helpful with the typing and checking of the manuscript.

My thanks are due, too, to Mr Ronald Segal for his patience in awaiting the completion of this book, which was substantially delayed by my arbitrary expulsion by Sir Roy Welensky and Mr Winston Field from the then Federation of Rhodesia and Nyasaland in October 1963. In the event, it went to press before the 1965 elections in Basutoland and Bechuanaland, and I have been able merely to indicate their course and results in the brief notes which have been appended.

Finally, my debt to my wife defies description. Without her this book would not now be published. Its errors of fact or judgement are, of course, mine alone; I can only hope that it will help to make the three Territories better known at a time when their peoples are daily more in need of good friends.

JACK HALPERN

London, January 1965

Foreword

There are countries whose claim on the attention of humanity lies not in lavish natural resources, the large number of their inhabitants, or their strategic value in some potential conflict, but in their want, the very powerlessness of their condition. Such are the three High Commission Territories of Basutoland, Bechuanaland and Swaziland, still under British rule but advancing with deceptive ease to independence. Some eighty years of diligent imperial disregard have reduced them to no more than economic satellites of neighbouring South Africa, whose markets they supply with such of their produce as they can spare, and whose mines and factories and farms they supply with their men.

So appalling a dependence would be dangerous enough if the three Territories possessed a system of government approved by the rulers of South Africa; that they should be developing a system instead considered altogether repugnant and even hostile, that their very separate existence should be opposed, makes the character of their approaching independence uniquely vulnerable. What will they do? If they persist in promoting popular government, South Africa must fear the effect on her own deprived peoples and subject the Territories to strong, even irresistible pressures. If they accept a system of government which South Africa approves, they must adopt a subservient tribalism that will make their independence meaningless and all enjoyment of individual freedom impossible. If they draw closer to South Africa, they must sever themselves from African sentiment in the rest of the continent as well as from their own popular aspirations; if they draw away, they must prepare themselves for siege and conceivably mass starvation. Whichever way they turn, the direction they face is cruel.

Such, it seems, is to be the last scene of Britain's imperial play, though one would scarcely credit it from the common British comments on the action so far. Improbably, from a multitude of speeches by British politicians and officials, from the memoirs of former colonial servants and the application of academic apologists, a myth has emerged – of a Britain that stumbled upon her colonies by mistake, as in some thick historical fog; retained them with reluctance and at enormous cost; developed their economies and indigenous administrations as an act of disinterested service; and released them as soon as their citizens appeared properly prepared for independence.

One does not have to reduce British rule to the desolating presence of Belgium in the Congo to chart a vast discrepancy between such comment and the facts. For with what in the world but the expansion of power and wealth is colonialism concerned? Britain seized or accepted under her protection such parts of Africa as were economically or strategically of some advantage to her; she developed such industry and cash crop agriculture as would make her rule profitable if possible and, if not, at least cheap; she encouraged such education and training as in the main would facilitate government and commerce; and when repression promised to be more costly in the long run than retreat, she released her captives with much of her influence and most of her investments intact. Such service as she gave in the preparation for self-government was a by-product of the direct imperial purpose, not part of a secular crusade. If she left some of her colonies better equipped to face the modern world than she had found them, she did so in the process of extracting considerable wealth over the years for herself; if she showed herself willing to cut her losses when they began to outweigh her gains, it was because on the whole she was not stupid.

What disinterested service lay in developing the Zambia Copperbelt, or mining gold and promoting cocoa cultivation in Ghana? But without cheaply exploitable minerals or easily marketable crops, the three High Commission Territories received no more substantial investment than imperial protection. They were merely strategic real estate, limiting the expansionism of others and, subsequently in addition, offering South Africa an inducement to conduct herself congenially. Yet the Territories could not be permitted to cost Britain anything, and since their only realizable assets seemed to lie in the abundance of men whom poverty made readily available for export, Britain encouraged the recruitment of migrant labour for use by South African mines, factories and farms, so serving the dual purpose of relieving imperial responsibilities and cultivating cheaply the fields of British investment. It was a profitable partnership with white supremacy in South Africa, but one that events in Africa and the world beyond have made it necessary now to dissolve. With the geographical situation of the three Territories less a strategic advantage than a political embarrassment, with the cost of continuing to administer them an increasing nuisance, and with demands by their inhabitants for independence an adequate excuse, cut-price disengagement offers obvious attractions. They are attractions which Britain, or those able to influence her, must resolutely resist.

Basutoland, Bechuanaland, and Swaziland must be granted their independence – but with a democratic system of government firmly established in each, with the provision of sufficient aid to produce a significant measure of economic strength, and with clear guarantees of assistance in the event of any clash with South Africa. Britain, indeed, faces her most strenuous test in the three Territories – not because they are among the most valuable possessions she has ever had, but precisely because they are among the least, whose proper development carries the risk of a break between Britain and South Africa, and so an end to the prosperous appeasement of apartheid. If Britain fails the test, because it is so much easier and cheaper in the short run to fail, she will have done more than discard over one million people to the consequences of her greed and neglect. She will have exploded her own pretensions to an ultimately constructive mission in Africa; she will have blasted her own past. Those three weak Territories in Southern Africa are much more than themselves; they bear the burden of a whole imperial myth. And it matters to the future of Britain no less than to her past that in her treatment of the Territories now she should give some reality to the myth.

RONALD SEGAL

Part One

Introductory

1 A Slight Case of Kidnapping

One dark, misty night in August 1961, a party of six masked men in plain clothes secretly crossed the mountain border from South Africa into Basutoland and made their way to an isolated hut standing 683 yards inside British territory.

Inside the hut three men were sleeping. One of them, Anderson Ganyile, had sought refuge in Basutoland nearly a year earlier after being banished without trial to a remote area of South Africa for his resistance to the policy of apartheid. With him in the hut now were his brother and a friend.

The masked men rapped on the door, demanding admittance, and one of them announced that he was its absentee owner. Then they broke the door open and rushed into the hut. As they did so, one of them let out a scream of pain: he had been greeted with a glancing blow in the face from an axe. The fierce fight which ensued ended when one of the masked men flourished a revolver and threatened to shoot Ganyile and his companions if they didn't come quietly.

Handcuffing and gagging their captives, the masked men forced them at gun-point to walk across country towards the six-stranded barbed wire fence which marks the international border, carefully avoiding the Basutoland mounted police border post a thousand yards away. Then, having negotiated the fence, the party drove off into the night in two waiting cars bearing false number plates.

Anderson Ganyile and his two companions had been kidnapped on British territory by the South African political police, but it was to be three weeks before anyone else had the slightest idea of what had happened. Ganyile's isolated mountain hut was rarely seen by casual travellers, and he had kept himself aloof from the nearby border post, which the kidnappers had been so careful not to disturb on the night of 26 August.

Anderson Ganyile had long been regarded as an enemy by Dr Verwoerd's Government. A member of the Pondo tribe, he had been expelled from Fort Hare University College for opposing the introduction of Bantu Education, which Bishop Trevor Huddlestone has rightly called Education for Slavery. Politically active, he had then been among the hundreds arbitrarily imprisoned by the South African Government during the State of Emergency which followed the Sharpeville massacre in 1960. Released after four months, he had returned to his home in Pondoland, and there become one of the leaders in the Pondo resistance movement to the stooge Bantu Authorities system, a resistance so strong that the Government had declared a State of Emergency in Pondoland in November 1960.

On 7 November, Ganyile had been arrested in Pondoland and immediately deported to indefinite banishment on a remote farm called Frenchdale, where several African leaders were rotting their lives out already without charge or trial. One deportee whom Ganyile found at Frenchdale, a deposed chief, had been there for twelve years.

In Ganyile's own words:

There is nothing whatever to do at Frenchdale. All the people can do is sit in their huts and rot. I was informed that the Government supplied rations to the value of £1 10s. per month and ten shillings cash monthly for the maintenance of the people detained there. . . .

For a twenty-five-year-old militant this had been no enchanting prospect. Ganyile had escaped from Frenchdale in December 1960 and made his way for refuge to Basutoland. He had reported to the British authorities, and applied for a permanent residence permit, which is mandatory after the three months' temporary residence which is open to any visitor.

Having complied with the Basutoland regulations, Anderson Ganyile had then lived undisturbed at Quacha's Nek until he was kidnapped on 26 August 1961. For three weeks thereafter, no one missed him.

On 15 September, however, a scribbled note reached Ganyile's friends in the South African resistance movement. It read: 'Kidnapped in Basutoland on 28/6/61 at 10.30 p.m. by 6 policemen from the Union. We were three and are all now in KD and appeal to friends. We know and can identify our kidnappers. Yours, Powers.'

Powers was the pseudonym used in his political work by Ganyile, and the note was unquestionably in his handwriting. KD is a common way of referring to Kokstad, a town in the Transkei area of South Africa.

A friend of Ganyile's who received a message at this time hurried to his hut; almost everything in it seemed to have been thrown about and a blanket was covered with dried blood. He immediately reported to the Basutoland police post at the near-by village of Quacha's Nek, who took possession of the blood-stained blanket. This was on 15 September, and the first official theory was that Ganyile and his friends had been the victims of ritual murder.

The story of the kidnapping was broken a few days later with banner headlines by *New Age*, a small and courageous anti-apartheid weekly, now banned, published in Cape Town. Ganyile's jail note was photostatically reproduced on its front page. In the week following, senior officers of the South African police, including the chief of the political police, Colonel Prinsloo, and the border area commandant, blandly denied any knowledge of a kidnapping.

The British authorities, for their part, were prompt with statements and conclusions comforting to the South Africans. It had taken the Basutoland police six days to decide to send Ganyile's blood-stained blanket for analysis to the South African Institute for Medical Research.* Yet one day later, on 22 September, Basutoland's Government Secretary declared that 'the (Basutoland) Executive Council was not aware of the alleged (kidnapping) incident'.†

Moreover, within a week after Ganyile's note had been published, Basutoland's then Resident Commissioner, Mr A. G. T. Chaplin, stated that investigations so far had disclosed that it was most unlikely that South African police had entered Basutoland to kidnap the three men.‡

At the lower levels, however, at least one South African official

---

* Information from statement by the Institute's Director, published in *Contact* on 8 March 1962.

† *Cape Times*, 25 September 1961.

‡ *New Age*, 28 September 1961.

was less discreet. A police station commander at Kokstad told a lawyer who was trying to trace Ganyile that 'three Basuto were brought in about a fortnight ago'. When the lawyer persevered with his inquiries, a police sergeant told him: 'This is a Special Branch matter. Ring them. I do know about this. Ganyile is not here. He is being held somewhere in the Transkei.'*

The Special Branch proved inaccessible to the lawyer, and both the British and South African authorities remained quite unmoved by the sergeant's statements when *New Age* published them on 28 September.

Nor did Sir John Maud, Britain's ambassador to the Republic of South Africa and High Commissioner for Basutoland, the Bechuanaland Protectorate and Swaziland, discernibly lift a diplomatic finger when *New Age*, which was the recognized voice of the African National Congress Alliance in South Africa, followed these revelations by warning:

Britain is strong enough to get Ganyile out of prison tomorrow. If she fails to do this, Africa will accuse Britain of joining hands with Verwoerd to help keep a South African freedom fighter in jail.

Meanwhile, the South African Government continued officially to ignore the whole affair. After Ganyile's kidnapping, it had committed him and his two companions to jails in the Transkei area, there to be held indefinitely, with neither charge nor trial, at the pleasure of the police. They were, in fact, in solitary confinement and being interrogated.

Unofficially, the South Africans brazened out their embarrassment. *Die Burger*, an official organ of the ruling Nationalist Party, reported on 27 September that 'in Government circles' the kidnapping was regarded as 'complete nonsense'. It had been told on good authority that if the three men were in custody they must have been caught in South Africa and not in Basutoland.

By now, however, the case was beginning to attract wider interest. British newspaper correspondents had taken up the reports in *New Age* and in *Contact*, another courageous anti-apartheid paper, which in turn led South African English-language papers to report it more fully. The leader of Basutoland's major political party, Mr Ntsu Mokhehle, strongly

* *New Age*, 28 September 1961.

demanded action in the Basutoland National Council to secure the return of the three kidnapped men, and in South Africa the former Secretary-General of the banned African National Congress, Advocate Duma Nokwe, sent the British Labour Party leader, Mr Hugh Gaitskell, a cable which read in part: 'Appalled this South African aggression within British borders and the failure of British protection. Appeal strongest action.' Representatives abroad of the banned South African anti-apartheid organizations took up the matter.

Friends in Britain did try to take action, and on 29 September Mr Bernard Braine, Britain's Under-Secretary for Common-wealth Relations, received a delegation of M.P.s which included Mr Fenner Brockway and Mr Jeremy Thorpe. Mr Braine told them that the British Government had 'insufficient evidence to establish that Basutoland's borders had recently been violated by the South African police', but that 'investigations were still going on'. The M.P.s nevertheless gained the clear impression that 'the Minister was most anxious that an inquiry should be pursued with vigour and speed'.*

It soon appeared, however, that the only people who would actually do anything to find Ganyile and set him free were his friends and fellow-opponents of apartheid both in South Africa and in Basutoland, who felt – and indeed were – threatened if Ganyile's kidnapping were allowed to go unchallenged, for this would put an end to Basutoland as an island of freedom and refuge in South African territory.

In Basutoland, a demand was made in the Legislative Council at the beginning of October for the creation of a British commission of inquiry which would demand facilities from South Africa to visit Ganyile and to take his evidence. Within the week, this demand, made by Mr Khaketla of the Freedom Party, was forcibly backed up by the leader of the majority Congress Party, Mr Mokhehle, in personal calls on the Resident Commissioner and the Paramount Chief.

Then, on 5 October, it was announced that an application for *habeas corpus* would be made to the South African Supreme Court by Ganyile's uncle. His mother had collapsed on hearing of her son's arrest.

* Hansard, House of Commons, 16 November 1961, column 640.

Meanwhile, misgivings about the thoroughness of the investigations conducted by the Basutoland police were hardly allayed when the then editor of *Contact*, Mr Patrick Duncan, visited Ganyile's hut on 3 October and found, two and a half weeks after the police search, pieces of blood-stained cardboard which seemed to have been used as shutters for the windows.*

It was now nearly three weeks since the story of Ganyile's kidnapping by foreign agents on British territory had been published, and nearly six since the event itself. Yet almost another full week was to elapse before even an exploratory official approach on the matter was made to the South African Government by the British ambassador. And when Sir John Maud moved at long last on 11 October, he kept his modest request for information so close a secret for so long that an anxious public in Basutoland and South Africa only learned about it on 16 November through Private Questions in the House of Commons.

There Mr Bernard Braine made two curiously ambiguous statements. First he told the House that a 'reply is awaited' to the ambassador's request for information. Then, a few minutes later, when hard pressed by members of the previous protest delegation, Mr Braine declared: 'The South African Government have replied to the ambassador, but as the matter is before the South African Courts it is *sub judice*.'†

It was perhaps understandable that Mr Jeremy Thorpe, the Liberal M.P., who had interviewed Mr Braine seven weeks earlier, spoke of 'evasiveness and procrastination', and asked the Minister, if he persisted in sheltering his officials, to do the only honourable thing and to resign. Mr Fenner Brockway, who had also gone on deputation to Mr Braine about Ganyile's kidnapping, promised to pursue the matter further at the first opportunity in view of Mr Braine's 'very unsatisfactory answer'.

In the meantime, the application for what amounted to an order of *habeas corpus* has been brought in South Africa on 13 October. It was heard at Grahamstown by Mr Justice George Wynne, and the court's sessions were observed by an official of the British embassy and an officer of the Basutoland police.

Ganyile's uncle and advocate produced an overwhelming

* *Contact*, 19 October 1961.
† Hansard, House of Commons, 16 November 1961, columns 639–40.

8

prima facie case for assuming that Ganyile was in custody, and asked for him either to be returned to them or for the Government to supply full details as to his arrest, present whereabouts, and the charges against him.

Ganyile's advocate naturally stressed the extreme urgency of the application, but Mr Justice Wynne said that he would 'take time' to give a decision and adjourned the court for five days to allow for the original of Ganyile's note from prison to be handed in as evidence. When this had been done on 18 October, he adjourned the court again to await his judgment, which he was to take another eight weeks to reach.

In all this, as observers and British M.P.s had not been slow to point out, a fundamental aspect of the rule of law was involved, as well as a question of international aggression. Yet the British authorities had given no sign of taking any diplomatic action whatever, and doubts and suspicions about their role and intentions understandably spread rapidly.

In mid October a group of South African political refugees in Basutoland accused the Basutoland Government of deliberately sabotaging 'for political reasons' an inquiry into Ganyile's kidnapping, and complained of the administration's 'alarming indifference' to the whole case.

We as refugees [they said], would like to draw the attention of the British Government and of the whole world to the fact that our security under the British Flag is threatened and the fundamental English Common Law is flagrantly being violated by its supposed custodians.*

On 19 October Mr Patrick Duncan, son of a former governor-general of South Africa, charged Britain with avoiding her obligations as the Protecting Power for Basutoland. Specifically, he accused the British authorities of ignoring evidence in their possession and of being unwilling to press their legal right for a commission to interview Ganyile. As Ganyile had not been brought before any South African court for remand, it followed that he was held in the Transkei, where alone special laws made remand unnecessary.

African and liberal suspicions of British inaction rose to a peak

* *New Age*, 19 October 1961.

when no attempt was made to check *Contact*'s revelation on 16 November that one of its correspondents had been told 'by an official of the Union Government' that Ganyile was, on 25 October, being held in solitary confinement at Umtata jail in the heart of the Transkei.

'The British and South African Governments seem to be joined in a conspiracy of silence concerning the alleged kidnapping of Mr Anderson Khumani Ganyile by South African police from Basutoland on 26 August last,' *New Age* wrote accusingly on 23 November.

In fact, silence on all official fronts was the only response. Sir John Maud said nothing, Mr Justice Wynne said nothing, and on 11 December the Lord Privy Seal, Mr Heath, told Mr Fenner Brockway in the House of Commons that the South African Government had not replied to official British requests for information.

Also, on 11 December, having taken two months to consider this urgent matter, Mr Justice Wynne refused the court application. Mr Peter Charles, Q.C., the observer whom the International Commission of Jurists had sent to investigate the Ganyile affair, commented:

'The judgment by Mr Justice Wynne is a curiosity of legal literature. He dealt with this comparatively straightforward application for a rule *nisi* affecting the liberty of the subject in a judgment of seventy-two typewritten pages.' After attaching 'some sinister significance' to aspects of the presentation of the petition, the judge ruled that any alleged kidnapping in Basutoland was irrelevant and 'came to the remarkable conclusion that Ganyile's application "is manifestly an abuse of the process of the court"'.*

Fortunately, the decision by Mr Justice Wynne was subject to appeal to a full bench of the Supreme Court Division. 'The matter,' noted Mr Charles approvingly, 'was dealt with with unprecedented celerity. An appeal was noted, a full bench was convened and, in the course of the same week, i.e. on 15 December

---

*'South African Incident – The Ganyile Case' (International Commission of Jurists, Geneva 1962, pp. 13). An outstanding report in which the commission's secretary-general, Sir Leslie Munro, pays a well-deserved tribute to Mr Peter Charles, Q.C., Leader of the Salisbury Bar and a sometime Acting Judge. Mr Charles died shortly after the Report's publication.

1961, the full bench heard and allowed an appeal and issued a rule *nisi* substantially in the terms asked for by the applicant.' The comments made by the Judge President on Mr Justice Wynne's delay and judgment were, to put it mildly, scathing.

The South African Minister of Justice was called upon to justify Ganyile's detention before the Supreme Court on 18 January 1962.

This swift and dramatic defence of liberty by the South African Court did nothing, however, to stir the British Government into public action in the same cause.

When the Ganyile affair was raised once again in the House of Commons by Labour and Liberal Party spokesmen on 22 December, the Government refused to press for an immediate reply to Sir John Maud's inquiries, made two and a half months before and repeated in the preceding week without result. Nor would it give an undertaking that a British official would attempt to interview Ganyile, whose whereabouts were now allegedly known. When the *sub judice* nature of the issue was produced yet again by the Government's spokesman, Mr Thomas, to justify British inaction prior to the Supreme Court judgment, Mr Harold Wilson sprang angrily to his feet from the Labour front benches:

Since this *sub judice* excuse has been used to drag this business on for over four months . . . may I ask the Honourable Gentleman whether he will not take this matter a little more seriously than he has done so far ? Will he see that a complete investigation is made within the Protectorate concerned to collect, before it gets completely cold, all the evidence on this most wicked episode ?

To which Mr Thomas replied for the Government:

The matter was *sub judice* until last Friday when an order has been made reversing the decision and we hope to have a reply from the South African Government.

But this simply wasn't good enough for Mr Wilson, who protested:

But what was *sub judice* was the application for the release of the men under South African law. Is the Honourable Gentleman aware that what was not *sub judice* was the simple question of fact whether British territory was violated by the South African raiders who undertook the operation? Surely there is nothing *sub judice* about that ... some member of the Government could have been getting on with the job?

Mr Thomas then blandly replied:

We have been asking for information for some time. Our concern was to find out whether or not this territory was violated. We hope now that we shall have a reply.*

A few days later, on 22 December, Ganyile was brought before the magistrate's court in the Transkei capital of Umtata for a preparatory examination on charges of attempted murder and incitement to murder. No evidence was led, and the case was remanded first to 5 January, and then, still with no evidence being led, to 19 January.

Ganyile's appearance in court on 22 December was the first time that anyone outside of prison had seen him since he had been kidnapped on 26 August. He was now allowed for the first time to consult a lawyer. On 10 January 1962 an Umtata firm of attorneys applied for bail on his behalf. In support of this application, Ganyile told in an affidavit the whole story of his kidnapping and subsequent detention in solitary confinement for over four months.

Counsel for the State opposed the bail application but filed no replying affidavit. It was only from the State Counsel's argument that Ganyile could deduce that he was to be charged with attempted murder because he had used an axe to defend himself against being kidnapped. No hints were given relating to the charge of incitement to murder.

Nevertheless, the Senior Magistrate of Umtata granted Ganyile bail of £200. This was a courageous decision in a country where all magistrates are paid civil servants, dependent for promotion on the Department of Justice. It so happened that the magistrate, Mr Potgieter, was also an Afrikaner.

On 11 January 1962 Anderson Ganyile was released from prison. Nothing whatever had in all this time been heard of his brother, Ingleton Ganyile, or of Mohlovoa Mtseko, who had been kidnapped with him.

On 12 January Mr Peter Charles, Q.C., the International Commission of Jurists' observer, told the Press that his organiza-

* Hansard, House of Commons, 18 December 1961, columns 933–4.

tion was particularly interested in the fate of these two men and that he was having inquiries made into their whereabouts. On the following day, they were released from two jails in the Transkei, where they had been held in solitary confinement. The head of the political police in the Transkei, Captain D. Rossouw, explained to a reporter that the men had now been released because they had finally answered questions satisfactorily. There was, the captain said, 'nothing to it at all'.

By now, however, few newspaper readers either in Britain or in South Africa would have agreed with the disingenuous captain. Mr Justice Wynne's fantastic judgment, its dramatic reversal by the Supreme Court, the murder charges then brought against Ganyile, Mr Charles's arrival, and now the opportune release of Ganyile's two companions, suggested that there was a great deal to it all.

With the Ganyile case now headline news in responsible British newspapers, matters had in fact gone so far that even the British ambassador was prepared to display public interest in Ganyile. Between 15 and 17 January an official of the British embassy in Cape Town visited Umtata and saw Ganyile. It was now twenty-five days since Ganyile's public appearance in the Umtata magistrate's court and exactly four months since his disappearance had been reported to the Basutoland authorities. The International Commission of Jurists' report merely notes drily: 'At this stage (15 January 1962) it was clear that the British Government was actively interesting itself in the case.'

The crucial date of 18 January, on which the Minister of Justice had been ordered to show cause before the Supreme Court why Ganyile had been detained, was now almost at hand, and it was only when, on 15 January, the Minister filed affidavits with the court that the world had its first official word from the South African Government about the Ganyile affair.

The South African and the Basutoland mounted police regularly exchange information on persons of interest to either force, and there is a good deal of free passage over the border near which Ganyile's new home was located.

According to the affidavits which the South African Minister of Justice filed with the Supreme Court, his political security police became aware of Ganyile's presence at Quacha's Nek, and on 10 August 1961 an unnamed informer signed a statement alleging that Ganyile was organizing subversive activities in Pondoland from Basutoland. These activities, according to the anonymous informer, included the boycotting and killing of chiefs, sabotage, and the killing of Government informers and witnesses for the prosecution in Pondo unrest cases. On the basis of this and other reports, a Sergeant Steyn of the South African police issued a warrant of detention for Ganyile on 27 August.

Under the Transkei's Proclamation 400 of 1960, anyone suspected of knowing anything about anyone else's suspected intention to commit any conceivable offence can be arrested by any policeman of sergeant's rank or higher and detained indefinitely without charge or trial until he has answered any and all questions asked of him to the satisfaction of the police. This, according to the Minister of Justice, was the law under which Ganyile was arrested and held. Mr Charles aptly commented that it 'must surely be one of the most remarkable laws in force anywhere in the civilized world'.

The Minister of Justice submitted that Ganyile's arrest and detention under South African law were valid, and asked for the *habeas corpus* application to be dismissed with costs. He considered the allegation of kidnapping in Basutoland as irrelevant and therefore did not reply to it.

It looked as though there might yet be a legal fight, but the denouement now came with a rush.

Late on the night of 17 January 1962, following a meeting of the South African Cabinet, the Department of Justice announced that the proceedings against Anderson Ganyile had been abandoned, that Ganyile would be allowed to return to Basutoland and that the South African Minister of Foreign Affairs had informed the British ambassador of this and conveyed to him the regret of the South African Government that the incident had taken place.

The official statement went on to explain that on the night of 26 August 1961 South African police had been searching for four suspected murderers of a certain native chief and had crossed the Basutoland border unwittingly in heavy rain. The police had reached a hut in which the suspected murderers were hiding, had established that the hut was inhabited, had knocked on the door, and informed the inhabitants that they were the police. The door had been opened, and when they had entered, one of them had been hit in the face with an axe and seriously injured. There had been three Africans in the hut who, after a struggle with the police, had been taken to the police car at the foot of the mountain on the road. Only after the incident had it been established that Ganyile was one of the three Africans. The Attorney-General was satisfied, following a comprehensive investigation by a senior police officer which he had ordered, that the police had acted in good faith. It was estimated that the distance by which the police overshot the border was 500 yards, but a surveyor had established that it was 638 yards.*

On 18 January the Government attorneys wrote to Ganyile's attorneys offering to pay Ganyile's costs, which – after the Government's statement – remained the only question at issue. The *habeas corpus* proceedings thus ended.

On 19 January the Department of Justice abandoned the proceedings against Ganyile in the Umtata magistrate's court. A second official statement laconically declared:

As it has now been established that the arrest of Anderson Ganyile had taken place within the borders of Basutoland, the Attorney-General at Grahamstown has decided not to proceed against Ganyile in the preparatory examination of murder and incitement to murder.

With this move by the South African Government, Ganyile lost the opportunity of replying to the allegations that he had been organizing subversion, murder and sabotage in Pondoland from Basutoland.

On the same day the Minister of Justice withdrew the order for Ganyile's detention under the Transkei's notorious Proclamation 400, and Ganyile was allowed to return to Quacha's Nek in Basutoland.

It is very rarely indeed that the apartheid State publicly reverses its actions on a major issue, and there has probably never been an international incident in which it has made so public and humiliating a climb-down.

It is, of course, patent that the South African Government had been deliberately lying during the Ganyile affair. The Minister

* East London *Daily Despatch*, 18 January 1962.

of Justice, Mr Vorster, subsequently settled out of court for an undisclosed amount the action for £10,000 damages which Mr Ganyile was bringing for assault, false arrest and false imprisonment against the South African Government and the individual policemen. It is fair to conclude that in settling out of court Mr Vorster admitted that his six policemen could not have thought that they had any powers legally to arrest Ganyile.

Mr Charles, in the Report of the International Commission of Jurists, pointed out that even the South African Department of Justice had not said that at the time the police entered the hut, or at any subsequent stage, the police were unaware that they were in Basutoland. Indeed, in the circumstances, it appears impossible that they did not know that Ganyile had been captured in Basutoland, at the latest when they recrossed the border fence and returned to their cars.

As for the bringing of murder charges and their subsequent withdrawal on 18 January 1961. Mr Charles declared himself satisfied that it had been known to the authorities from 25 August 1961 that the arrest of Anderson Ganyile had taken place in Basutoland. The only difference which could be drawn was that the criminal proceedings had been instituted as a result of the court order on the *habeas corpus* application and that they had been dropped because of the international repercussions which resulted when the facts were exposed and because of representation made by the British Government.

It is the effectiveness of these belated representations by the British Government which concern us in this book, even more than the deeply disturbing conclusions which Mr Charles allowed himself to draw about South African police, officials, and law. He spoke of 'the spirit of lawlessness which seems to prevail among certain members of the Special Branch of the South African police'. He also believed that the early denials by police officers 'can be explained only by deliberate mendacity on the part of the senior officials concerned, or by the fact that the comparatively junior police officers who carried out the operation did so on their own initiative and concealed from their superior officers the fact that they had made an eruption into neighbouring British Territory. Either explanation,' said Mr Charles with careful understatement, 'is disquieting.'

He also had some scathing things to say about the higher officials of the South African Department of Justice, whose attempts 'to brazen out what had been done, when the facts were indisputably established, reflects a disquietening contempt for standards of international law'. As for Mr Justice Wynne, his 'delay of two months in dealing with an urgent application affecting the liberty of the subject was deplorable. In every other respect, however, the South African judicial officers and legal practitioners who dealt with the matter added lustre to the deservedly high reputation enjoyed by the South African courts and those who practice before them, among lawyers throughout the world who are familiar with the working of the South African system.'

But what of the British Government and of its representatives in South Africa, who then simultaneously governed the High Commission Territories of which Basutoland is one? Mr Charles pointed to 'representation made by the British Government' as having been one of several factors which finally led to the climb-down by the South Africans. He also recorded that only by 15 January 1962 had it become 'clear that the British Government was actively interesting itself in the case'. Yet the Basutoland authorities had been informed of Ganyile's kidnapping exactly four months earlier, on 15 September 1961.

What might not have been achieved had the British Government resolutely interested itself in the case four months earlier! All they did, in fact, until action by others had brought the appalling facts to light, was to make it easy for the South Africans contemptuously to ignore for over three months the polite little British requests for 'information'. In the meantime, Government spokesmen in the House of Commons simply stonewalled.

Why should this have been so? Basutoland is a British colony officially set upon a course of non-racial democratic development which is in sharp divergence from that of the South African State which completely surrounds it. The long and fine British tradition of granting refuge to political refugees is officially upheld in Basutoland, and it was as such a refugee that Anderson Ganyile was allowed to settle there by Her Majesty's High Commissioner for Basutoland, the Bechuanaland Protectorate and Swaziland.

But Her Majesty's High Commissioner happened also to be her Ambassador to the Republic of South Africa, in which Her

Majesty's loyal subjects have invested some £1,000,000,000. Could it be that a conflict of interests made Her Majesty's Government and ambassador follow for four months a policy which came dangerously near to looking not like masterly but like servile inactivity?

We shall return to this problem of Britain's conflicting interests in South Africa, but certainly nothing could illustrate more clearly than the Ganyile affair the crucial importance of Britain's not only claiming to uphold freedom in the High Commission Territories but of being publicly seen to be doing so.

On 29 January 1962, Mr Harold Wilson said in the House of Commons:

Since the police officers concerned must have known within a few hours that they were in the wrong country, and since this occurred last August and it has taken four or five months to find that the charges which have been laid were not appropriate, will the Honourable Gentleman make absolutely clear here and now that the apology we have had is not sufficient for everything that has happened and that the Government will firmly stand behind Mr Ganyile in the matter of compensation for this quite illegal detention?

Mr Godber, a senior spokesman for the Government, replied only:

We have made it quite clear that we take a very serious view of what has happened. As to Mr Ganyile's application for compensation, I think that it should go forward in the normal way. He is a South African citizen and should make this application through the courts.*

The importance of the court action which led to Ganyile's return to Basutoland and, even more, of the unprecedented apology given by the South African Government to Britain, grows with every day. For the crucial significance of the Ganyile case is that it confirmed three things: the right of those opposing apartheid to seek asylum in the British High Commission Territories; the willingness of the British Government to grant them political asylum; and the impotence of the South African political police once that asylum has been granted.

It would be hard to exaggerate the importance of these precedents for democratic South Africans of whatever colour –

* Hansard, House of Commons, 29 January 1962, columns 701, 705.

though, ironically, their significance is perhaps even greater for whites than for blacks. An African, despite the rigid controls and checks to which he is daily subjected in the Republic, can flee and even re-enter the country with relative ease.

To the apartheid State, an African is primarily a cipher with a document. If he is humbly dressed and subserviently spoken, and if he has an authentic looking and properly endorsed 'pass' document, he passes as 'just another kaffir'. It would seem that this applies even to political leaders whose photographs have appeared dozens of times in the newspapers, usually, of course, sporting a well-cut suit. But exchange that suit for a ragged blanket, the natty shoes for gaping cast-off plimsolls, grow a scraggly beard, carry a well-forged pass and – above all – say '*ja, baas*', and the trick is done. Or so it would seem.

The most dramatic example of this transfiguration was certainly Mr Nelson Mandela, the former secretary-general of the now banned African National Congress. Mr Mandela is a prominent man in more ways than one. Not only has he been a well-known lawyer and leading politician for many years, but he is also a six foot two inch former boxing champion. Yet for almost two years he treated both bannings and restrictions with contempt, slipping out of and into South Africa with apparent impunity. It is no secret that the route he used was the now famed Escape Route to the North: by car or, even better, on foot across the long South Africa–Bechuanaland border; then, if funds permit, by chartered private plane from the northernmost landing field in Bechuanaland, at Maun, across neighbouring Northern Rhodesia and into now independent Tanganyika; and from there, to Accra, Cairo, London or, in fact, anywhere. Eventually, Mandela was arrested in South Africa in 1962. But others still travel the route he used.

This Escape Route was pioneered during the State of Emergency which followed the Sharpeville massacre of Africans by the South African police in 1960. As police swoops began, leaders of the African National Congress Alliance and the rival Pan-Africanist Congress took refuge in ever-increasing numbers in the High Commission Territories. No passports were at that time required for entry, and any visitor could stay for up to three months without applying for a special permit.

The South African Government, which had preferred no

charges against most of those who had fled to avoid probable arrest, objected to these 'safe bases' within or on their borders, and tried to push the British authorities into returning the refugees. When this, despite considerable blustering by the Nationalists, produced no results, Verwoerd's Minister of Justice stated in the South African Parliament that the State of Emergency could not be lifted until the 'Communists and agitators' in the British Territories had been apprehended. In the meantime, the South Africans bolted the proverbial stable door by setting up armed police road blocks at main entry roads into the Territories, and by mounting much publicized mobile patrols along the borders.

The British Government, to its credit, stood firm on extradition, as indeed it was obliged to do under international law, but then promptly marred its record by trying to impose political restrictions on the refugees.

Thus in Swaziland, which had received the largest contingent of refugees, the British authorities demanded that each of them sign an unprecedented undertaking which effectively deprived them of all normal political rights.

Each refugee was to undertake that,

in the exceptional circumstances of my presence in Swaziland, I shall, so long as I remain in the Territory, refrain from taking an active part in the politics of this Territory or of either of the other High Commission Territories or of any other territory bordering on any of the High Commission Territories.

The expression 'taking an active part in politics' was obligingly defined for the refugees by Swaziland's Government Secretary to include:

(i) writing for publication or causing to be published in any manner any matter of a political nature;
(ii) making a speech relating to any such matter; and
(iii) taking any part in the creation, direction, organization or activities of any political association.

What such an undertaking would mean to South African refugees can be imagined. As they pointed out in a memorandum sent both to the British Prime Minister and to the High Commissioner in Cape Town, they would have been prevented from agitating even for the release of their husbands, wives and families detained without warrant in South Africa under Emergency Regulations.

They would have been prevented from calling for the ending of the South African State of Emergency, or from calling attention to their financial and material plight even in the British Press. And, finally, they would, under pain of criminal penalties and deliverance to Dr Verwoerd's political police, have been prevented from defending themselves against malicious and distorted hate-attacks not only in the South African Press, which circulates widely in Swaziland and the other two Territories, but also in Swaziland's own white-settler Press.

For the large group of refugees who were 'sitting it out' in Swaziland were made anything but welcome by the majority of the Territory's white inhabitants. For the most part, these whites are farmers of either South African origin or connexion, and in the two weekly Swaziland papers which existed to reflect their views, they made their feelings about the refugees plain. The refugees, whites and Africans together, had taken over a new block of flats in Mbabane, the Territory's charmingly situated capital, and had wrily dubbed them as 'No. 10, Downing Street' and 'Belsen'. Several of the white refugees were of Jewish descent, and the nasty racialism which bubbled up in many of Swaziland's whites included the anti-semitic variety. Typical of the comment in the now defunct *Swaziland Chronicle* were two paragraphs of 'Pub Chatter' in which 'Bar Fly' said:

There are too many refugees in Swaziland, the Passover is over, time some of them passed back. . . . Might mean saving Mr Goldblatt (a local Jewish businessman) another block of flats.

This paper, in particular, the refugees pointed out, 'waged a persistent campaign to whip up local feeling with fabricated allegations of misconduct, abuse of hospitality and sedition', urging that the refugees should be promptly expelled.

Although their three months' permit-free 'visitors' period was expiring for increasing numbers of the refugees, all but one of them, Mr Patrick van Rensburg, refused to sign the requested declaration.

An extended, polite but grimly dogged correspondence ensued between the refugees, led by a former South African member of

Parliament, Mr Sam Kahn, on the one hand, and the British officials, led by the High Commissioner, Sir John Maud, on the other. Sir John held that the refugees' refusal to sign the demanded undertaking entailed an admission that they intended to 'engage in active politics in the Union and in Swaziland'.

The refugees made it clear that they did

not intend to exploit (British) hospitality by converting Swaziland into a base from which to launch 'subversive and seditious' attacks upon our country. . . . Nor do we hold to the concept that we are to organize and control the affairs and activities of Union political bodies from here. But we cannot accept restrictions upon our right to defend ourselves when publicly attacked in the Press.

Questions were asked in the House of Commons; some firm assurances of non-repatriation for political offences were squeezed out of the very reluctant Minister of State for Commonwealth Relations, Mr Cuthbert (now Lord) Alport; and in the end the refugees stayed until the emergency in South Africa ended without giving the demanded undertakings.

That they did is of more than historical interest today. A steady trickle of refugees has continued to reach Swaziland and the other two Territories month by month, and is becoming a renewed wave now that a further concentrated Government attack is being made on opponents of apartheid in South Africa.

During the 1960 emergency in South Africa over thirty whites and blacks, including Bishop Ambrose Reeves of Johannesburg, found temporary refuge in Swaziland; nearly as many are known to have fled into Basutoland; and a large number, including Mr Oliver Tambo, the leader-in-exile of the banned African National Congress, and Mr Ronald Segal, the editor-publisher of the influential, since-banned anti-apartheid quarterly *Africa South*, used the Escape Route through Bechuanaland to freedom.

Some of these and subsequent African refugees have stayed on in the High Commission Territories, and have, after obtaining residence qualifications, become active in politics and trades unionism. Their reception has varied from the hostility of many Swaziland and Bechuanaland whites to the first warm welcome of Basutoland's militant politicians.

As those who remained have settled down, local reactions to

them have changed, and usually cooled. This applies particularly to Basutoland and Bechuanaland, where some of the politically experienced and sophisticated black South Africans, who have usually maintained their home contacts, have come to be regarded as a threat by the local African politicians. Thus in Basutoland the country's leading politician, Mr Ntsu Mokhehle, has for some time been engaged in a bitter vendetta against refugees, many of whom were leading members of South Africa's banned African National Congress. Mr Mokhehle has had to fight a challenge to his leadership from some of these South African politicians, and he has not relished the experience.

Similarly, in the Bechuanaland Protectorate, there has occurred a split in the Bechuanaland People's Party, in which the continuing connexions of its Secretary-General, Mr Mutsamai Mpho, with the banned African National Congress in South Africa has played a crucial role. This dispute reached such proportions that the deputy-president of the party, Mr Matante, was publicly accused of having kidnapped a South African A.N.C. refugee and dumping him back across Dr Verwoerd's border. Mr Matante, who has helped many refugees to pass on to freedom through Bechuanaland, has strongly denied the kidnapping allegation, although he does admit to ordering the man concerned to move on out of the country. The split in the party has in fact been carried over into court actions.

Even this, however, may be seen more as an aberration than as a basic attitude. Whilst some of the African political leaders in the High Commission Territories would doubtless prefer to have the South Africans pass through their territories rather than see them settling down, no African in these territories would deny the refugees at least help in transit. On the contrary.

It is the very fact that the Territories offer a refuge from Dr Verwoerd's persecution which points the difference in their political systems, under British protection, from the South African apartheid State. It is, of course, true that from any democratic point of view, the High Commission Territories leave, as the United Nations has learnt from their African leaders, a great deal to be desired.

We shall presently examine these shortcomings in some detail and view them against the background of generations of British neglect. But to understand the South African attitude today towards these Territories, we must look at the contrast which, with all their imperfections, they provide to Dr Verwoerd's white supremacist State.

When, on one occasion several years ago, I went to Basutoland with an African friend from Johannesburg, the first thing he did on crossing the border was to jump out of the car and throw his 'pass' into the air. In the Republic, every moment of an African's life is controlled by the hated pass. In the Territories, men come and go as they please. In South Africa, the law states that the black man is the inferior of the white. In Basutoland, the white man only stays on sufferance, and in all three Territories the law is increasingly becoming the same for all.

In South Africa no African can vote for the country's Parliament. In Basutoland, elections on the basis of universal adult suffrage have brought the country to the verge of independence. In Bechuanaland, black and white have voted together, with no racial or other qualifications, to elect a Government which will exercise a considerable degree of internal power. And in Swaziland, elections to the country's first Legislative Council have made at least a beginning of a non-racial common roll.

Where Africans are discriminated against in every possible way in South Africa, racial discrimination in public places has been outlawed in Swaziland, is soon to be prohibited in Basutoland and is being partly broken by law in Bechuanaland. Where, in South Africa, any serious opponent is named as a 'Communist' and persecuted accordingly, Basutoland has a legal Communist Party.

As the whole machinery of South Africa depends upon effectively controlling the African and isolating him – with, increasingly, the whites as well – from the outside world, the Nationalist Government clearly cannot afford to have liberal enclaves within or on their borders.

Refugees leaving South Africa permanently are only one aspect of the danger, and possibly the one least worrying to Dr Verwoerd. After all, he is prepared to grant at least some of his white opponents one-way exit permits, having apparently got past the point of worrying about what they will say abroad.

Much more worrying to Verwoerd is the use of the Territories as a safe haven by South Africans and as possible bases of operations against the Nationalists. The Nationalists may control the Press in South Africa, but they cannot stop literature coming into the country from the Territories.

In the streets of Maseru I have bought copies of *World Marxist Review* and the Proceedings of the 22nd Congress of the C.P.S.U., and the Communist Party of Basutoland is planning to set up a printing press in the Territory.

Furthermore, the British Government is preparing to set up independent broadcasting stations in each of the Territories, which could give the possessors of even the most modest medium-wave sets in each country – and in South Africa – access to objective world news and thus make nonsense of the slanted news bulletins put out by the South African Broadcasting Corporation.

Together with all this, the High Commission Authorities have of late been taking an unprecedentedly emphatic stand in safeguarding the liberties of South African refugees passing through the Territories. In the past, those who had passed through Bechuanaland and into the Federation of Rhodesia and Nyasaland had been apprehended there by federal immigration officials who obligingly escorted them back on trains through part of Bechuanaland and handed them over to the South African police. But in November 1962, the Bechuanaland police, acting on direct instructions from Sir John Maud, boarded a train in the Protectorate and freed one coloured and two African men who were thus being returned in handcuffs to South Africa.

As a result of this firm action, the Federal Government decided that in future it would merely escort illegal immigrants from South Africa by train back to the Bechuanaland border, and then leave them to their own devices. This was done in the same month with twenty-seven further South African refugees, and the Bechuanaland authorities permitted them to remain at least temporarily in the Protectorate. An extremely important precedent was thus established, though by March 1963 the Federal Government had found a way of by-passing British fair play. With the Bechuanaland Protectorate, which provides South Africa's only rail link with the north, closed for purposes of repatriation, Federal officials took to trucking captured refugees by road to Beit Bridge on the South African border with Southern Rhodesia – a practice which the latter country is now following.

It is, of course, disturbing that the British Commissioners of the Territories continue to cast about for ways in which to limit the political activities of refugees, and that in Swaziland the restrictive conditions which South African refugees refused to accept during the 1960 emergency are now imposed as a matter of routine.

ADVISE AND CONSENT

Refugees can, however, create circumstances so provocative as to undermine their own position and to push their hosts into limiting their freedom of action and even of speech. There has, in fact, only been one case of this happening to date, but its repercussions have been profound.

In the last week of March 1963, Mr Potlako Leballo, a leader of the Republic's banned Pan-Africanist Congress, announced to a Press conference that he had 150,000 underground P.A.C. members under his command in South Africa, and that these men were about to stage a general uprising. Announcing that he had taken over the leadership of the P.A.C. movement from its imprisoned founder, Mr Robert Sobukwe, Leballo proceeded to equate the P.A.C. with the terrorist Poqo movement in South Africa. Poqo had been responsible for bloody riots in the town of Paarl in which several whites were hacked to death. 'What they call Poqo is P.A.C.' Mr Leballo announced. 'Poqo is not an organization – it is a slogan. Poqo and P.A.C. are one and the same thing.' He went on to allege that Poqo members had, against his orders, been responsible in 1962 for the hacking to death of five whites at Bashee Bridge in the Transkei.*

Understandably, Leballo's statements caused a furore in South Africa – and in Britain. It was recalled that he had been one of Robert Sobukwe's chief lieutenants in the P.A.C. Both men had previously been active in the African National Congress, but had broken away in 1957. It was the P.A.C. which had called the peaceful demonstrations which had resulted in the massacre of unarmed Africans by the South African police at Sharpeville in 1960, and

* *Sunday Express*, Johannesburg, 31 March 1963.

Leballo had subsequently served a two-year hard labour sentence. On his release, he had been banished to a remote spot in Natal, but had appealed successfully against this on the grounds that he was a native of Basutoland. He had been allowed to leave South Africa for Basutoland, and had set himself up in Maseru as the leader of the P.A.C. Being a Mosuto by birth, he required no residence permit from the Basutoland Government.

But political jail sentences were not the only ones that Leballo had served in South Africa; he had also been sentenced for fraud, forgery and uttering. He has, too, a reputation for personal instability which may account for his calling the Maseru Press conference in the first place, for the obviously exaggerated claims which he made, and for the denials with which he followed them a few days later. Certainly the Johannesburg *Sunday Express*, which some time before had disproved Leballo's widely publicized allegations that Robert Sobukwe was critically ill and being ill-treated in prison, did not on 31 March hesitate to call him a 'liar, fool, and braggart'.

Be that as it may, Leballo's announcement that he was about to direct a mass uprising in South Africa from Basutoland inevitably led to considerable tension between the South African and British Governments. Although the Republic's Foreign Minister, Mr Eric Louw, said that statements by private individuals like Leballo were not a basis for official protests to the British Government,* Dr Verwoerd's official Nationalist Party Press promptly urged that South Africa should prevent such a situation on its borders 'even at a very high price', and that South Africa could not be expected to tolerate the apparent impotence of the Basutoland authorities to 'obstruct Leballo in his devilish work'.

In point of fact, Dr Verwoerd had to wait less than a week before the Basutoland authorities moved dramatically against Leballo. On 1 April, All Fools' Day, they raided his home and P.A.C. office in Maseru, officially on the suspicion that he might be breaking the law by being in possession of arms and ammunition. Two carton-loads of documents were seized from Leballo's home and office, and only fifty rounds of small-arms ammunition found in extensive raids on the homes of P.A.C. members and their office. A warrant was issued for Leballo's arrest on a charge of

* *Evening Post*, Port Elizabeth, 29 March 1963.

27

incitement to public violence. He managed to flee into the mountains and evade a national man-hunt, but at least thirteen other leading members of the P.A.C. were arrested by the Basutoland mounted police. Simultaneously, the South African police, who had been camping on the Basutoland border and searching all cars and trains since Leballo's threats, sealed the border completely.

A Basutoland Government spokesman strongly denied that the police action was the result of pressure from the South African Government, or that the Republic had been consulted about it. It was, the spokesman said, a 'purely local action', carried out with the approval, though not on the instructions, of Sir John Maud, the High Commissioner and British Ambassador to South Africa.*

Well-informed journalists on the spot who also had excellent South African contacts painted a different picture. Thus the correspondent of the conservative and highly reputable Johannesburg *Star* reported on 2 April:

The swoop on the Pan African Congress headquarters in Maseru yesterday afternoon was the first stage in a combined operation by the South African police and the Basutoland police to rid the territory of the Pan African Congress. . . . If the police operations are successful, a spokesman said today, it 'would rid Basutoland of the P.A.C. for good'.

On 2 April it was revealed that amongst the documents which the Basutoland police had seized from Leballo's premises was a list of just over 10,000 P.A.C.–Poqo members in South Africa. Asked by reporters whether this list would be handed over to the South African police, a Basutoland Government spokesman replied: 'No comment. It is obviously a matter of security.'†

In the early hours of 3 April, a series of raids was launched with pin-point accuracy on members of the banned P.A.C. throughout South Africa. The men arrested were alleged by the South African authorities to be cell-leaders of P.A.C.–Poqo or to be furthering the aims of a banned organization.

By 5 April, both a senior officer of the Basutoland police and Major-General Keevy, the Commissioner of the South African police, had emphatically denied that the South African police had been associated in any way with the action taken by the British

---

* *Rand Daily Mail*, Johannesburg, 3 April 1963.
† *Rand Daily Mail*, Johannesburg, 4 April 1963.

authorities in Basutoland, and this denial was repeated on behalf of the British Government when questions were asked in the House of Commons.

On 5 April a senior officer of the Basutoland police also said that there was no question of the list of P.A.C. members being handed over to the South African authorities.*

On 27 April General Keevy of the South African police told the Johannesburg *Sunday Express* that the capture of Leballo's female secretary had led to the uncovering of the Poqo plot for an 'uprising'. According to the general, this African woman was on her way from Maseru to Bloemfontein on 29 March to post letters to 150 cell-leaders all over South Africa, instructing them to rise against the whites within two weeks. The seizure of her briefcase, filled with these letters, accounted for the widespread arrests in South Africa in the next few days.

General Keevy denied that the Basutoland police had tipped off the South African police about the ring-leaders after their raid on 1 April on Leballo's office. The reputed 10,000 names on the captured list were never disclosed to the South African police.

'Because of Leballo's threatening statements, and reports that he was plotting a revolution in South Africa, it was decided to watch and control all road and rail routes leading out of Basutoland,' General Keevy said. 'As a result we picked up Leballo's secretary and also about fifteen of his main leaders, his regional commanders, in fact, who were either on their way to see him or returning from his headquarters with personal instructions for the contemplated plan of action in South Africa.'

The general also let slip the tantalizing titbit of information that the British authorities were told earlier in the year of Leballo's activities, but declined to take action at that time.

It has in fact been admitted by the British authorities that there is cooperation between the Basutoland and South African police forces, but with the rider that this 'is strictly limited to normal liaison on purely criminal matters'. Now if this were true of two neighbouring democratic countries, it would in no way be remarkable. But it sounds, to say the least, a little too disingenuous when one remembers that in South African law almost any political

* *Rand Daily Mail*, Johannesburg, 6 April 1964.

protest or organization by Africans can be considered 'a purely criminal matter'.

In fact, the Commissioner of the Basutoland mounted police, Brigadier Kitson, admitted to me in an interview in 1962 that his force reports to the South African police on the activities of South African political refugees in Basutoland, and that the South Africans reciprocate by watching and reporting to him on expatriate Basuto 'who might make trouble'.

This revelation will certainly not surprise political refugees in Basutoland, nor, for that matter, those in Bechuanaland or Swaziland. For there is, in addition, ample evidence, including photographs, that South African plain-clothes police come and go freely in all three Territories, and that they do so on active duty.

As it happens, I can testify to this from personal experience. When I was collecting some of the material for this book in Basutoland during 1962, I was given every cooperation by Sir John Maud, the then High Commissioner, and by Mr Chaplin, the then Resident Commissioner. In fact, I carried official letters of introduction from both, and that from Mr Chaplin, in addition to stating the purpose of my visit, requested all Basutoland officials to give me their full cooperation. Despite this, the Basutoland Special Branch, acting on behalf of their South African counterparts, made inquiries about my activities in the Territory. And after I had stayed with a trader in the mountains, members of the *South African* Special Branch twice visited his premises to make inquiries about me.

If a journalist who has been vouched for by the High Commissioner and the Resident Commissioner is investigated in this manner, one can well credit the detailed and sworn accounts by political refugees of the closest cooperation between the South African and the Basutoland police.

Brigadier Kitson made his extremely important admission to me before the Leballo affair, and it would be naïve to expect the authorities in either country publicly to repeat it after the suspicions of the whole world had been sharply aroused by the South African raids which followed hard on the heels of the seizure of the P.A.C. list in Basutoland.

General Keevy of the South African police has given the world a story about the arrest of Leballo's secretary which might, given

Leballo's egocentricity and arrogance, seem plausible – until one learns from other and more level-headed P.A.C. leaders that this woman had in fact been arrested and jailed in South Africa *more than a week before* the date on which the general claims she was seized with the letters to P.A.C. leaders. On 29 March she was still in a South African jail.

Access to the relevant police records being impossible, it is the word of the P.A.C. leaders against that of General Keevy – and the British authorities. But the South African Government and its top police commanders proved themselves brazen enough liars in the Ganyile affair, and in view of the information given to me by Brigadier Kitson, there is ample reason for questioning the disingenuous denials of the Basutoland authorities.

It is in any event interesting to note that by August 1963, when the High Commissioner had begun to take a firmer stand on protecting refugees in the Territories against arrest by the South African Police, it was announced that the arrest warrant for Leballo had been withdrawn. Leballo then reappeared in Maseru on 12 September, after having been in hiding for $5\frac{1}{2}$ months.

Mr Ntsu Mokhehle, the leader of the Basutoland Congress Party, was emphatic that the withdrawal of the arrest warrant was an after-effect of the stinging motion of no confidence in the Basutoland Government which had been moved a little earlier.

Leballo was to be arrested to appease South Africa, Mr Mokhehle claimed, but the British now knew that the Basuto were acutely dissatisfied with the way the British authorities handled relations between Basutoland and South Africa.

Perhaps we shall learn the final truth of this whole profoundly disturbing affair when Mr Mokhehle or another Mosuto becomes Prime Minister of independent Lesotho – always provided that he would find the relevant police and Government files intact.

In the meantime, there can be little doubt that Leballo, by becoming the first political refugee in the Territories openly to threaten violence against South Africa, spurred the British authorities into introducing the presently operative Prevention of Violence Abroad Proclamation, which makes it a serious criminal offence to plan or advocate violence against the South African régime, or even to do anything which might incite others to do so.

The next move by the British authorities against a political refugee in the Territories did not, however, have even the provocative impetus of the Leballo affair.

On 5 June 1963, the Colonial Office in London announced that Mr Patrick Duncan was to be banned from all three High Commission Territories. Mr Duncan, the son of a former Governor-General of South Africa, had a distinguished record of peaceful opposition to apartheid, for which he had been to jail, was the chief proprietor and editor of *Contact*, an outspokenly liberal and strongly anti-Communist South African fortnightly paper, and had been a prominent member of the South African Liberal Party. When, in 1963, a banning proclamation by the South African Government confined him to the magisterial area of Cape Town and limited his freedom as a journalist and politician in other ways, he fled to Basutoland, where he had earlier served as an officer in the administration and where he proposed to publish *Contact* if the South African Government should ban it.

Shortly after obtaining refuge in Basutoland, Mr Duncan resigned from the South African Liberal Party, largely because he felt that the unyielding and increasing repression by the South African Government of all effective opposition had rendered the party's absolute rejection of violence untenable. A little later he announced that he had been accepted as a member of the Pan Africanist Congress, the only white man ever to be so received. He also withdrew from *Contact*, and set up as a trader in a mountainous area of Basutoland.

The announcement of his banning from Basutoland and the other two Territories came as he was on a private visit to London with his family. It was baldly justified by the Colonial Office in a statement that his presence in the Territories would be prejudicial to peace, order and good government.

But, as Mr Christopher Mayhew, M.P., said in a letter which *The Times* published on 10 June,

it is clear that this action has been taken because of Mr Duncan's known opposition to the South African Government. Everyone realizes that the South African Government is following policies which will lead the country and all its peoples to catastrophe. Britain has a great opportunity in the three High Commission Territories to show how things ought to be done. But here we have the Government ejecting a liberal-minded resident of Basutoland for no better reason that that he is *persona non grata* to the Verwoerd régime. This is to abdicate to the South Africans responsibilities that properly fall upon the British Government. It is particularly regrettable that the Government chose to announce this decision three days after Parliament rose for the Whitsun recess . . . it is to be hoped that Mr Sandys will look closely into this matter and refuse his assent.

The Colonial Secretary, however, did nothing of the kind, and Mr Duncan remains barred not only from Basutoland, where he had made a new home and invested money in his trading store, but also from Bechuanaland and Swaziland. In 1964 the South African Government followed up the British initiative by depriving Mr Duncan of his passport.

The indignation of Mr Duncan's friends had barely begun to cool when the British authorities in Bechuanaland acted against South African refugees there.

In May three white South Africans, Mr and Mrs Jack Hodgson and Mr Michael Harmel, who had been under house arrest in Johannesburg had fled to Bechuanaland and been granted temporary residence permits. Mr and Mrs Hodgson, who were British subjects and held valid British passports, refused, however, to accept the condition that they must abstain from politics during their stay in the Protectorate, and on 5 June they were informed that they would become illegal residents when their temporary permits expired on 14 August. They were ordered to leave Bechuanaland by that date.

The Hodgsons had, like Mr Harmel, been named and banned under South Africa's notorious Suppression of Communism Act and were veterans of the anti-apartheid struggle in that country. They now promptly sent a cable to the Colonial Secretary, Mr Duncan Sandys, saying:

Our situation consequence of consistent unequivocal struggle against apartheid. Physically and financially unable to comply with order to leave Bechuanaland by 14 August. What you do with us now will indicate where your Government and Territorial authorities stand on the issue of apartheid.

In Johannesburg, a British High Commission spokesman

announced that 'there is no question of returning them to the Republic'. The Hodgsons, however, say that they had been reliably informed by Lobatsi's District Commissioner that if they were to cross into Southern or Northern Rhodesia Sir Roy Welensky's federal authorities would almost certainly arrest them and return them to South Africa. The only other way out was by charter flight, costing some £540 to Tanganyika, and they had no funds.

With British M.P.s taking a keen interest in the fate of these two British subjects in a British Protectorate, a grim test of doggedness now began. Their permits duly expired on 14 August, but already before this date their determination was tested by an attempt – made by a senior member of the political police in Pretoria – to kidnap them from the flat in which they were living in Lobatsi.

The attempt failed and the Hodgsons stayed on, to be arrested by the Bechuanaland police on 3 September and tried on the charge of being illegally in Bechuanaland. For lack of funds and available lawyers, both were forced to conduct their own defence. Both were found guilty, and their fines of £50 and £30 paid by the Bechuanaland Peoples' Party, led by Mr Mpho, a former fellow-member of the Republic's Congress Alliance.

They were then left temporarily at liberty, but after a bomb had nearly destroyed a Landrover belonging to one of their close political associates, they were declared prohibited immigrants, taken into protective custody, and on 20 September were flown to England at the Government's expense. As the International Commission of Jurists has pointed out in a memorandum to the U.N. Special Committee on Apartheid, the 'no-politics' which the Hodgsons refused to accept 'are never imposed on supporters of the South African régime who wish to reside in the Territories'.

This outcome of the stand taken by Jack and Rica Hodgson was undoubtedly influenced by the unprecedented crisis and world-wide publicity which erupted over the issue of refugees in Bechuanaland during August 1964. This crisis had three aspects, which became inter-related. The Hodgsons' case was its minor aspect: world-wide interest centred on the flight to freedom of Arthur Goldreich and Harold Wolpe and on the kidnapping at the same time in Bechuanaland and forcible return to South Africa of Dr Kenneth Abrahams. For the sake of clarity, I shall separate the two stories.

In July 1963 the South African police raided the home of Arthur Goldreich in the Johannesburg suburb of Rivonia, which was used as the underground headquarters of the banned African National Congress and its sabotage group, the Spear of the Nation. Goldreich, a talented young artist and industrial designer, was arrested in the raid together with a group of underground leaders who were subsequently arraigned together with Nelson Mandela in what became known as the Rivonia Trial, and sentenced to life imprisonment. The Rivonia raid was followed by police swoops throughout South Africa, in the course of which they arrested Harold Wolpe, a young lawyer and veteran of the anti-apartheid struggle.

Goldreich and Wolpe were held in the cells of Johannesburg's police headquarters in Marshall Square, and the news that they and two Indians, Moosa Moolla and Abdulhai Jassat, who had been similarly arrested, had escaped from there on 11 August constituted an enormous humiliation for the South African police. It later emerged that they had bribed a young Afrikaner constable to let them out, making it appear as though they had overpowered him. According to the South African authorities, the constable had been promised £2,000; in the event, he got six years' imprisonment.

But an even greater humiliation awaited the South African police. The most intensive man-hunt in the history of South Africa was mounted to recapture the escaped men; a particularly close watch was kept on the borders of the High Commission Territories, which were their obvious targets of refuge; and a price of at least £1,000 each was placed on the heads of Goldreich and Wolpe.

Nevertheless, after evading the police drag-net for over two weeks, Goldreich and Wolpe, disguised as priests, reached safety in Swaziland. From there, they flew by charter flight into Bechuanaland on 26 August, where an East African Airways plane was to collect them together with other refugees. The British authorities, to whom they reported on landing, granted them temporary asylum, to the unbridled fury of the South African

35

authorities and the excitement of the world Press, whose representatives flocked into the Protectorate to cover one of the news stories of the year.

A Dakota airliner of E.A.A. duly arrived, and was scheduled to leave with the two men and other refugees, of whom there were at the time approximately 100 in Bechuanaland, at 7 a.m. on 29 August. But at 2.15 a.m. residents sleeping near the airport were awakened by the sound of an explosion, and rose to find the Dakota in flames.

In the white-frequented pubs of Francistown there was unconcealed satisfaction. 'Pity some of those bastards weren't on the bloody plane,' one man said to me, and he was typical. So hostile, in fact, was the attitude of most whites to Goldreich and Wolpe that after the sabotage of their plane they felt obliged to leave the grossly misnamed Grand Hotel and shut themselves away in the town's jail.

It was there that they gave me the first Press interview since their escape from the South African police.* The two men were in an agonizing position; E.A.A. had cancelled a replacement flight for the burnt-out Dakota, communications with their contacts in Dar-es-Salaam were tenuous, and all telephone calls and cables had, for lack of independent Bechuanaland facilities, to be routed through South Africa. The asking price for a local charter flight which might barely reach Mbeya was £600, but even if they disposed of this sort of money they could not be sure that a local pilot would not bring them down in South African territory and claim the large rewards on their heads. To most Bechuanaland whites, such a man would have seemed a hero. And to cross the Zambesi at the narrow point at which Bechuanaland has a common border with Northern Rhodesia would have meant walking straight into the arms of Sir Roy Welensky's officials, who – it was not unreasonable to suppose – would return them to South Africa.

Both men were deeply worried about their families: Wolpe's wife Annemarie had been interrogated for fifteen hours by the South African political police, and Goldreich's wife Hazel had been detained under the so-called Ninety-Day Law. Their children,

* The *Observer*, 1 September 1963 and the *Sunday Express*, Johannesburg, of the same date.

Goldreich had just learnt, had also been interrogated by the South African political police.

On 8 August, Goldreich and Wolpe made their way before dawn to the landing strip at Palapye, accompanied by a police escort. There they were picked up by a Cessna light aircraft, chartered from East Africa, which left them on another landing strip at Kasane in the northernmost corner of Bechuanaland whilst the pilot went on to refuel at Livingstone in Northern Rhodesia. Despite the assertion by the Federation's Director of Civil Aviation, Colonel H. M. Barber, that if the two men had landed only to refuel they would have been quite safe, Goldreich and Wolpe had satisfied themselves that it was in fact the intention of Sir Roy Welensky to detain them if they landed on federal territory. From Kasane their plane went directly on to Elizabethville in the Congo, and on to a hero's welcome in Dar-es-Salaam and Britain. Throughout their stay in the Protectorate, the Bechuanaland authorities, and especially the Francistown District Commissioner, Mr Phil Steenkamp, had behaved with courtesy and correctness towards them. Their two Indian fellow-escapees from Marshall Square made their way independently to Swaziland and thence to Britain, so that the humiliation of the South African authorities seemed complete. Barring the sky-hatch against future refugees, Dr Verwoerd unilaterally promulgated in September regulations controlling aircraft flying into and out of the Territories, as well as inter-territorial flights passing over South Africa.

'HAT TRICK'

Fresh salt was, however, being rubbed into Dr Verwoerd's self-inflicted wounds at the same time through the case of Dr Kenneth Abrahams.

Dr Kenneth Godfrey Abrahams, a South African twenty-six-year-old coloured medical practitioner, had been politically active in Cape Town, and in September 1963 moved to South West Africa to practise amongst the Basters of the Rehoboth district, a coloured community from which his wife came. South Africa's administration and virtual incorporation of South West Africa, which borders on Bechuanaland and is a former League of Nations

Mandated Territory, is being challenged before the International Court of Justice, but for the moment South Africa's repressive law runs there.

The South West Africa administration suspected Dr Abrahams of being a member of the anti-apartheid South West African Peoples' Organization. He was charged with being illegally in South West and found guilty. Before his appeal could be heard, police arrived with a warrant, issued in Cape Town, for his arrest. But when they tried to arrest him, the Baster Council of elders threatened bloodshed. The police were forced to retreat. Until his arrival the Basters had been without a regular doctor, and a few days later the South African Government gave him an indemnity, saying that he could remain in South West even if he lost his appeal, provided that he continued with his practice.

Dr Abrahams had, however, fled with three Baster friends into Bechuanaland by that time. Shortly after his party crossed into British territory, a sergeant of the South African police demanded their return from the Bechuanaland police border post, but this was refused.

The Bechuanaland authorities issued Dr Abrahams and his companions with residence permits for one month after providing them with a police escort to the nearest centre, Ghanzi. On 11 August Dr Abrahams informed the police that they were leaving by road for Lobatsi, and duly set off in a truck driven by a white Bechuanaland transport contractor, Mr Taljaard. They never arrived at Lobatsi.

When next heard of, Dr Abrahams and his companions, who included Mr Hannes Beukes, a leading elder of the Baster Council and the father of a recent petitioner to the United Nations, had been charged in the South West African magistrate's court at Gobabis with leaving the territory illegally, and Dr Abrahams had been flown to Cape Town in a South African Air Force aeroplane and there charged with sabotage.

What happened to them on the rough, lonely, long road which winds through practically uninhabited, dry shrub country between Ghanzi and Lobatsi? How had they fallen into the hands of the South African police?

Its Commissioner, General Keevy, stated categorically that the party had been arrested by a police patrol 'in the Gobabis district [of South West Africa], near the Bechuanaland border'.*

Mr Taljaard, the white driver of the truck in which they set out from Ghanzi, told a story of their meeting another truck carrying three Coloured men on the road, of Dr Abrahams chatting with these men, whom he appeared to know, and then transferring to their truck after telling Taljaard that he was no longer required. Though one rarely sees another vehicle on that lonely road, Taljaard claimed that he did not notice in which direction Dr Abrahams and his friends then drove off.

But a quite different story exploded on to the front pages of South African and British newspapers in Cape Town. After Dr Abrahams's mother had seen him in the local police cells at Woodstock on 15 August, his wife Lottillie alleged that he had been kidnapped in Bechuanaland by agents of the South African police and taken forcibly back into South West.

South Africa's Minister of Justice, Mr Balthazar Vorster, who had been interned during the Second World War because of his pro-Nazi activities and support of sabotage, promptly replied that this allegation of kidnapping was 'sheer nonsense'.†

But newspapers in and out of South Africa were quick to recall similar statements made after the kidnapping of Anderson Ganyile by South African policemen in Basutoland. As the Port Elizabeth *Evening Post*, edited by a courageous and outstanding journalist, Mr John Sutherland, said on 17 August:

In both [the Ganyile and Abrahams] cases political refugees badly wanted by the South African authorities were involved. In both cases the refugees fled to British territory and subsequently disappeared from there in mysterious circumstances. In both cases the refugees turned up in South African jails after their disappearance. And in both cases the South African authorities claimed (originally) that the men had been arrested on South African territory.

There were, however, two crucial differences from the Ganyile case. First, the hunt for Goldreich and Wolpe had centred international attention on the position of anti-apartheid refugees and on the High Commission Territories towards which these two

* *Evening Post*, Port Elizabeth, 17 August 1963.
† *Rand Daily Mail*, Johannesburg, 21 August 1963.

were at that time obviously heading. Thus the news that Dr Abrahams had been arrested, and the subsequent allegation that he had been kidnapped, received immediate and widespread publicity. And secondly, the British authorities, aware of this publicity, and possibly having learnt something from their scepticism and procrastination in the Ganyile affair, reacted with promptness and firmness. It also so happened that the new High Commissioner, Sir Hugh Stephenson, was in Bechuanaland when Dr Abrahams disappeared.

It was immediately announced that a full-scale investigation into Dr Abrahams's disappearance by the Bechuanaland police had been ordered, and the Protectorate's Information Officer, Major Allan Donald, told reporters: 'I can assure you quite categorically that the Bechuanaland police did not connive in this [disappearance]. Dr Abrahams was reported to be in Bechuanaland, and the next thing in the custody of the South African police.'* Meanwhile, British Labour Party M.P.s were asking questions about the case in the House of Commons, which is always the quickest way of stirring a colonial administration into action.

In South Africa, the handling of the case was taken over by the British embassy, which had been ordered to report to the British Government. By 17 August, a British consular official described the situation, not without some traditional understatement, as 'red hot'.

On 19 August, Dr Abrahams's lawyers brought an urgent *habeas corpus* application against the South African Minister of Justice in the Cape Supreme Court, together with a petition that their client be returned to Bechuanaland. Dr Abrahams's petition ran to eight typed pages. Filled out with some minor details which emerged later, it read except for its sober, legal language, like something out of a Wild West thriller, complete with masked men, cowboy hats and low-slung hip holsters:

On the morning of 11 August, Dr Abrahams and his three companions left Ghanzi for Lobatsi in Mr Taljaard's truck. In the truck with them were Taljaard, another unknown white man, and two of Taljaard's African employees.

About one mile from Ghanzi, and approximately 100 miles

* *Evening Post*, Port Elizabeth, 17 August 1963.

from the Bechuanaland–South West Africa border, they were hailed by three white men standing next to a parked truck whose number plates had been covered over with sacking. The three men asked Taljaard if he could take them to Lobatsi, and he signalled to them to climb on to his truck. At this, three other white men, all wearing masks, jumped into the back of Taljaard's truck. One, who was subsequently identified as the son of a South West farmer called Heydenreich, was sporting jeans with a low-slung holster on one hip, a dagger sheath on the other, and wore a stetson-type hat. This colourfully dressed individual ordered the men in the truck to 'get up'. Dr Abrahams refused, and one of his companions, realizing what was happening, leapt to his feet and shouted in Afrikaans: 'I, Hermanus Chritoffel Beukes,' a phrase which he apparently uses frequently, 'will rather die today than give in to you.'

The 'cowboy', feet apart, dagger in one hand and revolver in the other, replied: '*Maans Beukes, jy gaan vandag vrek!*' (Maans Beukes, today you will die!)

The masked men then forcibly ejected Beukes and another of Dr Abrahams's companions from the truck. Two of them were assaulted and handcuffed, and Dr Abrahams told that he would be shot if he resisted. All four men were then transferred, together with some of Dr Abrahams's luggage, to the parked truck, which one of them was able later to identify as Heydenreich's since the sacking at one time slipped off its number plates.

Taljaard then drove off and the kidnappers' truck started, with three of the whites sitting in the rear and keeping their captives 'covered' with one or more guns.

No sooner had the truck gone 100 yards or so, however, than a puncture was discovered, causing panic amongst the kidnappers, especially when their jack failed to work properly in the soft sand which constitutes roads thereabouts. The captives were made to help with holding up the back of the truck whilst the wheel was changed. When the spare wheel also proved to be flat, there was a further flurry of excitement, but it was successfully pumped up.

With Heydenreich driving and repeated stops to check the way with passing Batswana, they proceeded by side paths and part of the main Ghanzi–Gobabis road until they reached the international border fence on an isolated farm. The captives' handcuffs had by this time been loosened, and some of them were made to hold down the fence while the truck drove over it.

As soon as the border had been crossed, young Heydenreich said to Beukes: 'We are now in South West Africa and I am *baas* (master) to you.'

Near Buitepos, where the local police post is situated, two of the kidnappers left to pick up a vehicle parked in some bushes. The captives recognized one of these men as a sergeant of the South African police.

At Buitepos, two of the remaining men changed into South African police uniforms, whose numbers were again noted by Dr Abrahams's companions. Then, with young Heydenreich driving, they all proceeded to his father's farm. Old man Heydenreich emerged on his farmhouse *stoep* with a rifle and two dogs, but was told that they were not necessary as the captives were *'heeltemaai mak'* (quite tame).

At the farm they found a vehicle belonging to the Buitepos police post guarded by an African constable, whose number they again noted. The captives were well treated, in fact old man Heydenreich engaged the equally voluble Beukes in a discussion which lasted from 2 p.m. to 9 p.m. Heydenreich tried to make Beukes see the error of his ways, telling him of everything which the Government was doing for the benefit of non-whites and saying that it was wrong for Beukes and his son to encourage the United Nations to meddle in local affairs, which could be settled by the people of South West themselves if they 'talked things over'. Beukes, who likes nothing better than a discussion, put his views at length, neither convincing the other but both maintaining an amicable tone.

At 11 p.m. the captives were taken to the Buitepos police post, where they spent the night in a cell also occupied by a Bushman. The next day, 12 August, they were taken to Gobabis in police vehicles, accompanied by two sergeants of the Special Branch from Windhoek, the capital. *En route*, one of the policemen read out a warrant of arrest to Dr Abrahams on a charge under the so-called Suppression of Communism Act, and his companions were formally arrested for leaving South West without a permit.

At Gobabis, Dr Abrahams was immediately brought before Mr J. Kriel, the local assistant magistrate. He told the magistrate that he and his companions had been kidnapped in Bechuanaland, that he wanted to see a lawyer and get in touch with relatives at Windhoek and that he wanted bail.

According to Mr Kriel, the charge sheet did not say where Dr Abrahams had been arrested, nor by whom: 'Although it was not officially stated in court, I understand that the arrest was made by the South African police,' Mr Kriel subsequently told the *Rand Daily Mail*.* 'Abrahams asked if he could appear in a court at Windhoek, but the prosecutor said that *arrangements had already been made* for the trial to take place in Cape Town. I accepted the prosecutor's argument.' (My italics.)

This was less than thirty-six hours after Dr Abrahams had set out in Taljaard's truck from Ghanzi for Lobatsi. Yet *arrangements had already been made* for a Cape Town trial, and by 4 p.m. of the same afternoon a Dakota of the South African Air Force had landed at Gobabis. It immediately refuelled and took off with Dr Abrahams aboard for Cape Town, where he was lodged in the Woodstock jail.

'At every opportunity since then,' he concluded in his petition to the Supreme Court, 'I have informed the police of my abduction, and demanded release and to be able to return to Bechuanaland, but my protests and demands have been ignored. At no time did I voluntarily cross the border from Bechuanaland into South West Africa, nor did I at any time willingly accompany the six persons referred to or any of them, but did so only under compulsion and threats.'

Some minor details, such as the 'cowboy' dress affected by young Heydenreich, were not included in the petition to the Supreme Court and emerged only a little later, but the petition as it stood was quite sufficient to satisfy Mr Justice Diemont that Dr Abrahams had established a *prima facie* case. He felt, however, that the three respondents named by Dr Abrahams should have an opportunity to investigate the allegations made and to controvert the facts if they wished to do so.

On 20 August Mr Justice Diemont therefore issued a *rule nisi* calling on the Minister of Justice, the police commander at Woodstock (where Dr Abrahams was being held), and the Attorney-General of the Cape (who was charging Dr Abrahams with

* *Rand Daily Mail*, Johannesburg, 19 August 1963.

sabotage) to show cause by 5 September why Dr Abrahams should not immediately be released from custody and returned to Bechuanaland, and why the Minister of Justice or all three should not be ordered to pay the costs of Dr Abrahams's application.

On the same day, the case moved up to another level with the delivery to the South African Government of a note by the British ambassador from his Government. Its contents were not disclosed.*

With the issuing of the *rule nisi*, a fascinating prospect opened up before the international Press corps, which was by this time concentrating on the Abrahams case whilst waiting to see whether Goldreich and Wolpe would reach safety or not. For if the judge were to rule after 5 September that the submissions to be made in writing by the Minister of Justice were insufficient to resolve any dispute over the facts of the case, he could order it to be sent to trial. Witnesses could then be called by Dr Abrahams as the petitioner in the case and by the judge himself, and these would almost certainly include the men kidnapped with him, who were being held in custody in South West, the drivers of the two trucks involved, and the Resident Commissioner of Bechuanaland who had granted the refugees political asylum. An international *cause célèbre* seemed in the offing.

But before the due process of law had time to move further, an extraordinary international diversion was staged by the head of the South African security police, Colonel H. J. van den Bergh, which promptly heightened yet further the tension between Britain and South Africa.

Calling a special Press conference, Colonel van den Bergh launched an unprecedented attack on the British Government and the Bechuanaland authorities for allowing Bechuanaland to be used, 'wittingly, in my opinion', as a 'free port for runaways, Reds and saboteurs'.† He claimed that 'so-called political refugees', escapees and hundreds of young African sabotage trainees were being given 'red carpet' treatment in Bechuanaland, 'presumably with the full knowledge of the authorities there'.

'The Bechuanaland authorities provide guest-houses for them,'

---

* *Rand Daily Mail*, Johannesburg, 21 August 1963.

† *Sunday Times*, Johannesburg, 25 August 1963; *Sunday Mail*, Salisbury, 25 August 1963; *Rhodesia Herald*, Salisbury, 27 August 1963.

the Colonel said (Dr Abrahams and his companions had initially stayed in such a guest-house, which was the only accommodation available in an area which has few homesteads, and certainly no hotels), 'and even allow planes to land at Francistown to pick them up for their journeys north. In fact, there is one continuous red carpet for South African saboteurs from Lobatsi to Northern Rhodesia. Bechuanaland is not only a haven for political refugees but a base for sabotage against South Africa. If we know these facts, it seems inconceivable that the British Government and its Resident Commissioner in Bechuanaland should not know them.

'I am not,' the Colonel added 'attacking the British or Bechuanaland authorities in any way. I am merely giving you the facts.' One of the 'facts' which he then added was that hundreds of young Africans were being sent out through Bechuanaland as political refugees. 'They are going to the northern States and to Peking, Moscow, Cairo, Algiers, Ethiopia and other centres for the A.N.C. and P.A.C. on three months' special training in guerrilla warfare and sabotage. They are promised heaven by their Communist sponsors,' Colonel van den Bergh alleged, adding with heartfelt indignation, 'and most have never even come to the notice of the police.

'We are always arresting them either coming or going from South Africa. The Bechuanaland authorities must be 100 per cent aware of what is going on.'

He then proceeded to name a number of 'notorious Communists' who had escaped imminent arrest by passing through Bechuanaland, amongst them Mr Michael Harmel, Mr Joe Slovo 'who was primarily responsible for the local training of all races in sabotage methods', and Mr J. B. Marks. Colonel van den Bergh also alleged that Mr Jack Hodgson who with his wife had been ordered ten days earlier to leave Bechuanaland, was also one of this group and was the 'chief escape officer for all A.N.C. members and Communists leaving South Africa'. (The Hodgsons had for some time before their flight from South Africa been under house arrest, requiring special permission, as banned people, to communicate with any other banned person, including each other.)

But if Dr Verwoerd had hoped to lessen British pressure over the Abrahams case by letting Colonel van den Bergh off the leash, he was mistaken. On 26 August Goldreich and Wolpe reached Bechuanaland.

On 28 August a Foreign Office spokesman announced that Mr Peter Smithers, the Parliamentary Under-Secretary for Foreign Affairs had summoned the South African chargé d'Affaires in London and had expressed to him the British Government's 'serious concern' over the case of Dr Abrahams. At the same time the Colonial Office announced that the conclusions of the special investigation being made into the case by the Bechuanaland police would be made available as soon as this was completed* (though this was never done).

As the *Rand Daily Mail* pointed out on 29 August in a leading article headed '*Another Ganyile?*':

The admonitory phrase will not have been used lightly by the Foreign Office, which obviously has some reason to believe that everything was not above board. The grave consequences for relations between Britain and South Africa over the Protectorates are clear enough ... unfortunately the Opposition in the House of Commons will give Mr Macmillan's Government no quarter on this point. It is well briefed on the facts and will demand a much stiffer attitude from the Foreign Office in the future. This can be a diplomatic situation of the greatest delicacy.

But, as in the Ganyile case, firm British pressure brought a denouement with a rush.

On 27 August an application by Dr Abrahams for bail had been refused, and he was remanded in custody until the still unformulated charge of sabotage against him was due to be heard on 10 September.

Then, on 30 August, the Minister of Justice announced that Dr Abrahams and his companions would be returned to Bechuanaland 'in the interests of good relations' with Governments of neighbouring States. At the same time Mr Vorster denied that they had been kidnapped from Bechuanaland by the South African police.

In an affidavit to a full bench of the Supreme Court, Mr Vorster said that the Abrahams case had two basically important aspects: that of legal proceedings 'prospective and pending', and that of

---

* *Rand Daily Mail*, Johannesburg, 29 August 1963.

good international relations between South Africa and adjoining states.

On the legal side, 'the charges are of a very grave nature, including sabotage so serious as to involve the security of the State and the safety of all law-abiding citizens'.

Earlier, the Attorney-General had explained that Dr Abrahams was to be charged with being chairman of a guerrilla warfare organization known as the Yu Chin Chan Club: 'I am informed that this is Chinese for guerrilla warfare and is also the name of a book written by Mao Tse-tung relative to guerrilla warfare.'

In his statement, Mr Vorster asked that because of the assurance that Dr Abrahams and his companions would be returned to Bechuanaland Dr Abrahams's application for a writ of *habeas corpus* be dismissed with costs. (Later, the court dismissed Dr Abrahams's application on just such a technicality, and ordered him to pay £300 costs.)

'It appears,' said Mr Vorster, 'that no member of the South African police,' was in fact concerned in the alleged kidnapping. 'What is beyond dispute is that no instruction or authority in regard to Abrahams on Bechuanaland territory was at any time issued by the South African police. On the other hand, there are indications that civilians may have been involved in *Abrahams's removal from Bechuanaland* to South West Africa.' (My italics.)

The South African Government wanted to maintain good relations with all Governments of neighbouring States, and believed that to detain Dr Abrahams in the circumstances would not help good relations. 'It has accordingly been decided to return him and his companions to Bechuanaland.'*

It was a far cry from the minister's earlier pre-judgement that all allegations were 'sheer nonsense'.

On 31 August Dr Abrahams was flown from Cape Town to Gobabis in South West Africa in a South African military aeroplane, where he was joined by his companions and driven to the Bechuanaland border. The Bechuanaland police took them to Ghanzi, where he was reunited on the next day with his wife Lottillie, whom the enterprising *Rand Daily Mail* had flown up from Francistown in a chartered aeroplane. They are now in

* *Evening Post*, Port Elizabeth, 30 August 1963.

Zambia, where Dr Abrahams obtained a post in the medical service.

It was probably Vicky, that superlative political cartoonist, who summed up the Abrahams affair best. In a cartoon widely syndicated by the London Express Service, he showed Dr Verwoerd standing, with a bunch of keys, in front of a heavily barred cell. On the wall is a framed quote from one of his many past speeches: 'Our policy of apartheid can best be described as a policy of good neighbourliness.' Spreading his arms in pained innocence, the good doctor is now saying: 'We've never kidnapped anybody – and to prove it, we've just sent him back again!'

The whole affair had proved to be a clear-cut triumph for very proper British firmness, and the respect which Britain thus earned was increased by her equally proper behaviour at the same time over the Goldreich and Wolpe case. And then, within weeks, the British authorities promptly went ahead and blotted the fine page they had written in their copy book.

Dr Verwoerd and his supporters had been left smarting under their self-inflicted débâcle, and began to apply considerable pressure to Britain for a revision of extradition arrangements with the Territories which would include political refugees against whom 'criminal' charges were pending. In South Africa, of course, most political opposition can draw 'criminal' charges, and Britain has refused to play this South African game. But it was not long before she brought into operation in Bechuanaland a Prevention of Violence Abroad Proclamation which could lead to the imprisonment of persons in the Protectorate calling for any campaign against apartheid. Britain also failed, despite public and advance warning, to make any protest when the South African Government in September 1963 unilaterally limited the freedom of aircraft flights between the High Commission Territories. When a refugee family of P.A.C. supporters, including two small children and accompanied by two student refugees, defied the South African regulations by flying from Basutoland to Bechuanaland in October, the Bechuanaland authorities first imprisoned them and then did South Africa's work for it by making them fly back to Basutoland.*

This looked very much as if the British authorities were

* *Sunday Times*, Johannesburg, 15 September 1963.

'cutting the pipe-line' and appeasing the South Africans; an impression which was strengthened by the otherwise inexplicable banning from Bechuanaland of Mr Joe Slovo and Mr J. B. Marks, who had passed through the Protectorate some time before but who had been specifically named by Colonel van den Bergh of the South African political police in his calculated outburst during the Abrahams affair.

As long as she insists on retaining control over security and internal affairs in the High Commission Territories, Britain will of course continue to find the problem of political refugees, which increases with every further turn of apartheid's repressive screw, a difficult and even invidious one. As with all threatened totalitarian régimes, the South African Government's hatred of internal opposition is increasingly matched only by its paranoia towards the outside world.

For all the assurances given by the Commissioner of the South African police in the Abrahams court case that 'strict instructions have been issued to all officers and men that no border incidents of any nature whatever should be permitted to take place', the real attitude of the régime is reflected by the editorial with which *Die Burger*, the official Cape Town newspaper of Dr Verwoerd's party, topped a series of increasingly violent and hysterical party comment during the Abrahams case. 'It must be obvious that an underground war that recognizes no borders [*sic*] also necessitates underground defence,' *Die Burger* declared. 'South Africa will perhaps have to go deeply and professionally into this business, for no games are being played by the other side. The less that is said in public about such countermeasures the better it would be, but one aim should probably be to deprive the revolutionary of his sense of security once he has left South Africa. For that the South African defence will have to develop long and skilful arms in the knowledge that when the life of a nation is involved unorthodox methods have always been orthodox.'* And this from the paper which traditionally reflects the views of the 'moderate' wing of Dr Verwoerd's party!

The asylum and transit rights which Britain rightly grants in Basutoland, Bechuanaland, and Swaziland to opponents of apartheid, underline the visible and constant reminder to the

* *Sunday Times*, Johannesburg, 1 September 1963.

Republic's Africans and white liberals that these Territories, for all their democratic shortcomings, provide the possibility of a different and better way of life in southern Africa for all races. The Territories not only proclaim that Africans are entitled to the full weight of their numbers in governing themselves. They increasingly demonstrate that Africans are capable of exercising these rights responsibly and competently.

Sir John Maud, when High Commissioner for the Territories, described them as 'shop-windows of the British way of life'. It is a telling phrase, for even if the windows are somewhat shabby and poorly stocked for the moment, Britain has pledged herself before the United Nations to make Sir John's image good.

Clearly, where the British way of life differs so radically in its basic assumptions from those now imposed on South Africa, there must be friction between the two countries for as long as Britain fulfils its responsibilities to the Territories.

2 The British Responsibility

Britain's responsibilities to Basutoland, the Bechuanaland Protectorate, and Swaziland are clear – and extensive. Some confusion is sometimes caused by the fact that Britain has chosen to call only one of the Territories a Protectorate while Basutoland and Swaziland are officially described as Colonies.

None of the three Territories was ever conquered by force of arms, and Britain came into all three of them with the agreement of the inhabitants. Britain indeed entered Basutoland at the persistent urging, over years, of Moshesh, the founder of the Basuto nation, but the Basuto today still resent being called a Colony. They argue, with considerable justice, that they originally entered into a treaty of allegiance with Britain that promised to protect their country, and that therefore Basutoland should have been classed as a Protectorate.

But whether they are called colonies or protectorates makes no difference to Britain's clear responsibilities today. First and foremost, of course, Britain is responsible for the territorial integrity of the three States. And secondly, but no less importantly, Britain is, under her declared policy for her remaining colonies, responsible for bringing the peoples of all three Territories as rapidly as possible towards independence, ensuring meanwhile that the well-being of their inhabitants is promoted as far as possible.

Few colonies have shown more clearly than the High Commission Territories that this British colonial policy is of very recent date. In fact, the key to the history of all three Territories is that for forty years of this century the British Government worked on the underlying assumption that they would be incorporated eventually into South Africa. Each Territory was poor and, except in terms of the migrant labour that it provided for South African farms and mines, highly unprofitable, and Britain spent as little money and energy on them as possible. Sooner or later, the assumption was, they would be taken over by South Africa, and provision for this was made in the Act which created the Union of South Africa in 1910. In the meantime, provided there was no trouble with the inhabitants, the less money spent on them the happier the British taxpayer – and the British Departments of State – would be.

When the British, having fought and won the Boer War, made their generous peace with the South African Republics, they followed this up by creating the Union of South Africa, a unified self-governing white-ruled State between the Cape of Good Hope and the Limpopo. But the British were uneasy about handing over also Basutoland, Bechuanaland and Swaziland, which they had undertaken to protect. They wanted, at any rate, to wait until they felt sure that the interests of the people of these Territories would be safeguarded as part of the Union. The Africans of the three Territories had made their objections to incorporation known in no uncertain manner. The Basuto in particular, who had had experience of Cape administration between 1871 and 1873, had sent delegations to protest in London. Thus, although the Act of Union made provision, in a schedule, for the incorporation of the Territories, the British Government made it quite clear that this procedure could not become effective unless the British Parliament was consulted and the wishes of the inhabitants of the Territories considered.

The white South Africans were not very happy about this condition, but although the Boer War was the first twentieth-century illustration of the maxim that the best way to win the peace is to lose the war, they formally accepted the situation. A schedule was made to the Act of Union which also laid down very clearly safeguards which would protect the rights of the Territories' Africans in the event of a transfer taking place (similar provision was also made for the incorporation into South Africa of Southern Rhodesia).

It was not long, however, before the South Africans began their diplomatic offensive for incorporation. The incorporation of Bechuanaland was raised as early as 1913 by South Africa's first Prime Minister, General Botha, who was concerned chiefly to prevent Bechuanaland from falling to the British South Africa

Company, with its visions of a Greater Rhodesia, and the British Government reassured the South African premier.

The First World War intervened, but in 1919 Generals Botha and Smuts tried to take up the incorporation of Swaziland. The British Government, privately and publicly, reaffirmed the promises of 1909 that nothing could be done unless the Territory's Africans were consulted.

At this stage, the South Africans fully accepted that transfer was dependent upon such consultation, but tried subtly to change the meaning of the schedule which would give special protection to these inhabitants if transfer took place. The British firmly resisted these moves too, and for a few years the matter rested there. The South Africans were busy establishing their own constitutional independence, which they achieved with the passing of the Statute of Westminster in 1931 and the South African Status Act of 1934. The latter established the Union Parliament as a 'sovereign legislative body', and the South Africans, led by General Smuts as Minister of Justice, returned to their demands for the Territories. From 1933 to the outbreak of the Second World War, the attack never flagged.

But since the British Government, despite some vaccilation, ultimately stood firm on the constitutional position and its frequently repeated pledges of consultation, the South Africans shifted their ground to the economic sphere. They argued, quite rightly at the time, that transfer would benefit both the Territories and the Union economically. And, to add point to their argument, Prime Minister Hertzog in 1934 hinted for the first time at the threat, which Dr Verwoerd has today made explicit, of economic sanctions.

Economic sanctions could be a most telling South African weapon, for, quite aside from their long neglect, Swaziland is the only one of the three Territories which is not obviously poor. Basutoland, in particular, depends heavily on the earnings of its migrant menfolk labouring in South Africa; at any given time, forty-three per cent of its adult male population is away earning money in the South African mines and on farms. A large number of Botswana similarly work in South Africa.

This dependence on migratory labour can never be wholly solved if all the Basuto are to be based in Basutoland, but it is an indictment of British neglect that General Hertzog could, in 1934, phrase his implied threat in almost identical words to those used by Dr Verwoerd in 1961.

'It can, therefore, be seen,' General Hertzog wrote in 1934 to Britain's Secretary of State for Dominion Affairs, 'that if these Territories are still for any length of time to remain outside the administrative control of the Union it will become increasingly difficult, if not impossible, for the Government of the Union to extend to their inhabitants the enjoyment of the rights and privileges of citizens in the labour and other markets of the Union'.* In 1935, further unease was created by the official setting up of a British–South African Committee to prepare the Territories for closer association with the Union.

Once more a world war intervened. General Smuts divided South Africa by entering the war on Great Britain's side and, amidst the multiple problems posed by opposition to the war – led by leaders of the country's present Government – and armament efforts, the issue of incorporation was shelved. In fact, South Africans fought in some war theatres with African units recruited from Bechuanaland, Basutoland, and Swaziland. But Smuts's hopes, expressed in 1944, of gaining British assent for post-war transfer, if only in return for South African war services, were frustrated.

When Smuts went, the Nationalist Prime Minister, Dr Malan, took up the attack. He warned the new Churchill Government in 1951 that 'foreign treatment' might be meted out to Africans from the Territories, but to this Mr Winston Churchill, as Prime Minister, on 22 November 1951 gave the unequivocal reply, much quoted since, that transfer could not take place 'until the inhabitants of the Territories had been consulted and Parliament had had an opportunity of expressing its views'. In 1953 Dr Malan nevertheless issued an ultimatum that their transfer to South Africa had to be achieved within five years. These threats were not made good, but Malan's successor, Mr Strijdom, kept up the psychological pressure.

In 1961, twenty-seven years after General Hertzog first hinted

* Letter from General Hertzog to Mr J. H. Thomas, Blue Book; Basutoland, The Bechuanaland Protectorate and Swaziland, History of Discussions with the Union of South Africa 1909–39, Cmd 8707; p. 48.

at sanctions, Dr Verwoerd told the Orange Free State Congress of his party that until recently it had been assumed that the Territories would one day become part of South Africa's Bantu areas, and Africans from them had therefore been accorded the same privileges as natives from South Africa's own native territories. However, during the premiership of Dr Malan, Britain had started developments in the Territories towards their independence. Since then, and particularly since South Africa's withdrawal from the Commonwealth, relations with the Territories had to be placed on the basis of relationships with a foreign State.*

The threat first made in the thirties is to be made real in the sixties, but under what changed political circumstances! It is surely ironical that it was Dr Verwoerd, the most fanatical of all Afrikaner nationalists, who should have earned the strange distinction of becoming the first Prime Minister in South Africa's history to admit finally that the Territories were legally lost for ever to his country.

This historic admission does not, of course, put paid to South African ambitions for the Territories. In fact, it must merely increase the republican Government's desire to see these shop-windows of freedom either smashed or absorbed into their own State. But South Africa's departure from the Commonwealth has finally ended the long and increasingly acrimonious debate between it and Britain about an ultimate transfer of the Territories.

As a result, the new relationship between South Africa and the Territories has now reached the stage of foreign States, though it remains one partly comparable to that which will exist between member countries of an increasingly integrated European Economic Community. The customs union and common currency continue in force, and migrant labourers from Basutoland and the other two Territories are still admitted, though only under permit, into South Africa, provided that they work only in mines or on farms. The richer, though still poor, pickings of the cities are closed to them, as to all 'foreign natives'.

Other consequences of this 'foreign' status have already been formalized by both the South Africans and the British in the legislation of both countries which defined their relationships after South Africa left the Commonwealth. Many of these new

* *The Times*, 18 September 1961.

regulations are proving irksome both to South Africans and to the people, black and white, of the Territories, but invariably they hit the latter harder than the former.

It will soon no longer be possible for people living in the Territories to enjoy the benefits of what has amounted to dual citizenship. Until now, white South Africans resident, say, in Bechuanaland, have been able to choose where they pay their income tax and have enjoyed a vote in both countries. Following fresh South African legislation, however, the Bechuanaland authorities in 1962 gave them a year in which to make up their minds which citizenship they wanted to keep, with members of the Bechuanaland Legislative Council required to make an immediate decision. Interestingly enough, the representatives of Bechuanaland's white, Afrikaans-speaking farming communities have all opted for British citizenship. The only Council member to opt for South African status when faced with the choice has been an African, Dr Molema, who in South Africa was Treasurer-General of the African National Congress in the stirring, Defiance-Campaign days of 1952. For the time being, however, there are no similar provisions in Swaziland or Basutoland.

Under recent South African legislation, passports are now required for entry into the Territories. Border control posts have been set up by the South Africans at the main road points of entry, where before only an occasional South African police patrol harassed the traveller. Given the long and tortuous nature of the borders, this does not make it impossible for South African refugees to slip across into sanctuary, but it certainly makes things more difficult, especially for whites, who lack the protective anonymity provided in South Africa by a black skin.

On the crucial economic front, then, little has changed so far. The two countries maintain common currencies, and, above all, the agreement under which South Africa allocated to the Territories a fixed share of its customs revenues remains in force.

With Britain starving the Territories of funds, this customs agreement is of the greatest importance, especially to Basutoland, which obtains half of its annual revenue from this source.

There would, of course, be no legal bar to South Africa's abrogating this customs agreement at any time, and the Basuto, in particular, are far from allowing themselves to be lulled into a sense of security because it remains in force for the moment.

In fact, a possible pattern of future South African intentions may be discernible in the way in which the Republic is already trying to modify the customs agreement. Where until now it has handed over a lump sum to the British authorities, who have then doled it out to the Territories, South Africa now wants to pay each Territory its share directly. This would clearly enable it to differentiate in the future between the Territories. It would make possible, for instance, an attempt to squeeze Basutoland economically while leaving Swaziland, which has substantial South African – and British – investments, untouched.

The negotiation of the revised relationships were conducted on the British side by Sir John Maud, who combined the theoretically separate offices of British Ambassador to the Republic and High Commissioner for Basutoland, the Bechuanaland Protectorate and Swaziland, and there has rarely been an occasion which so clearly demonstrated the ambiguity inherent in this dual role. On the one hand, Britain has some £1,000,000,000 invested in South Africa, and this, if nothing else, means that her ambassador to the Republic attempts to maintain the smoothest possible relations between the two countries. On the other hand, the High Commissioner for the Territories has had to battle against South African hostility and resentment against the very separate existence of such countries and any attempts to further their development.

This dual role of Britain's representative in South Africa was understandably extremely unpopular with the Africans. Resentful as most of them have always been of colonial rule, which they regard as something quite different from the British protection for which they originally asked, Africans protested that they had been given a ruler who did not even reside in any of their Territories. Worse still, he resided in the enemy camp, where he maintained apparently most cordial relations and delivered himself of elegant declarations on British–South African friendship. Then, from time to time, he visited one or other of the three Territories and delivered himself of equally warm and elegant declarations on Britain's determination to promote their interests and to help them towards early independence.

Those who defended this arrangement pointed to the close

identity of economic progress in South Africa and the Territories. They argued that precisely because Britain had such large, if indirect, economic power in South Africa, a greater chance of concessions for the Territories would lie with a High Commissioner whom the South Africans would not wish to offend. And they pointed to the efficiency and economy of an arrangement which avoided an inevitable duplication of work and liaison.

It is the last argument which really explains how this unique combined office of ambassador and colonial Governor came to be established, for Britain was anxious to spend as little money as was compatible with the maintenance of law and order in the Territories. But whatever the historical reasons and earlier justifications for this dual arrangement – and even the latter were cogently criticized thirty years ago – it became rapidly less satisfactory as the Territories tacked politically away from South Africa.

The more their political and economic development was stimulated, the clearer it became that they are really three separate Territories which, while they share underlying economic and political problems, have quite separate and specific needs. These differences will become clear as we examine each Territory; and certainly once Britain allowed at least one of the Territories to move towards independence, she undermined the concept of one man as the ultimate authority for all three. The post of High Commissioner was abolished at long last in 1963.

Today Britain is firmly and publicly committed to policies which lead in the opposite direction from Dr Verwoerd's. But how far can Britain go, and how fast? At what pace can progress be made without its leading to South African economic warfare against the Territories, or even to an outright physical attempt at annexation? Are Britain's responsibilities to the Territories so far-reaching that she must push to their logical conclusion policies which raise the possibility of an armed clash with South Africa? To find an answer to this ultimate question we must look briefly at how Britain came to rule Basutoland, the Bechuanaland Protectorate, and Swaziland.

Basutoland first came under British protection in 1868 and under imperial rule in 1884; Bechuanaland joined it as a British Protectorate a year later in 1885; and Swaziland, whose independence was first guaranteed by Britain in 1881, had this promise renewed in 1884.

These years of 1884–5 were the precise ones during which the European Powers, meeting at the Berlin Conference, agreed between themselves on the carve-up of Africa, and this coincidence of dates has inevitably been noted by the present African leaders of the Territories. They, and their fellow Pan-Africanists, sporadically claim to see British responsibility for their countries as stemming from the time, only eighty years ago, when a rapacious Britain was determined, by fair means or foul, to colour the map of southern Africa a solid imperial red.

It therefore comes as an unpleasant shock to many Africans to be reminded that, in strict historical fact, Britain was most reluctant to assume responsibility for what became the three High Commission Territories: that the Basuto vainly petitioned Queen Victoria for protection from 1865 to 1867; and that, as late as 1895, the three major chiefs of Bechuanaland in a petition to the British Government declared, 'If you will keep us under the protection of the Queen we will give you a part of our country'.

This picture of Britain as a reluctant imperialist is one which is still being projected vigorously by some senior officials in the Territorial administrations, and it has as its corollary the position that British responsibility towards the Territories is a limited one, resting on altruism. Therefore, the argument runs, the Africans and the world have no right to attack Britain for what it has failed to do for the Territories. If the United Nations does not approve of what Britain is doing, then Britain should wash its hands of the whole unrewarding affair. Let the United Nations do better, and let the Africans see how they get along without British protection and help.

This point of view was tartly put to me in private conversation by a senior British official in Basutoland, during a discussion of criticisms at the United Nations of British rule in the Territories. 'We never wanted these Territories in the first place,' the official proclaimed. 'They've been nothing but an embarrassment and financial drain to us, and now we're getting kicked for carrying and protecting them all these years. What we should do is to say to the United Nations: "Very well, gentlemen, you say that we're nasty imperialists. All right, *you* can take over. We don't want these Territories, and never did. Now *you* go ahead and provide them with financial subsidies and experienced administrators. And *you* can protect them against South Africa."'

On the face of it, this seems a telling line of argument, and its acceptance would certainly minimize Britain's responsibilities to the Territories.

It is, however, far from being the real picture. For whilst it is strictly true that, before the precise moment that the Territories came under her flag, Britain was reluctant to accept responsibility for them, it was Britain who in the first place had created a situation whereby, without British protection, they would be either devoured by the Afrikaners or gutted by Rhodes's untrammelled imperial commerce.

Fundamentally, the Territories in their modern form have been shaped by the interaction of two nineteenth-century conflicts, which also drew the map of the remainder of southern and central Africa. First there was the conflict among the Bantu tribes of the subcontinent themselves and secondly there was the long drawn out battle for power, land and, later, minerals, between these tribes, metropolitan Britain, and the white settlers, especially the Boers. The conflicts between the tribes were already in spate as the white men manoeuvred, and inevitably the latter exacerbated the former. Increasingly, in fact, white land-grabbing and conflicts forced displaced and dissatisfied tribes into war with each other and at certain stages, opposing Boer and Briton bid for the armed help, or at least the neutrality, of rival Bantu groups.

At its sunrise and set, British imperialism in southern Africa was a full-blooded affair; in its middle period, which saw the Territories come under the Union Jack, it may have been anaemic; but at all except perhaps the earliest times it was confused and even contradictory in its detailed operation.

It is with the middle period that we are chiefly concerned. As de Kiewiet has put it, 'Since 1840 the attitude in England towards colonial questions had undergone striking changes. The prevailing mood was opposed to any increase of imperial responsibilities.'*

The history of the Territories is, of course, so inextricably interwoven with that of South Africa that its deeper understand-

* *A History of South Africa – Social and Economic*, C. W. de Kiewiet, O.U.P., 1950, p. 65.

ing demands a study of the wider field. Here we can sketch in only the boldest of outlines.

For quite some time after Jan van Riebeeck established the first settlement at the Cape for the Dutch East India Company in 1652, the southern tip of Africa was regarded as little more than a provisioning station. Gradually, its strategic importance, commanding the sea route of trade to India, increased, but the permanent and expanding settlement of the sea-lane provisioners inevitably produced, at the beginning of the eighteenth century, the problems of remote control from Europe. First Holland and then Britain, the two maritime powers, wanted obedience at the Cape, and later the latter wanted control, too, along the expanding settled coastline.

The early part of the nineteenth century was one of expansion in South Africa, with Britain repeatedly involved in wars against Africans who disputed the advance of the settlers and their absorption of ever-increasing areas of land. Although their absolute cost may have been small, these wars involved Britain in bother and expense, which were not eased by the growing insubordination against British rule and taxation of the white settlers themselves.

Bands of these settlers moved ever deeper into the interior and farther along the coast, and Britain's governors at the Cape, poorly equipped, tried vainly to maintain at least formal authority over them. As the settlers moved, clashes with the Bantu tribes developed, either preceded or succeeded by trade and double-dealing. Meanwhile, however, new patterns of international trade and interest had their effect on public opinion at home. Slavery fell from favour, and the power of commerce and treaties made the rule of the gun less direct.

In 1836 the Boers at the Cape began their Great Trek from British control, and two years later emigrant Boers founded the Republic of Natal. Though the British pursued them for a time, annexing Natal in 1843 and proclaiming British sovereignty between the Orange and the Vaal Rivers in 1848, the home Government grew increasingly disturbed at the unprofitable expenditure of men and, above all, of money which this entailed.

By mid century, Britain's tactics, if not her underlying motives, had changed radically. As Lord Hailey puts it:

Throughout all the discussions on South African affairs during the middle years of the nineteenth century there runs one insistent theme – the necessity to avoid any form of commitment, however much it might be justified by other considerations, which might involve Great Britain itself in military expenditure.*

The reduction of military expenditure took on the greatest importance, and it had its corollary in the granting of self government, so that henceforth any responsible colony had to foot the bill for the consequences of its own alliances or adventures.

'There was an unspoken alliance,' says de Kiewiet, 'between the conviction of the disciples of free trade that it was unprofitable to govern colonies that could govern and pay for themselves and the assurance that the proper place for British regiments was not on colonial frontiers where they too readily became the instruments of local ambitions.'†

Thus in 1848 a draft constitution for a self-governing Cape Colony was on its way to England. But before it could be proclaimed, war broke out again in two areas, on the Basuto border for the Orange River Sovereignty and on the frontier of the Eastern Cape.

It is here, with Basutoland, that we come to the present High Commission Territories.

* *An African Survey*, Lord Hailey, revised 1956, O.U.P., p. 323.
† *A History of South Africa – Social and Economic*.

Part Two

History

3 The Birth of a Nation – Basutoland

Basutoland is a tiny, mountainous country of stark, jagged beauty, and great contrasts, roughly the size of Belgium. Only a quarter of the country lies less than seven thousand feet above sea level; the other three-quarters are highlands, rising in rugged leaps to 11,425 feet in the Drakensberg, or Dragonmountains, which form the eastern boundary with Natal. Scenically, at least, its snowcapped mountains justify the description of an African Switzerland.

It was over these Drakensberg that, early in the nineteenth century, there fled the remnants of Natal tribes, broken in war by Shaka, the great warrior chief of the Zulu. Hot on the heels of the refugees across the Drakensberg followed Shaka's pursuing *impis*, looting, ravaging and devastating everything settled in their path. Shaka's wars became known amongst the tribes as the 'Wars of Calamity', and for the small groups of Africans which his *impis* found settled in the rich Caledon Valley, today forming the north-eastern border of Basutoland and South Africa, the description proved no exaggeration.

This bloody conflict was an African one, and through it there emerged one of the great African figures of the nineteenth century, Moshesh, the father of the Basuto nation. When Shaka's *impis* blazed their trail of blood and havoc across the mountains into what is today Basutoland, Moshesh was a little-known son of a minor chief, living by the cattle-raiding and minor warfare which was the pattern of the time and area.

Having himself been defeated in battle by the forces of a formidable local warrior queen, the young Moshesh, who nevertheless had already made a name for himself as a raider, moved his headquarters to the natural mountain fastness of Thaba Bosiu, the Mountain of the Night.

Here, too weak as yet to take on major foes, he made safe his

3,000 followers, and promptly began to display that talent for diplomacy which was to make him the most outstanding African figure of his time. By a discreet paying of tribute to Shaka, and to his successor, Dingaan, he freed himself from attack by the terrible Zulus.

His strategy was imaginative and successful. Where he could, he temporized with stronger neighbours. When he was attacked, he fought intelligently and well from his fortified mountain. Then, having won, he either absorbed weaker groups or opened conciliatory negotiations with intrinsically stronger foes.

Moshesh also displayed early a talent for learning from his enemies. In 1830 he was attacked by the Korana who, though a rag-bag lot of mixed bloods and 'desperados of any race, black, brown or coloured', were made formidable by their rifles and horses. Moshesh beat off the attack, but this first encounter with firearms and mounts made a deep impression on him. From that time on, he acquired as many rifles as he could, and from this early encounter the Basuto were to become the best horsemen in southern Africa. They came to use the horse in warfare far more than any other African tribe, and, while their speed and firepower made illegal cattle-raiding so tempting to them that it led eventually to their near-downfall, it also made the Basuto formidable fighters.

By about 1831, Moshesh had, through a series of alliances, allegiances, battles, treaties and absorptions become the acknowledged leader of most of the previously distracted Basuto clans. And at about this time, too, the first white hunters and pasture-seeking Boers made contact with him.

Moshesh was illiterate, but he displayed throughout his life a keen appreciation of the power of learning. Having heard of the educational work of white missionaries, he invited three members of the Paris Evangelical Mission into his territory in 1883. With Moshesh's help, these Frenchmen established a mission station at Morija, and thus began the process which has made the Basuto of today the most literate Africans on the sub-continent.

The French missionaries were to become true and lasting friends of the Basuto, but Moshesh soon learnt that not all contact with the white men was so pleasant.

In 1836 the advance parties of trekking Boers from the Cape

reached the Caledon Valley, and from that time began the bitter and protracted fight over land between the two peoples which was to end only with British protection.

The Boers had left the Cape mainly to escape governmental control and to find new lands, and in the Caledon Valley they came upon the finest corn-land in southern Africa. At first they were content merely to graze their cattle on the borders of and within Moshesh's territory. Some of them made Moshesh small presents, which Moshesh, by African custom, regarded as signs of gratitude for the temporary permission he had granted them to graze their cattle on some of his lands. The Boers, however, regarded these presents as having bought them permanent ownership of the land.

The conflict did not take long to materialize. Within three years, in 1839, Moshesh addressed what was to be the first of many complaints against the Boers to the Governor of the Cape Colony. He was curtly told that the British had no control over the Boers in the interior. Then, in 1842, when it seemed that a rival chief might allow a largish party of Boers to settle on territory which Moshesh regarded as falling within his rule, he asked directly for British protection, with a letter written in the French used by Moshesh's Paris evangelical missionaries.

This request of Moshesh's happened to suit a new strategy adopted by the British, who had decided that if they could not themselves control the interior, they would at least encourage the establishment of buffer states. Hence, in October 1843, Sir George Napier, the Cape Governor, signed an agreement with Moshesh which recognized the latter as 'a friend and ally' of the Cape Colony, and laid down in rough outline the extent of his territory. Moshesh undertook to maintain peace and order within this area and not to disturb the neighbouring Cape Colony, in return for which he was to receive £75 a year.*

This recognition of Moshesh and his people as 'a friend and ally' of the British Cape is still regarded by many Basuto today as forming the basis of British–Basuto relations. They argue that Britain never acquired any right to rule Basutoland, since the Napier Treaty made it a Protected State, and not a Protectorate or still less, a Colony.

* *The Map of Africa by Treaty*, E. Hertslet, 1909, vol. 1, p. 184.

As Britain subsequently vacillated in its relationships with the Basuto, and as it revoked some of the succeeding treaties unilaterally, the Basuto have, in theory, considerable backing for their argument. But there is also much to be said on the other side, for, as we shall see presently, Moshesh's attitude towards treaties had its own peculiarities.

Meanwhile, however, Moshesh was given no reason to doubt the new relationship of an alliance with Britain. In fact, the Napier Treaty was confirmed by that Governor's successor in 1845. A British Resident was appointed in Bloemfontein to control the country up to the Vaal, and a fresh provision of the confirmed treaty obliged Moshesh to provide a small force for the Resident's use.

Then and over the years that followed, the cause of conflict between the Boers and the Basuto remained the same: the rich lands of the Caledon Valley. Both claimed the land, and both used it. Without a clear and mutually respected line of demarcation, conflict was inevitable.

But on the Basuto border 'the Dutch had come with their cattle and the Basuto had come down from their hills at about the same time. From the beginning settlement filtered so irregularly into the rich cornlands that no line could succeed in separating white farmers from black herdsmen.'* The problem was hardly eased by the fact that the whites were part-ranchers and the Basuto traditional cattle-raiders. The new British Resident at Bloemfontein, Major H. D. Warden, attempted demarcation, in what became known as the Warden Line, but failed at the time to have it accepted.

Conflict and strife continued beyond the Orange River, and when Sir Harry Smith became Governor of the Cape he decided, as a professional soldier, that the only way to put an end to it was to place the whole area firmly under British rule. Both Boer and Bantu were to be firmly governed.

Sir Harry, an extraordinarily active and decisive man, made a lightning tour beyond the Orange River to acquaint Britain's future subjects with his intentions. In a brief interview in January 1848, Sir Harry assured Moshesh 'that he would remain inde-

* *A History of South Africa – Social and Economic*, C. W. de Kiewiet, 1950, O.U.P., p. 77.

pendent and would be allowed to govern his tribe according to his own customs. On this assurance he agreed to come under British jurisdiction.' As a result of a similarly brief interview with the Boer leader Pretorius, Sir Harry returned to the Cape under the almost certainly mistaken impression that the Boers too had agreed to his scheme.

In February 1848 Sir Harry Smith proclaimed the Queen's sovereignty over all the territories north of the Orange River as far as the Vaal, 'including the countries of Moshesh . . . and other minor chiefs'.*

But the printer's ink had not long been dry on the proclamation of the Orange River Sovereignty when Pretorius, the Boer leader, took up arms in July and seized Bloemfontein. Moving swiftly, Sir Harry brought up troops from the depleted Cape garrison and broke the forces of Pretorius in August.

This apparent success had, however, two consequences which undermined Smith's long-term intentions. His proclamation of the Orange River Sovereignty made good tactical sense as part of a wider strategy of imperial expansion into the southern African sub-continent. But the British Government at home was becoming increasingly reluctant to extend its physical responsibilities. Expansion meant soldiers, and soldiers meant money. Sir Harry's victory over Pretorius reinforced the point.

Britain preferred to let the colonists govern themselves, though naturally under the British flag, and to let them foot the bill for their own policies of expansion, if that was what they were bent on doing. 1848 saw not only the Orange River Sovereignty; it also saw the dispatch to London of a draft constitution for self-government at the Cape.

Thus Sir Harry Smith was pursuing a policy which involved the extended and direct operation of what has been termed the imperial factor in South Africa, whilst the tendency of the home government was to diminish this very same factor. At the same time, the shrewd Moshesh must have noted that as the Cape came closer to self-government the number of British troops there was being reduced. A future Governor would have precious few forces at his disposal to move in aid of the Basuto or against the Boers. Moreover, Moshesh's experience of succeeding Governors must,

* Hertslet, op. cit., p. 212.

even at that early stage, have made him realize that Smith possessed not only unusual incisiveness but even rarer military talents. The conflict over the land continued despite the defeat of Pretorius. In fact, friction, land-disputes, raiding and reprisals were on the way to becoming endemic. There was only one sure answer which lay within Moshesh's powers. He began to equip his people in earnest with arms and horses, obtaining them in exchange for Basuto cattle, and contemporary records suggest that within a few months Moshesh could have mobilized a force of 7,000 mounted men, nearly all of them armed with muskets.

It may have been the knowledge of this increase in Basuto fighting power which, more than the scanty forces at the disposal of their new British sovereign, prevented large-scale attacks by the Boers; in any event no major clash occurred for four years. It was, in fact, typical of the times that during these years Moshesh's old enemy, Pretorius, appealed to him for military help against the British, and it was equally typical of Moshesh that he refused to give it. He might clash with the British authorities on the spot, but he always regarded himself as the 'friend and ally' of Britain which the Napier Treaty had officially made him.

Tension rose dangerously between Moshesh and the British Resident at Bloemfontein, reaching a peak when Moshesh helped a raiding party of an allied tribe to defeat Warden's pursuing forces.

The Government in Britain was now confirmed in its intention of cutting down responsibilities – and therefore expenditure – abroad. 'In the counsels of Whitehall economy prevailed over strategy. It was decided to curtail the area of British responsibility in South Africa.'*

The independence of the Boers living north of the Vaal, which hence became known as the Transvaal, was recognized by the Sand River Treaty of 1852. It remained only to abandon the Orange River Sovereignty, and with it 'the countries of Moshesh . . . and other minor chiefs'.

By this time, however, Moshesh was no longer regarded by the Basuto or the British as a minor chief. In fact, his old enemy, Major Warden, regarded him as the major cause of the sovereignty's troubles, and although the sovereignty was about to be

* De Kiewiet, op. cit., p. 67.

abandoned, Moshesh had to be taught what law and order meant. The new Governor, Sir George Cathcart, felt that such a lesson to the upstart Moshesh would also serve as a warning to others. Ignoring the token restitution which Moshesh offered for the damage done by raiders from his territory, General Cathcart presented him with a demand to which Moshesh could not possibly have submitted. He was to hand over 10,000 cattle and 1,000 horses, and he was to do so *immediately*. Forced by Cathcart to choose between humiliation and ruin or war, Moshesh prepared to defend himself.

Nothing could have been more vindictive than Cathcart's ultimatum, and he followed it up by sending the largest force he could raise against Moshesh to enforce his terms.

Cathcart had, however, reckoned without the difficulty of textbook fighting over rocky, difficult ground against the mounted and armed Basuto whose home it was. There were small but significant numbers of casualties on both sides, but the British failed to dislodge the Basuto in a full day's engagement.

That night Moshesh displayed his mastery of diplomacy. Victorious, he sued for peace. In what has rightly been called the most politic letter ever penned in South Africa, the undefeated Basuto chief wrote: 'You have chastised; let it be enough, I pray you; and let me no longer be considered an enemy of the Queen.'

This master-stroke of diplomacy succeeded. Moshesh was spared the possible disaster of having to make his men face a renewed attack by the British, and was hailed as a victor. His prestige and fame spread throughout South Africa.

But he could not alter the main course of British action, and in August of 1854 the British Government formally withdrew its sovereignty and authority beyond the Orange River. Pretorius and his fellow Boers were now free to establish the Republics of the Transvaal and the Orange Free State. It meant, as de Kiewiet has put it, 'that the Trekkers were free to manage their own relations with their native neighbours'. The self-governing Cape would under the British flag, go its way; the Boers theirs. 'The Great Trek had conquered. South Africa was a land divided.'*

In making this great division, the British could not, at this late stage, be bothered to finalize an agreed dividing line between

* De Kiewiet, op. cit., p. 66.

Moshesh and his now triumphant Boer neighbours. The British withdrew and left behind them an undemarcated Basutoland border which could only explode sooner or later into violence.

Moshesh's known strength, and the relative sanity and personal friendliness of the Orange Free State's first president, Hoffmann, held the teetering balance of uneasy peace for a while. But when Hoffmann was succeeded as president, the hunger of his struggling, inefficient farmers for the rich Basuto lands, increased by their resentment at sporadic cattle raiding, took command.

In 1858 the Free State commandoes struck at the Basuto. They scored a limited initial success, but once again the mountain fastness of Thaba Bosiu held. Striking back, Basuto raided the Free State farms which the commandoes had left undefended. Ill-disciplined at the best of times, and with winter setting in, the Free Staters had to sue for armistice, and called in Sir George Grey, the new British Governor at the Cape, as mediator.

Sir George, who was to become a friend of the Basuto, came up from the Cape, but Moshesh refused to meet him. When Grey laid down the Warden Line border between Boer and Basuto, Moshesh signed the settlement only under the strongest protest, making it clear that he would not be permanently bound by its terms.

For seven years a sort of peace endured, punctured almost continually by Basuto cattle-raiding into what they still considered their rightful lands. Reprisals followed raids and raids reprisals. Moshesh was growing older, and the Free Staters stronger through reinforcement from the Cape.

Moshesh had never accepted Britain's unilateral renunciation of the Orange River Sovereignty; for he found it hard to accept the British dictum that 'wars cancel treaties'.

Increasingly fearful for his people's future after his own death, he used the visit of Queen Victoria's younger son in 1860 to send her a personal plea for resumed British protection. A year later he renewed his suggestion, proposing for the first time that the Queen should send an agent to live with him, to be 'Her eyes and ears'.

The British representative to whom this suggestion was addressed was yet again a new one – the rapidity of official succession in South Africa hardly added to the chances of a consistent policy or of stability – but he had the courtesy and sense to send two commissioners to find out what Moshesh, who had a reputation amongst whites for intrigue and sharp dealing, was about. Fortunately both commissioners spoke Sesuto. They came away convinced of Moshesh's sincerity, and were equally clear that what he wanted was to be protected but not to have his country ruled for him. He wanted a Queen's Agent – to this day the Resident Commissioner is known as the Queen's Man in Sesuto – but not magistrates. He told the two Commissioners, in words remembered by the Basuto today: 'If the Government sends magistrates, the Basuto will not understand; it will be like a stone that is too heavy for them to carry.' But the Queen's Agent could 'practise the Basutos, and gradually teach them to hear magistrates while he is helping me in political matters'. There was to be no confusion over who ruled the Basuto. 'I will be under the Queen as her subject, and my people will be her subjects also, but under me . . . so that the Queen rules my people only through me. . . . I wish to govern my people by Native law, by our own laws; but if the Queen wishes after this to introduce other laws into my country, I will be willing; but I should wish such laws to be submitted to the Council of the Basutos; and when they are accepted by my Council I will send to the Queen and inform her that they have become law.'*

The new Governor, Wodehouse, pressed the British Government to appoint the agent whom Moshesh had requested, but London continued to fear that additional commitments of any sort would lead to additional expense. The situation was allowed to drift and, with the Basuto continuing to raid and the Boers to occupy 'their' land, it inevitably went from bad to worse.

In 1863 Brand, the new president of the Free State, persuaded Sir Philip Wodehouse to mediate between his people and Moshesh's. Again it was the disputed border which wrecked the attempt. The Free Staters, reasonably enough by their lights, stood by the Warden Line to which Moshesh had been an unwilling and temporary party. Moshesh, on the other hand, claimed the return of large but loosely defined areas of 'lost lands'.

Wodehouse stuck, with minor changes, to the Warden Line. But, as both sides knew, he could only make suggestions as a

* *The Basutos*, G. Langden, p. 315.

73

mediator. He could not enforce anything. Only arms could do that. The Trekkers had deliberately been set free to manage their own relations with their African neighbours, and in 1865 they proceeded to do so by force. It was their second war against the Basuto within seven years, but this time the Free Staters were more prosperous and better armed.

At first their tactics were again unsuccessful. They tried vainly to take the mountain stronghold of the Thaba Bosiu. Both sides suffered heavy casualties, and Moshesh appealed again to Wodehouse for British protection. But he felt unable to accept Wodehouse's conditions, and the fighting was resumed.

Now, however, the Free Staters changed their strategy. Instead of launching a frontal assault on a well-defended natural fortress, they captured the Basuto cattle and grain reserves in the surrounding countryside. Their success was electrifying. Crowded into a small and largely mountainous country, the Basuto could not survive for any length of time without stored grain, cattle and new harvests. One of Moshesh's chief lieutenants made a separate surrender to the Boers, and from his territory Thaba Bosiu became vulnerable. Moshesh was forced, in 1866, to sign the Treaty of Thaba Bosiu, in which he recognized the surrender to the Free State of the territory held by his defected lieutenant, Molapo.

The Free Staters had won a rich victory. They had forced the Basuto to give up more than half their arable land, and it was wonderfully rich land in the river valley. The remaining rocks and mountains of Basutoland were of no real interest to farmers and ranchers, and the Boers began to establish themselves in their new domains, for whose riches there was keen competition amongst themselves. The Basuto on these lands were driven out or kept on merely as labourers, and the French and Wesleyan missions were closed down for having supported the Basuto.

This mission expulsion added to the uneasiness which some members of the British Government felt at the possibility that the Free Staters might, from their new position, push through to an ocean outlet on the eastern seaboard, but no action was taken by London.

Moshesh, however, was rallying his forces and waiting for the harvest. Then, in 1867, though undermined by the disloyalty of his eldest son, Letsie, he renewed the fight. It went badly, and within a short time the Basuto were near the end of both their physical and moral tether. Almost down but not quite out, Moshesh made a last desperate appeal to Wodehouse at the Cape for British protection on practically any terms.

It had become clear to Wodehouse that the British Government was morally responsible for a great deal of the Basuto's troubles. For years the British had vacillated. They had practically guaranteed strife by unilaterally pulling out of the Orange River Sovereignty without leaving a clearly demarcated border between Boer and Basuto. In 1866 they had agreed to send an agent to Moshesh, but within months had retreated from the undertaking.

Pestered by influential friends of the arbitrarily expelled missionaries; afraid of a possible Free State breakthrough to the sea if the whole of Basutoland was captured; and with financial savings about to be made by the grant of responsible government to the Cape, the imperial Government listened to Wodehouse's urgings. In December 1867 he was able to announce that Basutoland was to be incorporated into the colony of Natal.

Moshesh had at last achieved his wish, but he was almost past caring. Thousands of his people were starving, while further thousands had fled the country. Thaba Bosiu still stood, but most of his other strongholds had fallen. 'The country is dead; we are all dead; take us and do what you will with us,' he said to Wodehouse after the news reached him. It was at about this time that he reportedly made his famous statement: 'My country is your blanket, O Queen, and my people the lice on it.'* It seemed a Pyrrhic victory.

The Free Staters were furious. They felt that they had a claim by settlement to a good deal of the valley land; the Basuto had never ceased to raid far and wide for cattle, ignoring the British award tax which Moshesh had signed. Now, with the final victory over the Basuto within their grasp, the Free Staters were to be cheated of their prize by an imperial Government which had specifically renounced any rights in the area. It was more than they were prepared to stand, and they renewed their attack, capturing one of Moshesh's last strongholds with most of his remaining cattle.

* *The Basuto of Basutoland*, E. A. T. Dutton, p. 44.

But this, in turn, was something which Wodehouse could not allow. On 12 March 1868, he issued a proclamation declaring that the Basuto were, as of that day, 'admitted into the allegiance of Her Majesty' (the phrasing is important), and that 'the tribe of the Basutos shall be and shall be taken to be for all intents and purposes British subjects, and the territory of the said tribe shall be, and shall be taken to be, British territory'. Basutoland had finally been annexed.

Faced at last with a clear British stand, the Free State agreed to negotiate an agreed border, and gave back to the Basuto some, though by no means the major part, of the valuable land it had seized by arms. The border then laid down has been maintained in substance ever since.

The consequences of British surrender to the Great Trek had worked themselves out on predictable lines. The Trekkers had settled matters with the Africans by force of arms, and even though Britain had prevented total conquest, the Basuto had lost most of their good land.

The most telling footnote to the period must be Lord Hailey's, who wrote with unaccustomed asperity:

It is typical of the Colonial Office of the day, that it should have taken alarm at an article of the Convention [finally settling the war and the border] which appeared likely to involve some expenditure on compensation for the farms given up by the Free State, and it withheld ratification of the Convention until President Brand agreed to expunge the article.*

On 19 March 1870 this was finally done.

Moshesh, the Old Chief of the Mountain, died within three months of the treaty's ratification. Perhaps ninety years old, he had been in poor health for some time, and had declined rapidly in the past year, but he had lived long enough to see his wish of British protection fulfilled and to prevent his people from being totally 'broke up as the Hottentots were'.

Britain's troubles with Basutoland were, however, far from ended. Having annexed, or rather re-annexed, the country, and having at long last established an agreed border with the Free State, Britain had to decide on who was to administer it. The

* *Native Administration in the British African Territories*, Part V, by Lord Hailey, H.M.S.O., 1953, p. 43.

imperial Government certainly had no wish to do so; it would cost money.

The original intention had been to make Basutoland the responsibility of Natal. Moshesh and his eldest son, Letsie, had earlier reacted to this proposal by protesting that they wanted to be under the Queen and not 'to go into prison', for the white Natalians taxed Africans and were generally repressive.

Letsie, a weak but ambitious man who was far below his father's calibre in all respects, had now succeeded to the paramount chieftaincy. But this did not give him anything approaching the powers of an absolute ruler.

The system that Moshesh had so laboriously constructed was nearer to a confederacy, with regional chiefs enjoying a good deal of independence and with most major decisions taken only after full consultation. Most of the main chiefs, were now, it is true, sons or close relatives of Moshesh, but this only increased the rivalry between them and Letsie. They were by no means agreed upon the sort of administration they preferred; in fact, what the chiefs wanted then, and have continued to want, was to preserve their rule and privileges while Britain protected them against the Boers.

Britain, however, paid small attention to the chiefs. By 1871 preparations to give the Cape Colony responsible government were well in hand. Natal was nowhere near to such independence, and the British Government, anxious that the costs of native administration should be off-loaded on to self-governing – and self-financing – settlers, decided that the Cape should administer Basutoland. It was not thought necessary even to consult the Basuto chiefs about this, and in 1871 the Cape Legislature simply passed a formal Act of Annexation.

The Basuto chiefs vociferously opposed the terms of this Act, which created a system of direct rule through the appointment of resident magistrates in Basutoland and so cut down drastically the powers of the chiefs. On the surface, however, law and order were restored in the Territory, and for a time growing prosperity papered over the deeper conflicts. The diamond mines had opened in near-by Kimberley, and thousands of Basuto flocked there for short spells to earn money. At home, the use of the plough spread and, with settled conditions, crops increased dramatically.

But underneath the prosperity the Basuto felt far from secure. They had too recently been near to extinction, and even the simpler amongst them had learnt by bitter experience that the Queen's Government could change its mind suddenly about protection. Guns or their lack had been decisive in the past, and were likely to be so again. Most of the diamond-field money left over after drink went on guns; some of the minor chiefs went to the diamond fields themselves, to earn the necessary money. Basutoland became 'the central powder magazine of South Africa'.*

In Basutoland, the sale of guns without a permit – and the sale of liquor under any circumstances – had been forbidden by the Cape Annexation Act in 1871, but the new laws were widely disregarded, as were the further provisions of the proclamation passed by the now quasi-independent Cape in 1887. In effect, these two proclamations turned Basutoland, at least administratively, into a Native Reserve.†

Fundamentally, the Cape Government – and all succeeding white governments in South Africa – saw the Native Reserves as limited areas of inferior land in which the black man might be permitted to scratch for survival and from which he could, as demand developed, be made to work for the white man through subjection to tax. It was central to this policy, of course, that the Reserves should not become centres of potential military strength, and, in the late nineteenth century, that they should not be able to continue playing rival European groups off against one another by giving or promising their support in war.

This sort of support had been repeatedly solicited by – and given to – both Boer and Briton. If this competition was to be stopped the black men had to be disarmed, and this is what the Cape Government decided to do. Behind the decision lay the fear of a general African uprising which, with good reason, had haunted both Briton and Boer almost since their arrival in South Africa.

In many cases it involved the disarming of Africans who had stood by Britain either through neutrality or with their arms in past wars and skirmishes, and it caused a great deal of bitterness.

The Basuto opposed the disarmament policy from its first announcement, and they were confirmed in their worst fears by

* *A History of South Africa*, E. A. Walker, Longmans, 1947, p. 358ff.
† Hailey, Part V, p. 48.

the inexplicable idiocy of the Cape's Prime Minister, Sir Gordon Sprigg. This dignitary made a special trip to Maseru in October 1879, to tell the Basuto chiefs that they were to be disarmed. The Basuto had gathered in a large *pitso*, or general meeting, to hear the Governor, and one can imagine their feelings when he announced not only the disarmament policy but also that the tax on every Basuto hut was being doubled and that a large chunk of Basutoland was to be opened to white settlement.

It had been a cardinal tenet of Moshesh's policy that no white men should be allowed to own land in Basutoland, and it is one of the country's greatest assets in achieving modern political progress that this policy has been maintained to the present day. In fact, all land in Basutoland has since Moshesh's day belonged to the nation, and not to any chief or individual.

The chiefs in Sprigg's day had been deeply unsettled by having their powers to allocate land taken away by the British and given to the High Commissioner. Now the motives behind this move became clear to them. Britain was about to betray them a second time.

The wars with the Boers had been fought over land and, as they saw it, the Basuto had lost their richest lands because Britain had unilaterally decided to quit the Orange River Sovereignty. When the Basuto were at their last gasp, Britain had agreed to take their diminished country back under its protection, but had arrogated to herself the allocation of Basuto lands. Now, delivered up to the white Government at the Cape, the Basuto were to be disarmed – and the white settlers let in.

It was more than Basuto flesh and blood, already plagued by overcrowding and drought, could bear. All but one of the chiefs, though less than united amongst themselves on other issues, refused to disarm. Sprigg moved against them, and the Gun War began. It dragged on for seven months, cost the Cape Government £4¾ million, and ended in complete failure.

The Gun War saw only one major engagement, which the Basuto, under Moshesh's grandson Lerotholi, won. For the rest, it was a protracted series of skirmishes, raids and sieges. But it aroused echoes in the Africans of neighbouring territories, whose simultaneous risings, though limited, forced the Cape Government to deploy yet more men and money.

Not a single British soldier fought in the Gun War. Sprigg had ignored strong misgivings and even warnings from Britain when he announced his disarmament policy; he asked for no British help, and would have been most unlikely to get it if he had.

The Basuto victory, however, was weakened by two factors. The defection of one of their chiefs led to something of a civil war within the Gun War, and they needed a respite to harvest their crops. An overcrowded and drought-prone Native Reserve was not an ideal base for an extended war.

Both sides accepted British arbitration in 1881, and the peace terms did little more than save the face of the Cape. Disarmament was to remain the policy, but Basuto could legally retain their guns at a registration fee of £1 for each. White settlers were not to be allowed into the territory.

In the general unrest, however, the administration in Basutoland had been greatly weakened, and most of the chiefs neither surrendered their guns nor paid the tax. Three chaotic years followed, with the victorious chiefs revenging themselves against war-time defectors, and at last the Cape persuaded a reluctant British Government to take the troublesome Basuto off its hands in 1883.

But the British had learnt one lesson from the arbitrary way in which they had handed the country to the Cape in 1871. This time the British consulted the Basuto, and it was with their consent that, on 18 March 1884, the Basuto finally became British subjects directly under the Queen.

4 Empire Through the Desert – Bechuanaland

It is significant that the final acceptance in 1884 by Britain of responsibility for Basutoland coincided almost exactly with the setting up of a British Protectorate in Bechuanaland, the second of the present three High Commission Territories.

We have seen that, in the struggle for land and power which constitutes so much of South Africa's early history, the Basuto were little more than pawns in the game between the British and the Boers. The imperial red of Britain's queen varied in intensity according to the dictates sometimes of her bishops but finally of her financial castles; the Boers aspired throughout to paint the chessboard a dominant white, reducing the black squares to a couple of worthless corners.

But where in Basutoland the queen's bishops and castles acted, so to speak, at one or two removes, they played out the drama more directly in Bechuanaland.

The great importance of Bechuanaland lay, and largely continues to lie, in its being what Cecil John Rhodes called 'the Suez Canal to the North'. The Scots missionary, Moffat, was the first to open up what came to be called the missionaries' road, winding its undemarcated way along the fertile strips of Bechuanaland which adjoin the Transvaal and the great Kalahari desert, then as now the home of the Bushmen. Livingstone, Moffat's son-in-law, pressed farther along this 'road', and it was only when its strategic significance was first realized by Rhodes, and its blocking threatened by the Transvaal Boers, that Britain was persuaded to bring Bechuanaland under its protection. This was in 1885, one year after Basutoland came under British rule.

As both Bechuanaland and Basutoland are, effectively, part of South Africa, each territory was, of course, affected by the same broad conflicts between black and black, black and white, and white and white. Swaziland, too, was involved in these conflicts, but the connexion between Bechuanaland and Basutoland was particularly close since the Africans of these two territories shared a common ancestry.

The early history of Bechuanaland's tribes is shrouded in legend, but their Sotho, or Basuto, origin is certain. Like the Basuto, the early Bechuana tribes felt the impact of Shaka, the great and ruthless Zulu warrior genius. As the lesser groups and tribes were driven before Shaka's *impis*, they became predatory raiders in their turn. Amongst the most ferocious of these driven-turned-driver groups were the followers of an amazon called Mma-Nta-tisi, who swept from near Basutoland into Bechuana territory. But her pillage was to seem mild compared with that wrought later by Mzilikazi, the founder of the Matabele nation.

Mzilikazi was one of Shaka's chief captains, but he decided not to return home after embezzling the loot of a particularly profitable raid, and moving north-eastwards, he established himself for a period of pillage near Zeerust, on the border of the present-day Bechuanaland Protectorate.

The composition and distribution of Bechuanaland's eight main tribal groupings today stem largely from this bitter time of Mzilikazi's raids. So does the strong missionary influence on the territory, especially that of the London Missionary Society. It was in 1820, while Bechuanaland was torn by internal strife and outside raiding, that Robert Moffat, the great missionary from Scotland, established himself at Kuruman, in the country later to become known as British Bechuanaland, which is today incorporated in the Cape Province of South Africa. Within three years the existence of his mission station and of his host tribe were threatened by Basuto raiders from the south, and Moffat, always a man of action as well as of God, mobilized the help of Griqua half-castes living 100 miles away. With the aid of their firearms, the attackers were overwhelmed.

This triumph, however, would have been hard to repeat against the far more organized and formidable *impis* of Mzilikazi, and the mission, from which Moffat's son-in-law Livingstone was to strike out in exploring the interior, would almost certainly have been razed had Moffat not struck up an extraordinary relationship with the bloody Mzilikazi. Over the years, Moffat established a remarkable ascendancy and influence over the tyrannical and extremely gifted chief, and as a result, whilst most of the rest of Bechuanaland shuddered and bled under his raids, Kuruman remained inviolate, until Mzilikazi in turn suffered telling defeat at the hands of the Boers in 1837 and withdrew across the Limpopo River to become the first ruler of Matabeleland, in the south of present-day Southern Rhodesia.

It was, however, to be some time before the victorious Boers took a direct interest in Bechuanaland. For many years after Mzilikazi had moved on, internecine strife worsened the tribal chaos which he had created. Robert Moffat continued his work at Kuruman, and David Livingstone, who had married Moffat's daughter Mary, set up a station of the London Missionary Society further north, where he remained until the early fifties.

Meanwhile, the tensions between the British home Government, its subjects at the Cape and the Afrikaners who had trekked from the Cape into the interior were shaping circumstances. In 1852 Britain formally recognized the independence of the Transvaal, and in 1854, as we have seen, withdrew her sovereignty from all lands beyond the Orange River. But, in recognizing the Transvaal, as in recognizing the Orange Free State, Britain failed to lay down definite boundaries. The Transvalers had long been concerned about their western border, along which the missionaries' road ran to the Zambesi, and with their own independence finally recognized, they laid claim to the road and the Bechuana lands surrounding it.

The London Missionary Society, spurred on by David Livingstone, vigorously opposed the Transvaal claim, but Britain was attempting to limit her responsibilities, and took no direct action. For a time, indeed, the Transvalers succeeded in closing the road to the interior altogether by means of an agreement with one of the Bechuana chiefs. Suddenly, Bechuanaland roared into prominence when a Boer commando raided Chief Sechele's territory in Bechuanaland and there ransacked Livingstone's house in his absence. Through Livingstone's involvement, the raid and the Boers themselves became notorious in Britain, but the British Government, still pursuing the policy of withdrawal, showed no interest in Chief Sechele's subsequent attempts to appeal to Queen Victoria for support against the Boers.

Even today the missionaries' road, along which the railway runs to the Rhodesias, is South Africa's only rail link with the rest of Africa, and it was Rhodes's realization of its importance which marked his emergence as one of the major political figures in South Africa. He saw that if the road were closed, by the Transvalers or anyone else, it would not only lose the Cape the trade it was already conducting with the interior, but would prevent Britain from expanding farther into the heart of Africa. Beyond the Limpopo lay the great territories of Matabeleland and Mashonaland, and if the missionaries' road were closed, he, or Britain, would be unable to annex them and so link the Cape to Cairo in an unbroken imperial line.

The Boers of the Transvaal, under President Kruger's stubborn leadership, may not have seen as far ahead as Rhodes, but they realized the importance of the missionaries' road nevertheless. When gold was discovered in the Tati area of Bechuanaland in 1866 their determination to control the road and its surrounding territory increased, to harden further when the Kimberley diamond rush, affecting the southern part of Bechuanaland, started in 1868.

The Transvalers tried unilaterally to annex the Tati gold area together with the surrounding country, so formally closing the road, and tribal appeals to the British for assistance in controlling the inrush of gold diggers were ignored despite strong missionary support. It was only because the Transvalers simultaneously laid claim to a strip of land leading to the sea at Delagoa Bay and thus came into conflict with the rival claims of both the British and the Portuguese that Britain refused to recognize the annexation of the Tati area as well.

In 1874 the British Government received a formal request for protection from the chief of yet another tribe, the Thlaping, in Bechuanaland, and the situation took on fresh urgency when this was followed in 1876 by an appeal from Sechele of the important Bakwena and Khama III of the increasingly important Bamang-wato.

Khama, who became known as the Great, is rivalled only by Moshesh of the Basuto as the leading African figure of the late nineteenth century in South Africa. The Bamangwato have become well known in our own time through their Regent,

Tshekedi Khama, and the deposition of his nephew, Seretse Khama, from the chieftainship when he married a white English-woman. Both Tshekedi and Seretse are in direct line of descent from Khama the Great, and inherited, as we shall see, some of his remarkable qualities.

Khama was born and grew up a pagan, but his father allowed him to attend the first school which Lutheran Christian mission-aries had established in the Bamangwato tribal territory. Although Khama learnt and absorbed tribal lore as a boy, he was deeply influenced by his schooling, and as a young man in his twenties he was baptized. Khama means antelope, and in many ways the name fitted the handsome, athletic and brave young man. Even at this stage of his life, he showed the thoroughness and energy which were to raise him to greatness. Conversion was not for him a mere formality, but a complete and deep change in his way of life. He renounced all pagan ways completely, adopted the western dress which missionaries have so arrogantly equated with Christi-anity, and stuck to his new beliefs despite growing and increasingly open opposition from his father, even refusing to obey his father's instructions to take a second wife.

The ensuing conflict between pagan father and Christian son was bitter and at times threatened to end in violence. But Khama survived several attempts on his life by his father and brothers, displaying throughout at least outward charity and respect for his father. Despite his own defiance of them, the tribal traditions of filial loyalty had bitten deep, reinforced perhaps by the new ideas of Christian forgiveness. For his part, the tempestuous old man, who had described his own heart as being 'proud, proud, and always angry', recognized in his quieter moments his son's great quality. 'We think like that,' he once said, as he drew a circle in the sand; 'but Khama thinks like that,' and he drew a straight line.

When Khama finally succeeded to the chieftainship on his father's death in 1875, he changed the whole life of the tribe, outraging its most cherished customs. All alcoholic drink was outlawed; witchcraft, the killing of one of twin children and other traditional practices abolished, and the paying of bride-price and polygamy forbidden. Schools and a church, by now under the London Missionary Society, were established at Khama's extremely large, new royal kraal, in which a telegraph office was opened.

This enthusiastic affirmation by Khama of what he saw as the best in the white man's world, however, could not isolate him and the Bamangwato, any more than their neighbours, from the white man's greed. The appetite of the Boers for land was insatiable, and the Bechuana tribes, who knew what had happened to Africans around them under white rule, feared the loss of their land above everything. Even though the Kimberley diamond rush drew off many whites from the Tati gold diggings, others remained in Bechuana territory and claimed land there. Tensions between them and the tribesmen flared up periodically in minor clashes, and when Sechele and Khama appealed to Queen Victoria for protection in 1876, they pleaded that the Boers 'are cruel amongst us black people'. But this appeal, too, was ignored, despite even more impressive missionary support. Britain, in any case, had her hands full enough in dealing with the Boers of the Transvaal itself. Despite the reluctance to increase her direct responsibilities she annexed the Transvaal in 1877, only to be forced, after the Boers rose in 1880 and inflicted ignominious defeats on the British, to restore it to independence in 1881.

The settlement of that year laid down borders for the Transvaal, but the war and its winning had bred a new defiant spirit amongst the Transvalers, and they pushed beyond their territory in search of new lands. As they trekked into Bechuanaland, they set up the two tiny new Republics of Stellaland and Goshen, which threatened to block the missionaries' road completely. Not far to the west of these 'mushroom' Republics lay the Kalahari desert, and Rhodes saw that if Stellaland and Goshen were allowed to exist, with the Boers carving out ever more of Bechuanaland for themselves, the interior would be lost to British expansion – and trade.

The British Government saw the force of this argument but, still smarting under the defeat inflicted by the Transvaal, was committed to a policy of withdrawal. If the Cape, on the urging in its Parliament of Rhodes, wanted to annex Bechuanaland, well and good; it was the Cape Government's responsibility and not Britain's to secure Cape interests.

What finally swung Britain into action was the totally unforeseen intrusion of Bismarck's Germany into southern Africa. For a long time, Britain had regarded southern Africa as a cosy, if frequently troublesome, family concern. The issue was usually whether the home or the colonial Government should annex 'empty' lands; that other European powers might step in to provide a third way out of these disputes had apparently never entered an official head in London.

It had, however, entered the heads of German merchants, and they put it into Bismarck's. In 1883 a Bremen merchant hoisted the German flag over land he had purchased from African chiefs in South West Africa, and a German warship dropped anchor offshore to protect his property. There was dismay in London. But Britain, involved in other imperial disputes, especially over Egypt with France, came rapidly to the conclusion that it could not antagonize the Germans. In 1884 London agreed to a German Protectorate over the coast of South West Africa.

Bismarck's shock-treatment, however, had its effect. London's reluctant eyes were now fully opened to the importance of the road to the north. For if Germany were to join hands across Bechuanaland with the Transvalers, or with her own and Portuguese agents in east Africa, the Cape – and Britain – would be permanently cut off from the interior.

Rhodes until this stage had shown nothing but contempt for the feeble and indecisive 'imperial factor'; what he wanted was to secure the road, Bechuanaland, and the lands beyond it decisively for the Cape. But in the new circumstances of imperial clash, and with the British Government at last brought by Bismarck to the realization that its policy of withdrawal had failed, Rhodes, facing difficulties of his own in the Cape, was happy to let Britain act.

In March 1885 Britain proclaimed a Protectorate over the whole of Bechuanaland, and the missionaries' – and traders' – road to the interior was secured. Britain still intended that Bechuanaland should be given to the Cape, but detailed agreement with the Cape Government could not be reached, and burgers of the 'mushroom' republic of Stellaland were not happy with the idea. So, in September, the southern part of Bechuanaland was declared a separate Crown Colony, and it was ten years before this area, known as British Bechuanaland, was finally incorporated into the Cape. It remains part of South Africa today.

In all this, the African chiefs counted for little. Bigger forces than their tribal fears were now urgently at work. Britain did, it is true, make separate treaties in 1884 with the chieftains of the southern tribes whose land was later incorporated into the Cape, and both Khama and other Bechuana chiefs had repeatedly, if imprecisely, asked for British assistance or protection. But these requests were disregarded until Bismarck moved. In essence, the settlement was a carve-up by white men, between the imperial Government, its colonists on the spot and the troublesome Transvalers.

Even when Britain did decide to secure the way to the north, it was anxious to limit the resultant direct responsibility – and, of course, expenditure – as much as possible. After it had split off the two southern territories in 1885, Britain assumed jurisdiction in the rest of the Bechuanaland Protectorate only over British subjects.

The road was the thing. Most of the lands surrounding it were considered 'unsuitable for European colonization', and when the first Assistant Commissioner was sent to the Bechuanaland Protectorate in 1887, he was told 'not to interfere with Native Administration; the chiefs are understood not to be desirous to part with their rights of sovereignty, nor are Her Majesty's Government by any means anxious to assume the responsibilities of it'.*

This attitude was maintained even after the passing in 1890 of the Foreign Jurisdiction Act, which gave, in the words of a later court judgment, the British sovereign 'unfettered and unlimited' power to legislate for British possessions. In terms of this Act, an Order-in-Council was published on 9 May 1891 authorizing the High Commissioner to provide in the Bechuanaland Protectorate 'for the administration of justice, the raising of revenue, and generally for the order and good government of all persons'. It is this Order-in-Council that remains the legal basis of British authority in the Bechuanaland Protectorate today.

In exercising his powers, however, the High Commissioner was also clearly instructed to respect native custom, insofar as it did not clash with the 'due exercise of Her Majesty's power and jurisdiction'. He was simultaneously cautioned to limit as far as possible the obligations which proclamations might incur and, in

* Cmd 5237, 1887.

a dispatch accompanying the Order-in-Council, directed to leave the chiefs and their subjects almost completely alone and to confine his jurisdiction as far as possible to Europeans. When magistrates were appointed a month later, the same policy directions were given.

Thus it might be thought that Khama and his fellow chiefs had gained what they wanted – British protection for the continuance of their traditional ways and tribal government. But whatever pleasure they may have felt at obtaining this British protection was short-lived. Their fears for their lands were fired afresh, and with good reason, when Rhodes founded his British South Africa Company in 1889. The granted application for the company's royal charter specified 'the development of the Bechuanaland Protectorate and the North', and in the year of the company's foundation Rhodes was already negotiating with the Colonial Office for a contribution towards the official running of the Protectorate.

Rhodes had by this time established his ascendancy over the world's diamond production by gaining control of the Kimberley fields. Pursuing his dream of empire, Rhodes had played politics not only in the Cape and the Transvaal, but also in London, and had pressed on into the interior. Lobengula, the King of the Matabele in what is today Southern Rhodesia, gave Rhodes's agents a concession for the exploitation of all minerals in his lands, which Rhodes believed would provide a new El Dorado to rival that of the by-then booming Witwatersrand gold fields. Lobengula was promised in return rifles, ammunition, an annual gratuity, and – presumably a tribute to the reputation of the white man's technology – a steamboat to be used on the Zambesi River.

Rhodes rightly felt that he had struck a good bargain with Lobengula, and later ignored the chief's Renunciation of the 'steamboat agreement'. But what Rhodes needed if his imperial possessions were to be exploited was to push the railway system through into the interior.

There was only one route this railway could take. The missionaries had marked out their road through Bechuanaland; the traders had followed; with the Transvaal on one side and the inhospitable Kalahari desert on the other, trains could go no other way. So Rhodes began to manoeuvre for a take-over by his

British South Africa Company of the Bechuanaland Protectorate. He wanted to replace 'the dead hand of Downing Street' with his own energetic grasp.

The British Government, still willing to have even minimal administrative – and potentially larger financial – obligations taken off its hands by men on the spot, favoured the idea. But Khama and his fellow chiefs regarded it as the prelude to their extinction. They had the support in high places only of the High Commissioner, Sir Henry Loch, who let London know unequivocally that handing Khama and his tribe over to Rhodes's commercial company would be 'a breach of faith such as no government should commit'. But Rhodes had more powerful friends closer to court.

The chiefs had been disabused of many illusions about the British mission in Africa, but they still preferred British rule to the land-hungry Boers or the land-snatching company. Also, they differentiated even then between the Government, and especially the Queen, in London, and the local administrators. Khama especially realized what his descendants were to confirm from bitter experience: one of the main obstacles to obtaining even minimal justice was the lack of communications. The missionaries, Moffat, Livingstone, and Mackenzie, had given them a faith in the ultimate justice of British public opinion, and they revered the Queen. They decided to visit London and see her.

The three senior Chiefs, Khama III of the Bamangwato, Bathoen I of the Bamangkwetse and Sebele I of the Bakwena, arrived in England in 1895 where, aided by two missionaries, they mounted a judiciously selective and increasingly successful lobbying and public relations campaign.

Their objections to Rhodes's company were simple. In Khama's words:

We fear that they will fill our country with liquor shops, as they have Bulawayo and some parts of Mashonaland and Matabeleland . . . and we fear also because we hear the words of the Makalaka and Matabele, who live under the Company, and we see that these people don't like their rulers.

To the British Government Khama said simply:

There is no government we can trust as we can trust that of the Great Queen. We pray you, therefore, not to throw us away as if we were troublesome children who would not listen to their mother's words.

The Queen herself, when she received the three chiefs at Windsor Castle, was much taken with them, and especially with the devoutly Christian Khama. She presented them each with an inscribed bible, and her interest and sympathy undoubtedly helped to swing the initially unsympathetic Government to the side of the chiefs.

A compromise settlement was reached. The chiefs agreed to cede to Rhodes's company a strip of land needed for the building of the railway. In return, they remained under British administration, with the explicit assurance that they would 'continue to rule their own people much as at present'.

5 Machtpolitik – Swaziland

If the early history of Bechuanaland was largely one in which its Africans became mere pawns in the struggle for land and lines of communications between the British and the Boers, that of Swaziland introduces in addition the beginnings of the Machtpolitik rivalry between Britain and Germany in Africa.

In Swaziland, the reluctance of the British in the latter half of the nineteenth century to extend their responsibilities in South Africa was seen at its clearest. For years, Britain, in so far as she concerned herself over the then independent Swazi at all, was interested in them merely as minor allies in fighting tribal wars. The territorial ambitions which the Transvaal Boers developed on the rich pasture lands of Swaziland hardly worried Britain, and at several stages she was quite ready to hand the Swazi over to the Boers. But the Transvaal's interest in Swaziland lay in more than its winter grazing and in the extravagant concessions which could be obtained by fraud or from a venal Paramount Chief.

After its first eclipse, the landlocked Transvaal Republic, re-established in 1881, began to look for an outlet to the sea, and planned a coastal railway to run through Swaziland. For a time, despite the hostility of the Transvalers towards her, Britain was prepared to see their ambitions realized, subject to certain small qualifications, but the Transvalers, under President Kruger, rejected all qualifications and, against a background of growing tension with Britain, decided to play Machtpolitik by inviting Germany into South Africa. It was only then that Britain finally denied the Transvaal a protectorate over Swaziland, and broke Kruger's hopes of an independent outlet to the sea. And it was only as a result of the conquest of the Transvaal in the Boer War that Britain finally accepted responsibility for Swaziland and made it the British Protectorate which it remains today. In all this, the

Swazi were, as was the fashion of the times, barely consulted and, where it suited the white power-groups, any objections they had were simply ignored.

The Swazi formed a distinct tribe only at the beginning of the nineteenth century. Their forerunners had moved southwards in the great Bantu migration from central Africa, and settling in country which was then only sparsely, if at all, occupied by other Africans, they had absorbed smaller clans and forged alliances through diplomatic marriage.

The early Swazi, like the Basuto and the Bechuana, felt the impact of the Zulu explosion from Natal, though they suffered raiding rather than conquest. Indeed, the Swazi, though they avoided outright wars, were expert fighters in their own right, and in the one major clash which occurred with the Zulu they came off best.

By 1840 the Swazi kingdom or confederation of clans covered more than twice the present area of the country, and it was in that year that Mswati, who was to unite his people, extend their territory and then sign two huge chunks of it away, acceded to the Paramount Chieftainship.

A few Europeans had by then reached Swaziland, but none had settled there, and when Mswati came to manhood he ruled over purely African country. He unified and strengthened the clans and built up a Swazi fighting force which earned the respect of his African neighbours. But white men were already setting in motion forces which were to dwarf the Swazi regiments and make Swazi independence a counter in the contest for trade.

The Great Trek of Boers from British control at the Cape had begun in 1836, and by 1843 the struggle for the control of the coast and the interior had led to Britain's absorption of Natal, on Swaziland's border, as a Crown Colony. In 1852 the independence of the Transvaal was recognized, and by 1860 the South African Republic of the Transvaal was established.

The Portuguese were in possession of Moçambique and, whilst the borders were ill-defined, the Swazi began effectively to find themselves in their present hemmed-in position between Natal in the south, the Transvaal in the north and west, and the Portuguese in the east.

For some considerable time the Paramount Chief, Mswati, though aware of white power, seemed to have looked upon the

British and the Boers less as enemies than as possibly useful allies in his troubles with Zulu raiders.* When, not long after he came to the throne, he found himself threatened by Zulu pillage, he appealed to Britain for protection through Sir Theophilius Shepstone, her Agent General in Natal, and Shepstone influenced the Zulu to leave the Swazi alone, though no formal treaty of protection was concluded.

With his southern borders thus more or less secured, Mswati greatly extended his lands and influence to the north and west. At the height of his reign the lands and chieftains owing allegiance to the Swazi and, for the most part, integrated through military service and intermarriage with the Swazi proper, was perhaps three times the size of present-day Swaziland, while Mswati's *impis* even penetrated into what is today Southern Rhodesia.

Not seeing the ultimate threat which Boer land ambitions were to pose for the Swazi, Mswati in 1845 sold a large area inhabited by subject tribes to the 'Dutch South Africa Nation'. He was paid for this in cattle which, then as now, are a rural African's 'bank', and he received further cattle when, some time later, he signed a document handing over to the mushroom Lydenburg Republic the large stretch of territory which today forms the district of Lydenburg in South Africa.

Mswati's relations with the Boers were indeed so good, or Mswati himself was so confident of being able to use them for his own ends, that in 1864 Swazi *impis* helped the Transvalers to smash the opposition of tribes in the Lydenburg area which refused to acknowledge Boer rule. Here, for once, Africans wrote a wry footnote to their own later history of subjugation and oppression.

It was during Mswati's long reign, which lasted from 1840 to 1868, that white men began to enter Swaziland in significant numbers. Some came as traders, others as adventurers, and in 1844 there also arrived the Rev. James Allison, a Wesleyan missionary, in response to a request made by Mswati's father. Today missions play a major part in Swazi life, but Mr Allison was no more successful in this first attempt at settling in Swaziland than he was to be on his second in 1874.

As time passed, more and more of the whites who came to

* Hailey, Part V, p. 360.

Swaziland were Transvaal farmers looking, as they still do, for winter stock grazing in Swaziland's more temperate conditions. Today one of the chief Swazi resentments – and one of the country's obstacles to agricultural development – are the South African farmers who own large tracts of Swaziland and who, instead of farming there the year round and thus helping the country's production, use the land purely as winter grazing for their stock.

It was, in fact, with the granting of the first of a long series of land concessions to white farmers that Swaziland's troubles, and the end of its effective independence, began.

The first recorded personal land concession was given by Mswati in September 1860 to one Coenraad Vermaak, who – in return for some thirty head of cattle and an annual rent of £5 – acquired some 1,000 square miles of land and, interestingly, was placed by Mswati as chief over the Swazi in that area.

At the time this seemed to be no great matter, and one can safely assume that Mswati would hardly have envisaged large numbers of white men being 'placed' in the same way, for this would have undermined the whole structure of Swazi life and his own rule. When Mswati died in 1868 he was still a truly independent Swazi ruler. He was to be the last.

By 1868 the Transvaal Republic was compensating for its precarious economic condition by making grandiose new land claims which, to mean anything, had to be accompanied by claims to water. But there was more at stake than the desire to ensure a supply of water when in 1868 a Transvaal Volksraad Proclamation laid claim to a strip of land one mile wide on each side of the Great Usutu River from the Republic, all the way through Swaziland, to the sea at Delagoa Bay, then, as now, in Portuguese hands.

The landlocked Republic had begun to dream of an independent outlet to the sea that would transform its whole relationship with the British, who controlled both the Cape and the Natal coastlines. With an independent lifeline to the sea, the Transvalers could afford to defy the detested British, and the whole power struggle between the whites in southern Africa would be transformed.

The claim to the Usutu River was made simultaneously with other grandiose claims to territory in the north and west of the Transvaal and these claims evoked immediate protests from both the British and Portuguese, who rejected the Volksraad's Proclamation. But Boer bluff and blustering did lead to the signing of a Boer–Portuguese treaty which defined the border between Portuguese East Africa and the Republic as running along the Lubombo Mountains, thus including Swaziland in the Transvaal. Britain protested against this Boer attempt at annexation, which consequently failed, but the desire for an outlet to the east coast continued to attract the Transvalers.

Mswati was succeeded by his seven-year-old son, and when the boy was poisoned in 1874 the dispute over the succession led from intrigues to actual clashes between rival factions. The Swazi, unlike many tribes in southern and central Africa, do not automatically recognize the ruler's first wife as the Great Wife and therefore as mother of the next ruler. Instead, as in Bechuanaland in the days before its chiefs adopted monogamy, a sort of royal family council would meet after the King's death and decide which of his many wives outranked the others. Her son, or a boy whom she would adopt from one of the lesser wives if she had none herself, would then be named as heir.

To the Swazi, their King is mystically identified with the health of his people and the all-important fertility of the soil. Mswati, like other Swazi Kings before and after him, had a large number of wives, taking new ones until shortly before his death, and the choice of the most senior wife after his death was considerably complicated by disputes arising from rival family and clan connexions centring around traditional ascendancies.

According to almost all non-Swazi authorities, including the redoubtable Lord Hailey,* it was at this stage that the Transvaal Boers actively intervened, sending in a commando whose armed presence helped to stop the factional conflicts and led to the choice of another minor son, Mbandzeni, as King. At the same time, with the armed Boers at their elbows, some of the chiefs entered into what has been called a 'closer understanding' with the leader of the Transvaal commando, an 'understanding' which included ratification of the land concessions granted by Mswati and provided for an offensive–defensive alliance. This agreement – if it ever existed – was, however, never ratified by the Transvaal Volksraad, and Hailey, in any case, believes it 'open to doubt

* Hailey, Part V, p. 360.

whether this carried the assent of a number of the responsible chiefs in Swaziland'.

The Swazi, on the other hand, deny the whole story. They assert that the admittedly severe conflicts over the succession did not occur until five years after Mbandzeni as a minor had been chosen and that the issue was settled without any intervention by the Boers.*

Whichever version is correct does not, in the event, much matter, for the Transvalers, whilst having their eye on Swaziland as the obvious route to an independent harbour on the eastern seaboard, were at that time practically bankrupt and themselves in a state of internal anarchy. The British Government did not at this stage want to see the Transvalers gain an independent outlet to the sea, but also did not want to get involved in extending its own responsibilities any further than necessary. The feeble Boer condition suited Britain perfectly and made any firm action over Swaziland unnecessary.

Thus when the British did annex the Transvaal in 1877, they did little more in Swaziland than send a few officials there. The British did, however, encounter the same trouble in subduing the Swazi's hostile neighbour, Sekukuni, as the Boers had encountered, and the Swazi duly helped the British against him as they had helped the Boers. It may be that some gratitude for this military help influenced the British to insist upon a guarantee of Swaziland's independence being written into the treaty which re-established the Transvaal Republic in 1881, though it is more likely that this was a precautionary move against any renewed Boer ambitions of breaking through to the coast.

In any event, both the British and the Transvalers agreed to 'recognize the independence of Swaziland within the boundaries laid down in the conventions' of 1881 and 1884. To the Swazi, however, this was small enough comfort, for the white men fixed these boundaries so that a large slice of Swaziland, with its thousands of Swazi, became part of the Transvaal.

As the sober Annual Report of the Swaziland Administration for 1960 puts it:

These arbitrarily defined [northern, western and southern] boundaries

---

* Hailey, Part V, p. 361.

encroached on land to which the Swazi laid claim and account for the number of Swazi now domiciled in the Transvaal Province of the Union of South Africa.

What was more, the conventions did not prevent – and did not aim to prevent – the Transvaal Boers or other Europeans from acquiring land or other rights within the Swazi country. Nor is there any formal written record of objection by Mbandzeni and his leading chiefs to these concessions, though their descendants today sometimes aver otherwise.

Certainly no other single question is as important and bitterly disputed in Swaziland to this day than that of the concessions granted by Mbandzeni. Gold had been discovered in north-western Swaziland in 1879, and immediately a rush took place to obtain mining concessions from the Swazi King, with Europeans settling permanently in Swaziland from 1880 onwards. What followed is a lurid story of bribery, deceit, venality, corruption, and fraud without parallel even in southern Africa.

In return for gifts and money, champagne for his wives and councillors, and greyhounds for himself, Mbandzeni blithely signed away concessions for almost every conceivable commodity and right in Swaziland. Concessions were not only given for land, minerals, trading, postal, and telegraph services, but also for the operation of refreshment bars on the railways that other concessionaires were to build. The Paramount Chief eventually even signed away to white men the right to collect all taxes due to him, and allotted, sometimes several times over, monopolies to manufacture dynamite, woollen and linen goods, cement, even gas and electricity.

In the five fantastic years before Mbandzeni's death in 1889 he and his council were netting more than £12,000 a year from the granting of concessions, and this when British pounds really bought something. In fact, they bought the concessionaires' rights to just about everything conceivably worth having in Swaziland several times over, though no one seems to have any record of how Mbandzeni and his cronies spent the estimated total of £70,000 which they took during their concession régime.

In the sober words of the 1907 Swaziland Annual Report:

Practically the whole area of the country was covered two, three or even four deep by concessions of all sizes, for different purposes, and for greatly varying periods. In but very few cases were even the boundaries defined; many of the areas had been subdivided and sold several times, and seldom were the boundaries of the superimposed areas even co-terminous. In addition to all this, concessions were granted for all lands and minerals previously unalloted or which having been allocated, might lapse or become forfeited. Finally it must be remembered that over these three or four strata of conflicting interests, boundaries, and periods, there had to be preserved the natural rights of the natives to live, move and cultivate and hunt.

The last sentence at least, places the actions of Mbandzeni and his council of chiefs – for they were together responsible for the concessions – in a somewhat better light. They granted concessions, yes. But they had no intention whatever of permanently handing over the country's assets to outsiders.

In fact, Swazi law and custom did not recognize the alienation of national assets. What the chief might do was to allow others the use of assets such as land for a time, but the assets themselves remained always the property of the nation. Mbandzeni and his chiefs recognized this, and in most cases granted use for what amounted in effect to a ninety-nine-year leasehold. Then, too, most of the concessions which Mbandzeni signed contained a clause reserving the Paramount Chief's 'sovereign rights' over the land involved and purporting to protect the Swazi from 'detrimental interference' by those receiving the concession.

The existence of such qualifications, even if they were only inserted *pro forma* by unscrupulous fortune hunters to give the semblance of reassurance to an ignorant native ruler, indicate that Mbandzeni did try to make the fundamental Swazi position of national ownership clear to the white men who swarmed around him, pressing gifts and riches into his willing hands in return for a fat stake in what promised after the finding of gold to become a new El Dorado.

In any case Mbandzeni was, to judge from contemporary accounts, no ignorant fool, and he did have some knowledge of the ways of the white world which came pressing in upon him. Nor did he take the decisions on the granting of concessions alone; they were assented to, and often discussed, by his council of chiefs and thus did carry the nation's formal authority.

At the same time, as Lord Hailey has pointed out,

there must have been in those concessions much of which the Paramount and his chiefs could not really appreciate the meaning. The land concessions dealt with principles of land tenure, as for example leasehold, freehold or private ownership, which were based on concepts unknown to them; the concessions relating to mineral rights or the grant of a trade monopoly of the privileges of banking or the use of scientific processes in mining all related to a field of operations even more unfamiliar to them. But there were others regarding which one is unfortunately obliged to conclude that Mbandzeni had placed undue reliance on the good faith of the European Advisers or Secretaries.*

The white concession hunters not only intrigued against the Swazi, they intrigued and fought amongst themselves and pestered Mbandzeni with their rival promises and offers. As the official historical version has it:

A cosmopolitan crowd of concession seekers arrived in search of every conceivable right from the Swazi ruler. The tenacity with which the Europeans sought for concessions, as well as the intrigues and controversies which divided them, not unnaturally confused the Swazi.†

Mbandzeni, moreover, could hardly have realized that the whole political future of his country would be shaped largely by the fights amongst whites over the concessions which he granted with what the Secretary of State for the Colonies described in 1892 as 'a reckless prodigality, unparalleled even in the history of South Africa'.‡

At first there was a loose if fairly clear division between the concessionaires. Farmers from the Transvaal sought lands and grazing rights, whilst, after the discovery of gold, Britons and other foreigners pursued mining and trading monopolies. Some 100 whites came to live in Swaziland, most of them unscrupulous characters, and as they began to stake their claims to Swaziland's actual or potential riches, they soon came into conflict with the lesser Swazi, flouted the authority of the chiefs and in general lorded it over the Africans.

In theory, the independence of the Swazi had been guaranteed by both the Boers and the British in the conventions of 1881 and 1884. But the Boers soon showed that they regarded these

* Hailey, Part V, p. 363.
† Annual Report of Swaziland for 1960, p. 93.   ‡ Hailey, op. cit., p. 363.

conventions as meaningless scraps of paper, and pressed ahead with their objective of absorbing Swaziland altogether. The Transvaal Government obtained from Mbandzeni major concessions which gave it a monopoly over the building of railways and telegraphs, the operation of postal services and, crucially, the levying of licences and customs for the whole of Swaziland. In 1886 the Boers even tried to push Mbandzeni into repudiating any obligations towards Britain and into recognizing only the Transvaal Government.

Mbandzeni was too shrewd to fall into this trap, and already concerned about the consequences of the in-fighting amongst the white concessionaires in Swaziland, he told the British about the Boer manoeuvre, and appealed in 1886 for British protection. The British, as we have seen, however, did not want to assume any increased responsibilities in South Africa, and they simply ignored Mbandzeni's request.

Rivalry amongst the concessionaires steadily increased, and in 1887, backed by some of the less unscrupulous amongst them, Mbandzeni again appealed to the British to intervene by appointing a British Resident. He was again rebuffed.

Realizing that he needed help from somewhere to deal with the concessionaires, Mbandzeni then turned to his old military ally Sir Theophilius Shepstone, who in 1887 sent his son, Theophilius Shepstone jun., as resident adviser and agent, to deal with the contending Europeans. This was, however, an unofficial appointment, liked neither by the British mining and trading interests, who had invested substantial sums in Swaziland, nor by the Boer farmers.

Shepstone, who was to play a shady part in Swazi affairs, organized the election of a committee of concessionaires, and persuaded the Paramount Chief to give it a Charter of Rights so that it might sort out the concessionaire squabbles. Mbandzeni had five appointees on the committee, and retained a right of veto over its decisions, but the whole project was undermined from the beginning by the internecine quarrels of the whites.

Though increasingly harassed and anxious, Mbandzeni continued to grant concessions which in 1889, the last year of his life, became more fantastic than ever in their scope. The Transvaal had already gained a monopoly over communications, customs, and licences. Now, with its income rocketing from the goldfields which had opened on the Witwatersrand in 1886, President Kruger was more than ever set on achieving an independent outlet to the sea.

Whilst the land-locked Transvaal had been poor, it had been held financially at the throat by the old-established Cape and Natal, which controlled the coastal harbours, customs and the developing railway system from the coast to the interior. The British colonies screwed every bit of possible advantage out of their historical and geographical advantages and were in great measure responsible for stunting the financial growth of the Transvaal and Orange Free State Republics.

Parasitic greed at the coast blocked attempts to create a customs union of the four territories which, if successful, would have changed the history of South Africa through its political consequences.

But the Cape and Natal continued to bleed the Boer Republics through arbitrary customs and tariffs. Bitter resentment at this treatment lay behind Kruger's determination to open an alternative outlet to the sea, and when gold was discovered on the Witwatersrand he suddenly had the means with which to get his own back on the parasitic British colonies on the coast.

In the most illuminating and masterly sentence ever written on South Africa, Professor de Kiewiet has summed up the country's history in eleven words: 'South Africa has advanced politically by disasters and economically by windfalls.'* The discovery of gold in 1886 was the prime example of the economic windfall, and enabled Kruger to spurn the Cape when the Transvaal's new financial power belatedly brought that colony to its senses on customs and tariff arrangements.

Railway lines were now pushing rapidly towards the Transvaal, with Kruger's eyes fixed on the one which would at long last connect him with a non-British port at Delagoa Bay in Portuguese East Africa. Of course, it would be better still for the Transvaal to have a port under its own control, and it was here that the importance of Swaziland lay. Beyond Swaziland lay Kosi Bay. If the British could be persuaded to cede the bay to the Transvaal, and if Swaziland could be brought fully under Boer control, a

* *A History of South Africa – Social and Economic*, p. 89.

railway could be pushed through to the coast and the Transvaal's complete independence finally secured.

In 1889 Boer control of Swaziland came within grasping distance when the Transvaal obtained, through an intermediary, one of the most incredible of all Mbandzeni's concessions. In return for an annual payment of £12,000, the revenue concession which Kruger now obtained gave his Government the right to collect and keep all the private revenue due to the Swazi Paramount.

With young 'Offy' Shepstone still the Swazis' adviser on European affairs, a group of concessionaires conveniently petitioned the Transvaal Government to take over Swaziland. Kruger promptly responded, and asked for the Boer–British convention to be suitably amended. Britain's man-on-the-spot, realistically impressed by the tremendous control over Swaziland which Mbandzeni's concessions had already given to the Transvaal, arranged for the creation of a commission to look into Kruger's request, which he favoured in principle.

Swaziland seemed within Kruger's formal reach, but at this stage Mbandzeni panicked. He dismissed Shepstone and, through a new adviser, requested British protection. At the same time, carrying his old weakness to the point of absurdity, he gave Hermann Eckstein, a Johannesburg German who was a friend of Kruger, an incredible concession which effectively surrendered control over Swaziland's foreign policy. Then, early in 1889, he died.

The Transvaal tried to reach a speedy and profitable settlement with the British; but Britain's attitude towards Transvaal control hardened under pressure from companies and chambers of commerce at home, who saw some £2 million of invested capital vanishing. Moreover, if Kruger's demands were granted, the northern interests of Rhodes's British South Africa Company would be threatened. Britain would therefore agree only to a system of dual control, and this, together with guarantees of Swazi independence, was embodied in the convention of 1890. The Queen Regent of the Swazi, who ruled until one of Mbandzeni's two minor sons gained his majority, agreed to the creation of a provisional Government committee to deal with white interests in Swaziland, and nominated 'Offy' Shepstone to represent the Swazi on it.

But this agreement gave little to the Swazi, for the two white powers had agreed between themselves that Swaziland was henceforth to be treated like a delinquent ward. Even if the Swazi agreed to allow one white side or the other to make further inroads on the pathetic remnants of Swazi independence, such arrangements would have no force unless both the British and the Transvaal Government agreed to it.

True, the provisional Government committee was not to intervene in purely native affairs, while Swazi ownership and sovereignty over land was to be respected (subject, of course, to the protection of all existing rights). Any further land concessions were to require both British and Transvaal consent. But the Republican monopoly over railway construction and communications was recognized.

A court which functioned in the most dubious way examined the validity of concessions given by Mbandzeni, but it did not concern itself with whether any concession had been obtained by fraud. All it required to establish was whether the concession documents had been properly drawn up, and whether 'the concession was against public morals'.

Conveniently, two of the court's three judges retired, and the remaining judge found that of 364 concessions 352 were valid. Of the twelve disallowed, one was for gaming houses, which the learned judge clearly considered to be 'against public morals'. But he found quite in order a concession which granted otherwise unallocated grazing rights over most of Swaziland in return for £50 rent a year.

Rarely can Britain have lent herself to a more sordid farce, but worse was to come. Hoping to limit Transvaal ambitions in other directions, Britain rapidly moved towards appeasement of the Boers over Swaziland and abandonment of even the dual control system.

In 1893 Britain agreed to let the Transvaal try and take over 'the rights of powers of jurisdiction, protection and administration over Swaziland, though without incorporation thereof into the South African Republic'. In other words, Britain was ready to hand over Swaziland as a Protectorate, despite the admission by both white sides that the proposed action conflicted fundamentally with the guarantee of Swazi independence given in 1890. The

British conscience was to be salved by the inclusion of provisions for the protection of Swazi law and custom where whites were not involved and of what little land and grazing rights were left to the Swazi.

It looked like a neat deal, but the Queen Regent of the Swazi and her council promptly saw through it. They not only refused categorically to give their assent to the proposed arrangement, but they sent a delegation to England to plead for British protection.

In London, this Swazi delegation was treated to a classic display of British official hypocrisy. With their minds already made up to hand over the Swazi to the Boers, British officials warmly assured the Swazi petitioners of Britain's deepest goodwill towards their people and expressed Her Majesty's Government's deep regrets that obligations under already existing treaties precluded acceptance of the proferred Swazi allegiance.

Then, on 10 December 1894, the British and the Boers arranged the Transvaal take-over by ignoring the need for Swazi assent altogether. In the words of the official account, they 'dispensed with the necessity to consult' the Swazi,* and arranged the matter between themselves in a convention. It could hardly have been simpler.

Of course, the observance of native law and custom was guaranteed (provided that it did not conflict with the white man's laws) and the remnants of Swazi land and grazing rights were to be protected. Moreover, there was to be no question of incorporation. Kruger's Republic was merely given 'all rights and powers of protection, legislation, jurisdiction, and administration over Swaziland and the inhabitants thereof'.

The Swazi, of course, have protested from that day to this that they were not parties to the 1894 convention, and indeed that they actively opposed it. But, as the restrained and conservative Lord Hailey wrote:

In the practice regulating these matters the recognition accorded to a change of national status has more frequently depended on the decisions taken by exterior powers than on the wishes expressed by the inhabitants of the country concerned.†

* Swaziland Annual Report for 1960, p. 95.
† Hailey, Part V, pp. 367–8.

At the beginning of 1895 the Transvalers dispatched their own Resident Special Commissioner to administer Swaziland, and he shortly started trying to collect the hut tax for which the white men had made provision in their convention of the previous year. The Swazi, who had never before been taxed, understandably objected. Later, too, the Transvalers altered the convention so as to make the Swazi and their chiefs subject to the white man's criminal law.

But in the meantime more important developments affecting Swaziland were taking place. The British–Boer disposition of the country seemed complete, and all that remained to fulfil their bargain was for Kruger to get his ocean outlet at Kosi Bay. Despite rising tensions between Englishmen and Boers in the booming and increasingly arrogant but somewhat bewildered Transvaal, Britain was still prepared to make Kosi Bay available to Kruger. But she was not prepared to hand it over to him completely and insisted on retaining ultimate rights to the bay.

By then, however, Kruger felt strong enough to play for all or nothing. He wanted not only Swaziland under his control, but also unfettered sovereignty over Kosi Bay. To have the use of a British-controlled harbour was not independence.

To achieve this he in effect invited Bismarck's Germany into South Africa in January of 1895. Kruger's right-hand man went on a visit to Berlin, German officers began to appear in the Transvaal, and German warships arrived at Delagoa Bay.

Britain had already suffered one traumatic shock when the Germans had suddenly staked their claim to South West Africa. If now German South West linked up with the Transvaal and the Transvaal in turn were allowed to absorb Swaziland and to breakthrough to the sea at Kosi Bay with German support, a fatal German–Boer axis would be established straight across South Africa. The Cape and Natal would be cut off from the interior and the old Bantu dream of driving the white man into the sea might be realized for the British by the Boers and the Germans.

This was too much to bear even for a Downing Street intent on limiting its commitments. Britain reacted sharply, and Kruger lost his chance of gaining unfettered control over Swaziland. Some two months after the Transvaal's special commissioner took over in Swaziland, Britain annexed Tongoland, and thus permanently forestalled any chance of Kruger concluding his own agreement with the Kosi Bay territory's African ruler. The Transvaal was cut off from the sea except by express British agreement, and the rising tensions between the Transvaal and Britain made it highly unlikely that this could now be negotiated. In fact, the negotiations over Kosi Bay were never renewed.

When the Boer War finally broke out in 1899, the Transvaal Administration was withdrawn, and the Swazi, on Britain's advice, remained neutral throughout the conflict. On its conclusion, the victorious British took over all the Transvaal's rights. The Queen Regent of the Swazi asked that her country should be annexed by Britain, and a special commissioner was sent with a small force of police to take over the administration of the country. With the promulgation of an Order-in-Council in 1903, Swaziland at long last came under undivided British rule, completing the tryptich of the High Commission Territories.

6 The Locust Years

Having reluctantly assumed responsibility for the High Commission Territories, Britain proceeded to neglect them totally for fifty years. Such development as has taken place, whether political, economic, or social, is, in all three, effectively a post Second World War phenomenon, and many of the difficulties and bitter problems which Basutoland, Bechuanaland and Swaziland present today are directly attributable to the indifference, dishonesty, evasiveness, and deliberate neglect which characterized Britain's policy towards them for half a century.

This neglect was, of course, most visible in the economic sphere, and remains so even today. Until 1945 Britain spent nothing on economic development. But perhaps even worse in its effect on their African peoples, was Britain's prolonged failure even to work out a policy for what was then called native administration.

We have seen that Basutoland came under direct British control in 1884, that Bechuanaland came under British protection in 1885, and that Swaziland joined them in 1903.

Yet Lord Hailey, certainly no radical critic, could report of the Territories – 'It was not until 1927 that the imperial Government began to give any sign of a practical interest in the means necessary to improve the local economic and social services.'

Even then, there was, by 1931, 'no evidence of any consideration being given by the British Government at this stage to the policy to be observed in regard to their development or their political future'.*

It is worth while quoting Lord Hailey at a little greater length on the half century given over, in some instances quite literally, to the locusts, for his conservatism and accuracy are such as to have made his *African Survey* (first published in 1938) and his

* *An African Survey*, revised 1956, Lord Hailey, p. 271.

later, officially commissioned, *Native Administration in the British African Territories* (of which Part V, published in 1953, is devoted to the High Commission Territories), the accepted authoritative texts for British Governments.

Hailey observes, with typical dryness, that the Territories

were from the first regarded in a different light from the Colonial dependencies in Central, East, and West Africa. . . . For many years such control as was exercised over the three Territories appeared to be the concern of the authorities in the Cape or Natal rather than of Great Britain herself.

In short, although Britain had taken them finally under its wing, it still hoped that the colonial governments would pay, and was happy in that case to let them rule. Even when, a little later, Britain had to provide and pay for administrative staff in the three countries, she never thought of providing them on the level, or of the quality, usual in the Colonial Service elsewhere in Africa, meagre as that too often was. Instead, it was found cheaper and easier to employ South Africans locally. This practice is only now being breached. The great attraction – aside, of course, from cheapness – of 'locally' recruited officials, was that they supposedly 'had the advantage of previous knowledge of the South African environment' [*sic*]. Equally, as Hailey also puts it, they 'with some rare exceptions, had no acquaintance with the policy or procedure of rule prevailing in the British Colonial dependencies elsewhere in Africa'.

From the beginning, the system, if it can be called that rather than 'an arrangement of convenience', adopted by the British was what came to be known euphemistically as 'parallel rule'. This amounted to no more than leaving the chiefs to run their tribes and territories, while the administration collected taxes from them, and, in a last resort, kept order. How the chiefs ruled, or how their subjects fared, was no concern of the British 'administration'. As long as the taxes were forthcoming, and as long as there was no political trouble which they could not themselves suppress, the chiefs were left to get on with the job. As long as they didn't worry the British Treasury, the British wouldn't worry them.

The political crisis in Swaziland which for over three years prevented the creation of even so rudimentary a modern political institution as an advisory legislative council, was caused largely by the stubborn resistance to democracy of its Paramount Chief, whom the British for long encouraged to strengthen his almost feudal powers. As a result, even in 1963, he was still in a position to prevent any agreed formula of political advance for his people into the modern world.

As Lord Hailey described it, the parallel rule practised in the Territories was

a system in which the Government denied to itself the power to intervene in the administration of a wide range of matters intimately affecting the welfare of the majority of the population, while a relatively small ruling class, highly tenacious of its position *vis-à-vis* the Government, could combine to render ineffective any measure projected by the latter for the betterment of the people at large.*

In the early days, of course, this refusal to interfere with the chiefs could be seen in England as a benevolent policy, which preserved for the tribesmen their traditional way of life.

The British Government for its part was well content to meet the demands of the humanitarians at home, and, in the case of Bechuanaland, to further the bold designs of imperialists such as Rhodes, and to achieve both these objects at no cost and very little trouble to itself.†

When, later, the Union of South Africa had been established and the imperial factor removed, continued neglect was justified by talk of legal obligations. As two of the first modern and well-informed critics of the system put it in 1931,

Britain as a matter of policy attempted to disguise the change in her position. She has preferred to leave the administration in the hands of the chiefs and encourage the idea that she cannot do otherwise without a change in the legal status of the territory.‡

All this was, of course, in large part an expression of the underlying assumption that the Territories would, in the never too distant future, be transferred to South Africa. If the Territories were in any case soon to be transferred, why spend the British

* Hailey, Part V, p. 134.

† *Problem Territories of Southern Africa*, Sir C. Dundas and Dr H. Ashton, S.A. Institute of International Affairs, 1952, p. 50.

‡ *Britain in South Africa*, No. 2, Bechuanaland Protectorate, M. L. Hodgson and W. L. Ballinger, Lovedale, 1931, p. 31.

taxpayer's money on them? And why stimulate the development of African political institutions which, as elsewhere in Africa, were intended and could only lead to eventual self-rule? South Africa, after all, was pursuing a different sort of native policy.

In a book published in 1932, Mr Leonard Barnes wrote,* after visiting them, of 'the economic and biological stagnation of the High Commission Territories' and of 'the spirit of sloth [which] has infected the Administration'. The 'guiding principle' followed by the administration was 'that the territories exist to supply the requirements of the Union's labour market, without any claim for reciprocal benefits and regardless of the effects on the vitality, the tribal organization or the economic condition of the territories themselves'.

Describing, in Bechuanaland, a process which characterized British actions in all three Territories, Mr Barnes noted:

The British authorities stepped in ... declaring their intention of interfering as little as possible with tribal law and custom. Their first subsequent act was to tax the tribes and demand from them something they had never possessed – namely, money – thus immediately imposing a profound modification of tribal custom. The imposition might have been balanced by a simultaneous offer of the means of making money, i.e. by stimulating tribal economic development. ... If conditions made an effective offer of the kind impossible, then there was only one logical alternative. That was to recognize that the tribe would have to go outside the tribal system to acquire the money, and that acquisition would *ipso facto* necessitate some measure of detribalization.

Mr Barnes was not so naïve as to believe that the British administrators had not, from the beginning, realized that taxation would drive the Africans from their homes to work for the white man. That was the precise and conscious intention, in the Territories as in South Africa. But he was right in pointing out that the British administration refused – which it continued to do until 1947 – even to think about what migratory labour was doing to African life. The administration became the *reductio ad absurdum* of indirect rule.

Aside from the question of their transfer to South Africa, nobody outside the Territories really knew much about them, and

---

* *The New Boer War*, Leonard Barnes, Hogarth Press, 1932. This short book remains extraordinarily interesting. Many of Leonard Barnes's criticisms are still relevant today.

those whose job it was to know were the very people responsible for their neglect.

In Basutoland, at best, the Government sought to advise, not to administer.

The reason for stagnation was not far to seek:

In Basutoland, the chiefs and the European administration and traders alike think the country lucky in having Union [of South Africa] industry hard by to take the overflow of unemployed and provide them [at a price] with cash to bring back. And to Union eyes it appears fitting that Basutoland should thus make a fat contribution to the supplies of labour unsophisticated and unorganized enough to be ignorant of its proper value.

In Swaziland, where similar considerations were aggravated by the presence of white settlers, two-thirds of the African productive manpower had, by 1932, been driven by taxation and land-shortage and the lack of cash markets at home into permanent exile. The Swazi were so taxed that they were 'as a community . . . paying, in point of fact, more per head for the privilege of European government than any other native south of the Nile', whilst 'to put it with brutal candour, the European has drawn large subventions from the pockets both of the Swazi and of the taxpayer of Great Britain'.

In Bechuanaland in 1932 'the country only keeps itself going by sending its manhood abroad to seek employment'. 'The Government, with its habitual penchant for the line of least resistance, has always favoured this dispersion, as simplifying the fiscal problem; and annual report after annual report complacently announces that "the Protectorate offers a large field of operations for recruiters of native labour for work on the mines and elsewhere outside the territory".'

As for the general morale of the African population, 'the Bechuana natives, as a group, are today cowed in spirit by the harshness of their chiefs, chilled by the vacillations of British administration, and perplexed at the disintegrating changes in their old life which they feel but cannot understand'.

Britain, to suit her own convenience, had in practice affected chieftainship more than it claimed, to the detriment and not the advantage of the ordinary tribesmen. The democratic interplay and checks of traditional tribal discussion in Kgotla, when every adult male was entitled to speak, had been undermined. In earlier days, an unpopular or corrupt chief risked exile or even assassination. Now the chief had been 'materially strengthened but morally weakened by the Government which stands between him and the consequences of failure or neglect. . . . Paradoxically, one effect of British protection has been to make tribal rule not only less self-sufficient (that was perhaps inevitable), but actually harsher and more capricious. There has been a real loss of personal freedom among the Bechuana since the British came.'

Looking around in 1932 for entries on the positive side of the British ledger, Leonard Barnes found precious little:

The British came into the Bechuana country to keep the Boers out, and they have ever since been inclined to suppose that in safeguarding the Bechuana peoples from outside aggression their duty has been done. . . . The British have rendered valuable veterinary aid; they have provided such medical services as the country could afford to pay for [sic] and very recently they have established two good hospitals and given some assistance in boring for water. But the old tribal life is disintegrating under their hands, and so far they have done nothing either to repair it or to put a substitute in its place.

Now it might be argued that the lack of progress in the Territories at this and preceding times, whilst regrettable, must be seen as part of the general failings of British African policy, and that there was nothing peculiarly reprehensible about its operation in Basutoland, Bechuanaland, and Swaziland. But this argument simply doesn't square with the facts, and both Hailey and Barnes, men of very different outlook and temperament, refute it decisively. As Hailey, himself an enlightened administrator, pointed out, the Territories were always regarded differently from the colonial Dependencies in central, east, and west Africa.

It was their being embedded in South Africa that caused this difference of approach, and South Africa, quite aside from any other considerations, had a flourishing mining industry, whose overwhelmingly British shareholders were more than happy to have the Territories and especially Basutoland used as a reservoir of cheap migrant labour.

Even when the decision *was* made to reform the system of Native Administration, the British Government's spirit of sloth and excessive regard for the susceptibilities of the chieftainship led to a sixteen-year delay before these intrinsically limited reforms were fully implemented in all three Territories.

A growing local demand for the improvement of the procedure of the Native Courts combined with a tardy recognition by the British Government of its responsibilities for the expansion of the social and economic services led in the early thirties to the introduction of a series of reforms which followed the model of the Native Authority system then holding the field in most of the British dependencies.*

It could hardly be put more euphemistically. Even then, the reforms introduced to Bechuanaland in 1934 did not come into full operation until 1943; Basutoland got its reforms only in 1938; and the struggle with the Paramount Chief which resulted from the introduction of very limited reform for Swaziland in 1944 ended only in 1950. Furthermore, by the time that it was implemented in 1945, the Native Authority system was already becoming recognized or actually replaced as out of date in Britain's other African territories.

The tardy reforms introduced from 1934 onwards were not, of course, advocated as measures preparatory to the introduction of political self-rule. Nor did the British Government make any announcement before the Second World War specifically applying to the Territories its general intention of bringing all its colonial possessions to self-government. And if Britain wasn't going to antagonize South Africa before the war, she certainly wasn't going to do so during it, when she was grateful for the help of South African soldiers – and was helped by units from the Territories.

The war did, however, stir ideas and hopes of freedom and of an end to colonialism throughout Africa, and led Britain, in 1945, to set up the Colonial Welfare and Development Fund. It was only with its founding that the Territories began to receive anything approaching significant economic help from Britain, and it was only after the Nationalist victory in the South African elections of 1948 that Britain finally began to move towards its present position of advancing the Territories towards the publicly stated object of democratic self-rule and eventual independence.

* *An African Survey*, revised 1956, Lord Hailey, p. 272.

7 A Ripple of Democracy

The Basuto are unique in several ways. Alone amongst the African peoples and tribes of southern and central Africa, they have made of themselves a mountain nation; they have become natural horsemen and developed the unique and widely sought-after Basuto pony; though completely surrounded by hostile, white-ruled territory they have never allowed white men to own land in their country; and they have led most, if not all, of Africa in literacy.

But the Basuto are also remarkable for the strength of the tradition which combines democratic participation in government with a strong Paramount Chieftainship. And this tradition is highly relevant to the solution of Basutoland's problems today.

Basuto democracy has its roots in the *pitso*, or general assembly, in which every man is entitled to have his say, and even where decisions seem to have been made by the chief, in reality they have depended upon assent by a majority of his people. This is neatly expressed in the old and often quoted Basuto proverb, *morema ke morema ka batho* – a chief is a chief by the people.

Even Moshesh, the creator of the Basuto nation and its first *Morema E Moholo* or Supreme Chief, never claimed to be an absolute ruler. In announcing his laws, he stressed that they had been enacted 'by the advice and with the concurrence of the great men of the tribe', a concurrence usually obtained through a *pitso* which was either local or, on major issues, national.

In building up the nation, Moshesh at first made it a sort of confederation of various clans, each ruled by a chief owing allegiance to him. Later, he welded these units more closely together, and strengthened his own rule, by 'placing' his sons and other close relatives over different areas of the country. Thus instead of a series of semi-independent barons, an effective monarchy was established, but Moshesh never attempted to make it an absolute one. The chiefs remained chiefs through the people.

There were, therefore, indigenous democratic foundations on which the early British administration could build. In 1880 a Cape M.P. who knew the Basuto and spoke their language could urge the development of the 'strong democratic element' which he found to be a 'natural African product' in Basutoland.

In a fascinating passage written in 1879, Lord Bryce went so far as to compare Basuto democracy with the Greek model:

Once a year the Commissioner meets the whole people, in their national assembly called the *Pitso* – the name is derived from their verb 'to call' – which in several points recalls the *agora*, or assembly of freemen described in the Homeric poems. The Paramount Chief presides, and debate is mainly conducted by the chiefs; but all free men, gentle and simple, have a right to speak in it. There is no voting, only a declaration, by shouts, of the general feeling. Though the Paramount Chief has usually been the person who convokes it, a magnate lower in rank might always, like Achilles in the Illiad, have it summoned when a fitting occasion arose.

I was struck by the freedom and intelligence with which speakers delivered their views. One observed: 'This is our parliament, though it is a very disorderly parliament, because we are all mixed up, young and old; and we cannot accept any measure without discussion' ... (another) wishing to excuse any vehement expression which he might use, observed: 'We have a proverb which says that a man who makes a mistake in a public assembly cannot be killed.' In this proverb is the germ of the English 'privilege of Parliament'. It is easy to gather from the whole proceedings of these *Pitsos* how much more popular government has been among the Basuto than it was among the Zulus or Matabele.*

The system did not, of course, work wholly in quite this ideal way. Succession to the chieftainship in Basutoland is inherited in the male line through the first, or main, wife, and ever since the time when lesser chiefs copied Moshesh's technique and began to 'place' their own relatives in positions of authority, the chieftainship began to proliferate to an unhealthy degree. But one of the safeguards which the common people retained against a chief who refused to heed their counsel was for them to replace him with a more popular younger brother or son.

* *Impressions of South Africa*, Lord Bryce, 1879, pp. 424–5.

Moshesh himself formalized the sacred rule that the land belongs to the people and not to any individual, and that the Paramount holds it in trust for the whole nation. Similarly, the subordinate or local chiefs administered the land for their people. Each chief allocated and periodically re-allocated land for grazing and farming, and had the right to call on the tribe for voluntary labour on the tribal lands. He also combined these executive functions with judicial ones, and every chief had his own court where he tried both civil and criminal cases.

The system was, of course, plagued since its earliest days by disputes over succession and, sometimes more importantly, jurisdiction, and even Moshesh could not count absolutely on the allegiance of his 'placed' relatives. Indeed, on Moshesh's death, the nation was rent for some time by dissension. The British, faced with settling these problems, if law and order were to be maintained, saw that the strengthening of the Paramount Chieftainship was both the best way of achieving this minimal aim and of limiting their own expenses and direct responsibilities.

The Basuto had fought simultaneously a civil and an external war; their crops had been exhausted; cannibalism had been rife and their country and they were pretty nearly ruined.

As the Basuto have themselves put it:

For a considerable period the energies of the Administration were largely absorbed in the task of settling inter-tribal disputes. If the Basuto were to continue to be a unified nation it was essential to enforce the supremacy of the Paramount Chief over insurgent chiefs of lesser rank. It was therefore the policy of the early Administration to maintain the Paramount Chief as the head of the indigenous Basuto organization. The Basuto have cause to be grateful for the successful achievement of this policy; the position of the Paramount Chief as the symbol of national unity and the custodian of Basuto tradition is now so firmly established that it is taken for granted.*

In fact, the British administration supported successive Paramount Chiefs to such an extent that their position became not only consolidated but virtually unassailable.

The British left judicial and executive functions in the hands of the chiefs, except for serious crimes such as homicide, which went

* *Report on Constitutional Reform and Chieftainship Affairs*, Basutoland Council, 1958, p. 19.

to magistrates' courts, and the chiefs were also made responsible for the collection of tax, in which the assurance of a five per cent rake-off for themselves presumably spurred them on to greater efforts. This arrangement, together with the powers left to the chiefs to retain, ostensibly for the tribal good, the fines which they imposed in their courts, also saved over the years the expense of paying them any salary. Thus a sort of self-financing Basuto administration was set up side by side with the British one, limited only by the ability of the tribesmen to pay fines and their willingness to render labour.

The British imposed the tax, the South Africans across the border provided work and a pittance from which the tax could be saved, and the chiefs, for a percentage, collected it.

For more than fifty years, Britain's policy in Basutoland was thus one of *laissez faire*. The country's population, with peace and the tenuous beginnings of rudimentary health services, grew; its economy, in the meantime, was transformed from a pastoral subsistence to a money one; and the chiefs, fighting for their fiefs against rival claimants, increasingly abused their position to amass personal wealth. As ward chiefs took over the custom of 'placing' their relatives, they either displaced existing chiefs or cut up areas under their own control to provide fresh fiefs.

Inevitably, as the competition between chiefs became keener, many of them abandoned the custom that a chief's wealth existed only to be shared with his people. They continued to demand the traditional services, such as unpaid labour, but they stopped giving anything in return. Some went even further and transformed their courts into petty racketeering concerns. Unreasonable orders were issued, and defaulters heavily fined. Sometimes a chief would even enter into cahoots with cattle thieves in return for a share of their loot. Understandably, dissatisfaction grew over the years, to reach a climax in the thirties.

Meanwhile, many years of patient negotiation by the British led in 1903 to the creation, by unanimous consent at a national *pitso*, of the Basutoland National Council. The national *pitsos* had begun to be largely ceremonial affairs, for as the matters with which the Paramount Chief had to deal multiplied, it became increasingly difficult to have each one discussed nationally, and the Paramount came to rely more and more on a small circle of advisers.

The Basutoland National Council was established as a purely advisory body 'for discussing the domestic affairs of the territory', meeting under the Resident Commissioner. It had 100 members, ninety-four of whom were nominated by the Paramount and included the major chiefs, while another five were nominated by the Resident Commissioner, and the Paramount himself sat in as the chief counsellor.

This composition naturally made the council, on the whole, a conservative body, but its discussions did receive healthy outside prodding after a body of commoners formed themselves into the Basutoland Progressive Association. This association was the first to press, in 1919, for part of the National Council to be elected. The request was rejected.

Then came the Great Depression, whose impact on Basutoland was worsened by a very bad drought in 1923-4. The British Government at last felt moved to take a look at the economy and finance of Basutoland, and commissioned Sir Alan Pim to report.

Pim emphatically condemned the Basutoland administration's policy of parallel rule, which he castigated as one of

non-interference, of preferring allegiance, of leaving two parallel governments to work in a state of detachment unknown in tropical Africa . . . the Government and Native organization still work practically independently of each other, and no attempt has been made to combine them into a real system of Government, or to make such modification in the Native system as would render it capable of dealing with the changing conditions of modern times and with the effects of the introduction of a money economy and of contact with European institutions.*

Sir Alan Pim recommended the transplantation to Basutoland of the policy of 'indirect rule', by then established in Nigeria and Tanganyika. This meant, in his view, that, 'The control from below which previously operated to secure at least a minimum of just government must disappear under a system of protection and must be replaced by control from above'.

Even given the best will in the world, the problem was, of course, a very difficult one. Despite dissatisfaction, loyalty to

* *Financial and Economic Position of Basutoland*, 1935, Cmd 4907.

chieftainship still carried much traditional weight in Basuto life, while dissatisfaction with the gross shortcomings and abuses of power by the chiefs themselves found vocal expression only through a small 'middle-class' of teachers and traders who never thought, at this time, of any mass following. And the one body which did campaign for following amongst ordinary people, the *Lekhotlala Bafo* or Commoners' League, was in favour of returning to even more direct and extensive chiefly rule. Above all, the administration needed to decide on an active, rather than a passive, policing policy. What this policy should have been, if there had been a courageous, informed and competent administration, was succintly put by the Basutoland Council years later:

The policy of 'control from above', advocated in the Pim Report, defeated its own object, and fostered conditions under which 'dualism' was to become a major problem . . . the reformers of 1938 failed to take adequate account of the growing influence of the Basutoland National Council: what was needed was less emphasis on indirect rule and control from above, and more emphasis on encouraging the growth of responsibility and initiative in the hands of Basuto organs of self-government.*

What the administration did instead was to fumble, and so it – and, more importantly, the Basuto – got the worst of several worlds. In 1938 it introduced, by proclamations rushed through the Basutoland National Council, reforms in the chieftainship structure. The number of chiefs was limited; they and the Paramount were given statutory responsibility for maintaining Basuto law and order; and the recognition of the Paramount was placed in the hands of the High Commissioner, with both of them sharing the responsibility for the placing and deposition of other chiefs.

These measures had fundamental weaknesses, and much of the beneficial effect that they might have had at the time was lost by procrastination. Conditions had hardly changed at all for fifty years in Basutoland; now that reforms were proclaimed, the administration waited for another eight years to implement them effectively.

In fact, the agreement of the Paramount Chief to the 1938

* *Report on Constitutional Reform and Chieftainship Affairs*, Basutoland Council, Maseru, 1958, p. 37.

measures was brought by an understanding that no immediate changes would be made in practice. They weren't.

There were too many chiefs, and hence too many courts. But when the administration gazetted its list of recognized chiefs, very few existing petty chiefs were omitted. 1,340 chiefs, sub-chiefs and headmen were recognized, each entitled to hold a court, and this inflated number was not reduced until 1946. Meanwhile, the list contained inevitable inaccuracies, and those who felt themselves, often with cause, to have been unjustly excluded felt understandably bitter. The situation was not helped when in practice District Officers continued to recognize and work through ungazetted chiefs.

One of the advantages claimed for indirect rule has been that it encouraged indigenous local government. But local government cannot function without local finance. Hence, elsewhere in Africa, Native Treasuries were established under indirect rule. In Basutoland no treasury was provided for in the 1938 reforms, and it was, in fact, only after a National Treasury was established in 1945–6 that the reforms of 1938 became effective. The number of chiefs entitled to hold courts was reduced in 1946 from 1,340 to 121 and again reduced in 1949 to 107. It stands today at sixty-three, and it should be said that these reductions were made with the consent, and latterly at the urging, of the Basutoland National Council.

Then, too, with the establishment of a National Treasury came two crucial reforms in the way that the chieftainship functioned. Chiefs were paid a fixed salary so that they no longer needed to support themselves on the extraction of court fines, the seizure of stray livestock and the enforcement of tribal labour. British administrative officers were given the power to reverse, on appeal, the decisions of the Native courts, and court fees were introduced, eliminating a great deal of unnecessary litigation (though some Basuto objected that this hampered a traditional method of airing grievances).

The difficulties of attempting piecemeal legal reform from above without tackling the basic social and economic problems, however, are well illustrated in the way that these reforms were received.

Many of the lesser chiefs had felt insecure since 1938, when the

Administration took powers to 'de-stool' them. Nevertheless, as long as they were recognized, they had the prestige of rank, seen by all in their power to hold courts. Now a new criterion was established, salary. But fixed salaries were paid only to the Paramount and to the twenty-two principal or ward chiefs. The rest had to rely on getting a cut from a limited overall sum, and the very complicated way in which this was allocated made the multitudinous lesser chiefs dependent on the often haphazard judgement of the District Officer and on caprices of the ward chief and his advisers. The payment of salaries, therefore, hardly lessened the feeling of insecurity among the lesser chiefs and headmen, in fact it was heightened by contemporary, if limited, increases in the stature, influence and representative nature of the Basutoland National Council.

In 1943 the council itself recommended that an effectively elected element be introduced in its membership through the creation of District Councils. These councils, themselves partly elected, were to prepare 'motions' for the National Council to consider, and were indirectly to elect nine of its 100 members. By the time this reform was legalized in 1948, however, the District Councils' indirectly elected national representation was increased to eighteen, and this was further increased to thirty-six in 1950. Various associations were also given representation through joint nomination by the Paramount Chief and the Resident Commissioner.

Thus by 1950 the Basutoland National Council's 100 members, presided over *ex officio* by the Resident Commissioner, were made up of:

(a) the Paramount Chief

(b) five members nominated by the Resident Commissioner, and

(c) ninety-four members nominated by the Paramount Chief, of whom: thirty-six were indirectly elected by District Councils, and six were elected by various associations namely one each by the Agricultural Union, the Progressive Association, the Teachers' Association, the Traders' Association, the Leper Settlement [*sic*] and the ex-servicemen.

In the meantime, too, the National Council had increased its powers. It still remained, in law, a mere advisory body. But, in response to pressure from the council, both the administration and the Paramount Chief had bound themselves to consult it.

In 1944 the High Commissioner agreed 'to consult the Paramount Chief and the Basutoland Council before Proclamations closely affecting the domestic affairs and welfare of the Basuto people and the development of the Basuto Native Administration are enacted'. He stressed, of course, that an extremely wide range of decisions, including those affecting Europeans, fell outside of this definition; but the agreement formalized a limited advance.

The Paramount Chief, also at the urging of the council, fell into line with a formal declaration in 1944 that 'it is the policy of the Paramountcy to consult the Basutoland Council before issuing orders or making rules affecting the welfare of the Basuto people and the administration of the Basuto'. By 1948 the council had also succeeded in persuading the Paramount to accept an advisory council, and had then established some indirect check on National Treasury expenditure, as well as making local taxes imposed by the Paramount Chief dependent upon its approval.

Thus the council gained in power and became, at the urging both of outsiders and of its own members, partly representative. These developments were approved by the British administration, but they were not the result of any general plan and did not point to any defined objective, as Lord Hailey observed as late as 1953.

The British ignored the transformation of the Basuto economy and abuse of their power by many chiefs; the middle-class commoners and the more progressive chiefs pressed for reform, and the administration agreed to changes here and there whilst putting off their effective implementation for years. Consistently the British ignored demands for the creation of a Legislative Council, though this was the only logical result of their own declared policy. Neither the world war nor difficulties of finance can explain or excuse the contemporary administration's record of delay and dither.

It reflects well on the more progressive minority within the chieftainship that the National Council was itself amongst those to agitate for its own reform. It also so happened that in subtly limiting the power of the Paramount Chief, the progressive councillors and commoners outside were helped by an intense dispute over who should succeed Griffith as Paramount when he died in 1939. It seems clear that Griffith had intended his eldest son, Bereng, to be his successor. But the Sons of Moshesh backed Seiso, a younger son by Griffith's second wife, and the British Government recognized him. He died, however, within a year, and once again the Sons of Moshesh passed Bereng over. Instead of him, they appointed the senior widow, Mantsibo, as Regent for the two-year-old boy of the Bereng house whom they chose as heir. This boy, Constantine Bereng Seiso, is today the Paramount Chief, Moeshoeshoe II.

The dispute over the Paramountcy was very bitter, and its scars can still be detected in the country today. Bereng challenged the appointment of Mantsibo as Regent in the High Court but lost.

Embittered and desperate, like other unrecognized or dissatisfied chiefs, he sought help in ancient Basuto magic and medicine, and in 1949 he was executed for complicity in the gruesome 'medicine murders', which made Basutoland notorious in the immediate post-war years.

From olden times, Basuto had made special protective or *diretlo* medicine from the still living body of a victim selected for the purpose and subsequently killed. After the reforms in chieftainship and native courts became effective in 1945, the incidence of such *diretlo* ritual or 'medicine' murders increased to almost epidemic proportions. Between 1895 and 1938, only twenty-three suspected 'medicine murders' had been reported. Between 1938 and 1950 there were seventy, and of these thirty occurred in the two years 1947 and 1948.

There can be no doubt that a large number of lesser chiefs, bitter about official non-recognition or fearful of being deposed, resorted to 'medicine murder' to reinforce or restore their position and prestige through magic. For despite the long history of Christian missionary work, a great many Basuto still stuck openly to their tribal religions, while many others, though ostensibly Christian, understandably still felt the pull of these old beliefs. At times of conflict or distress such an underlying faith may sooner or later have been expected to rise again to the surface.

Thus the post-war resurgence of 'medicine murders' was linked with the hastily imposed and inadequately considered attempts at administrative reform in Basutoland. For all that, they had the rather gruesome virtue of focusing public attention at home and in Britain on some of the Territory's problems. Mr G. I. Jones was appointed to inquire into the murders, and produced a very valuable and wide-ranging report.*

It is, of course, impossible to ascribe all the murders to the crisis over the chieftainship. By their secret, magic nature, such crimes are hard to investigate. They are frequently not reported to the police, and witnesses are, understandably, difficult to trace once a mutilated corpse has been discovered. Lord Hailey has pointed out that chiefs and headmen were by no means the only ones involved in the post-1938 cases, and that some of these murders were most probably 'commercial' ones involving 'witch-doctors' who wanted to stock up with exceptionally potent and therefore expensive magical medicine.

Still, there is the law of supply and demand, and if the 'doctors' thought that they could get higher prices for *diretlo* medicine after 1938, there must have been an increase in anxious clients. One cannot say that the growth in post-war 'medicine murders' was wholly due to unsatisfactory administrative reforms and failure to meet political frustration, but there is every reason for assuming a strong connexion.

And any attempt to root out the gruesome practice had to fail unless it fundamentally improved the economic and social life of the people.

In retrospect, the administration seems to have been almost perverse in its refusal to face the challenge of thinking out and implementing basic, integrated reforms leading to Basuto self-rule. The problems were, of course, many and massive, and each new administrator was burdened by the failings of his predecessors. Furthermore, very few first-class, let alone brilliant, minds could be found in the administration of the Territories. Neither the prestige, nor the challenge of the posts, let alone the low pay, attracted good minds. Second-rate South African and ex-police officers were the rule rather than the exception. So, to some extent, the administrators were victims of their own inadequacies,

* *Report on Basutoland Medicine Murder*, G. I. Jones, Cmd 8209, 1951. On ritual murder in Basutoland, see also *The Basuto* by Hugh Ashton and *Native Administration, Part V*, Lord Hailey (pp. 130–32). For related types of murder in Swaziland, see *The Swazi*, Brian Marwick, 1940.

which the British Government's meanness and indifference almost guaranteed as the norm. Those few administrators who were first class, some seconded from the Colonial Service, were starved of funds and frustrated by the underlying policy assumption, still operative after the war, that nothing much needed to be done for the Territories since they would soon be incorporated into South Africa. But even allowing for all this, the refusal over the years of the Basutoland administration to listen to the demands of the Basuto chiefs and commoners for a Legislative Council cannot be excused.

In 1953, Hailey – by that time, the officially recognized expert on Native administration in Africa (he had produced his monumental work, *An African Survey*, in 1938) – published a report on Native Administration in the High Commission Territories,* which had been commissioned by the Secretary of State for Commonwealth Relations.

He was scathing about the lack of past policy and the absence, even at that time, of 'any general plan or defined objective'. He was emphatic in stating the urgent need for a Legislative Council to be introduced.

Hailey's strictures undoubtedly helped to shake the Commonwealth Relations Office and the High Commission itself into some kind of action, and only two years after receiving the report the Government appointed Sir Henry Moore, a former Governor of Kenya, to head a committee of inquiry. Unfortunately, the terms of reference made no mention of a Legislative Council; Moore was to inquire into the complex structure of local government, and its relations with the central government. This did not, however, prevent the Basuto from pressing the need for a Legislative Council on him in every possible way. Every Basuto body which gave evidence stressed this need, from the Sons of Moshesh and the Progressive Association through the Basutoland African Congress and the *Lekhotla la Bafo* to the African Teachers' Association.†

* *Native Administration in the British African Territories, Part V.* (The High Commission Territories: Basutoland, The Bechuanaland Protectorate and Swaziland), H.M.S.O., 1953.

† For an excellent summary of their memoranda, the Moore Report, and a brief outline of the historical background of Basuto institutions until 1955, see *Basutoland Enquiry*, Isobel Edwards, Africa Bureau, 1955.

This, apparently, left Moore unmoved, and he produced a report* which has been aptly characterized as 'an unimaginative document, lacking both political forethought or political wisdom'.†

Its recommendations had, of course, certain obvious purely administrative attractions. It proposed to make the Paramount a constitutional ruler, made the revolutionary suggestion that in certain circumstances the inalienable tradition of hereditary chieftainship should be set aside, and proposed the creation of a Land Board, 'to supervise the allocation of lands'. To Basuto eyes, this seemed a direct attack on chieftainship and tribal rule, whose continuance all the witnesses had supported. It should be said, however, that Moore was quite right in warning of 'the obvious dangers of vesting unfettered control of so precious an asset as land indefinitely in chiefs or headmen'.

Opposition from the Basuto to the Moore Report was immediate and practically unanimous, while a second major grievance was the refusal of the Moore Commission to consider the introduction of a Legislative Council which was widely demanded by both chiefs and commoners.

The Moore Committee attempted to meet the bitter criticism of its refusal even to mention the words Legislative Council in its report by shielding behind its terms of reference. Yet it did make recommendations on the grant of legislative powers to the Basutoland and District Councils. As Isobel Edwards has aptly commented:

How the Committee is in a position to make recommendations on the question of a subsidiary legislative function of the Basutoland and District Councils, but is unable to discuss or even to accept evidence on the wider and more important issue of the main legislative functions of the Basutoland Council, is an administrative and constitutional riddle that baffles the imagination.

When the Resident Commissioner insisted on putting each of the report's 200 paragraphs to the National Council, a deadpan farce ensued. Each paragraph was duly put and debated, and each paragraph, no matter what its particular relevance, was duly

* *Basutoland: Report of the Administrative Reforms Committee*, 1954.
† *Basutoland Enquiry*, p. 25.

rejected on a vote. As the *Observer*'s Cyril Dunn reported: 'If the date had been printed on the report, they'd have rejected that as well.' The Resident Commissioner gave up after paragraph 47, told the councillors, who included the Territory's senior chiefs, that they were 'naughty boys', and sent them home.

They went, but before going sixty-six of the 100 councillors wrote to London asking that the Resident Commissioner and the other senior officials responsible for this fiasco be recalled. The Resident Commissioner and the other three top officials concerned were transferred within a year, but as they were all promoted, any punitive assumptions would be shaky. The British administration, however, did have the good sense to see that it was futile to proceed in the face of such stiff and unanimous Basuto opposition. The report was dropped.

This was a triumph for the Basuto, whether in the council, the Sons of Moshesh, the various associations, the *Lekhotla la Bafo*, or the Basutoland Africa Congress, which had cut its political milk teeth on the anti-Moore campaign. Considerable attention had been focused on Basutoland by this whole episode, and, unlike the publicity over the earlier medicine murders, it was favourable.

Sensing its advantage, the Basuto Council passed, in September 1955, a motion requesting 'that the Basutoland Council be given power to make laws in all internal matters, such laws to be confirmed by the Paramount Chief'. The motion also proposed that the Resident Commissioner and his staff should guide and advise the council in policy, and that the British administration 'should deal with external affairs on behalf of Her Majesty's Government'. The Secretary of State replied in May of the following year that he was prepared to consider proposals for internal self-government from the council, but that any powers granted could not extend to non-Basuto in Basutoland.

This was a great step forward, marred only by the obvious intention to give whites in the country special status. The council went about framing its democratic reply. It asked for opinions from all the District Councils. The Paramount Regent also had her say, urging acceptance of the British conditions, which would have formalized legal apartheid in Basutoland. Then the Basuto Council set up a Constitutional Reform Committee, stressing in its terms of reference that the exclusion of non-Basuto from future

Legislative Council jurisdiction was not acceptable. The Reform Committee was instructed to 'show what the position will be if the Secretary of State's reply were accepted as it stands'. Then the Council, with the agreement of the Resident Commissioner, set up another committee to look into the whole question of chieftain-ship affairs.

The two committees shortly decided to produce a joint report, and appointed Denis Cowen, professor of comparative law in the University of Cape Town, to be their legal adviser. They pro-duced, in July 1958, a most impressive report* on which, in effect, the country's next constitution was based. Sensibly, the British Government yielded to practically unanimous Basuto opinion, and agreed that the Council's jurisdiction, however limited, should extend to all those living in Basutoland, Basuto or not.

Under the new constitution, there were to be eighty members of the Basutoland Council, of whom half would be indirectly elected. Direct elections were to be held for District Councils, in which anyone who had been resident in Basutoland for six months, maintained a home in the country and paid tax, would be entitled to vote. Since all adult, able-bodied men had to pay tax, Basuto-land was accordingly given, in effect, universal adult male suffrage. Conversely women, who were not generally liable to tax, were effectively unenfranchized. The nine District Councils, thus popularly elected, were then to act as electoral colleges and in turn choose the forty elected members of the National Council.

To these elected members were to be added twenty-six *ex officio* ones – the twenty-two principal ward chiefs, and four senior government officials – while fourteen nominees of the Paramount Chief completed the tally. The Council itself was to elect an outsider to be its President (who by agreement was Mr Walter Stanford, a former Liberal member of the South African Parlia-ment, now a member of the South African Progressive Party).

The qualifications for membership of the Council were to be the same as those for the District Council franchise, with the addition of literacy in Sesuto. Both elected and nominated members might be suspended by the High Commissioner after consultation with the Paramount Chief, and no one could be a member who had

* *Report on Constitutional Reform and Chieftainship Affairs*, 1958.

within the preceding five years completed serving a jail sentence of twelve months or more without receiving a free pardon.

The powers of the Council were to be carefully limited, and it was not to control the Executive Council, whose own powers would be no more than advisory. The High or Resident Commissioner might act against the Council's advice whenever either 'consider[ed] it right to do so', though in that event they would be obliged to report their reasons to the British Secretary of State. The Executive Council itself was to consist of the Resident Commissioner plus his three senior administrators *ex officio*, one nominee of the Paramount Chief from the Legislative Council membership, and three members elected by the Council. The Resident Commissioner was to have an additional casting vote, thus giving the officials a majority vote, and its non-official members were to be subject to arbitrary suspension by the authorities.

Both the Resident Commissioner and the Paramount Chief would be generally obliged to consult the Executive Council, but there was a wide range of exceptions to this rule, which for the Paramount Chief included chieftainship affairs and the withholding of his assent to a Bill passed by the Legislative Council.

A separate college of chiefs was to be set up, consisting of the twenty-two principal chiefs, presided over by the Paramount, with the function of nominating future Paramount Chiefs, settling disputes over succession to lesser chieftainships and over chiefs' territorial boundaries, and – most important in a country where, by and large, the integrity of the chieftainship has sunk near to vanishing point – the investigation of misconduct or abuses by chiefs, with recommendations to the Paramount for the suspension or removal of offenders.

The first elections under the new constitution were held, to District Councils, in January 1960, and the poll was low, despite considerable publicity and campaigning; of a total electorate of 191,663 men and women of all races, only 35,302, or eighteen per cent, went to the polls. This could partly be attributed to there being no tradition of voting and to the extremely rugged nature of the country. But in the main, responsibility lay with the administration's refusal to arrange polling in South Africa, where forty-three per cent of the electorate were working, and the extraordinary arrangements that the administration made for postal voting by these migrant absentees.

The transparent excuse of organizational difficulty was given for the refusal either to organize proper postal voting or, more practicably, to have polling stations in South Africa; but the real reason quite obviously lay in the contrast which the Basuto, voting in South Africa – however indirectly – for their own Legislative Council, would have made with the denial of all democratic say to their South African fellow workers. As to the arrangements for the postal vote, which affected a majority of the electorate, they practically invited abuse. Each Mosuto voter in South Africa was, through a provided form, to advise a voting relative at home or a chief of how he wanted to vote, and the chief or relative would then cast his vote for him. Those who could not write were to get a friend to write home for them. With the powers and future of a largely corrupt chieftainship a major issue in the elections, this was patently absurd. But once the British had decided to hide all visual evidence of Basutoland's newly granted democracy from Dr Verwoerd's helots, they were obliged to resort to this ludicrous device.

Once again, even at the moment of granting advance, Britain's men on the spot devalued their own good work for fear of offending white South African susceptibilities. Once again, it was the Basuto who paid.

In Basutoland, the elections went off smoothly and resulted in a sweeping victory for the Basutoland Congress Party, which gained seventy-three seats with 12,787 votes, while the Basutoland National Party won only twenty-two (7,002 votes), the Marema Tlou Party sixteen, and Independents fifty-one. In the subsequent elections of National Council members by the District Councils, twenty-nine came from the B.C.P., five from the Marema Tlou, and one from the National Party, while five were Independents.

The elections were, despite the shortcomings in their organization, a political landmark. For the first time in South Africa's history, and in the very heart of the country, an election took place in which a decisive degree of political power rested in the hands of a predominantly black electorate. The supposed obstacle of widespread illiteracy had been overcome by the simple and effective device of having voters drop their ballot papers into boxes marked with colours allocated to different parties and candidates, and the electorate had behaved peacefully and responsibly. As *Drum* magazine said at the time, 'the first ripple of democracy has reached our people in Southern Africa'.

Part Three

The Territories Today

8 Khena Ka Khotso – Basutoland

Basutoland today is the paradox of the High Commission Territories: economically their ugly sister, she is politically their Cinderella, at least to modern African eyes. Completely surrounded by South Africa, Basutoland is viewed as an island of freedom by those who oppose apartheid, and this view is shared, in varying degrees, by the Basuto themselves. But to hundreds of thousands of Basuto their homeland, of which they are intensely proud, is also an island of poverty from which they must go into the apartheid State if they are to survive.

There is no obvious way in which Basutoland can keep going economically, even at its present low level, without this massive export – some forty-three per cent – of its labour to South Africa. At the same time, the underlying hostility of white South African racialists towards Basutoland increases with every fresh step which she takes towards genuine democracy and self-rule, for such progress reveals the fraud of Dr Verwoerd's supposedly self-ruling but effectively puppet Bantustans.

Yet, with official South African policy committed in principle to squeezing out 650,000 Basuto said to live in the Republic, Basuto political leaders, supported by the Paramount Chief, have gained their demand for further radical advance, not only to internal self-rule but to complete independence for their country in 1966.

Leading this demand has been Ntsu Mokhehle, president of the Basutoland Congress Party and likely, at the time of writing, to become his country's first Prime Minister when internal self-government is achieved early in 1965.

It is with this paradox, with the opposing pulls of acute internal political awareness and poverty on the one hand, and, on the other, economic dependence on a hostile, encircling, South Africa, that both the people and the British administration of Basutoland have had to live. It is an agonizing situation, without parallel in British colonial history, but it is one which the casual visitor to Basutoland's capital, Maseru, might easily miss. For Maseru, which by European standards is more of an upland village than a capital, is on the surface anything but agonized.

One enters Basutoland, on the main route, by crossing a girder bridge over the Caledon River, whose fertile valley lands were the object of the long drawn-out conflict between the early Boers and the Basuto. Until 1962 there was, except for an occasional police check, no control on the South African side of the border. Today there is a permanent South African border post (one of eighteen being established on Basutoland's borders), at which the documents of black and white travellers are carefully scrutinized. It marks the growing tension between the two countries.

Once over the bridge, however, and safely on the Basutoland side, little seems to have changed. Behind the modern, cleanly ceremonial entrance arch with its splendid slogan, *Khena Ka Khotso* – Enter in Peace – the Union Jack flies, and a well turned-out sergeant of the Basutoland mounted police salutes with great smartness and passes the visitor smoothly through.

A sergeant may, of course, have an occasional attack of officiousness, as on the occasion in 1962 when I presented myself in a car with Rhodesian number-plates. Having duly signed the car and passenger entry register, which also informed me that the police-man presenting it was an authorized border control official, I was about to drive away when he asked, 'Have you a passport, sir?'

Having, over many years, passed in and out without ever hearing such a question, I told him in amazement that I did indeed have a passport. Would he like to see it? Yes, please, sir. Everything was in order, but *my* suspicions were aroused.

'Tell me, Sergeant, do you always ask people now for a pass-port? And what do you do if they haven't got one? I mean, what about refugees from South Africa?'

'Oh, sir, if they haven't proper papers, we send them back.'

Deeply disturbed and mentally composing an exposé cable to my paper, I sped along the couple of tarred miles into Maseru, where I had an appointment with the then Resident Commis-sioner. My story drew an indulgent smile and a shake of the head.

'Was it a fat sergeant? That must have been old — again. We sent him over to the Coronation and so had to promote him, otherwise he really wouldn't be a sergeant, and he sometimes likes to impress visitors with his own importance. It must have been your Rhodesian number-plates. No, no, of course we haven't started asking people for passports or turning them back. As you know, anyone can come in and stay for three months before he has to register in any sort of way. But we'll have to have a word with Sergeant —. After all, it wouldn't do if such a story appeared in the *Observer*, would it? Now, how can we help you with this book you're writing? We'll do everything we can. After all, it's about time that the world knew a little about our needs.'

It was, in many respects, an illuminating little episode, typical of the easy-going and friendly paternalism of many 'old hands' in the Basutoland administration. Jogging along from year to year, doing their best on a shoe-string budget, they have – with a few notable exceptions – grown increasingly distressed as 'their' once-sleepy country has become a cockpit of international tensions. They have played difficult situations 'off the cuff', as they have long played overall policy. In the post-war years they have learnt, through some admittedly rough experience, to fear the Press inquiries which might lead to that ever-threatening bane of the colonial administrator's life, a Private Member's Question at Westminster. But they have remained, withall, devoted and genuinely ready to help in providing information where the interests of 'their' territory might – in their judgement – be furthered. Inevitably, the pressure of recent events, and especially of internal political advance, have pushed many of Basutoland's expatriate administrators into new postures and attitudes to match those of the administered.

As one leaves the Secretariat and walks down Maseru's single shopping street, even the buildings and the movement of people show that the administration has today ceased to be the only major power in the land.

Maseru, though it is the capital of a strikingly beautiful, if often harsh, mountain country, could hardly be called a pretty little town. It is, in fact, probably the ugliest place in Basutoland, aside from being, with 6,000 inhabitants, the country's only large population centre. But Maseru is certainly picturesque. Bathed in the clear highland air of its 5,100 feet, unpolluted as is the whole country by factory chimneys, Maseru's street scene is a vivid juxtaposition of tribal Africa, colonial Britain and South African trading.

Jeeps, and Landrovers, British, French, and American cars vie for passage with Basuto horsemen, many wearing conical, woven straw hats. These hats are as typical of traditional Basuto dress as the gaily and distinctively patterned blankets (originally designed in Manchester) which, draped over the shoulders during the day, keep off the biting mountain air at night. Besuited African officials greet their equally staidly clad white superiors, though a few of the latter may, in the summer, wear shorts and stockings pulled to a respectable British height near the knee.

Near the entrance to Maseru there stands, just past a boldly advertising modern garage, the rambling white sanctum of the Club. It is white both figuratively and literally, for while it did by 1962 have one absentee black member, political consciousness has so developed amongst Maseru's Africans that they are no longer interested in being vetted for membership now that the Club's colour bar has at long last been dropped. So, on its premises, one sees only pink wives and children, with the men coming to sink 'sundowners' in the late afternoon.

But in Maseru's only hotel men and women now come and go (though to buy hard liquor they have needed a permit), and the occasional one will come with a white friend to perch on the stools in the cosy pub. Four years ago it was different, and today the liquor permits too are being abolished by the Legislative Council.

Coming to the modest Anglican church, the visitor is almost at the old post office, with a clock which has told the same fixed time since it stopped many moons ago. It faces the Maseru branches, one across the corner and one across the road, of the two groups of trading stores which dominate the country's retail trade. Both are South African owned. A chemist, a bakery, with a curio shop as a sort of annexe, wholesale stores, two South African banks, government offices to left and right in plain single-storey buildings, another garage, an African café, and one is practically at the end of Maseru's main street. Up to the left is the Legco building and beyond that the airstrip, to the right is the hospital and the High

Court and the police; help and chastisement on one side, debate and the great outside world on the other.

It is only when one comes to the very end of the main road that one reaches two very different buildings which house two of the most important forces in the country: the large Roman Catholic cathedral, backed by its schools, and the small, squat concrete box which is the national headquarters of the Basutoland Congress Party.

The Roman Catholic Church is the largest religious group in the country. It dominates Basutoland's education, has until recently owned and did rule the Pius XII University College, and has been a major, if behind-the-scenes influence in politics.

There can, however, be no doubt that the Basutoland Congress Party, known by its initials as the B.C.P., has been the strongest political force in the land. Despite defections, it has commanded the largest group amongst the elected half of the National Council members, and has thus had a powerful voice in legislative debate. And the B.C.P.'s voice is heard even further afield, in more important councils. Its president, Mr Ntsu Mokhehle, became in 1958 a member of the Steering Committee of the All-African Peoples' Conference.

Today, at the age of forty-five, Ntsu Mokhehle is a heavy-set, physically impressive man of prickly temperament. Very intelligent and able, but intolerant of opposition and criticism, he has come to identify the continuation of his own leadership with the good of the country.

In recent years, he has beaten off with grim and often vindictive determination what he has believed to be challenges to his leadership, and whilst some of these, such as that made by the Communists, undoubtedly existed, others may have been less real. In the process, Mokhehle has built up a considerable personality cult around himself, modelling himself in this, as in a great deal else, on his friend Kwame Nkrumah.

To many in the British administration, and even to many sympathetic visitors, Mokhehle seems to make a point of being surly, suspicious and often deliberately rude, leading many to believe that he is anti-white. Some of his recent speeches leave little room for doubt that this is so. He can, however, be extremely charming to white and black alike, even though the charm is switched on a little too obviously. On the rare occasions when he relaxes, he can be teasing, and sometimes humorous, in a friendly way.

With all this, he generates, far beyond any other politician in Basutoland, the impression of leadership, the indefinable but palpable impact which makes one feel that one is dealing with a man who matters, a man of power. His devotion to Basutoland and its people smoulders within him, however surprising or even dismaying its outbursts may sometimes be.

Ntsu Mokhehle's life and political career have both shaped and summarized modern politics in Basutoland. He was born in a small lowland village, from which his family takes its name, in the Teyateyaneng district on 26 December 1918. His father, a moderately wealthy sheep-owner, was for many years a civil servant who rose to become one of the first inspectors of schools in Basutoland, and Ntsu, unlike so many young Basuto boys, was put to school early. In Basutoland the herding of livestock is the responsibility of young boys, and the common pattern has been to send them out to herd sheep and goats for long stretches of time in winter pastures on the mountains. Thus even if they start school in the summer, which is by no means usual, they cannot continue it in the winter, and it is common to find boys of fourteen or fifteen, freed at last of their herding duties, attending school for the first time.

Young Ntsu, however, whilst he herded sheep from the age of seven, wasn't sent up into the mountains, and attended a little village school. From there he was sent to the big Anglican mission school of St Agnes, which was at that time run by a Father Wrenford, a reputedly saint-like and ascetic priest who nevertheless believed in stern discipline.

Returning home in 1934 after completing his primary school course, the young Mokhehle went back to herding, until in 1935 he was admitted to a South Africa secondary school, St Matthews, in a Native Reserve near Grahamstown. There were, at that time, no secondary schools in Basutoland, so that 'going to the Union' was, for the tiny number of bright boys who reached secondary school at all, the normal process.

While still in school, at the age of nineteen, Mokhehle began to write for a small, independent Basuto paper called *Mochochonono* (The Comet), articles about the sufferings of his people, the white traders' life of ease, and the fallacy of regarding Africans as being mentally inferior to whites.

In 1940, almost twenty-two years old, he went to Fort Hare, the African University College set up and run jointly by various missions and the South African Government. Though it was segregated, Fort Hare was, in those days before the bitter farce of Bantu Education, a proper University College. It was also becoming, in Mokhehle's day, the breeding ground of militant African nationalism.

In his second year, Mokhehle helped to lead a students' strike, and in 1942 he was expelled for leading a further strike together with Oliver Tambo, now Deputy-President and leader in exile of the Republic's African National Congress. He joined Basutoland's pioneering nationalist and anti-colonial organization, the *Lekhotla la Bafo* (Commoners' League) led by the extraordinary Josiel Lefela, and when in 1944 Fort Hare decided to re-admit him, he took his degree in science. After a little teaching, he won the then hardly heard of distinction – for an African – of bursaries for further study from both the Basutoland Government and the South African Council for Scientific and Industrial Research, and went on to the even rarer distinction of taking his M.Sc., with a thesis on the parasitology of birds.

By this time he was becoming seriously involved in South African politics, and had joined the Youth League of the African National Congress. This was to be a crucial move in more ways than one. The Youth League was not only to instil into the A.N.C. the idea of racial Africanism (whose ultimate fruit is today's dissident anti-white Pan-Africanist Congress, led by the now imprisoned Robert Sobukwe). It also mastered the techniques of modern political in-fighting and lobbying to such effect that its leaders became the 'king-makers' of the A.N.C. When, in recent years, Mokhehle has beaten off, with no holds barred, successive challenges to his leadership in Basutoland, it was with personal experience of such struggles within the African political movement of South Africa.

The activities of the A.N.C. Youth League bound Mokhehle through personal friendship to men like Oliver Tambo and Nelson

Mandela who later became the leaders of the South African Congress Alliance. Mokhehle founded the Basutoland African Congress with their help and seemed, like them, to have discarded Africanism for non-racialism. But he was soon to go back on this evolution. Today a fervent Africanist once more, he regards his early comrades as his bitterest enemies.

Meanwhile, after a short spell of teaching in the small South African town of Ermelo, Mokhehle went back once again to Fort Hare, to become the first African to gain the diploma of the Union Education Department. Thus uniquely qualified, he returned to Basutoland to take up a teaching career – although the pay was lower there than in South Africa. Within a few years, he became president of the Basutoland Teachers' Association and of the Basutoland Sports Association.

In 1952 he founded and became first president of the Basutoland African Congress. The congress was modelled on and inspired by the African National Congress of South Africa, whose former president, Dr J. S. Moroka, gave an opening address pleading for racial cooperation. Mokhehle, in his presidential address, came closer to what moved the Basuto: the fear of incorporation into South Africa.

We must organize our Congress – we must cause it to exert its influence in towns, in villages, in churches, in the offices, in the buses, in the trains and among the workers of all classes. We must influence other working organizations. We must expose the underground dealings of the Union and our government on this question of incorporation.

But the congress, despite Mokhehle's exhortations, made little headway in its first three years of formal existence. The authorities indeed considered Mokhehle so little a threat that in 1955 he was, at the early age of thirty-seven, appointed principal of the Maseru primary school.

But at this stage Mokhehle got some gratuitous help for his incipient congress from the South African authorities. Two extremely talented young teachers, Ezekiel Mphahlele (who became an author and university lecturer in Nigeria and is now abroad working for the Congress for Cultural Freedom) and Zeph Mothopeng (who became prominent in the Pan-Africanist Congress of South Africa) were expelled from South African teaching and nationally black-listed because they had opposed the introduction of Bantu Education. Showing considerable independence, the Basutoland Education Department gave these two young men jobs, and it was not long before they teamed up politically with Mokhehle. Aided further by periodic visits from South African A.N.C. leaders like Walter Sisulu, progress began to be made.

At this stage, too, Mokhehle was joined by Bennet Khaketla, a fellow-teacher who was also an author and an authority on the Sotho language, and the four men, led by Khaketla, started a home-produced English–Sotho monthly called *Mohlabani* (The Warrior). This paper, owned and edited by Khaketla, was to have a considerable effect in furthering political consciousness and, consequently, the congress cause in Basutoland.

Certainly *Mohlabani* shook the administration and white traders, if at first mainly on minor issues. One of them would be criticized by name for, say, using Government transport to go to a polo or cricket match, another for swearing at a teacher, a trader for cheating his customer. In 1952 such direct and personal criticism was unprecedented.

As Patrick Duncan, who was in the administration at the time, has put it:

Mohlabani had instantaneous and devastating effects. I can testify to the shocked trauma suffered by the small white community of Maseru when it appeared. Accustomed to learning from their Basuto interpreters that they were angels of light rescuing the Basuto from indigenous darkness, they discovered from *Mohlabani* that they were regarded as obstacles to the Basuto in the struggle for freedom and equality.*

The administration and the chiefs had each had their cosy little sphere and way of life. True, Josiel Lefela and his *Lekhotla la Bafo* had not only criticized Britain but had consistently challenged her right to administer the country. But this had been an attack on broad fronts of legality and principle. *Mohlabani* made everyone in the administration realize that they were being personally watched by critics who commanded a public platform. It did a power of good in more ways than one.

* Basutoland in Transition', Patrick Duncan, *Africa South*, vol. 3, No. 3.

Struggling through partly on their own earnings and those of their wives, Mokhehle and Khaketla kept the paper and Congress going (though Khaketla himself did not become a B.A.C. member for some years) with their early efforts mainly concentrated upon fighting the very limited proposals for political advance made in 1954 by Sir Henry Moore. As we have seen, the Basuto wanted to transform their long-established but still only advisory National Council into a legislative body, and they reacted strongly to Moore's refusal even to discuss this demand.

Today the B.C.P.'s policy towards the chiefs is ambivalent, largely because most of the chiefs themselves have given their support to rival parties. But in its evidence to the Moore Committee the Basutoland African Congress, as it was then known, fully backed hereditary chieftainship which it declared to be 'inseparable from the land rights of the people, since the land is also of the people, owned by the people for the people. The oneness of hereditary chieftainship and land rights of the people is elemental in any African society and so it is with the Basuto.'

Mokhehle also pressed strongly for a return in government to the intentions and political principles of 'the great King Moshesh of old', while indirect rule was condemned because it took power from the people and gave it to British officials, making the paid chief 'a mere government tool'. Native administration should be replaced by one central administration, for it was a forerunner of 'colour discrimination in multi-racial societies'.

Going further than any of the other bodies giving evidence, Congress demanded immediate responsible government, with an executive council responsible to the lower of two legislative houses. Mokhehle, through the Congress and through the Teachers' Association, was one of the leading spirits in the campaign for the total rejection of the Moore proposals, and he had gained a good deal of prestige by the time that this aim was achieved. It was a triumph for the Basuto, showing that they could no longer be fobbed off with inadequate, partial reforms.

In 1958 Mokhehle attended the All African Peoples' Conference in Accra and was elected a member of its steering committee, as representative of southern Africa. In the same year he visited Britain, which he liked, for the first time, and in 1959 again visited Ghana and then Guinea, for whose president, Sékou Touré, he developed a great admiration. In 1959, too, he joined a group of demonstrators, led by the Rev. Michael Scott, protesting non-violently in the Volta Republic against the French atom bomb test in the Sahara.

With the elections which in 1960 followed the granting of the new constitution, party politics proper came to have a direct meaning in Basutoland, and today's political line-up derives significantly from the positions that the various parties adopted in 1960.

The chieftainship figured largely, if subterraneously, in the campaign, for a struggle had already begun between the Regent and the Paramount Designate, Constantine Bereng Seiso. The stakes were large. Whoever was Paramount immediately after the elections would nominate fourteen of the council's eighty members. The Regent, uneducated, conservative and not very popular, was persuaded to try and retain power by her conservative advisers, amongst them Chief Leabua Jonathan, who in 1958 had founded the National Party. Her young step-son, she said, must first finish his education and marry; then she would step down.

Bereng, a tall, handsome and intelligent young man, was then a twenty-two-year-old undergraduate reading politics, philosophy, and economics at Oxford. He was urged to return home by a more progressive section of the chieftainship, and he immediately grasped the points at issue. Rightly refuting, in his quiet Oxford accent, the existence of valid traditional precedent for his step-mother's demands, he took matters into his own hands, decided not to sit for his finals, and returned to Basutoland with a public demand to be 'placed' immediately. Waging his private campaign with considerable dignity and firmness, he gained much popular support and emerged victorious. He had no wish to make the question of his 'placing' a party issue, but in so factional a situation it inevitably became one. In fact, the main pressure for his return and immediate 'placing' came from a party, the Marema Tlou, specifically formed in 1957 by Chief Seepheebe Samuel Matete to promote this object. Member of a family which had long provided advisers to the Paramount, Matete had been educated at Adams College in Natal, worked in the Basutoland administration from 1940 to 1946, and though himself a ranking chief after the death of his father in 1946, had become one of the early members of Congress. In 1954 he had been made an adviser to the Regent Paramount Chieftainess, but he had disagreed with her so strongly in 1956 that he had felt obliged to resign. Firmly convinced that Basutoland needed the return and immediate 'placing' of the young Paramount Bereng, he had then tried to press this policy on Mokhehle and the other leaders of Congress, and when they had refused to make this their main immediate concern – even though he was about to be elected its President – he had resigned from Congress altogether.

In the following year, 1957, Chief Matete formed the Marema Tlou Party – a name meaning the Elephant Choppers, derived from the proverb 'Unity chops elephants' – with its main formal aim 'to unite chiefs and commoners'. This to Matete meant the 'placing' of the young Bereng, and he is credited with much of the success in achieving this object. Furthermore, as a member of the old National Council, he served on the Chieftainship Affairs Committee which, together with the Constitutional Reform Committee, drafted Basutoland's constitution.

Supported by the more progressive element in the chieftainship and by an important conservative section of Basuto traders and teachers, the Marema Tlou won sixteen of the 162 District Council seats in the 1960 elections. These it converted, with the support of the by then triumphant pro-Bereng section of the chieftainship, into the disproportionately high number of five elected seats out of the forty elected ones in the National Council. Chief Matete, a powerful personality, himself gained one of these seats, and became one of the three members to be elected by the National Council to the Executive Council, where he was the Member for Local Government and Chieftainship Affairs. He is today reputed to be closer than ever to the Paramount Chief, who certainly owes him a great political debt.

The Congress, which Mokhehle and Khaketla (who had joined in 1958) had converted into the Basutoland Congress Party for the elections, skirted around the Paramountcy succession dispute. Its election programme, drawn up by Khaketla, pledged the party to 'strive for the maintenance and enhancement of the position, status and dignity of the Paramount Chief as the sole ruler of Basutoland', but guardedly promised to protect only the position of the principal chiefs. On the position of the lesser chiefs, whose misrule was – and is – still a popular grievance, the B.C.P. programme said nothing. Some of its speakers, however, tapped this source of discontent, especially where they suspected or knew that particular chiefs were backing rival parties, and the party, with the enthusiastic aid of its opponents, got the reputation of being hostile to chieftainship.

Many chiefs were, and are, understandably hostile to the B.C.P. in return. On the one hand, the B.C.P. election programme clearly implied that the Paramount should be no more than a constitutional monarch, a position which Mokhehle has since made explicit but which Bereng emphatically did not want to accept. Bereng himself wished to be an executive head of State, but the 1964 constitution – agreed to by delegates of all parties – frustrated this ambition. On the other hand, the chiefs have had good reason to distrust the growth of the District Councils, which have increasingly taken over their administrative functions. With the new B.C.P. the dominating elective element in the Councils, antagonism from conservative chiefs has grown, and Mokhehle, never tolerant of opposition, has given some of them the sharp edge of his tongue. Then, too, Mokhehle and the B.C.P. have always been closely linked with the outside world of Pan-Africanism and especially with Kwame Nrukmah, whose 'de-stooling' of chiefs in Ghana has not gone unremarked in Basutoland. A certain anti-white tone among some African leaders has also been carefully noted.

The B.C.P. programme in 1960 said nothing remarkable on race relations beyond calling for the rapid Africanization of the civil service. But many of its speakers tapped the rich popular vein of latent anti-white feeling. Favourite Mokhehle epithets like ticks and bloodsuckers were freely applied to white traders, missionaries and government officials. Khaketla, however, broke new ground in the opposite direction by holding a meeting for white residents in his constituency of Maseru to expound to them the Congress philosophy. Many of his audience remained suspicious, though at least one influential white resident, with substantial investment in the country, came away saying, 'Now Khaketla's a real smoothie. Khaketla and I understand one another.'* On the whole, Basutoland's small white community was pleased that, through the new constitution, they too would at last have some direct say in a country hitherto ruled only by officials and chiefs. But the more common attitude towards the B.C.P. was summed up by another influential white resident who said – 'I can tell you that the Europeans will vote against Congress. Those fellows are just waiting to cut our throats, you know.'† The reputation of being anti-white had stuck to the B.C.P., and it has grown, with reason, since.

For the rest, the B.C.P.'s programme was what might have been expected: the improvement of all social services, free and universal education, and unyielding opposition to South African influence in Basutoland. This last was connected with the B.C.P. demand for the nationalization of the currently very small diamond diggings, then in the hands of a South African mining magnate, Mr Jack Scott.

Basutoland has, on the showing of preliminary surveys, no obviously payable mineral deposits aside from some diamonds, but this almost every Mosuto refuses to accept. Hence the B.C.P. included in its programme a demand for a thorough, fresh geological survey of the whole country.

If there are no discoveries of payable mineral deposits, hopes of Basuto economic progress must rest on improving agriculture. Here the B.C.P. had a number of sound suggestions, but its programme was silent on the crucial but vexed question of land tenure. At present, with chiefs allocating and re-allocating land, there is no security of tenure, and many experts believe that this lack of security discourages individual peasant farmers from making substantial improvements.

But even if agricultural production were to be dramatically improved, Basutoland could not survive without exporting a great deal of its only surplus and obviously marketable commodity – labour. This is at present recruited in Basutoland, as in other African territories, mainly by local representatives of the Witwatersrand Native Labour Recruiting organization, an offshoot of the South African Chamber of Mines. The B.C.P. wants this

* *Contact*, 23 January 1960.
† *New Age*, 21 January 1960.

organization replaced by one run by the Basutoland Government.

The party called in 1960 for the introduction of cooperative movements, which are today, with Government direction, an important part of Basuto life; a national minimum wage, which Mokhehle later refused to back; the vote for all, including women though, in the interim, its slogan, 'votes for taxpayers', had excluded most women); and the encouragement of industries, which is a tall order in a very poor country without industrial electric power. Here the B.C.P. looks towards international help, especially from the United Nations agencies.

Like most of the parties and the Paramount Chief, Mokhehle believes that the British administration has, whether through sloth or deliberate policy, not exerted itself to obtain loans. Increased efforts have been made since 1960, not least by the Paramount Chief, and the marked increase by international agencies of advisory work in Basutoland since the elections has reinforced the conviction of most Basuto leaders that international agencies are practically queueing up to lend Basutoland money. These leaders do not seem particularly discouraged by the failure of any large sums to materialize so far.

Finally, taking a sideways swipe at the formation of the Catholic Party which was widely rumoured before the 1960 elections, the B.C.P. pledged itself both to 'recognize' freedom of religious worship and to 'work for keeping religion out of the political arena'. It takes, of course, more than one player to agree on the rules of a game, and the Catholic Church no more kept out of politics in 1960 than, a great deal more circumspectly, it did for some time after. In the event, the Catholic Party formed in 1960 was almost immediately abandoned, and the backing of Catholic churchmen was given instead to Chief Leabua Jonathan's National Party.

The Roman Catholic Church in Basutoland, which has latterly made such spectacular progress in 'Africanization' that it today has a Mosuto as archbishop, has for long been dominated by French–Canadian priests of the Oblates of Mary Immaculate. They have done splendid work in education and health, but have been characterized by reactionary social views which have latterly taken the form of hysterical anti-Communism.

As the 1960 elections approached, the Catholic priests reacted on two levels. The two local bishops issued a joint pastoral letter entitled, 'The Church and Politics – Duties and Responsibilities of Catholics in Basutoland'.* Citing modern papal authority, this painted a hair-raising picture of what would result if the faithful did not rally as voters to support 'good candidates, candidates who are acquainted with the laws of God and of His Church, and capable and desirous of having them respected'. Only if the faithful voted for, or themselves became, such candidates could the world be organized 'in justice and liberty, in love and in peace. . . . Such a world can only be guaranteed by a government which believes in God and accepts His holy law with love and submission.'

Catholics who failed to vote – 'a mortal sin' – or who voted for the wrong people would 'be accomplices wrought by unworthy candidates'. Such Catholics would be to blame if 'a tyrannical government compels children to attend its godless schools', or if it refused to subsidize Catholic schools. Catholic voters had to be particularly on their guard against ostensibly Christian candidates who 'in fact work hand in glove with the Communists or who give them the weight of their support'.

The point was presumably brought home to the Basuto faithful by a reminder that Pius XII had excommunicated whoever belonged to the Communist Party and that 'His Holiness Pope John XXIII has recently reminded all the Catholics of the World that they are not allowed to vote for . . . Communist sympathizers'.

But who, in Basutoland, were these Communist sympathizers? The bishops, who stressed that the Church 'is above and beyond all political parties', did not say, but many a parish priest was happy to give more direct guidance.

I have spoken with many Basuto Catholics who told me that their local priest forbade them to vote for the Congress Party, and to others who were specifically instructed to vote for the National Party. Archbishop 'Mabathoana has assured me that if such things occurred, it was never on the instruction of the Hierarchy. But many of the ordinary mission priests are simple and often politically ignorant men who, sheltered in their

* Published by the Catholic Centre, Mazenod, Basutoland, 1959.

mountain parishes, and accustomed to guiding every aspect of their parishioners' lives, had little difficulty in identifying for Catholic voters the good and evil in the elections.

In any case, the National Party made anti-Communism a major plank of its platform, whilst the B.C.P. made no mention of Communism at all, and the National Party received editorial support from the Catholic newspaper *Moeletsi*.* National Party speakers accused the B.C.P. of getting its ideas and its funds from Moscow, via Accra. It was widely assumed even in congress circles at the time that Mokhehle had been given £1,000 for the elections by the All African Peoples' Conference, and two microbuses and a new jeep, widely used in the campaign, were assumed to have come from the same source.

Hitting back, the congress paper *Mohlabani* alleged that the Catholic Church 'capitalises on the ignorance of its members' and declared 'The Church must quit the political arena and learn to confine themselves to matters of the soul'.

The man who, as leader of the National Party, naturally came in for a good deal of congress abuse was Chief Leabua Jonathan. A fat, rather jolly man of considerable intelligence, common sense, shrewdness and presence, he is a minor hereditary chief, being a great-grandson of Moshesh, the Father of the Basuto. Born a Protestant in 1914, Leabua Jonathan was educated at Morija, a Protestant school in Basutoland, but was converted to Catholicism as an adult. In 1933, on completing his primary education, he went, 'for the adventure' as he puts it, to work in the mines on the Witwatersrand, and was summoned to return home in 1937 to enter the Paramount Chief Regent's administration. Starting as a clerk, he rose rapidly to become president of the Basuto courts and assessor to the Judicial Commissioner.†

Whilst still only a chief's son, Jonathan stood for and won an elected place in the old Basutoland National Council. He was 'placed' as a chief in 1940, and though his 'caretaking' is a small one, he is noted as being one of the few chiefs who, whilst respecting tradition, is both progressive and popular with his people. He became an advisor to the Paramount Regent, but also served on the Constitutional Reform Committee of the National

---

* *Contact*, 23 January 1960.
† Then Mr Patrick Duncan, who later financed and edited *Contact*.

Council and became, in 1962, a member of the constitutional committee set up by the present council to draft a fresh constitution. In 1959 Chief Jonathan formed the Basutoland National Party, with the help of Chief George Bereng, who had been chairman of the Constitutional Reform Committee. Alleging that the B.C.P. was alienating the chiefs, the National Party undertook to work for the reuniting of the chiefs with the people and in its election platform, called for responsible self-government, though with great stress on the maintenance of the protective link with Britain. In 1962 Chief Jonathan gave his party's backing to the present Paramount's demand that he should be an executive, rather than a purely constitutional, monarch. But by 1963 he helped to formulate the 'quasi-constitutional monarchy' proposals of the constitutional committee, on which he served.

Like all of Basutoland's parties, the B.N.P. is vehemently opposed to any form of South African influence in the country. But it has clashed sharply with the B.C.P. over the latter's attacks on white traders, over the demand for what Chief Jonathan describes as 'premature and suicidal independence', and, until Congress swung to the same line, over anti-Communism.

Formal differences between party programmes do not, of course, necessarily define their different functions, and this is especially so in a country young to modern party politics like Basutoland, in which traditional loyalties and personalities count for a great deal. Thus the followers and opponents of the National Party and the Marema Tlou know that, despite their almost identical programmes, the two parties are different – because Chief Jonathan was too close to the old Regent to be in court favour today.

The fact that the only major programme difference between the two parties lay in the active anti-Communism of the National Party does, however, reflect a difference of original sponsorship. It gave, at a time when, unlike today, there was no Communist Party or known Communist in Basutoland, additional grounds for believing the Congress allegations that the Church was strongly behind Chief Jonathan's party. In fact, as I have been told by an extremely influential member of the Basutoland hierarchy, financial backing was given to the National Party through individual priests and not by the Church itself, but this makes little difference. The Catholic Church inspired and backed the National Party's formation. Priests also helped in organizing the campaign of the party's seventy-four candidates, a number generally thought 'astounding', since Jonathan, busy as an adviser to the Paramount, mounted only a token campaign himself, while the National Party possessed only one old car.

Despite the powerful backing of the Church (which did not, however, provide new transport), the National Party did very badly at the 1960 elections. Only twenty-two of its seventy-four candidates were successful, and only one member was elected through the District Councils to the National Council. Chief Jonathan himself was defeated, though he entered the council as a nominated member.

Under Chief Jonathan's continued leadership, the National Party has seized the initiative in petitioning both the British Government and the United Nations on various matters, and it pressed in this manner during 1961 for further constitutional advance. In 1962 the party urged that the Paramount Chief should become King of Basutoland, with the power to refuse assent to legislation or to send it back for amendment, together with a majority party cabinet system in a parliament elected on universal adult suffrage. Chief Jonathan himself stresses that cooperation with the chiefs in achieving reforms is essential, and that 'ours is the war of the tongue and not of the sword'. He has increasingly taken up cases of injustice – such as the position of the Indian community in Basutoland – in which the Church can have no direct, special interest, and it was one of his lieutenants who introduced into the Council the motion that land tenure in Basutoland be investigated by outside experts, an investigation which is now being undertaken. Furthermore, he was instrumental in obtaining votes for all women under Basutoland's 'self-government' constitution, a change which Mokhehle himself at one time opposed.

The Catholics, however, seem to have decided that the National Party is an unsatisfactory tool in the fight against Communism, whose spread they saw heralded by the increasing number of political refugees from South Africa and whose existence they saw triumphantly underlined when, in 1961, the Communist Party of Lesotho (Basutoland) was formed.

Thus Chief Jonathan and his National Party have been left to more or less their own devices, which still include anti-Communism but exclude support for any banning of the local Communist Party. Chief Jonathan himself has drawn a number of Protestants into the councils of his party, for which he claims a membership of 6,000, though he freely admits that the number of paid-up and card-carrying members is only a small fraction of this total. Though Chief Jonathan's membership claim is, characteristically, much more conservative than the inflated figures readily claimed by many other politicians, it is doubtful whether even then it can be substantiated.

Jonathan sees his party, which others have described as 'the party of moderation', as a 'conservative' one, in which thinking chiefs and commoners can find their natural home. It is true that Jonathan has owed his place in the Council to nomination by the Paramount, whose advisor on these nominations described the B.N.P. leader as 'Politician. Has ambition for leadership. Hard reader. Personality. Diplomat. Public speaker (Bismarck). Admirable.' And he has, in the Paramount's eyes, the virtue of being a fellow-Catholic.

But Chief Jonathan has been outclassed in the chieftainship stakes by the support which the Paramount has privately given to the Marema Tlou (now the Freedom-Marema Tlou) Party. After the Catholic priests stopped doing his organizing for him, Chief Jonathan took some time to build up his own organization, but today he claims to have eighty-one field organizers, each paid £8 a month. He relies for most of his funds on donations from well-wishers, who have included at least one foreign-owned and strongly pro-South African trading group, but his transport fleet was in 1964 limited to two Datsun vehicles and one Landrover.

The major support which Catholic clergy used to give to the National Party subsequently went to a crusading anti-Communist league called *Thaka Tsa 'Mesa-Mohloane*. This short-lived body, which claimed to be 'above all political parties and organizations', was the creature of the more reactionary Catholic clergy, who provided it with a good deal of money. Aside from having offices in Maseru, it managed to publish and to distribute widely a smear-sheet which 'smelt out' and denounced alleged Communists and their supposed sympathizers. A broadcasting station was even promised in order, amongst other things, 'to educate the shepherds by giving them evening lessons'. It seems, however, that with the approach of self-government the league's crude tactics and Catholic support became an embarrassment to the Hierarchy, and little is heard of it today.

The *'Mesa Mohloane* restricted its actual operations to Communist witch-hunting, and in one smear-sheet they concluded that Mokhehle was himself a dupe of the Communists.

This was patently absurd, but Mokhehle never reacted publicly to their alleged transcript of an interview which his full-time representative in Accra had given to *Pravda*. In this, quoted in the anti-Communist publication *Est & Ouest*, *Pravda* reported the B.C.P. representative, Mr Chakela, as saying of the published programme of the Communist party of Lesotho that ' I agree with its thesis'. He reportedly said also that the programme of the C.P.S.U. (the Soviet Party) provided a guide and source of strength to Basutoland Africans. Mr Chakela has denied to me the accuracy of this report, though he was unable to recollect what he had in fact said. But it is in any event significant that it was passed on to the *'Mesa Mohloane* by Basutoland Catholic priests. A senior member of the Hierarchy has admitted to me that the League's funds came through Catholic channels.

During the past two years the fastest-growing political group in the country has been the amalgamated Freedom-Marema Tlou Party, of which the Freedom half owed its separate existence to dissension within the leadership of the B.C.P. In the 1960 election campaign the prestige of Bennet Khaketla, who had drafted the B.C.P.'s programme single-handed, grew, and his victory in Maseru, the first result to be announced, was greeted with wildly enthusiastic demonstrations. In the National Council's internal elections for three of its members to sit on the Executive Council, both Mokhehle and Khaketla stood for the B.C.P., but only Khaketla was elected. He thus became the B.C.P.'s only 'Cabinet Minister', responsible for education and health.

The Executive Council is not responsible to the National Council, and in theory its members are elected as individuals, not as party representatives. Executive Council members have to take an oath of secrecy. This put Khaketla, who was also the elected deputy-leader of the B.C.P., in a difficult position towards

Mokhehle, who was in any case increasingly criticized within the party for his authoritarian attitude.

Some of this criticism of Mokhehle came from the strong branch of the B.C.P. in the Transvaal Province of South Africa, where most of the Basuto miners and industrial workers live. Some of the branch's leaders were also leading members of the African National Congress.

There is good reason to think that the leaders of the A.N.C., who had helped Mokhehle organize and build his party, and some of whom were his old comrades, assumed that with the B.C.P. election victory their own movement's influence had been extended. Mokhehle, however, proved recalcitrant. He wasn't going to be bound by past ties, and he set out to strengthen his position by forbidding B.C.P. members to belong to any other party as well.

Shortly before the B.C.P.'s 1960 conference, the first after the elections, Mokhehle alleged that he had discovered a plot to murder him. The police in Basutoland were sceptical, but a man carrying a long knife was arrested when he forced his way into the crowded conference hall.

The day before the conference, Mokhehle had the fourteen Transvaal delegates expelled for 'subversive activity', together with the B.C.P.'s national chairman, Mr O. P. Phoofolo, who had circulated a letter within the party canvassing support for the election of Khaketla as leader. The expelled were mostly veteran B.C.P.–A.N.C. members.

Mr Phoofolo's subsequent public challenge to Mokhehle to publish his canvassing letter was ignored. 'Apparently,' said Mr Phoofolo, 'if one canvasses for a candidate against his leader whom he is not satisfied with, he is called subversive and expelled ... B.C.P. policy is perfect and shall always get my support, *but the leadership is good-bye*.'*

Khaketla, who is a better speaker and administrator than a practical politician, denied any part in the campaign to have him elected leader. But Mokhehle, without mentioning Khaketla's name, made a speech attacking him. Delegates were warned not to be misled by a man's eloquence or good clothes (Khaketla is a smart dresser), and to vote only for men who would give all their

---

* *New Age*, 16 February 1961. (My italics.)

time to the party. Nevertheless, with the exception of the expelled former chairman Phoofolo, the whole executive was re-elected *en bloc*, including Khaketla as deputy-leader.

Mokhehle took this hard, and made fresh public criticisms of party leaders who kept company with government, who shared secrets with the imperialist oppressors, and who talked of going to church when they were needed for national service. Khaketla, unlike Mokhehle a devout Christian, had been unavailable for some Sunday morning meetings.

Only two days after being re-elected as B.C.P. deputy-leader at the conference, Khaketla resigned from the party. Mokhehle promptly said that Khaketla 'was never convinced of the B.C.P. policy'. The B.C.P.'s secretary-general, Kolisang, claimed that Khaketla had joined the B.C.P. in 1958 only because of the support it gave to his paper *Mohlabani*. (The B.C.P. subsequently started its own fortnightly, *Makatolle* – The Uprooter – hewing to the Mokhehle line.)

Khaketla retaliated by accusing Mokhehle of having plotted his 'political murder', of having 'his own little axe to grind', and of wanting to 'dictate how I shall worship'. He referred to the statement which Mokhehle had made to the Pan-African Youth Seminar at Tunis in April 1960 that 'We must look back to our own religion and weed out things that are not compatible with the present'.*

A month later, in April 1961, Khaketla formed the Basutoland Freedom Party, and was joined by others who had been expelled or resigned from the B.C.P., including Phoofolo. The Freedom Party's manifesto denounced the B.C.P. as having degenerated into a 'totalitarian' body whose 'power-drunk' leaders regarded 'criticism and opposition from within as sabotage' and were determined 'to dictate how party members shall worship'. The 'cardinal principle' of working with the chiefs had been 'radically departed from', with the result that 'most of the District Councils dominated by members of the B.C.P. are at a standstill'. The Freedom Party pledged itself to strive for cooperation with the chiefs and the administration in leading Basutoland to responsible government, while trying to inspire the confidence of overseas financiers and technicians whose money and skills were 'needed

* *Contact*, 23 March 1961.

so urgently' by the Basuto people. In a further manifesto published during 1962, the B.C.P. called for Basutoland 'to fulfil [its] noble destiny of being a leaven of freedom in South Africa'.

Khaketla retained his National and Executive Council seats and was joined by one council member. But his party made small progress – in part due to the strength, which he had himself helped to build, of the Congress machine; in part to Khaketla's own preoccupation with his Executive Council portfolios; and in part to his not being fundamentally a hustings politician.

Bennet Makalo Khaketla is pre-eminent amongst the Basuto as a political intellectual and theoretician. Born in 1913 in Basutoland of a peasant family, he qualified locally as a teacher and went on to take his B.A. in politics and the Sesotho language by correspondence. After working as a clerk-typist and a teacher, he spent some time in the Administration and then took to teaching again, this time in South Africa.

He returned to Basutoland in 1952 and edited the paper *Mohlabani* with great success. But though he worked closely with Mokhehle on *Mohlabani*, Khaketla did not for some time join Congress, reputedly because he objected to its then multi-racial outlook. In 1958, however, he became deputy-leader of the old Basutoland African Congress, and kept the position when it became the B.C.P.

A quiet, intense man of considerable intelligence, Khaketla is one of the greatest living experts on the Sotho language, for whose purity he cares passionately. He also has an excellent command of English and a head for detail. This made his contributions to National Council debates outstanding, and he has created an excellent impression at U.N.E.S.C.O.-sponsored international conferences on education. He is a good orator, whose relative lack of demagogic delivery does not prevent him from frequently indulging a strong anti-white streak. This would be no disadvantage in Basuto politics, but Khaketla's chief weakness is his lack of energy in grass-roots organizing. Anti-Communist, he nevertheless attended in 1962 a peace conference in Moscow.

In 1962 he tried without success to merge the formal remnants of his party with Chief Jonathan's National Party, and it seemed as though he had at most only a personal future in Basutoland politics. Since then, however, he has successfully merged the

Freedom Party with the stronger Marema Tlou, under the name of the Freedom-Marema Tlou Party (F.M.P.). The programme of the merged parties is roughly that of the Marema Tlou, and in general the new party, with the goodwill of the Paramount Chief, promises to constitute strong opposition to the B.C.P. in the self-government elections, despite internal divisions.

Through Khaketla himself and the Marema Tlou's five elected members, the party exercised significant influences in both the National and the Executive Councils. The F.M.P. has also been fortunate in recruiting Dr Seth P. Makotoko, who gave up government service to become its full-time secretary, and in obtaining, presumably through the support of the chiefs, three new vehicles. Chief Matete became the F.M.P.'s leader, and Khaketla his deputy.

In a mountainous country like Basutoland, transport is a prerequisite for effective political organization – or, indeed, for organization of almost any kind. Dr Makotoko began using his transport energetically to penetrate the country and met with considerable response. The F.M.P. has also absorbed a number of politically active people who resented or suffered under Mokhehle's autocratic and unpredictable rule in the B.C.P.

The F.M.P. was second to none in its demand for full and immediate self-government, which the Paramount had also demanded. Following his line further, the F.M.P. wanted to see the Paramount Chief as executive head of State. Dr Makotoko explained that this meant that the Paramount would concern himself with the implementation of laws but not with the legislature, and claimed that this would be better than if a vaccilating leader were to lead the Government in the usual democratic fashion. This may sound contradictory to outsiders, but it could have considerable plausibility and appeal in Basutoland. Certainly the F.M.P. has looked like becoming a force in the land and has given Khaketla a new lease of political life. At the London Constitutional Conference, he and the Marema Tlou leaders gave way on the Paramount's constitutional position in order to maintain Basuto unity.

Dr Seth Makotoko, who has proved himself to be a promising public speaker and a capable political organizer, learnt his politics in the Republic's African National Congress. Born in the Leribe district of Basutoland and now in his thirties, he is the son of a senior chief who was also a civil servant. Educated at the Basutoland High School, he matriculated and then found employment in Johannesburg, where he was privately sponsored by a white friend for medical studies at the University of the Witwatersrand (the Basutoland Government only helped him in the later stages). Whilst at university, he became a member of the A.N.C. Youth League, and after serving his medical housemanship in Natal, he joined the Basutoland civil service as a medical officer.

After becoming Secretary of the F.M.P. in 1962, Dr Makotoko made his first trip abroad in 1963, visiting West Germany, and in 1964 he attended the Addis Ababa Conference of heads of African States as an observer. There he presented a memorandum on behalf of the F.M.P. appealing to the heads of State not to forget Basutoland and its unfortunate position. But though Dr Makotoko did not associate the F.M.P. with the policies of the conference, the making of this appeal displeased some highly conservative members of the Marema Tlou. They apparently persuaded Chief Matete, who had originally agreed to Dr Makotoko attending the conference, to denounce his Addis Ababa appeal and to issue a counter-statement.

This precipitated a split in the F.M.P. A party conference was due shortly, but Chief Matete tried to prevent its being held before the London Constitutional Conference, or at least to prevent the election of a new party executive. A large party conference was nevertheless held in April 1964, but it was boycotted by Chief Matete and his followers. At this conference, Dr Makotoko was elected president of the F.M.P., Mr Khaketla declined nomination as vice-president but remained a member of the new executive committee, and a Mr Leanye became vice-president. Chief Matete thereupon held his own conference, which duly re-elected him president of the F.M.P., and so a permanent split in the party was confirmed. Present evidence, however, seems to suggest that Dr Makotoko's energetic leadership has achieved substantial support and that his more radical approach will strengthen opposition to the B.C.P.

Meanwhile, Ntsu Mokhehle's problems were by no means over with the hounding of Khaketla from the Congress Party. An increasing number of refugees have been coming to Basutoland from South Africa since 1960, some of them fleeing the police occupation of the Transkei and others the persecution of the African National Congress and the likewise banned Pan-African Congress. Many of those from the A.N.C. have been experienced political and trade-union organizers. At first they were welcomed into the B.C.P., but it was not long before Mokhehle became convinced that they were working to oust him from the leadership. Certainly some of the A.N.C. leaders in South Africa assumed, understandably if somewhat aggressively, that Mokhehle and the Congress in Basutoland should be fitted into the wider pattern, as they saw it, of South African politics. Once Mokhehle, in any case fearful of personal competition from such seasoned campaigners, jibbed, conflict was inevitable.

It has, largely by Mokhehle's choice, taken place on the two issues of Communism and Pan-Africanism, and it has come to have that intense, peculiar bitterness which only fratricidal conflicts breed. Mokhehle has become a compulsive anti-Communist and, following his anti-white streak, a supporter of the Republic's Pan-Africanists and therefore a bitter opponent of his early colleagues and their A.N.C. The most obvious sufferers in this conflict are the A.N.C. refugees in Basutoland, to whom Mokhehle has become actively hostile.

In 1960, at the B.C.P.'s eve-of-election conference, one of the chief speakers was Mrs Lilian Ngoyi, president of South Africa's A.N.C. Women's League. On the platform with her was Mrs Elizabeth Mafekeng, a remarkable trade-unionist who, to escape banishment in South Africa, had fled to Basutoland with some of her eleven children. People at the conference wept openly as Lilian Ngoyi, a superb speaker, held Mrs Mafekeng's youngest baby in her arms and told them that Basutoland's struggle and South Africa's were identical. Ntsu Mokhehle announced the formation of a fund to help Mrs Mafekeng and other refugees. Christian Action in London had donated £200, and all Basuto should support the fund 'as Basutoland is now the Jerusalem for all African refugees and all are welcome in Basutoland'.*

Eighteen months later Mokhehle declared 'I hate these so-called freedom fighters who are mostly Communist-inspired and

* *New Age*, 7 January 1960.

are interested in crippling the nationalist movements by their tricks and infiltration'.*

Similarly, his line on Communism has changed drastically. Speaking at a Lumumba memorial meeting in February 1961, Mokhehle said that in the existing circumstances anybody fighting Communism was an enemy of the African people and an agent of imperialism.† By September of the same year, he declared that 'Communists seek to cripple African nationalism'.‡

At the same time, he attacked all members of the A.N.C. who were in exile as 'cowards'; and denounced Mrs Mafekeng by name as an infiltrator and saboteur who was trying to organize Communist cells in Basutoland to take over the B.C.P. He spoke admiringly of the Republic's Pan-Africanist leader Robert Sobukwe, and denounced with vituperative bitterness Nelson Mandela, the underground A.N.C. leader. Mandela, said Mokhehle, had 'run away' to Basutoland after 'causing a mess' in South Africa.§ It was primarily to Mandela, widely admired and even revered for his courageous underground leadership which earned him the title of 'the black Pimpernel', that Mokhehle referred when he said 'I hate these so-called freedom fighters'.

Such accusations naturally sparked off extremely bitter replies, some from the underground Mandela. Mokhehle was denounced as a renegade and traitor who was destroying the African unity to which he had pledged himself in and out of Basutoland. His allegations that the A.N.C. was using Basutoland as a base and was trying to take over the B.C.P. were emphatically denied, as was his identification of the A.N.C. with Communism. As for his smearing of Nelson Mandela, the A.N.C. replied that 'Mr Mokhehle's bold statement (perhaps for the benefit of the South African police) that Mr Mandela has run away to Basutoland and was present at a meeting to discuss 'the conquest of the B.C.P.' is the most despicable slander and lie ever fabricated by what is supposed to be a responsible leader of a struggling people'.‖

The banned A.N.C. was in 1961 preparing for protests and a stay-at-home strike against the declaration of the South African

---

* *Contact*, 7 September 1961.   † *New Age*, 23 February 1961.
‡ *Contact*, 7 September 1961.   § *New Age*, 17 August 1961.
‖ *New Age*, 14 September 1961.

Republic in May. Mokhehle claims that four A.N.C. leaders, Nelson Mandela, Walter Sisulu, Moses Kotane and Joe Matthews had met the B.C.P. executive and had asked (a) for support, through letters to the Press, for the May protests; (b) that the B.C.P. and the banned A.N.C. jointly set up a printing press in Basutoland, which should not be used for Pan-Africanist literature; (c) that the B.C.P. organize anti-Republic demonstrations in Basutoland; and (d) that, instead of merely pressing for responsible government, the B.C.P. should demand independence. Mokhehle regarded these requests as 'interference' and rejected them all.

Mandela, on the other hand, categorically stated in August that he had not left South Africa since the May strikes. He stated that a meeting with Mokhehle had taken place in January 1961.

Behind all the heat and denunciation, Mokhehle did have two valid grounds for worry, if only about his personal position: talented South African refugees were exerting a growing influence in the B.C.P.; and the influx of refugee trade-unionists who promptly got to work threatened to create a new centre of power outside Mokhehle's control.

A.N.C. refugees had certainly become very active in the B.C.P. and, given their drive and experience, had rapidly made their mark. Mokhehle has never viewed rising potential leaders without suspicion. The A.N.C. men in Basutoland maintained their contacts with South Africa, and presumably continued to owe at least some allegiance to the underground organization at home.

Secondly, amongst the A.N.C. refugees were some who were widely regarded in Basutoland as Communist sympathizers, including John Motloheloa and the formidable Joe Matthews. Mokhehle suspected that the creation of a Communist Party in Basutoland was planned. In the event, he was proved right.

At the B.C.P.'s annual conference in December 1961, Mokhehle had the party's constitution changed so as to have himself elected party leader and president for five years, instead of the customary year. Mokhehle now also assumed absolute and arbitrary powers of expulsion and suspension, and the conference accepted that trade-unions were not to take any action without party authorization. Insofar as any justification was offered for these vastly increased powers of Mokhehle over the B.C.P., it was that they would enable him the better to conduct his openly declared war against 'the Communists'.

In February 1963 Joe Matthews found a bomb so fixed underneath his car as to have exploded had he driven off. Police investigations have not proved this to be connected with the B.C.P., or for that matter with anyone else, but it is an augury of how things might go in Basutoland. Joe Matthews has for years been the unrivalled target of Ntsu Mokhehle's anti-A.N.C. and anti-Communist denunciations.

Internal dissatisfaction with Mokhehle's autocratic leadership reached a new stage at the end of 1962, when Mr R. Matji, a B.C.P. member of the National Council, circulated a letter criticizing Mokhehle's leadership to the parliamentary caucus and the national executive of the party. In this letter Mr Matji, who is a veteran politician and a former A.N.C. leader, made a detailed analysis of trends within the party and suggested changes in the line it was following.

Mokhehle's reply was a mammoth torrent of abuse, and Mr Matji was expelled from the B.C.P. His letter, however, had a considerable effect, as had the fact that two other B.C.P. members of the National Council defied Mokhehle and criticized the labour legislation which was rushed through the Council with his support.

The gravest public setback for Mokhehle, however, came early in 1964, when no less than ten members of his parliamentary caucus – led by Chief Nathaniel Qhobela, a former deputy-leader and national chairman of the party – broke away from the B.C.P. in protest at Mokhehle's autocracy and inability to tolerate criticism.

Mr Mokhehle has denied to me that these men were expelled, claiming that they left after Chief Qhobela had been exposed as a spy for the Paramount Chief within the B.C.P. 'We don't expel people,' Mr Mokhehle told me, 'rather we organize around those who want to betray us and they wither away.'

Whatever the sequence of events, the fact remains that shortly before the London Conference in May 1964, Ntsu Mokhehle's parliamentary caucus had been reduced from its original twenty-nine members to only seventeen. Chief Qhobela and the other former B.C.P. members of the National Council had not, at the time of writing, formed a new party, but were acting as a loosely

coordinated group in the council, where they often found themselves voting with the chiefly *ex-officio* members or abstaining.
Most of them, however, claim to have carried their constituents
with them out of the B.C.P., but only the next elections can prove
or disprove this claim. If it is true, Mr Mokhehle and his B.C.P.
will have to look to their laurels.

In November 1961 the 'Communist Party of Lesotho'
(Basutoland) issued its formal programme, and threw both the
Basutoland and South African authorities into a tizzy. To understand the impact on South Africa of the emergence, in the middle
of the country but under British protection, of a legal Communist
Party, one must remember that to the Nationalists in the Republic
even the most modest real opposition to the sacred practice of
apartheid is 'Communistic', while Communism proper has
become an obsession in the Nationalist mind. The Communist
Party of South Africa had disbanded itself before the Suppression
of Communism Act outlawed it in 1950, and its members have
been mercilessly hounded ever since (as have, under cover of
anti-Communism, other effective opponents of apartheid).

For the British administration, anxious not to offend South
Africa but unwilling to copy it in legal anti-Communism, the
formation of the C.P.L. has been an acute embarrassment.
Whilst admitting this, however, the administration has, to
its credit, taken no action against the C.P.L., aside from saying
that in the event of an East–West conflict its members would be
interned.

To date, very few names have been openly associated with the
C.P.L. Its spokesman is John Motloheloa, a rugged, cheerful and
very hardworking refugee who, before coming to Basutoland in
1959, was a trade-unionist in South Africa. He was a member of
the Communist Party in South Africa, and in 1961, before the
C.P.L.'s formation, spent three months in Moscow. In Basutoland,
Motloheloa has made a scanty living by selling the South African
Congress-line, *New Age* (subsequently *Spark*), *Fighting Talk* and
Liberation (all of them now banned or strangled in South Africa),
and Soviet publications. It is quite a sight, in the streets of
Maseru or in remote mountain villages, to see the indefatigable
Motloheloa trying to sell blanketed tribesmen copies of *World*

Marxist Review or the Proceedings of the 22nd Congress of the C.P.S.U.

Motloheloa, who is a likeable, quipping, friendly man, seems to have made a point of acting the public clown. But he is a good orator for all that and has a considerable, if purely personal, popularity. The brain behind the party is reputed to be Joe Matthews, though his name has never been formally associated with it.

He is the son of the revered Professor Z. K. Matthews who, having become South Africa's chief African academic – he was even for a time acting principal of Fort Hare University College – resigned in protest against Bantu Education, was one of the accused in the notorious Treason Trial, and is now a senior staff member of the World Council of Churches in Geneva. Born in Durban in 1929, Joe Matthews was educated at St Peter's, the school of the Community of the Resurrection in Johannesburg, which was closed, whilst he was there, in protest against Bantu Education. Influenced by Oliver Tambo, later A.N.C. deputy-president, who taught at the school, Joe Matthews joined the A.N.C. Youth League on its formation in 1944, presided over its first national conference in 1948, and became its national secretary in 1951. Here and at Fort Hare, where he took his degree in 1950, Matthews came into early contact with Mokhehle.

He left his law studies at the University of the Witwatersrand in 1952 to become a leading organizer of the Defiance Campaign, was banned in 1953 under the Suppression of Communism Act and earned under it two suspended jail sentences. Having served his articles as an attorney, he was arrested and charged in the Treason Trial in 1956, thus rejoining his father. After his acquittal, Joe Matthews fled to Basutoland in 1960 to escape arrest during the South African Emergency, and now practises in Maseru as an attorney. He has since acquired a British passport and travels abroad frequently from Basutoland.

Highly intelligent, well-read, sophisticated, quick-witted, and possessing considerable charm and a sense of humour, Joe Matthews is one of the outstanding products of the African National Congress and a leading theoretician of African resistance. He has travelled widely in Europe and behind the iron curtain.

The generally high opinion of Joe Matthews's intelligence and capabilities is not, however, shared by Ntsu Mokhehle. At first, like several other A.N.C. refugees, Matthews was welcomed by Mokhehle, who today says that his suspicions were first aroused by the fact that Matthews, despite his keen interest in the B.C.P., never appeared at any of its meetings. Mokhehle claims that he finally proved that Matthews and Dr Arthur Letele, another prominent refugee, were behind leaflets trying to undermine his leadership. Contemptuously, Mokhehle said to me of Matthews:

I knew him at Fort Hare – a 'small boy', a chatterbox, just like his father. He's been deceived by other people into thinking he's intelligent and a good planner. Well, he tried to take over my party from me. If someone really capable had been trying to undermine us here, it would have been done much better.

Joe is foxy, but a politician can't be foxy. He must never say things that won't have a ninety per cent certainty of happening – the people don't forget. Everyone makes one major mistake, and the people understand that, but not twice. That's why my party has grown slowly – I never say anything which won't happen or which can't be fulfilled.

A tall statement.

Mokhehle today accuses Matthews of having earlier tried to build up Khaketla to take over the leadership, and of later having inspired riots in Maseru in order to point a lack of militancy on the part of the B.C.P. leadership. In fact, Mokhehle uses Joe Matthews and 'the Communists' as scapegoats for every failing of, and challenge to, his own leadership. But there certainly has been an attempt to infiltrate the B.C.P., and this attempt has been able to draw on Mokhehle's weaknesses and resentment at his personal autocracy.

The programme which the Communist Party, the only legal one south of Nigeria, issued in November 1961 naturally aroused great interest. It claimed that the reason for the party's creation was that the existing organizations were inadequate for coping with the 'new phase' of the struggle for independence. They had 'represented mainly chiefs or peasants or middle-class intellectuals'. The country was poor and had no industries. What was needed now was a Basuto party 'representing the most advanced class, the working class'.

Thus the C.P.L. would 'act as an independent party of the

workers and peasants of Lesotho, aiming at a Socialist Republic of Lesotho. It [would] work for a united front with the B.C.P. and all other progressive forces.' Full immediate independence was demanded, with United Nations membership, an army, a national bank and currency system. In 'fighting against our common enemy, aggressive white South African Imperialism', the party calls on the Basuto to 'maintain close friendly relations with the progressive movements in the Republic of South Africa such as the South African Communist Party and the African National Congress'.

There were brave words about relations with South Africa:

The party will demand that the [South African] Republic unequivocally recognize the independence and integrity of the country. It will demand a new arrangement with the mines and other Union employers to pay adequate wages, guarantee safety conditions and trade-union rights. It will propose that Basuto diplomatic officials take adequate measures to enforce such arrangements.

Even more interestingly 'the party will demand that negotiations be opened to provide Lesotho with an outlet to the sea in return for territories wrongfully included in the Republic by British imperialism'.

Finally, 'the party will be organized on the basis of democratic centralism, on collective not individual leadership, and the subordination of the minority to the majority once a decision is taken'.

It is a strange document, whose unreality may be judged by the fact that there is hardly any 'working class' in the Marxist sense resident in Basutoland, and that the country depends for economic survival on South Africa's absorbing its migrant workers and on the receipt of customs dues from the Republic.

The C.P.L. has so far operated in an equally strange way. Even after its first Congress was held, in secret, at Maseru in May 1962, the only name officially associated with it has been John Motloheloa's. He speaks as secretary of an unidentified central committee. The party's prolonged failure to hold public meetings has been widely and adversely commented on; its first public meeting was held only in March 1963, sixteen months after its programme was issued.

Individual members have told me that the reason for this approach is the necessity for the C.P.L., because of its small size at present, to work within the B.C.P. and the trade-unions. But it would seem to have got for the party the worst of both worlds.

By announcing its existence, the party has put many people on their guard and has provided an ideal scapegoat for both the Catholics and Mokhehle. It has put, amongst others, the Administration and the Paramount Chief to thinking how it might be suppressed. Unless there is any physical trouble or outright sedition, the administration will not do this, but senior civil servants rather hope that the Paramount or the National Council might do the job for them.

Nothing has come of the C.P.L.'s reported intention of applying for a site to start a printing works, and of its 1962 decision to publish a paper to be called *Mosebetsi* (The Worker). Within the country, it does not seem to dispose of any monies.

There is, obviously, no reliable estimate of the C.P.L.'s membership, but the highest it has been put at is 600. Its public impact has, so far, been negligible, but it has, by its mere existence, inflamed relations between Basutoland and South Africa.

Aside from one trade-union and the small but militant Basutoland African Students' Association, the only body which has responded to the Communists' call for a common front has been the *Lekhotla la Bafo*, or Commoners' League, an unusual organization centred around an extraordinary man, Josiel Lefela.

To meet Lefela today, one has to go up to the small village of Mapoteng in the Teyateyaneng district, where he lives with some of his sons. He looks like nothing so much as a biblical patriarch: his strong, heavily lined, intelligent face surmounted by a woolly thatch of white hair, he walks, draped in the traditional Basuto blanket, bent over a stick. He is seventy-five years old, and has been in trouble ever since he started the *Lekhotla la Bafo* in 1919.

Lefela has always been a visionary, dreaming and working to restore the independence, honour and lands which he believes white men, and the British in particular, stole from the Basuto. He started the *Lekhotla la Bafo* to preserve Basuto national rights and to improve the lot of the ordinary peasant. He worked by 'speaking to the people through meetings and to the chiefs and government through correspondence', and had rough handling from both the latter. But his influence slowly spread as, through sheer force of personality and footslogging perseverance, he gave peasants the courage once again to resist oppressive and unjust chiefs in the old tribal way. Lefela has always been a Basuto traditionalist. He probably knows more about Basuto history than most chiefs put together, and will, despite an excellent knowledge of English, speak to strangers only through an interpreter.

Leaving primary school at standard two, he has educated himself and has read to an amazing degree, so much so that the enormously long petitions which in recent years he has been sending to people like Khrushchev, Nehru and Eisenhower, are peppered with more esoteric footnotes than many a historian's thesis.

Lefela made a writer of himself, but found difficulty in having his articles published because they were so bitterly critical of the whites, and in particular of the British and South African administrators, as well as of the chiefs with their misrule and exploitation of the peasants. It was here that in 1928 he first came into contact with the Communists in South Africa who, themselves moving towards backing a 'black Republic', published Lefela's writings in their paper *Umsebenzi*, and relations were maintained until the Communists were banned in South Africa in 1950. Lefela admires Soviet Russia and the South African radical movement has always had a soft spot for Lefela, though it found his tribal conservatism hard to take. He has been against the chiefs because they misruled, not because he was against chieftainship. On the contrary.

Over the years, Lefela organized the peasants, led demonstrations, issued propaganda, and gained the reputation of being something near a prophet. His was Basutoland's first popular political movement.

Lefela's fundamental position, for which he makes out a strong historical case, is that the British have no right to rule in Basutoland, as Moshesh merely invited them to protect the country whilst he and his councillors would rule. Hence Lefela has refused to acknowledge the jurisdiction of British magistrates.

He campaigned assiduously against the recruitment of Basuto as soldiers in the Second World War, during which 21,463 enlisted in the High Commission Territories Auxiliary Pioneer Corps, and 1,105 lost their lives. Lefela felt on principle that the Basuto should keep out of a white man's capitalist war. He also became convinced that Basuto recruits were being deliberately sent to their death when, instead of being trained as infantry combatants, they were sent to north Africa unarmed to do menial work. (Some Basuto were later armed, and some served in artillery units, earning special distinction as members of a mule-using mountain regiment. Some were decorated, but they were denied commissioned rank.) For his persistent and highly vocal anti-war efforts, Lefela was detained for the duration. In 1955 he was jailed for nine months for sedition. He refused to recognize the courts which tried him.

Since 1948, he has tried to make his peace with the chiefs, whom he claimed the British were trying to destroy. The *Lekhotla la Bafo* gave evidence to the Moore Commission but not to the National Council's Constitutional Reform Committee. Today Lefela maintains that whites *a priori* want to kill off the Basuto. Taking the attitude that the Basuto have never lost their independence, he concludes that as the British usurped Basuto independence and are illegally ruling the country it is quite obviously absurd to petition them for the return of something they have stolen. Hence he will have nothing to do with anything less than a declaration by Britain of the restoration of complete self-government, and has denounced all the parties for having negotiated (except the Basutoland Communists, who were not then in existence).

Josiel Lefela's name still carries semi-prophetic weight in Basutoland, but with advancing years and increasing crankiness his organization has fallen to pieces and exists today only in the immediate district where the old man lives.

Alongside the development of Basutoland's political parties, an incipient trade-union movement has in recent years appeared.

The country has, as the official 1961 report puts it, 'no industries apart from small brickfields and the printing enterprises of the P.E.M.S. and R.C. mission, which together employ approximately one hundred Basuto. . . . Apart from employment in the Government Service and in trading stores there is very little work to be found in the territory, and this necessitates the regular exodus of workers to the Republic.'

A few people find work in garages, with transport companies and builders, and as domestics, but the number involved is insignificant. There is virtually no hired agricultural labour, the common system being for peasants to help one another out and for village work to be done communally under the chief's orders. This list of course leaves out of account the Native Recruiting Organization, which takes on vast numbers of men for employment outside Basutoland.

Thus the field for trade-union organization is relatively limited, though the wages paid in all spheres have, in a land of chronic unemployment, been so low that there is plenty to be done.

In order to obtain Colonial Development and Welfare Fund aid, Basutoland had to create trade-union legislation, and since 1942 all trade-unions have had to register under law. None did so until 1952, when the Basutoland Typographical Workers' and the Basutoland Commercial Distributive Workers' Unions were formed. By 1961 they had been joined by the Basutoland General Workers' Union, Motor Transport Workers' Union, and the National Union of Trained Artisans. In 1961, being covered under the same law, the Union of Employers in Basutoland was registered.

The High Commissioner has the power to prescribe minimum wages, but the Basutoland proclamations from 1953 to 1960 are innocent of any such move on his part, though of course the British administration is itself the largest employer of labour in Basutoland.

In 1957 'labourers employed mainly on roads and other public works, soil conservation works, etc.,' earned rates from 3s. 7d. to 6s. a day. In 1950 the rate had ranged from 1s. 9d. to 2s. a day. And in both years, as the annual reports calmly put it, 'Public works labourers work a fifty-four-hour week'.

This would give the father of a family who was lucky enough to get a public works job in 1957 the princely sum of £4 13s. 2d. for a 234-hour working month, or $4\frac{3}{4}$d. per hour. It could, one must suppose, be worse, for after all only seven years earlier the British Government was paying its Basutoland labourers $2\frac{1}{8}$d. per hour.

But one does understand the coyness which has prevented the Government from continuing with the publication of wage rates in the Basutoland Annual Reports after 1958. I understand that the rate current in 1963 was 5s. a day, or roughly 7d. an hour.

Whilst it still had the courage to publish these figures, the Basutoland administration (which has of course itself been starved of funds by Britain) added the disingenuous little note that

In considering these wages it should be remembered that every married man is entitled to lands on which to grow food, free occupation of a site for his house, and communal grazing rights for his cattle, and that the staple food of the average Mosuto of the labouring class is mealie porridge, samp and beans.*

The complacency and arrogance of this statement are truly frightening, coming as it does from 'men on the spot' who know all about the brutal land hunger which forces the 'average Mosuto of the labouring class' to work for such miserable pittances and which forces him to make do with mealie porridge, samp and beans.

Three years later Dr Munoz of the World Health Organization reported† that over seventy-five per cent of all Basuto were undernourished to a significant degree, and that 44·5 per cent suffered from endemic thyroid goitre. In the years 1951–7 the Basuto birth-rate had dropped from 30·6 to twenty-two per thousand, with lack of food, according to Dr Munoz, having made parents infertile. Infant mortality rose from 58·8 to 116 per thousand, while the one to four year mortality rate rose from 113·6 to 154·9 per thousand.

The actual financial situation which makes possible the paying of such starvation wages by Basutoland's Government is not the immediate fault of its administrators. But one is forced to wonder whether civil servants who, knowing the true situation, could blandly append the footnote quoted above were really doing all they could to influence the British Government into giving them increased funds.

Their false assumption that 'peasant' workers do not really

---

* *Colonial Reports: Basutoland, 1957*, H.M.S.O.
† *Report and Recommendations on a Nutrition Survey conducted in Basutoland*, Dr J. A. Munoz and Miss M. M. Anderson, W.H.O. Regional Office for Africa, South of the Sahara, 1956–60 (mimeographed).

need a living wage is precisely identical to that which the incredibly profitable South African gold mining industry has used to justify its exploitation of its migrant labourers, one in five of whom come from the High Commission Territories.

When a witness before South Africa's Lansdowne Commission into African mine wages asked whether a white miner with private means would not still be paid the rate for the job, the spokesman for the Chamber of Mines replied:

> this ignores the fact that the ability of the Native to earn a Reserve income is largely due to the fact that he is granted by the Union Government land to cultivate, and pasturage, with practically free occupation of both. In effect he receives a substantial subsidy from the Government which enables him to come out to work in the intermittent fashion which suits him.

The word by word similarity with the Basutoland Annual Reports is alarming. It lends depressing point to the British Government's claim in recruiting officials for the High Commission Territories that 'on retirement ... some officials find remunerative employment with industrial and commercial undertakings in South Africa for which their previous work and experience ... in these "Lands of Opportunity" have made them particularly suitable'.*

It should be added that the wages of the domestic servants working in the homes of Basutoland's administrators remained static from 1949 to 1957 at the £1 10s.–£5 a month range. The official reports add that 'food and lodging are *usually* provided in addition' [my italics], but fail to make it clear that the quoted wage levels are not statutory minimums.

Other monthly wage-ranges quoted in the latest available published form are those for store employees at £3–7 in 1949 and £5–15 in 1957; for artisans at £8–17 in 1949 and £15–26 in 1957; and for foremen at £5–8 and £6–18 respectively. They have risen a little, but not much, since then.

Meanwhile, the average wages of African miners in the South African gold mines, into which some 40,000 Basuto are forced every year through the poverty of their homeland, rose from 43·1 pence per shift in 1949 to sixty pence in 1955.

* *Lands of Opportunity*, Commonwealth Relations Office, 1958.

174

The difficulties of organizing workers for higher wages in a country like Basutoland are, of course, enormous.

Any attempt at strike action is bound to release the general tensions which are so close to the surface of everyday life of Basutoland, as Maseru's first general strike in 1961 illustrated. The strike was sparked off when two women were dismissed from the Maseru Club's staff 'for unsatisfactory service', one of them alleging she had been told that it was because she was pregnant. The rest of the staff, members of the General Workers' Union, stopped work. Some thousands of Basuto attended protest meetings, and when the club's committee refused to reconsider the dismissals, a one-day strike and boycott of all shops in Maseru was called for the next day, 14 March. Both were highly successful. Business came to a standstill, with tension rising as whites attempted to carry on African jobs.

The Government, on the urging of the B.C.P. and the Marema Tlou Party, began to negotiate with the club management, whose chairman was also the head of the Basutoland police Special Branch, and the strike committee. Immediately the situation was complicated by differences within the B.C.P. and trade-union leadership. Mokhehle urged people, on two successive days, to return to work as negotiations were in progress. The mass of strikers defied him, urged on by Jack Mosiane, the union's leader who was also an executive member of the B.C.P. Mokhehle earned the strikers' hostility when he informed the Government that the situation was out of control.

Armed police had been actively patrolling, joined by armed white civil servants, sworn in as 'specials'. There was no violence, but the Government claimed that there was a great deal of intimidation and brought to Maseru, with the Paramount Chief's help, 200 Basuto strong-arm men, officially described as 'chiefs' messengers', who were identified with black sashes made of police putties and then let loose 'to stop intimidation'. They went to work with a will, some of them armed with spears and axes and most with sticks. According to those on the receiving end, whatever intimidation there had been was more than fully revenged, and under police leadership, these 'black-sashers' also conducted extensive raids for permits and tax receipts.

After two days, the Government forbade all meetings of more

than three persons, and the Paramount appealed for calm. In a confused situation, the strike was called off late at night on the understanding that the two dismissed women would be reinstated by the club and that there would be no victimization of strikers. This was inadequately publicized, and a number of workers claim that on returning to work the next morning they were beaten up – by the Paramount Chief's men!

'The uneasy situation in Maseru,' says the Annual Report for 1961, 'persisted during the year.'

The strike highlighted the strength and divisions of the B.C.P. and trade-union leadership, as well as the resources of a shaken but determined Government. It showed the ordinary Basuto that by united action they could, despite widespread unemployment, bring normal life to a standstill for a while, though the strikers got nowhere with the demand for a wage of £1 a day which was introduced into the strike.

'The strike', as it has since become known, is still very much a live topic in Maseru. The first man to translate its lessons into action was Mokhehle. The man who had outbid him in popular appeal and had defied him by continuing the strike, Jack Mosiane, was a former South African trade-unionist and A.N.C. member whom Mokhehle had given overall direction of the not very important trade-union front. Mosiane was demoted, and Mokhehle laid down what has remained his trade-union policy. Unions having B.C.P. members would have to be under the B.C.P.'s control, and those who joined such unions would have to join the party. The workers' aims could not be achieved until political independence was won, and big wage increases or the question of a national minimum wage would have to await independence. The claim for £1 a day was an irrelevant importation from South Africa – it had first been raised there by the A.N.C. and its allies – which sowed disharmony in Basutoland.

By this time the rift between Mokhehle and South Africa's A.N.C. was widening rapidly. A number of other former South African trade-unionists had, like Jack Mosiane, really been responsible for livening up trade-unionism. But where Mosiane had worked in an established union, they had created the new Basutoland Workers' Union. With Mokhehle having thrown down the gauntlet they formed, late in 1961, the Basutoland

Congress of Trade Unions, or B.A.C.T.U. Only the Basutoland General Workers' Union belongs to this group. Mokhehle riposted by engineering, in February 1962, the formation of the Basutoland Federation of Labour, or B.F.L. (to which the five unions established earlier belong), and Mokhehle's brother, Shakane Mokhehle, became its secretary.

With the formation of these two groups, wider political conflicts entered the Basutoland trade-union field. In 1961 four members of B.A.C.T.U. were invited to Moscow for training by the Communist-dominated World Federation of Trade Unions, but the British Administration refused them passports. In 1962 B.A.C.T.U. affiliated to the South African Congress of Trade Unions, which has been associated with the W.F.T.U. before officially supporting the Africanist thesis that trade-unions in Africa should not affiliate to either the W.F.T.U. or the American-dominated International Confederation of Free Trade Unions.

This Africanist position has also been espoused since its formation by Mokhehle's Basutoland Federation of Labour, but the rival B.A.C.T.U. has felt unable to support Mokhehle's rider that local trade-unions must be subservient to the Basutoland Congress Party. The B.F.L. has also pursued an actively anti-Communist line.

In 1962 the American-dominated International Confederation of Free Trade Unions went so far as to send a representative, Mr Knight Maripe, to Basutoland. Maripe, born in Bechuanaland, is a former Southern Rhodesian trade-union leader who went into journalism. Having failed to bring the two warring groups together, he plumped with money and support for the anti-Communist Federation of Labour. He has suggested the creation of a new inter-territorial trade-union training centre, financed by the I.C.F.T.U.

Even with the best will in the world, the permanent solution of Basutoland's unemployment problem is beyond the powers of its present, or any future, administration.

But what has been painfully lacking is an imaginative approach to the question of public works. Expensive bulldozers are used where men with shovels and baskets would achieve the same result, if more slowly. Heavy lorries haul construction loads which men could carry, and so on.

Replacing machines with men may seem an inefficient approach, and so it is. But in Basutoland the position is rapidly becoming desperate, and it will become ungovernable when South Africa steps up the expulsion of 'foreign natives' to which it is committed. Only last year the Froneman Commission Report recommended detailed measures for the expulsion of all non-Republic Africans, and this report has been accepted by the South African Government. It will clearly not be possible for the mines to do without Basuto labour, but only half of the Basuto in South Africa work on the mines. It may be some time, too, before the Orange Free State farmers can be reconciled to parting with the Basuto labour on which they significantly depend, but the pressures are increasing. Certainly some thousands of Basuto are already being forced out of South Africa's urban areas.

The Government's only major move on the labour front has been the introduction, with the backing of the National Council, of new labour legislation in 1962.

The Trade Unions and Trade Disputes measure imposes severe restrictions on trade-unions, strikes and the settlement of disputes, and is based on South Africa's rightly notorious, so-called Industrial Conciliation Act and on certain British colonial statutes. The Employment Bill put forward at the same time introduces, *inter alia*, the 'ticket' system for mine workers in Basutoland. This 'ticket system' is one evolved in South Africa for migratory labour and has certainly not been to to their benefit. For the rest, this measure, too, is largely based on South African labour laws.

It should, however, be said that at its first annual conference in January 1963 the Basutoland Federation of Labour endorsed the Trade Unions and Trade Disputes Bill. It seems uncertain how far the delegates understood what they were endorsing, for whilst the Bill prohibited any union from financially supporting political causes, parties or individuals, the B.F.L. conference also resolved to support any political party representing the wishes of the Basuto and the workers. Similarly, Mokhehle and most of his B.C.P. members led the widespread support which Basutoland's new labour legislation received in the National Council.

PEASANTS ON HORSEBACK

Behind the politics and the elections, behind the trade-unions and their affiliations, there lies, of course, the poverty of Basutoland. Brutally, Basutoland could be summed up as being a tiny, mountainous, and terribly eroded country, called upon to support something like twice the population feasible from agriculture, but lacking almost every marketable material resource except a few diamonds and vast quantities of water which there isn't money to convert into the hydroelectricity that no one would be certain to buy even if it were produced.

Nevertheless all men are taxed and, as they must both pay up and eat, forty-three per cent of Basutoland's adult men are away from the country at any given time, working in South Africa and elsewhere. Some seventy-five per cent of the population left behind, composed chiefly of women, children and the aged, are undernourished, their efforts to scratch a living from the soil undermined by an old-fashioned system of land tenure, in which no individual has security and in which the chiefs abuse their rights to make temporary allocation of plots. The peasants apparently themselves oppose reform of the land-tenure system. The chiefs, who have been left with a fair amount of administrative powers, are for the most part in the grip of avarice, corruption, and drink, and have proved that they have neither the wish nor the will to reform themselves. Above them sits a young, intelligent, educated, and ambitious Paramount, who hankers after powers to match those of the Stuart kings of England.

Half of the population, which is nominally Christian, is caught in the unresolved conflict between tenaciously surviving old superstitions and tribal customs. Of those who are Christians perhaps half again are in the grip of the Roman Catholic Church, whose old, emphatic dogmas have been allied to a phrenetic, compulsive anti-Communism.

At best, only forty per cent of the population is reasonably within the reach of medical services, and those which exist are merely skeletal. Infant mortality is 116 per thousand: forty-four per cent of the Basuto have endemic goitre, and one Basuto in six suffers every year from pellagra, the horrible deficiency disease which cracks the victim's skin and frequently his mind as well.

Above all this, temporally if temporarily, has reclined the British Administration. Its legal powers absolute, its attitudes largely paternalistic and fatalistic, its economic outlook marked by a distaste for fundamental planning, its funds derisory, its political policy one of 'playing it off the cuff', its horizons have been bounded, as is Basutoland itself, on every side by South Africa.

The British Government, to whom alone the Administration owes allegiance, has welcomed the appointment of high-powered international economic survey missions, and has then largely ignored in practice their urgent recommendations.

In the hills, prematurely old men sit coughing their lungs out with the phthisis which, aside from a meagre wage and, if they are lucky, a pittance of £100–300 compensation, is all they have to show for years of grubbing gold out of the South African ground for white men. Now the South Africans are going drastically to reduce the number of Basuto who may work across the border, and there soon may not even be that. No one knows what there *will* be, but it won't, as far as anyone can see, be work and bread. Even now, as the population grows, more and more people must find work in South Africa or starve. From 1950–59, despite the lower rate of increase the population grew by nineteen per cent; the number of expatriate Basuto increased by eighty-five per cent.

That would be the brutal summing up, but, though true, it happily does not give the whole picture. Basutoland's economic and general position is grim, but it need not be as grim as it is. The Basuto themselves are stirring to this realization, alternately prodding and prodded by an Administration which in turn has partially pulled itself and been pulled out of its old rut.

The hard fundamental realities of course remain, and of them the most important is the land itself.

Agricultural land, livestock, water, scenery and people are Basutoland's principle resources.* Of the estimated total population of nearly one million Basuto,† at least 130,000, including

* For the factual information which follows in the rest of this chapter, I have drawn heavily and freely on the Morse Report (*Basutoland, Bechuanaland Protectorate and Swaziland: Report of an Economic Survey Mission.* H.M.S.O., 1960). Unless otherwise indicated, quoted opinions and conclusions are also taken from this source.

† Dept of Agriculture Annual Report, 1960.

20,000 women, live continuously out of the Territory, almost all of them in South Africa. Of these, some 59,800 Basuto men were in 1962 employed in gold and other mines in South Africa. The majority of non-miners labour for derisory wages on farms in the neighbouring Orange Free State, whilst the rest of the men and most of the women have been doing work, of one sort or another, in South African towns, from which they are now being expelled. The earnings of these migrants are a major source of income for Basutoland. For miners, there is an officially controlled system of deferred pay and remittances.*

Basutoland covers 11,716 square miles, four fifths of which is steeply mountainous terrain, almost without roads and negotiable only along bridle paths and tracks. One quarter of the estimated population of one million lives in these mountainous parts.

It is estimated that just under one million acres of land are under cultivation, which is all the land that is considered arable. Much but by no means all of the remainder of the country is grassland suitable for grazing, but the pressures of population growth is leading to more and more pockets of mountain land being cultivated, leading to increased soil erosion.

One has, as the Israelis have taught us, to be careful of estimating what is cultivable land; really detemined people can, given adequate funds, make nonsense of 'normal' criteria. For the moment, however, present estimates will serve.

Of some 160,000 families in Basutoland, perhaps 150,000, including those of men away, have some holdings of land. Very many of these holdings are, however, too small or poor in quality to be viable even in Basutoland's subsistence farming economy.

The allocation of lands is made by the local chiefs, and the supposedly typical Basuto family cultivates 5–10 acres, traditionally divided into three quite separate lots in order to give everyone some good and some poor land. A family may also have a small patch for a vegetable garden by its kraal.

On this basis, a family could make quite a reasonable subsistence living even with the old, grossly inefficient way of farming. But

* These in 1958 brought back into Basutoland £685,000 as well as £60,000 in tax which is automatically deducted from the migrant miner's wages. Total ordinary revenue in 1958 was £1,638,000, of which Customs and Excise handed over by South Africa, made up £777,114. Substantial licence fees are also paid by mine labour recruiters.

whilst these are the customary allotments, the pressure of a growing population on the land has led to very many families having only two lands, and frequently only one. Naturally, chiefs and headmen take the best and largest lands for themselves and often also for their families.

I have spoken with a typical peasant in the mountains who has to try to support a family of seven off one small and one medium 'land', and to another, whose case is by no means uncommon, who has only one largish 'land' for himself, his wife, mother, young child and two young brothers. Both were too poor to buy fertilizers even if they had wanted to or had known how to apply them properly.

11,700 of Basutoland's 161,230 households hold no land at all. Of those who do have land, 35·6 per cent hold less than four arable acres, and 75·5 per cent less than eight. Only 4·5 per cent have more than fifteen acres. Grazing is communal.

In theory, a peasant has some security of tenure once he has been allocated land. His chief is only supposed to withdraw his allocation if he fails to pay his tax, if he fails to make proper use of the land over an unspecified period, or if he moves his dwelling so as to make such neglect likely. But in reality these are thin safeguards, for the latter two depend on the chief's judgement. What is more, the chances of having one's lands reallocated increase in the remoter areas if one arouses the chief's jealousy by obvious improvements. Certainly the planting of trees or fencing is highly suspect, arousing fears of permanent claims to tenure.

The only appeal against improper reallocation lies to the Paramount Chief, but it takes a bold peasant to challenge in this way the chief under whose rule his daily life must be led, especially as an appeal is a protracted business in which it is ultimately the chief's word against the complainant's. There are, of course, no statistics, but extensive conversations with peasants and chiefs have convinced me that a substantial number of improper reallocations take place in which there is no legal redress.

The problems arising from this system of land tenure are fundamental to agriculture reform in Basutoland, and only two alternative broad solutions appear reasonable. Either individual security of tenure, inheritable by children, must be assured, or some way must be found of collective farming. It may be that some combination of the two is possible; certainly neither would significantly improve matters unless it were accepted by, or preferably came from the mass of the Basuto peasants themselves.

Peasants are traditionally conservative, and there is supposed to be widespread opposition to interfering with the tradition-rooted power of the chiefs to allocate land. Recent conversations with peasants in Basutoland make me doubt this very strongly. For instance, of eleven peasant farmers, chosen at random from a crowd in a trading store, with whom I had an extensive discussion in the Pitsiesnek area, all but two were in favour of taking land allocation powers away from the chiefs. Of the other two, one was an old man, and the other a representative of a local chief, who had been well looked-after himself.

Not all of those who wanted change were clear as to what alternative system they favoured, but the concensus of opinion was that the elected District Councils should make the allocations, which should be left undisturbed unless gross neglect could be proved in public discussion.

This, of course, brings us to the nub of the problem: the chiefs. It may be said that the power of the chiefs has formerly rested upon three legs: judicial, administrative, and land. Today the chiefs no longer have judicial functions, and the District Councils are progressively taking over the administrative functions which so many chiefs have neglected. By and large, the chiefs have long forfeited the affection and personal respect of their people. So, in a little while, all that will remain to them is the power to allocate land. Once that power goes, chieftainship in Basutoland will be finished, and the chiefs know it.

It is a moot point what the position of the Paramount Chief would then be; certainly he will lose many of his present formal functions. Being untainted by the abuses of the chieftainship in general, however, and looked up to by the mass of the people, he could unquestionably survive as a constitutional monarch, and has the personality and charm to be a popular one. As a constitutional monarch he might remain the symbolic owner of all land. If, for instance, District Councils were to allocate land (for which formal freehold title might not be necessary), the Paramount might be their final authority, and eventually the position might be reached in which the Paramount's 'ownership' of the land would be purely symbolic, as happened in Britain.

These are, of course, only tentative ideas concerning one way in which this very complicated and thorny problem might be tackled. Any detailed proposals would have to consider, for instance, whether bank credit could be obtained without individual free-hold title, and examine the relevance of the very promising progress made for a while under the present system by the banking institution of Basutoland's rapidly growing cooperative movement.

Tree-planting has long been recognized as one way of fighting soil erosion in Basutoland, but it has been hampered by vagueness over the ownership of trees planted by Government and by private farmers; the destruction of many trees by communally grazed goats; the chopping down of others by the peasants themselves; the absence of any trained forestry staff; and inadequate funds for official work.

With most of Basutoland lying over six thousand feet and a great deal of it between eight and ten thousand feet, the winter climate is bitterly cold, with a great deal of the country covered in snow. Since there are few trees, the people burn animal dung for fuel, thus robbing the soil of its finest manure. The shortage of wood is such that, without threshing flails, people use oxen to trample out corn.

Basutoland is not a potential forest country, but a great deal could be done by the Government, District Councils and individual peasants to grow at least sufficient timber for fuel and implements, simultaneously helping to stabilize soil in gullies or on mountains. But for this, too, clarification of land rights is required.

There is also the non-agricultural side of land tenure, at last tackled in 1962 by setting aside a limited area near Maseru in which intending industrialists may obtain extended leases. This move is, however, leading to renewed pressure from white traders for title to the land which has been 'lent' to them by the Basuto for their stores. And this in turn exacerbates Basuto fears that changes in land tenure will open the door for whites to 'buy up' their country.

Having struggled as hard as they have to retain their land, and with the demand for land rising amongst the whites in South Africa, the Basuto are not suspicious without cause. They have only to look at Swaziland to see what can happen when whites are allowed to buy land freely, and whilst of course most of Basutoland, unlike Swaziland, wouldn't interest farmers, there are parts which would. But it has become clear that something must be done to reform the present system, and the National Council has authorized the appointment of an expert outside commission to go into the whole question.

Clearly, however, reform of the land tenure system must be part of a broad attack on Basutoland's agricultural and social problems. As the Morse Commission says, 'a change in the land tenure system for arable land, taken by itself, will accomplish little. The favourable psychological environment that this should create must be given guidance through extension work, educational opportunities, and in other ways.' The 'other ways' are likely to include what amount to both an agricultural and a social revolution.

The Morse Commission is emphatic that 'the traditional system of land tenure is quite unsuited to the type of society Basuto leaders would like to create', and that, 'a modern, technologically advanced economy can only exist in an environment of modern law'. Largely preoccupied with current political issues, most Basuto leaders have not yet faced up to the challenges this raises, except in an *ad hoc* manner. But, says Morse, 'it is not possible to settle each case as it comes along – there must be established law for all to read and understand. . . . There is no need to abandon the tradition that land is a social asset, to be employed for the benefit of all, in favour of a purely private property system, for there are numerous alternatives, amongst them long-term lease and the conditional option for repurchase by public authorities after a term of years.' Whatever is eventually determined, it is certain that it must come from the Basuto themselves.

In the meantime, the struggle continues against soil erosion, which has devastated a large proportion of Basutoland. Travelling almost anywhere in the country means coming across hundreds of dongas or gullies, commonly six feet deep, cut into loosened and unbanked soil by rain floods. But such travel today also means coming across widespread signs of soil conservation work.

The only two natural features which Basutoland possesses in overabundance are steeply sloping land – four fifths of the total – and water. Three of South Africa's major rivers rise in Basutoland, which is the sponge area of the whole geographical region. Much of this mountain land is naturally prone to erosion. Much of it carries grass, but it is always vulnerable to overgrazing and to excessive trampling around sponges and cattle posts. As the grass cover decreases, the soil is loosened and runs off with the rains. And as pressure on arable lands has grown, more and more peasants have used patches of otherwise unallocated mountain grazing for ploughing, which has made matters worse.

The Government was shaken into action on soil conservation by the Pim Report in 1935, and Basutoland was saved in the nick of time from what would probably have been an irreparable loss of soil. But splendid as the work done by the Government has been, it has been limited both by lack of adequate finance and by lack of sufficient manpower to spread the word and adequately to supervise the maintenance of conservation works by the farmers once completed. Under these conditions, and given the increasing pressure on the land, it has been impossible to prevent the further spread of both donga and sheet erosion.

Today the Department of Agriculture has somewhat more, but still not nearly enough, money or men for this work, which in any case needs to be supplemented by active grazing control in both the foothills and mountains. If a successful attempt were made to enforce this by law and supervision (for which there is in any case not the manpower), it would set off explosive reactions amongst land-starved peasants with nowhere else to go. The Morse Commission is right in saying that however well-conceived soil conservation plans may be, they will be ineffective unless 'they are supported by wise policies and effective action' from the National Council. We are back with the need for a broadly based agrarian and social revolution, and with the apparently insoluble problem of too little land for too many people.

At present, the most promising developments in Basutoland are the 'progressive farmer' scheme and the growth of the cooperative movement.

If a peasant reaches a certain stage of advancement and has a little money, he can apply to the Agricultural Department to become a 'progressive farmer'. This is an excellent scheme launched a few years ago under which an approved candidate works for three years with a demonstrator from the department which, if he is judged fit, will help him to acquire tools and fertilizers so as to increase yields and improve the soil. Basutoland's Director of Agriculture has told me that he can take any unimproved land holding in the country and double its yield within one year, and he has proved this claim.

At the end of his first year of guidance, the 'progressive farmer' receives a certificate and badge at a ceremony, and at the end of a further two years he similarly becomes a 'master farmer'.

The department has decided to concentrate its limited resources on thus showing and helping people who have already proved that they both want to help themselves and are capable of being good farmers, and hopes that their example will ripple outwards. The scheme has shown great signs of promise since it was launched in 1959 – even women, in the absence of their migrant menfolk, are being drawn into it – and this has revealed one of its non-intrinsic drawbacks. There simply aren't the money and the trained demonstrators to keep up with even present demand for enrolment. In 1960, with then existing finance for training demonstrators fully extended, there were only 110 qualified demonstrators, who in turn could guide a maximum of 880 farmers every three years. In 1961 there were only 850 'progressive farmers'.

Following the praise and recommendations of the Morse Commission for the scheme, training facilities are being expanded, but a great deal more will have to be done if the 'progressive farmers' are to become a major influence.

The major drawback of the 'progressive farmer' scheme is, of course, that, as the Government has little money, its concentration on helping only those who have already made progress inevitably leads the ordinary peasant to feel that the Agricultural Department isn't really interested in helping him. This of course is not true. For even the best-intentioned Government, the choosing of priorities for scarce funds is always a painful problem, and the tone of recent Basutoland agricultural reports does give an impression of impatience with people who won't do enough for themselves.

The Department of Agriculture runs an enterprising research station in Maseru and a training school for demonstrators. In the past few years it has changed its policy from one of prosecuting offenders against soil conservation and agricultural rules. Helped by a belated realization of the need for modern public relations, which through a special sub-department now includes the production of attractive literature, mobile cinema and information vans, the new policy is on the way to changing the image of the department from one of a policeman enforcing imposed and often incomprehensible laws to something of a popular guide.

As with many other good Government intentions throughout the High Commission Territories, concern for all farmers can only be demonstrated if greatly increased funds and skilled man-power are made available by Britain, and if the men in charge of its spending are both professionally expert and able to communicate with the people they are supposed to serve.

Here Basutoland's cooperative movement has been fortunate in its registrar, Mr Bert Youngjohns, who has unobtrusively done much to guide and help the increasing efforts of farmers to band together and help themselves. As a result, Basutoland's young cooperative movement is today the model which the other two High Commission Territories can with profit belatedly follow.

The key to the recent and dramatic progress of the Basutoland cooperative movement has been the establishment of a central cooperative banking union.

If underdeveloped countries are to progress they must find ways of generating increased capital, which means increased production. 'Old hands' in Basutoland, as in other countries, have long despaired of getting subsistence farmers to grow crops for sale and thus getting the mass of the peasants into a cash economy without disrupting their lives. Such 'old hands' must be amazed by what has been achieved in a few years in Basutoland by the cooperative movement.

Basuto farmers have long been discouraged from growing for sale through the lack of trust, based on years of hard experience, which they have in many of the traders. In good times they are forced to sell at low prices maize which the trader then stores and resells to its growers in bad times at high prices. With wool, the other main Basuto product, traders are known to buy at less than proclaimed prices, in violation of the spirit of Government regulations, and to be very slack in their handling and grading. In 1960 traders officially made profits of twenty per cent on maize, twenty-three per cent on sorghums, twenty-nine per cent on wheat and 100 per cent on beans.

The dramatic quadrupling in one year of turn-over by the cooperative societies after the establishment in 1958 of the Co-operative Banking Union has provided the 'evidence that when markets are assured, and especially when the farmer trusts the marketing agent to serve his interests, the Basuto are willing to produce for sale rather than for family consumption alone'.

By providing assured markets for non-traditional but high-yielding and profitable crops like peas and beans, the cooperative movement is making an important contribution to the moderniz-ation of Basutoland agriculture, and by improving internal distribution it is helping to reduce the imports of maize by this maize-farming country.

Where, if a struggling peasant farmer wants to improve his lands, if he wants to experiment with new crops or implements, can he borrow the money? The answer, until very recently, was – nowhere. For, struggling along from year to year, with no title to his land and his only disposable assets his cattle, he was hardly a credit proposition to conventional bankers. Where banks *were* prepared to lend money in these conditions, their rates were inevitably very high indeed. As the Morse Report tartly observed: 'Many malpractices of the Basuto farmer can be attributed to the lack of resources to do anything better.'

Today, he has a chance to borrow on his good reputation amongst his fellow farmers by joining a credit cooperative.

Every applicant for a loan from the society is screened by its committee, who decide on two criteria: the judgement of the Department of Agriculture that the applicant is capable of making effective use of a loan, and on his character. As the society is collectively responsible for loans granted, the screening is a careful one, but it has the novel and crucial advantage that the applicant's standing among his peers is decisive. The application is then passed on to the Banking Union, and, if approved, both the local committee and the department visit and, if necessary, advise the farmer during the growing season. If he should reject their advice, the loan can be recalled, but 'as a rule farmers welcome inspection and advice'.

In reading official reports on the cooperative movement, one is repeatedly struck by this sort of phrase: 'Farmers welcome' inspection and advice; committees are 'quick to see' the need for ploughing back profits; the response of societies and members to a policy of accumulating capital rather than taking maximum dividends 'has been immensely encouraging'. Here, clearly, is something which the people feel is their own, which is visibly for their benefit and for their country's, and they respond to its challenge by taking and displaying responsibility and initiative. It is a unique venture in Basutoland, in which ordinary people are helping themselves, making the maximum use of the little financial help they have been able to obtain from the Government, and accepting guidance from officials because they know that it is both expert and disinterested.

That this desire of the people to improve themselves can, under inspired leadership, become almost religious in its fervour has been shown by a remarkable Mosuto, James Machobane. In the midfifties, Machobane developed a rather complicated system of intercropping, especially with potatoes, which he demonstrated would dramatically increase yields and, he believes, improve the soil. Inspired by his conviction that only self-help could save the Basuto, he launched his own private extension drive, demonstrating his intercropping methods and preaching the need for self-help, intensive cultivation, adult education and cooperative effort. The response amongst farmers in the northern areas of Basutoland was electric, and his work took on the overtones of a crusade.

Though officials were sceptical of his intercropping methods, they did realize the value of Machobane's ability to arouse great enthusiasm amongst the farmers. This led, in fact, to the beginnings of agricultural credit, for in 1958–9 a sum of £3,500, partly provided and partly guaranteed by the Government, was lent to Machobane's followers in order to let them test his theories. That year the weather was disastrous, with drought, frost and a glut of potatoes on the South African market; but nevertheless cash yields for maize were increased from the normal £4–5 to £25 per acre. On the due date, eighty-five per cent of the loan was recovered.

The Agricultural Department has nevertheless remained sceptical of Mr Machobane's methods, and efforts to establish exact comparison through controlled tests have been inconclusive.

Mr Machobane has founded what he calls the Machobane Mass Agricultural College, and through a movement called *mantsa-tlala* (dispel famine) combines mutual help with a sort of agricultural extension course by correspondence. In 1961, like the proverbial prophets, he received honour outside his own country, being awarded in New York the Lane Bryant International Volunteer Award (1,000 dollars awarded to foster voluntary projects for the benefit of mankind). Both President Kennedy and Mr Adlai Stevenson sent messages of congratulation. Whatever the merits of Mr Machobane's agricultural methods may finally be proved to be, he is living proof that the 'ordinary' Basuto farmer is willing and able to help himself and others to progress.

The need – as opposed to demand – for agriculture credit is as urgent in Basutoland, as it is in Bechuanaland and Swaziland. It has now been officially recognized for some years in Basutoland that the expansion of an agricultural credit system is the key-stone of agricultural progress in the Territory, and that the key to this credit system is the Cooperative Banking Union. The Cooperative and Agricultural Departments in Basutoland work in the closest cooperation, and the former's Banking Union has now taken over the granting of loans to 'progressive farmers'.

But the Union, excellent as its work has been, has been bedevilled by a shortage of funds. The members of societies do each buy at least one 10s. or £1 share, and in the course of time trading profits will give the Banking Union more resources. But at the beginning any such venture must lock up much of its capital and some of its borrowings in long-term essentials like buildings, storage and transportation. What any such organization needs in its initial stages is an outright grant to provide itself with these basic facilities and to give itself some room for manoeuvre. This has been recognized, and such a grant officially made, in other British territories such as Western Nigeria.

It is a telling commentary on the British Government's un-imaginative meanness towards the High Commission Territories that it should have been left to the Oxford Famine Relief Committee to make the Basutoland Cooperative Banking Union such a grant of £20,000.

With this grant, the movement has been able to continue its progress in Basutoland. It has not, of course, found its path always smooth, and further growth must add to the problems and snags already encountered, not all of which have been solved. Some of these are connected with the desire of societies to branch out rapidly, both into purchasing for their members and into general retail trading, which is a tricky business complicated further by the stranglehold which the two major expatriate chains of trading stores have on Basutoland. One very promising new venture has been the creation of a Mutual Savings Society for members and non-members alike, and which is making both a practical and a patriotic appeal. An artisans building cooperative has also got off to a promising start.

Unfortunately, if perhaps not surprisingly, some of Basutoland's political leaders have not been able to leave the cooperative movement alone, and a struggle for the control of the Banking Union has resulted. The senior African employee and seven others were expelled by the committee of the Banking Union, at a reputed cost of £2,000 for pay in lieu of notice and litigation. A confused period of elections and counter-elections followed, with the Basutoland Congress Party assuming control, being displaced by court order, and eventually assuming control again at fresh elections. Ntsu Mokhehle is now president of the Basutoland Cooperative Banking Union as well as of the Congress Party, whose members dominate the union's executive.

Disruptive as this power-struggle at the top has been, it shows that the Basuto politicians have realized what a tremendous force the cooperative movement can become in Basutoland. Having for the time being gained control of its key institution, they will now have to show how well they can run it for the benefit of the ordinary peasant farmer, by whose active participation the whole cooperative system must succeed or fail.

One hopeful possibility in Basutoland is the increasing of

agricultural yields. The Department of Agriculture believes that no single crop now grown in Basutoland is yielding more than half of the maximum possible per acre. Maize, which is the country's major crop, could be trebled from the present 'efficient' yield of three bags per acre (one bag per acre is common). Sorghum could be doubled from four bags, and so could the average yields of wheat and peas from three bags per acre. If this optimum output were achieved, the annual value of territorial production could be raised from its 1960 level of £4 million to £13 million.

Clearly, agriculture is and must remain Basutoland's basic activity. Yet in 1961, a bad year, with perhaps fifteen per cent of its population away, Basutoland had to import 153,030 bags of maize and maize meal, costing the country £355,250, and 1,532 bags of sorghum costing £6,500. This in a country where maize and sorghum are the staples of diet. Basuto farmers have shown that they want to increase their productivity and are capable of doing so, given disinterested guidance and financial help. They must be given these things.

The quality and quantity of wool and mohair, Basutoland's other two main exports, could also be improved far beyond their present levels, as could the export of cattle and hides, though with these commodities, as with others in agriculture, Basutoland is of course dependent on the fluctuations in world prices. Wool, which is Basutoland's only major export, is in any case under increasing international challenge by synthetic fibre.

For the moment, however, the main problem is to improve the quality of Basuto wool, the country's only major export, which is degenerating through cross breeding with inferior sheep. This is extremely serious in a country most suited to the production of the finest merino wool. The flouting in this respect by some Basuto farmers both of their own traditional precepts for stock improvement (the Laws of Lerotholi) and official advice drove the Agricultural Department in 1960 into the dramatic cry that 'it is difficult to find words sufficiently adequate to warn the Basuto nation of the seriousness of neglecting and failing to improve their heritage – the merino – the life blood of Basutoland and bearer of the "Golden Fleece"'.

Really fine merino wool looks like having an assured market, and if the Agricultural Department, the cooperatives and the

District Councils continue to work in increasingly close cooperation, it should be possible to improve both quality and quantity
again. In 1961 the export of 7·4 million pounds of wool earned
Basutoland £804,656, whilst in 1951 only 6·8 million pounds
earned £1·65 million.

Almost everywhere one goes in Basutoland, one finds goats, and
whilst these can be terribly destructive if, as is common, their
grazing is uncontrolled, they are the basis of a valuable mohair
trade. The world demand for mohair is on the increase, and by
the selective breeding which is officially encouraged it should be
possible to increase greatly the 1961 export of 1·27 million pounds,
which earned £364,314. The post-war improvement is shown by
comparing this with the 1946 figures of 1·37 million pounds fetch-
ing only £80,162.

Considerable as is the problem of persuading farmers to breed
sheep only selectively, it is nothing compared to the improvement
and culling of cattle.

This is not a problem unique to Basutoland; in most Bantu
tribal societies cattle are a prestige symbol and hence also the means
of paying bride-price. Most Basuto farmers would rather have a
large number of inferior stock than a small number of prime
animals. This is changing, but only slowly, for the old ways die
hard when there is in fact no satisfactory new way of life, rooted
in strongly-based and satisfying values, to replace it. Despite the
enormous migration of industrial labour out of and back into
Basutoland, the country remains pastoral, and many a young
man goes to the mines to earn the money to buy the cattle to pay
bride-price.

Nevertheless, through a combination of natural and social
forces, the number both of cattle and of livestock generally in
Basutoland has decreased. In cattle, the decrease between 1938
and 1958 has been from 450,000 to 360,000; in horses, from
88,000 to 81,000; in sheep, from 1,600,000 to 1,230,000; and in
goats, from 570,000 to 505,000. This may help in the campaign of
soil conservation, but it has not been due to changed attitudes
and it merely means that the people's resources have shrunk. As
much as seventy per cent of the cattle dying annually do so not
through market slaughter but through malnutrition, exposure,
old age, and disease. No dairy industry exists, and the milk for

Maseru's 5,700 inhabitants has to be brought from South Africa. Today Basutoland imports more cattle and livestock than it exports, and this trend is rapidly growing as Basuto forced to leave South Africa spend some of their money on stock to take home.

Yet it is officially estimated that a net cattle export of 35–40,000 head, valued at £700,000 to £1·2 million, could be achieved through 'the following of a sound policy of cattle husbandry and management, accompanied by improvement in grazing and watering conditions'.

The key word here is a value judgement – 'sound'. When this is applied to cattle, which are the pivot of tribal values, and to grazing in a land-hungry country, we are back with the wider problems of social and agricultural revolution.

I have dealt in some detail with the possibilities of improving agricultural production in Basutoland, for calculations may soon have to be made of how many Basuto must be found *lebensraum* elsewhere or starve. Certainly a great deal could be done to improve production in volume and value, and the country could, with relatively modest British help, support perhaps nearly its present population at subsistence level after the inflow from wages of migrants in South Africa had substantially dried up. This, of course, is only the roughest of guesses, but it is, if anything, an optimistic one. It would certainly involve many more able-bodied men in working on the land. Where the then excess women now on the land and the rest of the 130,000 men and women now working in South Africa would go, no one seems to know.

Faced with these questions, most Basuto pin their hopes on minerals and industrialization. It is worth while looking at both closely.

As Basutoland lies in an area of South Africa where coal and diamonds have been mined, and copper, nickel, and platinum prospected, most Basuto assume that their country must be mineral-rich. This hopeful, and at present almost unshakeable conviction, is negatively reinforced by the fact that no thorough geological survey of the country has ever been made. But the results of a reconnaissance survey carried out in 1938 were most disappointing.

Coal exists, but not in payable quantity. Limestone deposits are of poor quality. The possibility of discovering oil in depth was described as highly speculative. Aside from plenty of good road metal and building stones, the only remotely hopeful mineral prospect reported was that of pipes and fissures of kimberlite. This opened wide the floodgates of hope for diamonds, as, in the words of the 1938 survey, 'any kimberlite outcrop may be considered a potential source of diamonds'.

Less acceptable to the Basuto, however, was the geologist's conclusion that in Basutoland the outlook for finding diamonds could not be considered promising. He was unable to find anyone, Mosuto or European, who could show him a diamond from a definite Basutoland source. The so-called diamonds said to have been found in Basutoland had invariably proved to be quartz crystals. The most that the Government geologist felt able to say in 1938 was that other kimberlite pipes and fissures might be found 'with more promising results'.

It did not, in fact, take very long for this to happen. In the fifties some genuine diamonds were found, and the situation was considered sufficiently promising by a Johannesburg mining magnate, Colonel Jack Scott, for him to obtain from the Paramount Chief a concession to prospect for and win diamonds.

This outside interest fired afresh the diamond dreams of the Basuto, who have always been suspicious of letting Europeans prospect in their country. It has also led to a great deal of bitter dispute, and to anger at the thought that South African capitalists, exploiters of Basuto miners for decades, were now to wax even richer on Basutoland's diamonds.

Very few of the critics, however, have been able to suggest how the expensive work of prospecting and possibly establishing a mine could otherwise be done. The most common answer to this question is that 'the Government' should do it, thus keeping all of Basutoland's wealth for and in the country. This is sound in theory; in practice, a British Government unwilling to grant Basutoland adequate funds for desperately needed 'guaranteed' investments in agriculture would hardly be in the market for speculative, even if promising, diamond prospecting.

The Basuto, or more correctly the Paramount Regent and the then still largely conservative advisory National Council, were prepared to accept Colonel Scott personally. What they were against was giving concessions to other South African mining houses, and especially to the Oppenheimers' Anglo-American Corporation which, through the international De Beers group, controls the western world's diamond markets.

As Colonel Scott was himself the head of a large South African mining house, and as the industry is significantly interconnected, the Basuto were drawing a fine distinction by making the 1955 concession a 'personal' one.

But the furore was all the greater when it became known that it would be possible for De Beers to join a company which Scott proposed to set up in Bermuda to exploit 'his' Basutoland concession. The Bermuda company was dropped.

Between 1955 and 1961 Scott continued prospecting on a modest scale. It is officially accepted that he spent £600,000 and won £140,000 worth of diamonds.

Great as was the interest in diamonds which all this stirred, it became widely greater when Basuto began to find diamonds themselves on the surface of a remote mountain area called Letseng la Terai. Situated in an isolated mountain valley in the north-east of the country at an altitude of 10,100 feet, and accessible only via a precarious bridle pass or by air, Letseng la Terai became the scene of a diamond rush which fired the imagination of every Mosuto. Tales of fantastic finds swept the country, and from far and near men flocked there, with women camp-followers not far behind. Conditions became both grim and hectic in the cold, remote valley where every bit of food had to be brought up on mules, to be sold at astronomical prices, and where many ill-equipped Basuto hopefuls suffered real hardship in the bitter winter.

The Government, through the Paramount Chief in whom all land and mineral rights are vested, stepped in, and a system of controlled prospecting and pegging was rapidly established. Since the end of 1961, only Basuto concession holders are allowed to prospect, their number is limited, and sales to other than officially licensed buyers is prohibited. An emergency landing strip was constructed at Letseng la Terai by the Government in September 1961, which brought in both supplies and buyers, and a tented police post with radio was established.

A brief amnesty was declared in order to let non-concession holders sell their finds to licensed buyers, and between September and December 1961 diamonds worth £29,300 were officially bought. This may not seem a great deal. Its meaning to Basuto concession holders becomes clearer when it is remembered that, of this four-month total, £21,930 was spread amongst less than 500 people. The annual return of an above average farm at present is only £100.

Certainly these pickings were considered important enough to have the Letseng la Terai area excluded from the new prospecting and mining concession which Colonel Scott obtained from the Paramount Chief, with the approval of the National Council, as of October 1961, but which he dropped in 1964.

The agreement gave the Basuto the long-term prospect of taxing severely an industry which notoriously requires heavy initial capital investment which must be written off over a lengthy period. They were to get a little money for two years, ensure the spending in that time of a little more money in the country, and might or might not have got some training in the complex higher skills of mining. There was no hard guarantee that Basuto would in fact have been trained for skilled jobs.

Read together with the labour legislation which was subsequently passed by the National Council and which imposes the objectionable 'ticket' system on future Basuto miners, the outlook for the Basuto was not overwhelmingly bright in mining. Judging from the net cost of £62,860 a year incurred by Scott for prospecting, some critics of the agreement felt that had the Government been able or willing to take the gamble initially a better bargain might have been struck now with someone else later on. But aside from some reported but transient interest on the part of the Israelis, other risk investors with the necessary technical resources have been notable by their absence. And since Scott decided to pull out of the agreement in 1964, Anglo-American have turned down suggestions that they might take it over. At the time of writing, the mining rights were held officially by the Basutoland Factory Estate Development Company, a shadowy Government-sponsored body with neither the capital nor the knowledge to make any attempt to continue Scott's work.

POUNDING WATERS

Critics of the British Government who deplore its reluctance to finance mining operations are on much stronger ground when they slate its faint-heartedness and procrastination in doing something to harness and exploit Basutoland's most obvious asset: water.

Though in Basutoland conditions are authoritatively agreed to be 'ideal for the development of hydroelectric power', the only public electricity in the country comes from Maseru's thermal plant. If anyone thought of setting up a good-sized factory in the country, he would have to generate his own power. And whilst the country abounds in water, there is, for lack of channelling, no irrigation, though a good deal of land would benefit by it.

These paradoxes persist for lack of money, and not for any lack of detailed consultants' reports on how low-cost power and water could be obtained with relatively little capital investment.

Two of South Africa's largest rivers, the mighty Orange and the Tugela, have their source in Basutoland, as have the major tributaries of the Caledon River, which forms the north-western border with the Republic. A major part of South African farming, industry and towns depend upon the waters of these rivers.

At the same time the Orange Free State Province of South Africa, which borders Basutoland on the Caledon, suffers from a chronic shortage of cheap, clean water, a shortage accentuated by the post-war development of the Free State gold mines, which have themselves found it worth while to set up expensive plants to repurify their present high-price supplies. This same mining development, and that of ancillary industries, has created a great new demand for cheap electricity on Basutoland's borders. The story of how Britain's faint-hearted parsimony has caused Basutoland to miss a vast opportunity can be told in a few sentences.

The Ox-Bow scheme was proposed in 1956, to cost a total of £8·9 million. It would enable Basutoland to deliver huge amounts of clean water to South Africa at one third or less of current prices, and also to offer bulk electricity at a fractional cost. The first stage of the scheme would cost only £2,124,000, but would give Basutoland ample and very cheap power and water for any conceivable industrialization (in which cheap power is a strong attraction) and for irrigation. It would still allow substantial quantities of both water and power to be offered for sale to South Africa at cut-prices.

Britain, however, has not been prepared to proceed without prior assurances that South Africa would buy the Ox-Bow's water and electricity. As a result, nothing has been done except belatedly to set up the hydrological stations urgently recommended in 1951.

In 1963, the South African Government announced a £225 million development scheme for the Orange River which will more than meet the Free State's water and power needs. The South African Government has coolly and unilaterally decided what is to happen to the waters of the Orange. Though more than half of the waters to be used derive from the catchment in Basutoland, and though the Orange is an international river, Dr Verwoerd's Government has decided that it will use $97\frac{1}{2}$ per cent of this water. Basutoland will graciously be allowed to keep $2\frac{1}{2}$ per cent.

I have established that the British authorities were simply not consulted. They have politely and confidentially reminded South Africa of Basutoland's interest in the waters of the Orange; South Africa has ignored this reminder; and still the British authorities have made no public protest or comment.

If the South Africans are allowed by Britain to get away with what amounts to a monumental act of international piracy, a dispute would certainly arise between a self-governing or independent Basutoland and South Africa which would rival that between the Israelis and the Arabs over the waters of the Jordan, or that between Egypt and the Sudan over the Nile.

Yet Britain has made no protest whilst international and South African consulting engineers, reportedly appointed in 1963 by Dr Verwoerd, proceed with detailed plans. It is notable that two of the major consultants believed to have been appointed are British: Sir Alexander Gibb and Partners for canals and Sir William Halcrow and Partners for tunnels. And it is surely ironical that the latter firm was the one which in 1954 delivered to the Basutoland Administration a report on obtaining hydroelectricity and bulk water supplies from the Upper Orange. Nine years later, not even the urgently recommended hydrological stations, without which planning is impossible, had been set up.

If ever there was a cheap and practicable scheme, it is the Ox-Bow. The most eminent professional consultants have stressed for over nineteen wasted years that in Basutoland 'conditions are ideal for the development of hydroelectric power'. The Morse Mission, which included Brigadier C. G. Hawes, yet another eminent consulting engineer, described the Ox-Bow scheme as excellent.

With a production of 353 million kilowatt hours a year (at only 0·34d. per kWh), this scheme could supply forty million gallons of pure water a day to the Orange Free State and even to areas as far away as Johannesburg's vast mining and industrial complex. What is more, this water could be delivered in the Free State at 1½d.–10d. per 1,000 gallons, compared with the 2s. 6d.–5s. at present being charged there.

The Morse Mission was understating the case when it said that if Basutoland constructed the scheme, South Africa 'would be given enormous benefits at reasonable cost and Basutoland could develop its one real asset – water – with considerable advantage'.

Yet the British Government could not be tempted even though the cost of £8·9 million was based on the redemption of plant and equipment over only twenty years, of pipelines over twenty-five, and of civil engineering works over fifty years.

There was, of course, good reason for Britain to doubt whether the South African Government – left to its own devices – would officially contract to buy the Ox-Bow power and water. Dr Verwoerd hardly wishes to help Basutoland to become economically solvent, and the Ox-Bow scheme in full operation, if its power and water were sold, would have gone a long way towards achieving that. Revenue from water would have been at least £500,000 a year and might have exceeded £3,000,000, whilst electricity would have added a further £90,000 annually. (Basutoland's 1960–61 total expenditure was £4·98 million; its ordinary revenue, £3·72 million.)

Yet South Africa may have had little choice, if international law was to be observed. As the Morse Report clearly states:

The Orange River is international and any development on it, whether in Basutoland or in the Union [of South Africa], can properly be carried out only after discussions between the parties.

Moreover, no two groups in South Africa can exert more pressure on the Government than the farmers and the mines, and these are precisely the two groups which would have benefited most dramatically from the Ox-Bow scheme, cutting the costs of their operations and so earning increased profits.

Sir John Maud, Britain's Ambassador to South Africa and High Commissioner for the Territories, is on record as having composed an Ode to the Chamber of Mines, which he delivered most elegantly at one of its banquets. There is no record of any approach by Sir John on the Ox-Bow scheme to the chamber, which could on its own have bought all of the water involved.

There is a good deal of wishful thinking about industrialization in Basutoland, where it is almost universally believed that this would meet the need for employment. The obvious anomaly inevitably quoted is that Basutoland, a wool-producing and blanket-wearing country, has not even a blanket factory. Other possibilities raised by Basuto enthusiasts are a factory to can peaches, which are grown in the country, a tannery and a match factory.

Unfortunately, expert opinion is very well founded in its considered opinion that 'the opportunities for industrial development are not promising'.

Basutoland's population is not only small, it also has a very low purchasing power. The country has no source of cheap and abundant electrical power or skilled artisans and technicians. Its main requirements are the product of highly organized industry with which it is almost impossible for small units to compete. To top all this, it is limited in the imposition of possible protective tariffs by its customs agreement with South Africa, through whose good offices Basutoland annually obtains a disproportionately high sum which makes up half of its ordinary revenue.

For these reasons, even the obviously appealing idea of a blanket factory hardly bears examination. In the first place, only four per cent of Basutoland's wool production is of the low grade kind economically suitable for blanket production. Secondly, the costs of transporting it to a central factory in mountainous Basutoland would push costs too high. Thirdly, the Basuto are extremely fastidious customers, insisting on complex, multi-coloured patterns of which wide ranges are available in their traditional, near-by South African shopping centres. Finally, any Basutoland factory would have to meet the intense competition of the very large and highly organized South African blanket industry.

These detailed difficulties apply in large measure to other proposed industries. The Morse Commission considered that a small clothing factory, associated with a cotton mill in South Africa or the Rhodesias, might expand in stages to include a mill, producing low grade utility blankets from offsorts. Canning seems out of the question on any significant scale because of South Africa's enormous and highly competitive fruit canning industry. A plant for producing dehydrated vegetables might, however, be a proposition.

A number of small new channels for non-agricultural employment will, of course, develop if agricultural production and the cash income of farmers increase. The fact that none is spectacular should not be interpreted as meaning that they are unimportant, but they will leave the major part of Basutoland's vast and growing unemployment problem untouched.

Certainly what chances there are for the establishment of industry will never be tested until there is cheap and abundant electric power. The low price at which such power could be obtained from the Ox-Bow scheme would enable certain South African or Rhodesian fertilizers and alloys to be produced in Basutoland at a 3–7½ per cent saving in costs. But this highly speculative idea depends, once again, on the Ox-Bow scheme being implemented. Even if Britain's appeasement of South Africa forbids a legal dispute over the launching of the Orange River scheme, this must on no account be used as a pretext for not immediately proceeding with the first £2·12 million stage of the Ox-Bow plan. Not to proceed would be to compound the failure of the past. This relatively trifling outlay would give Basutoland 44·1 million kWh of electricity a year at a cost of well below 1d. a kWh. It would also make 7,860 million gallons of water available at only 1·64d. per 1,000 gallons. The plan involves relatively little storage construction and could thus be swiftly implemented.

There is a good deal of informed criticism of the South African Orange River scheme as at present outlined, and it may well be that it will take some years to reach the point of meeting the full need for cheap water of the Free State farmers. If this proves to be the case, there would still be a good chance of selling Ox-Bow water to those farmers. If not, then £850,000 needed for the building of a pipeline to the Caledon could be saved and used instead for sorely needed irrigation installations in Basutoland.

True, the scheme would then not be commercially 'sound'. The British Government would not get its money back for a very long time, if ever. But, after all, how much money has Basuto labour, driven by British neglect to South Africa's mines, not already given Britain?

It would be no bad thing if Basuto children had electric light for studying, if progressive farmers could use electrically driven farm machinery, if huts were heated by electricity instead of burning precious dung, and if water-powered pumps could bring irrigation water to the fields for the growing of more food.

And if, as seems at least possible, an economic siege should be laid in the future by South Africa against Basutoland, its position would be greatly strengthened by having ample and cheap supplies of its own electric power.

It is absurd to pretend that Britain can give Basutoland even a fighting chance to survive economically if she insists on making aid 'pay' by normal commercial standards. Basutoland is not a normal country, economically or physically, and Britain is not altogether without responsibility for this. The situation remains today as it was in 1960:

It is clear that if Basutoland's economic advancement is made dependent on the Union [of South Africa's] Nationalist government, the territory will continue to stagnate. Its politically ambitious and active African leadership, frustrated by economic barriers, may well become embittered. They will blame Britain for not being prepared to spend even £2·12 million in order to provide the prerequisite for economic, and therefore social, advancement.*

PILGRIM'S PROGRESS

The description of Basutoland as an 'African Switzerland' may be scenically apposite, but it does not extend to its people. Where Switzerland's major assets are the modern skills and education of its people, Basutoland has not even one technical college.

* James Fairbairn, *New Statesman* 6 February 1960.

The Basuto have long had the enviable reputation of being one of the most literate of African peoples, and certainly they have keenly appreciated education since the days when Moshesh, the founder of the nation, invited missionaries into his country to open schools. One of the first achievements of these missionaries was the establishment of printing works to publish books, religious tracts and translations in the Sotho language, for which they evolved an orthography. The Morija Press, which literally put Basutoland on the map, celebrated its centenary in 1961, but the tradition of printing goes back even further. This printing facilitated education and stimulated a Sotho literature, though one would like to know just what the Basuto of the 1860s made of *Pilgrim's Progress*, the first work to be translated and published.

There is accordingly a long tradition behind the pride which the Basuto take in their language and literacy. But in Africa literacy and education are relative, and today the Basuto are fast being outstripped by other African countries. Thus whilst it is true that perhaps ninety-five per cent of the children go to school *at some time*, very many of them remain only for two or three years.

Whereas the total number of students enrolled at primary schools in 1960 was 136,111 – probably the highest proportionately in Africa – the number enrolled at secondary schools was only 1,836. But even these figures do not give the full picture of wastage, which in 1960 looked like this:

1st year of primary	41,978
3rd year of primary	23,316
6th year (end of lower primary)	8,858
8th year (end of upper primary)	2,900
1st year of secondary	792
3rd year of secondary	306
5th year of secondary (sitting for matriculation)	67

The imbalance between boys and girls at school is also alarming.

While nearly all girls between ten and sixteen are at school, half the boys are absent, most of them tending cattle, so that while nearly all the female population of Basutoland will soon be functionally literate, only half the male population will be.

The British Government cannot feel complacent about its educational record in the Territory. Wide awake as the present Department of Education is, it is still hampered by lack of funds. As for the past, education in Basutoland has been the creation of the missions rather than of the British Government, which for decades starved Basutoland of the funds which its own experts declared were essential for healthy development.

Even in the period immediately following the Second World War, the attitude of the British Government was that expanded education should be overwhelmingly financed from Basutoland's own revenues. If the Basuto produced more and paid more in tax, then there would be more schools and teacher training. Until then, the British Government sincerely regretted that it could not find the £324,000 which a distinguished official commission considered essential. 1946 was admittedly a difficult time financially for Britain, but it was also supposed to be the dawn of a brave new post-war world, especially for colonial peoples.

As it is, the whole country of a million people had in 1961 only twenty-three secondary schools, and of these only four reached matriculation standard. Of 2,600 primary school teachers, more than 1,000, or over two-fifths, have no professional qualifications of any sort. Classes are large, and the teacher: pupil ratio has declined from 1:47 in 1950 to 1:54 in 1960. There are junior secondary school places for only half the children writing the qualifying examination. Poor as this is, it represents a very considerable expansion over only four years. In 1957 only seven schools offered the partial secondary education of three years, and in 1936 there was only one. Despite post-war building, it is still common in very many lower primary schools to see six classes in one large hall, which is used as a church on Sundays.

Nevertheless, some notable achievements must be chalked up to primary education in Basutoland. In this country of mountains and poor communications it is officially claimed that no child is beyond reasonable reach of a primary school, and education at this level is free. Parents have only to buy books, which cost from

8–10s. a year. Boarding schools naturally play a considerable part, and here parents must pay £16–30 a year, though this figure is subsidized.

A great deal of resentment has understandably been aroused when this very low *per capita* expenditure is compared with the relatively enormous amount spent by government on the hitherto segregated, English-medium primary schools for the children of civil servants. There were four such *schools* in 1960 for 113 pupils, whilst African *classes* average fifty-four pupils. Even greater resentment is aroused because of the very handsome educational allowances paid by government to enable expatriate civil servants to send their children out of the country for secondary education. No white children go to secondary school in Basutoland.

In a Sotho proverb, education is likened to a three-legged pot, standing on the legs of the missions, the people and the government.

It would be hard to over-emphasize the role which the various missions have played in developing the educational system which they started in Basutoland. Unlike other parts of Africa, ninety-eight per cent of Basutoland's schools are still run by missions today. The early stress on primary literacy, chiefly directed at religious instruction, was common to the whole of southern Africa.

Until roughly the turn of the century, Basutoland bore comparison with South Africa: since then it has increasingly lagged behind. This lag has been most painfully noticeable in secondary education. As late as 1936, there was only one secondary school in Basutoland, and that stopped two years short of matriculation.

It was only when Fort Hare in South Africa discontinued matriculation classes that, in 1939, Basutoland got its first proper high school. It was and remains a government school.

The criticism most commonly levelled against the missions in the educational field is that their schools have tended to be religiously exclusive, and that rival efforts at expansion have at times looked like a 'soul-catching' race. Thus even the tactful 1960 Report of the Education Department declares that

much of the notable improvement in accommodation and equipment standards in very recent years has resulted from healthy competition, but the Department has been hard-pressed at times to maintain the balance between denominational enthusiasm and genuine educational needs.

Such competition has been spurred by the planned and massive 'push' which the Roman Catholic Church has made since the Second World War in all spheres of Basuto life. In numbers of schools, the recent progress of the three main denominations has been:

	1945	1960
Paris Evangelical	459	465
Roman Catholic	334	448
English Church	82	130

From 1906 onwards, the government has given the mission schools some financial assistance, either through grants-in-aid or, increasingly, for teachers' salaries. But this help was until 1940 based on the assumption that what the missions could not themselves raise had to be met from Basutoland's budget, unaided by grants from Britain. The country was poor; its annual revenue only passed £½ million after the war; government help for education was small.

The Government was not only starved of funds but also of men. It was only after 1927 that Basutoland ceased to share a Director of Education with Swaziland and Bechuanaland. Education was cut back steeply during the Depression (spelt with a capital D in all contemporary Annual Reports), and by slumping customs revenue from South Africa. The steeply climbing cost of living swallowed up almost all of the limited increases in available funds.

Thus even if the Government had wanted to bring the missions under central control, it was in no position to flex its barely evident muscles. In 1946 an official commission could report of mission schools that 'no effective steps have ever been taken to control their foundation or regulate the quality of their work'. Until

1946 there was even a separate Catholic Teachers' Association.

Control was formally initiated in 1948, and today the Government pays the salaries of all teachers in recognized mission schools. Teachers' salaries have been progressively improved over the past decade in all three Territories, but even today the Basutoland Education Department lacks the staff for adequate control and inspection. In 1960 there were over 100 schools for each supervisor, who also had a heavy load of administrative duties. The situation is a little better, today.

The whole schools system has been put under great additional strain by South Africa's unilateral decision in 1953 to bar Basuto children from its schools. No one would in any case wish to see Basuto children brainwashed by South Africa's so-called Bantu Education, but the country is still far from receiving adequate compensatory aid, especially for secondary education, from Britain. Only £250,000 has been spent on education between 1940 and 1960 from the Colonial Development and Welfare Fund. This is equivalent to only £12,500 a year, and most of it has had to go into buildings and equipment.

The Basuto are hungry for education, though many parents still either do not realize the importance of uninterrupted attendance for boys or feel economically unable to do without their sons' labour in cattle-herding for long periods. But educational levies have been on the whole well received; District Councils have attempted with varying success to meet official expenditure on a £ for £ basis, and sufficient money has been collected by the Basuto to keep a Higher Education Fund providing a few bursaries for university study.

Education is today far and away the biggest single item of Government expenditure, but in a poor and long-neglected country this bears no necessary relation to the needs. In 1959–60 education took twelve per cent of total Government expenditure, but this, including British aid, meant only £353,000 in cash, or 51s. for each pupil enrolled. The system was only kept going because voluntary agencies spent a further £230,000, or 34s. per pupil.

Both the figures and the percentages have climbed steeply since, mainly because a long overdue increase in teachers' salaries was finally sanctioned. This increase was met largely by a special

T – H

British grant, but in future it will have to be met by Basutoland unless C.D. & W.F. allocations, or direct grants-in-aid, are increased.

Perhaps the most remarkable educational achievement in Basutoland has been Pius XII University College, which last year became the National University of Basutoland, Bechuanaland, and Swaziland (U.B.B.S.). From an extremely modest beginning in 1945, with four lecturers catering for five students in a single classroom, this R.C. institution grew under Roman Catholic auspices until in 1963 it had a student body of over 170 with a cosmopolitan staff of thirty-nine. Set in beautiful mountainous surroundings at Roma, some twenty-five miles from Maseru, the college today boasts an impressive group of handsome sandstone buildings, including hostels for almost 200 students. It has been offering degree courses in arts, science, social science, commerce, and education, as well as a two-year post-school certificate course leading to a junior secondary teachers diploma. Special courses in subjects such as public administration and local government have been run in consultation with the Government, and civil servants have been able to study at the college for the intermediate examination of the Chartered Institute of Secretaries.

All this was created in only fifteen years by the Catholics with token grants from the High Commission Administrations.

There are about the U.B.B.S. (or Roma University, as it is commonly called) four remarkable aspects: that a university college should exist at all in a small, poor, underdeveloped, and dependent country like Basutoland; that it should have been a Catholic university; that, run in an anti-apartheid country by an anti-apartheid denomination, it should have been obliged to limit its official student body to non-whites; and that it should for fifteen years have been so poorly patronized by the Government of the High Commission Territories whose peoples it seemed ideally placed to serve.

The fact that Pius XII existed at all and that it was a Catholic institution were inter-related. The Catholic post-war 'push' in education has already been noted, and Pius XII was one aspect of it. The 'apartheid' character of the student body resulted from the college's affiliation to the University of South Africa, which is an external-degree-awarding body.

The South African matriculation, or university entrance examination, is only equivalent to the British General Certificate of Education at 'O' level – South African schools in general have no sixth form – and education in the Territories has until very recently been linked with South Africa. Hence, Pius XII could not affiliate to, say, London University, as the university college in Salisbury has done. With the increasingly fanatical application of educational apartheid, the University of South Africa threatened to withdraw Roma's affiliation altogether if it admitted white students, and though a few have studied there nevertheless, latterly the South Africans have become more insistent.

This South African connexion has been a difficulty in general education as well, but the problem is well on the way to solution since the High Commission Territories introduced their own Junior Certificate examinations. The South African matriculation examination is likewise being replaced by British examinations.

The Catholic authorities were no happier about this obnoxious South African connexion than the students (half of whom are South Africans), but the problem has been to find an alternative. If entrance standards were raised to British levels, students would first have to go through a specially created two-year post-matriculation course. The college, already in dire financial straits, would have found the creation and staffing of this course difficult, and so would students. One alternative would have been affiliation to an American university, but changed curricula might have been unsuitable. The other alternative was for Roma to award its own degrees, and though this presented obvious difficulties for a tiny, isolated college, even under the benevolent eye of a British university, this was the solution reached.

The Basutoland Administration could have helped, had it not been for the Catholic nature of Pius XII. Though almost half the students were not Catholics, like two-thirds of the faculty, Pius XII was under absolute Catholic control. It was true that students obtained exemptions from the Index of forbidden books with relative ease, but the Index was part of the college, and while teaching was generally free, it was still subject to some limitation of subject and approach. Now, under new arrangements, the Catholics retain control over the college's faculties of theology and philosophy, and have their own hall of residence for Catholic students, so maintaining a Roman Catholic 'enclave', but the rest of the college has been secularized.

It looks very much as though it was financial need which finally solved the college's denominational problem. It was obviously uneconomic to run a university college for only 170 students and to employ forty lecturers, especially when running costs per student were £500–600 and fees only £100. Expansion to accommodate, at maintained standards, a student body of, say, 300 would have involved a capital outlay of something like £75,000 and additional recurrent annual costs of £50,000 for five years. The Roman Catholic Church has its own order of world-wide priorities, and it seems that Roma was not high on the list.

Now that overall denominational control has vanished, the British authorities will help to finance the college and will encourage more students from all three Territories to go there. In 1960 Roma had a student body of 167. Of these, thirty-four were from Basutoland itself, twelve were from Swaziland and only two from Bechuanaland, with all High Commission students holding bursaries that covered £90 of the £100 annual fees. Forty-one students came from the Rhodesias and Nyasaland, and seventy-seven from South Africa. Since then, the South African authorities have begun placing enormous obstacles in the way of African students from the Republic who want to study at Roma, where they can escape the bitter and humiliating farce of Dr Verwoerd's 'tribal colleges'. At least two students were refused passports to return and complete their courses at Roma at the beginning of 1964, and it seems unlikely that new students from the Republic will be allowed to enrol at all in the future. It remains to be seen whether the South African Government will make transit difficult for students travelling from Bechuanaland and Swaziland to Roma in Basutoland. If this were tried, it would be up to the British authorities to bring the strongest possible pressure to bear, for under present arrangements the students cannot even be transported by air without South African permission.

Understandably, rumours have, in this sort of situation, circulated amongst students at Roma that the authorities are trying to prevent a communications crisis by pandering to Dr Verwoerd. In March 1964, after a few lecturers had not been re-appointed, the university felt obliged publicly to deny that twenty of the thirty-five lecturers had been dismissed in order to please South Africa and thus keep the borders open. There was, the university authorities emphatically stated, no intention of turning U.B.B.S. into an inferior 'tribal' college, and whilst it was true that there were no faculties of politics or political science, these subjects were included in the curriculum.

The problem will now be to direct sufficient students to Roma from the three Territories. There is no common patriotism shared by the Swazi, the Batswana, and the Basuto, though the latter two peoples are related, and even Basuto students, isolated in their little mountain enclave, understandably prefer to study overseas. But overseas study is expensive, and once the Territories' bottleneck in secondary education is broken, it is doubtful whether even the Americans – or the Russians – will offer enough scholarships to accommodate all aspirants. There should thus be an important role for Roma to play in the future of all three Territories.

The future of Roma itself raises the question of where Basutoland's greatest educational needs really lie. Is an expansion of secondary education required in order to make possible a flow of university graduates? Certainly if the country is to make self-government, let alone independence, meaningful, it will need more than the 104 officially counted Basuto graduates it had in 1960. Of these, only fifty-nine were working at home, sixteen were doing post-graduate study, and twenty-one of the remaining twenty-nine were employed in South Africa. More graduates will be needed – and at home.

But the worst deficiency of Basutoland's educational system is not only the lack of qualified teachers, nor the resultant poor quality of education, nor yet the lack of ordinary secondary schools. The clearest need is for technical and vocational education, for there is not a single technical or commercial high school or college in the whole country, and until recently it was even impossible to obtain some commercial training in general secondary schools. There is one artisan training centre offering a five-year course in the building and engineering trades – this had an enrolment of 102 in 1960, when it also ran a one-year post-secondary school course in commerce – and a mission-run technical school which turns out village craftsmen in motor-mechanics, and blacksmithing, carpentry, and building and leatherwork. There are three craft schools training weavers for a struggling tourist industry, and that is all.

What Basutoland patently requires, therefore, is not to establish a university faculty of engineering, but to devote a major part of a dramatically enlarged secondary school programme to agricultural, technical, and commercial institutions. From the ranks of their students will come the great middle range of administrators, technicians, and scientific farmers on whose skill and devotion the tenuous hopes of Basutoland's viable independence must rest.

These needs are today widely realized in Basutoland. With primary education so relatively advanced, the National Council has decided to concentrate all future resources on secondary schools. This is a decision which some independent African countries have hesitated to take, for fear of the political repercussions from angry parents of excluded primary-school-age children.

It is hard to know exactly what most Africans expect from the magic of independence, but two of these expectations are almost universal: human dignity and schooling for every child. Where other African countries, however, could subsist even if education lagged, Basutoland must train and use its manpower or go under.

It is ridiculous to expect the Basuto, in their present poverty, themselves to finance the sort of programme which they need. In educational keenness and aptitude, they have more than proved themselves under very trying circumstances. Today, Britain must give them the educational tools without which they cannot even struggle to survive.

Urgent action is needed also to improve Basutoland's health services. Figures already quoted show the frightening incidence of malnutrition and its related scourges like pellagra.

This is all the more disturbing when one remembers how fortunate Basutoland is in being free, largely because of its climate, from tropical diseases like malaria, and bilharzia. The Basutoland winters are cold and dry, with the rainy season during the warm summer months, and the country has, by any standards, a healthy climate.

Because of poor nutrition, however, the Basuto have a very low resistance to disease, while in rural areas water supplies are so polluted that enteric diseases are common. Of preventable diseases, infants suffer from a great deal of gastro-enteritis, children and adolescents from typhoid and diphtheria, and all ages from tuberculosis.

Much would be done to improve nutrition if Basuto could be persuaded, as slowly increasing numbers are, to vary the crops grown, and above all to raise vegetables. Here there are two encouraging institutions.

The first is the long-established Basutoland Homemakers' Association which, established in 1935, has today some 160 women's clubs covering the territory. They are all-Basuto affairs, and give impressive proof of the progressive attitude of many Basuto women. Amongst their aims is the upholding of Christian standards in the home, the discussion of current affairs and the fostering of indigenous crafts. But most important, for health, the Homemakers emphasize the proper feeding of the family, the growing and use of vegetables, the rearing of good milk-cows, fowls and pigs, and cleanliness. Their excellent work was recognized in 1960 when the Homemakers' veteran president, Mrs J. Mohapeloa, was invited to attend a United Nations seminar in Addis Ababa on 'Women's participation in public life'. But, as in many other instances of Basuto self-help, the Homemakers' efforts have been hampered by lack of funds for a full-time organizer. The British Administration has felt able to find only £100 a year for them.

The nutrition of Basuto children has been so poor that in recent years U.N.I.C.E.F. has supplied tons of dried milk powder, donated by the people of Australia, Canada and the U.S.A. (It has also sent hospital equipment.) An increasing interest is being shown in Basutoland's health problems by various United Nations agencies, and the F.A.O., W.H.O. and U.N.I.C.E.F. are active. Staff is international. They included for instance, an Israeli expert, Miss Rivka Levitt, who advises the voluntary, interdenominational school-feeding organization; tuberculosis and other surveys have been made; and control projects are under way.

But, with all this help, the desperate shortage remains one of staff and equipment. On a *per capita* basis, Basutoland is worse off by far than Swaziland or Bechuanaland, as the following table for 1961 shows:

	Basutoland	Bechuanaland	Swaziland
People per doctor	21,300	14,500	8,900
People per hospital bed	700	350	400
People per nurse	12,300	2,700	1,900

Some of the nine Government and five mission hospitals in Basutoland are of a high standard, with two of them recognized as training hospitals by South Africa. Nurses and other auxiliary staff are trained in Basutoland, and an attempt is being made to cover the country with services radiating out from strategically placed hospitals. But two massive problems remain: how to serve the 250,000 people in the mountains, and how to obtain adequate funds.

This is a country whose 1960 official report admits that polio vaccinations were uncompleted 'due to the usual annual summer gastro-enteritis', and that the number of diphtheria cases reported 'has remained high because of the lack of sufficient field personnel to immunise children who are too far from dispensaries'.

Some £450,000 was spent on health by the Government in 1960–61, equivalent to nine per cent of total expenditure or roughly 14s. per head of resident population. This was an increase of nearly one third on 1958–9, and three times as much as ten years earlier, which will give some idea of what services have been like.

In addition, £60,000 was spent in 1960–61 on the running of an old-established leper settlement. Though a mental hospital is still only in project, Basutoland has the services of an African psychiatrist, which must make it nearly unique in southern and central Africa. He works in what is rather euphemistically termed a mental home.

A fascinating private attempt to bring medical services to remote areas is being made by BASOMED (Basutoland Socio-Medical Services Ltd). As its name states, this body, which has distinguished patronage, aims at a broad approach to health problems, but in its teething stage depended largely on the interesting personality of its founder and former director, Dr Carl van Aswegen. An unusual, British-trained Afrikaner, he gave up private practice to conduct BASOMED, basing himself near Maseru but going regularly into the mountains, either on horseback or by charter plane.

This and other private efforts seem, however, unlikely to make more than a dent in the medical needs of Basutoland. Once again it is money in substantial quantities and crash training programmes that are needed.

Against this background, it is interesting to note that the National Council has not in fact done very much since 1961, though it has talked a great deal. What it has done it has done slowly, as with the abolition of racial discrimination.

This could be ascribed to the preponderance of members nominated by the Paramount and of officials, which has left the largest party, the B.C.P., in opposition. It could also be ascribed to the 'dead hand' of the Administration, which can ignore the Council. But both these would be explanations highly charitable to the Basuto themselves.

It is true that on occasion the elected members of the Council have taken a commendably militant and constructive course, upsetting some hallowed colonial legislative practices in the process. Thus when the High Commissioner, Sir John Maud, opened the 1962 session of the council with a vintage version of the smooth, non-committal speeches which were his hallmark, the council revolted. An unexpected alliance of Mokhehle's Congress and Chief Jonathan's National Party moved a motion of no confidence in the speech from the Throne, on the grounds that Sir John had blandly ignored most of the real issues facing the country, failing to mention such pressing problems as the need for a Basutoland currency, the kidnapping by South African police of Anderson Ganyile in Basutoland, the threatened position of Basuto workers in South Africa, and economic development. The no-confidence move came within an ace of succeeding, and a slightly more tactful amendment by Chief Jonathan was lost by a single vote.

At other times, however, the unorthodoxy of moves in the

council has been less constructive. The B.C.P. in particular has been known to vote against amendments introduced with its agreement, and Ntsu Mokhehle has led an unpleasant campaign against the council's president, Mr Walter Stanford. Invited to assume the post in 1961, with the agreement of all parties, for an initial one-year term, Stanford was before very long being denounced in the council by Mokhehle as a tick and bloodsucker on the back of the Basuto. When, as president, Stanford also became chairman of the constitutional commission, this campaign was stepped up, though he survived with the backing of the Paramount, the Government, and the other parties.

At times, too, the whole embryonic party system has been threatened, as when chiefs have voted against Government measures, such as supplementary estimates, not in pursuit of any coherent policy but as a sort of blackmail to force the Government to increase allowances for council members.

There has, of course, been no lack of issues on which the British Administration has refused to act despite Basuto pressure in the council. But there have also been problems left untackled because the opposition of the Administration has been reinforced by sharp divisions of opinion amongst the Basuto leaders. The most disturbing of these problems concerns the right of entry and residence in Basutoland, and hence the position of political refugees from South Africa.

Basutoland's Entry and Residence Proclamation is a truly remarkable document which outrages almost every principle of personal and political liberty to which Britain supposedly subscribes; the draft of it was opposed in 1957–8 by a majority of members in the old, purely advisory National Council, but was nevertheless promulgated.* And now that the South Africans are demanding travel papers from Basuto entering the Republic, the High Commission Territories are moving towards retaliatory demands, which may complicate the position further.

So far, anyone has normally been able to enter Basutoland and remain there for three months, unless he was declared to be a prohibited immigrant; the problem has arisen with the acquisition of residence permits after three months.

* Petition from the Basutoland National Party to the Secretary of State for Commonwealth Relations, 1962.

Applications go first through a District Control Council, where the agreement and judgement of the local chief is crucial. Thus there are no uniform criteria in practice. This is bad enough, but there is also a Central Control Board, whose proceedings are not bound by court rules of evidence but whose chairman can put witnesses under oath.

Worse still, no decision of either District or Central Control Boards 'shall be open to question in any court on the ground that such board has failed to take into account any matter which it is required to take into account, or any point of fact or merit'.*

And then, to cap it all, there is a so-called Appeal Board which can decide, *on its own motion*, to revoke residence permits already granted by a lower board. Anyone having his permit taken away by the Appeal Board can appeal to – the Appeal Board. Thus this 'Appeal' Board is all powerful, and it consists of just two members: the Resident Commissioner and Paramount Chief or his nominee.

Despite repeated appeals and protests, the British authorities refuse to alter this iniquitous system, and have even defended it warmly, claiming without justification that it also has the support of 'the Basuto'. In point of fact, even the Paramount Chief has not bothered to attend the Appeal Board meetings, doubtless in the knowledge that if he disagreed with the Resident Commissioner, the decision would then go to the High Commissioner, who in any case possessed the power to grant his own special permits. The granting or revocation of permits can and does mean the difference between freedom and Verwoerd's jails to refugees. Yet until mid-1964 these two British officials, responsible to no one for their decisions, have held these permits in their absolute power.

There must, of course, be some system of control and of dealing with persons who, after being granted residence, may become a danger to the State. But this could well be met by making deportation subject to court appeal, so that at least a man would know the reason for any steps taken against him; it is insufferable that the same men should play judge and jury. If the spurious argument that the interests of 'the Basuto' are being somehow protected in this way is to be given any validity, 'the Basuto', through their

* Basutoland Entry and Residence Proclamation, 1958 (No. 13 of 1958, as amended).

elected representatives, must have a voice in final decisions. There can be no valid justification for the present system.

Amongst those who suffer under the Entry and Residence Proclamation is Basutoland's Indian community, members of which have been consigned to an administrative limbo.

The Basuto have always jealously guarded their land, and have steadfastly refused, since the days of Moshesh, to allow any of it to be bought by non-Basuto. This fundamental attitude was formulated in 1895 with Moshesh's 'Law of Trade', which has had a permanent effect on settlement by non-Basuto ever since. Its wording is both colourful and precise:

I, Moshoeshoe, write for any trader, whoever he may be, already in my land, and for any who may come to trade with the Basutos; my word is this:

Trade to me and my Tribe is a good thing; I wish to promote it.

Any trader who wishes to establish a shop, must first obtain permission from me. Should he build a house, I grant him no right to sell it. Further, I do not grant him liberty to plough the fields, but only to plant a small vegetable garden. The trader who fancies that the place he is sojourning belongs to him, must dismiss the thought; if not, he is to quit; for there is no place belonging to the whites in my land, and I have granted no white man a place, either by word, or by writing.

It was under these conditions that Europeans and, later, Indian traders came to Basutoland, and it is on the basis of this Law of Trade that the present Entry and Residence Proclamation excludes all non-Basuto from permanent residence rights.

But what is a Basuto? In terms of the proclamation, he must be an African. But many of the descendants of the Indian traders who came to Basutoland from the 1880s onwards have intermarried with the Basuto. They settled mainly in the Butha Butah and Leribe districts, and when jealous white traders incited British officials to have them expelled, Chief Jonathan, the father of the present leader of the National Party, accepted them as his subjects in Basuto law and custom.

There are today some 250 Indians in Basutoland, and perhaps 250 Indo-Basuto, or people of mixed blood. Some ninety per cent of them have been born in Basutoland, and a large proportion live as Basuto peasants, tilling the land under a chief. Only seventeen Indians are traders, and the remainder of the small community is employed in stores or in transport.

Before the Entry and Residence Proclamation of 1958, their position seemed perfectly clear, and even today Indians claim that they are regarded as Basuto under the Territory's Constitutional Instruments and its Basuto Tax and General Interpretation Proclamations. But these people now find themselves painfully caught in a bureaucratic cleft stick.

There are, first of all, the few old people who came to Basutoland many years ago as British subjects on British passports issued in India. Now the British Raj has vanished. They have not taken steps to formalize any changed status, assuming that as they were living in a British colony they remained British subjects. The Basutoland authorities maintain, however, that they must obtain Indian or Pakistani passports if they wish to travel outside Basutoland. But this they do not wish to do, even if they could, fearing that it would weaken their tenuous hold on residence in Basutoland. Their strict legal position appears to be obscure, but their human and moral rights seem clear. Most of them have been in Basutoland for very many years. As Indians, they are automatically prohibited immigrants in South Africa; they are afraid to leave Basutoland without being given British documents. What these people ask is not special rights in Basutoland, but British passports. It should surely be possible, in all justice, to thus secure their legal status in their old age.

Though the letter of the law may justify the Administration's attitude, even this is by no means certain. The Attorney-General for the Territories was unable to give me a clear ruling, and it is doubtful whether the Entry and Residence Proclamation applies to pre-1958 residents. But, whatever the legal niceties, the treatment of the Indians in Basutoland smacks of racial discriminaton against a minority group. South Africans have always been able to register as British citizens after one year's residence, and can still do so after five years' residence if they notify the authorities of their intentions before the end of 1965.

The Indian traders in Basutoland also allege that over the years officials have been in league with white traders to hamper them. In

1950 they even submitted a documented petition on this to the Resident Commissioner. He replied that the Administration was, in the interests of the Basuto, limiting expansion of trade by non-Basuto; and there is a nasty flavour to his additional observation that 'Although Indians of Basutoland domicile cannot enter the Union of South Africa they are able, for example, to return to their country of origin, India or Pakistan'.

The position of the children of Indian immigrants should be perfectly straightforward. Born in a British colony, these Indians are obviously British subjects, whatever the nationality status of their parents. Certainly there has never been the slightest shadow of doubt that this is the position of white children; and double standards cannot be allowed.

The most obvious injustice is suffered by the Indo-Basuto. Born in Basutoland of mixed parentage, they are nevertheless subjected to the letter of the law. Indefinite residence permits are grantable only to employees or traders amongst them, and so a substantial number of them who were born in Basutoland and live as Basuto peasants, have under the proclamation no residence rights whatever. Special permits are required for change of residence or employment, and deportation may result from the infringement of even a petty regulation. The rights of these people survive at the whim of officials, who are frequently alleged to deal differently with Indians than with Europeans, though the letter of the law is the same for members of both groups.

There is certainly no white case to match that of a prominent trader of Indo-Basuto parentage who recently had a charge laid against him for being in the land of his birth without a permit. It may not be without relevance that this trader, who is accepted as a Mosuto by the Basuto themselves, takes an interest in politics, nor that the charge was not pressed when newspaper publicity threatened.

The Basuto want to keep their land inviolate, but they are not as unreasonable as some British officials make them out to be. The Indo-Basuto are so far accepted by the Basuto as part of the nation that they are allocated land by chiefs. Why then should British officials rule otherwise?

There is no convincing evidence that the British Administration is really carrying out the wishes of 'the Basuto' in the illiberal aspects of its policy towards both the refugees from South Africa and the Indo-Basuto community.

It is, of course, true that some politicians, led by Ntsu Mokhehle, have become hostile towards a section of the refugees. But in many conversations with ordinary Basuto I always got the same response to my questions: the refugees didn't worry them; they were welcome, especially as the Basuto were themselves a nation of refugees; and whilst it was true that South Africa might threaten trouble for Basutoland as a result, that was, if anything, the best reason for not yielding to such white intimidation. It remains to be seen how these attitudes will be affected when Dr Verwoerd makes good his threats of 'retaliation', but the Basuto are a proud and stubborn people.

There is, of course, some resentment of both white and Indian traders by Basuto rivals, and the Paramount Chief has discriminated against even Indo-Basuto by refusing to renew their prospecting licences in the Letseng la Terai diamond diggings.

Hatred of any injustice is shown, however, in the language employed by Chief Jonathan and the National Party in petitioning the Secretary of State for Commonwealth Relations to instruct his officials to stop the 'persecution' of this 'very small minority group' and to alleviate their 'insecurity and hardship'. The British Government has ignored the National Party's request, made in 1962, for a commission of inquiry 'into the effects of the Proclamation, the granting of citizenship rights to the Indians who have been in this country before the passing of the Proclamation, and generally into the formulating of an Immigration Law which will not have the oppressive measures in the present law'. That law, it should be remembered, was promulgated despite majority objections in the old National Council.

The position of traders in Basutoland is a vexed one in which any resentment of the few Indians is insignificant compared with that widely felt against the two white groups which effectively control the Territory's commerce.

Both these groups, Frasers, and Collier and Yeats, are controlled wholly by British and South African capital, and both have been bastions of racial discrimination in Basutoland. In particular, the head of the bigger group, Lord Fraser of Lonsdale (formerly the Tory M.P., Sir Ian Fraser, and, himself blind, head of St Dunstan's League for the Blind) is notorious in Basutoland for his frank espousal of white rule in South Africa and his apologia for apartheid. His interests in South African mine stores and other Republican enterprises are today said to exceed his investments in Basutoland.

The present active hostility of many Basuto to the traders is of comparatively recent origin. In 1958 the National Council, commending the Administration's refusal to bow to the extended and persistent pressure of traders wanting title to 'their' land, stressed that the Basuto, 'seeking the path of civilized government', would never wish to take away without 'reasonable compensation' the 'privileges' which European and Indian traders had 'for so long enjoyed'. The Basuto were, 'moreover, not unmindful of the real advantages which the traders have brought to Basutoland; in addition to supplying material needs, they had greatly assisted in opening roads and communications, and have earned gratitude through oft-repeated acts of generosity in times of drought and stringency'.*

The feeling is rapidly growing now, however, that the traders, and especially the white giants, should give way to the increasing number of Basuto who want to enter commerce. As political consciousness among the Basuto has grown, so has resentment of the fat profits made and exported by these traders, of their stubborn delaying fight against Africanization, against their foreign control and especially against Lord Fraser's South African sympathies. Of the two groups, his has been the slower training Africans, though both have done tragically little, as the record of a comparable enterprise like the Booker Group in Malawi shows.

The staff relations of the big groups have long been poor, but a new pattern is now being forced on them since the Basuto have learnt to use the boycott weapon. When four workers were arbitrarily sacked by a Frasers store in 1961, their reinstatement was secured by a two-week boycott. Frasers, who reportedly planned to organize national counteraction by traders, capitulated when the boycott began to spread.

The situation of any but an enlightened expatriate firm trading in modern African conditions is bound to become increasingly

* Report on Constitutional Reform and Chieftainship Affairs, 1958, p. 22.

difficult, even where right may be on its side in a dispute. But the big traders in Basutoland have given little sign of profiting from the experience of similar groups elsewhere in Africa, and they may have to learn the hard way that Basutoland is not South Africa any more.

The efforts of Basuto to enter trading have been helped by the Paramount Chief's recent ruling that new trading licences are only to be issued to Basuto. But the fact that the 'big two' not only dominate retail trade, but also have a monopoly of the wholesale trade in the Territory hardly makes things easier for their aspiring, inexperienced and usually undercapitalized Basuto competitors.

It is because of these difficulties that there has been such strong pressure from its members that Basutoland's cooperative movement should branch out into retailing, but early efforts in this direction have not been successful. Where the cooperatives have done well, however, is in the supply of seeds and agricultural implements. In failing to carry such lines, the big stores have missed the chance of stimulating development in the country, and from their neglect cooperative opportunities have grown. Here is one chance amongst many for Britain's cooperative movement to lend a hand by helping to train staff and providing an expert retailing adviser and loan funds.

Whilst commerce, holding itself responsible only to its shareholders, neglects Africanization, the Administration hasn't done much better. It was only in 1962, seventy-six years after direct British administration began, that a Civil Service Training Committee was created, hard on the heels of Mokhehle's accusations at the United Nations of administrative racialism in Basutoland.

Few things have caused as much popular resentment in the Territory over the years as the racial discrimination which has been formally practised in its civil service. A great deal of pious and dishonest nonsense has been spoken by some local officials in denying that such racial discrimination existed. It is therefore refreshing to find Sir Richard Ramage, in an official report* compiled in 1961, frankly condemning 'the racial features of the present structure'.

* Report on the Structure of the Public Services in Basutoland, Bechuanaland and Swaziland, 1961, by Sir Richard Ramage, C.M.G.

In criticizing Basutoland's service, one must remember that it, like so much else in the country, has for decades been neglected by Britain, starved of funds and prestige and hence of good men. We have already noted the effects of the early 'cheap labour' policy with its recruitment of South African whites, and of the assumption that little needed to be done in a territory which was in any case soon to be incorporated into South Africa. It should, therefore, be said at the outset that, by their lights, many white officers have, over the years, displayed genuine devotion to and interest in their work, and that some have suffered relative hardship in the process. This admitted, it might well seem at times to the irreverent that, with the virtual disappearance of all of Britain's other colonies in Africa, the High Commission Service, and particularly that in Basutoland, has become the last refuge in which an impecunious would-be British squire can live as his betters used to do. Not that the administrators in the Territories have been well paid for the jobs that they have to do. It is, in fact, only with the reforms introduced recently that their pay has begun to match that which they could earn over the border in South Africa. But they have, if they wished, been able to lead an unusually pleasant life, and the British Government, in its recruiting propaganda, seems to have gone out of its way to stress this, and to perpetuate the most obnoxious sort of paternalism.

As the official recruiting brochure claims in its title, the Territories are 'Lands of Opportunity',* offering, 'to the right type of person . . . worthwhile work in colourful, and as yet, unspoiled countries'. Moreover, 'their African peoples are at an interesting state of evolution . . .'.

Due to the fortunate coincidence that all the Territories are bordered by South Africa,

almost all District Headquarters . . . are within two or three hours motor drive of modern shopping centres, which is doubtless a special attraction to the wives. Another is the privilege of a free journey by rail to seaside resorts on the coast of Southern Africa for officials and their families. . . . Many of these coastal resorts are so pleasant that on retirement some officers decide to make their homes in them.

* *Lands of Opportunity: Basutoland, Bechuanaland Protectorate, Swaziland.* Commonwealth Relations Office, London, 1958.

There is no mention of the fact that African colleagues do not enjoy these privileges. The brochure goes on to say:

But probably the most outstanding advantage of service in the Territories is that [an officer] can keep his family united during the school period. Within easy reach of the Territories are well-known private schools in South Africa which compare favourably with similar schools in the United Kingdom, while the fees charged average about one third less. Further, Government makes an allowance towards the expenses of education.

How is the recruit, thus lured, to anticipate the bitter resentment of African civil servants who have, on their lower salaries, had to make do for years with what limited educational facilities are available in Basutoland?

What the recruit *is* told, however, is that on joining he has a promising future. 'On retirement, which is, under certain circumstances, possible at the age of forty-five, some officials find remunerative employment with industrial and commercial undertakings in South Africa for which their previous work and experience in these "Lands of Opportunity" have made them particularly suitable.' [sic]

In the meantime, the new arrival will note with pleasure as he enters Maseru that, set amongst manicured playing fields, there stands the wide-verandahed Club. He will have gleaned from his brochure that 'there is provision for cricket, tennis, bowls, golf, hockey, polo, etc.', and that 'the costs are low'.

Given such advance conditioning by the British Government, it is sometimes hard to blame expatriate officials for so readily absorbing the attitudes of some old hands towards the Africans in their 'interesting stage of evolution'.

Fortunately, a breeze of change is now beginning to stir in the Basutoland Service, and most of the glaring racial injustices have been reformed, as of 1963, thanks to the implementation of Sir Richard Ramage's report. The Morse Commission, too, called Africanization 'an urgent matter', and suggested that every new expatriate recruit should have the training of Basuto civil servants made a condition of his contract.

Until 1963 all European officers were automatically given 'inducement pay' – or a third more in cash wages than Africans of equivalent status – even if they were normally resident in the territory. Ramage noted, with considerable understatement, that 'the racial operation of the inducement pay formula is causing serious and increasing ill-feeling amongst African staff generally and leading to political difficulties in all three Territories, especially in Basutoland'.

To make matters worse, European staff, including locals and South Africans, were automatically entitled to 'home' leave every two years, with full passages paid for their families. With 'local' leave conditions generous, a number of officials accordingly accumulated over 500 days' leave before their retirement, much of it earned in more junior positions on lower scales of pay.

To cap it all, for Africans, the service was as recently as 1960 parcelled into divisions, and though – like the franchise in Southern Rhodesia – these have ostensibly been non-racial, in fact the system 'has come to be regarded as a symbol of racial discrimination'.

Promotion into the 'upper staff list' of the civil service has been extremely slow and difficult for Africans but automatic on entry for Europeans. Moreover, once arrived, the Africans, of whom there were only eleven in 1962, have found in effect only a racial 'rate for the job'.

The list of justified African grievances is too long to enumerate here, but it has included other effectively discriminatory practices such as medical allowances, leave travel to the coast (in addition to 'home' leave), the extremely long promotion scales for the lower – and therefore African – grades, and the employment of the wives of white officials. It has been widely assumed in practice that such women are automatically endowed through their whiteness with executive capabilities and a much-vaunted 'sense of responsibility' which Africans only acquire after many years, if at all.

One has only to spend an hour or two in the Maseru Club to realize, not surprisingly, how very ordinary most of these women are, and to be struck by the extent to which they have acquired the Memsahib mentality. There seems to be something in the colonial situation which, while it can on occasion produce great devotion, much more commonly gives free rein to all the most unpleasant characteristics of the English middle classes. This is certainly the case with the womenfolk, who, surrounded by cheap servants and little distraction, as a rule become obsessively status-conscious, as well as uncomprehendingly arrogant towards 'the blacks'.

In Basutoland, of course, all this has been made many times worse by the very high proportion of South Africans in the service. Some of these, in fact, serve in Basutoland because they dislike South Africa's rabid racialism, but others could just as well be working in a South African Bantustan.

An idea of the importance of the South African element can be gained from the 1956 census figures, the latest available. Of the 800 European men (excluding missionaries) then in Basutoland, 115 were born in Britain, 150 in Basutoland, and 467 in South Africa.

It remains to be seen how the current implementation of the reforms recommended by Sir Richard Ramage affects both the local recruitment and advancement of Africans. The formal basis for near-equality of conditions and a non-racial service has been formally laid, but clearly much depends on both the facilities for training within the service and on the attitudes of those who supervise such training.

Quite recently, African civil servants aspiring to promotion were subjected to a battery of psycho-technical tests, one of which involved the using of somewhat difficult words to bring out their meaning. There were some sixty candidates, and most of them did poorly in the word test. But, their supervisor told me, the one word which every last man understood down to its finest nuance was – 'status'.

The official appointment policy now is to give preference to local candidates who can meet the minimal requirements, even if expatriate candidates have higher qualifications. It is high time. After more than three-quarters of a century of British rule, the highly literate Basuto in 1962 held only twenty-seven of their country's 130 senior civil service posts. On a wider classification, Basuto held 121 out of 325 'senior' posts.

In fairness to the Basutoland Administration, it should be said that it has gone further in Africanization than either Swaziland or Bechuanaland, though this reflects more on the failings of the High Commission Service as a whole than the virtues of Basutoland's section. Thus, in 1963, Basutoland alone could display an African District Commissioner, with a completely African subordinate staff. But how many is *one*? Similarly, Basutoland led the High Commission Territories with two Africans as commissioned officers in the Basutoland mounted police. But there are only two officers out of an establishment of twenty.

A sum of £60,000 was granted in 1962 to Basutoland by the Colonial Development and Welfare Fund for giving specialized training to Basuto civil servants, and plans for an Institute of Law and Administration await the grant of a further £160,000. This last is an essential project capable of yielding substantial human and economic returns on a small investment, but like so many other good plans in Basutoland, it will be shelved unless British governmental purse-strings are loosened.

The Administration, prodded by the National Council and formally re-organized by Sir Richard Ramage, is at long last aware of the urgent need for Africanization. Whether it will measure up to the realities of an African country on the verge of self-government remains to be seen. The first statement made in 1963 by the recently formed Civil Service Training Committee seems both idealistic and ill-judged in insisting that no diminution of standards should be allowed, 'even if this might retard the pace of Basothoisation'. But certainly, if a start is to be made in erasing the lamentable heritage of past racial discrimination and resultant resentment, the Administration must be given the funds for at least the training projects it has planned.

Today, the Basuto face their gravest crisis since the Boers beat them to their knees in 1868. They were saved then by being finally granted British protection. The question now is whether, in the face of renewed threats from the heirs of these same Boers, the Basuto can survive without the continuance of that same British protection and, equally important, British financial aid.

The prospect as it emerges from this survey is not encouraging, but it is certain that Basutoland could be in a far stronger economic position than it is today.

We have seen that there is tremendous scope for improvement in education, and especially for agricultural and technical education at secondary level. This, allied with the fostering of the cooperative movement, reforms in land tenure, and the extension of agricultural services, could lead to a significant and increasingly urgent rise in agricultural yields.

The prospects for industrialization are poor, and a much-publicized private South African corporation which was to raise £½m. (on a five per cent commission basis) has folded up after a short and unproductive life. But industrialization prospects would be immeasurably improved if Britain were prepared to make a £2½ million gesture of faith in exploitation of the country's ideal hydroelectric potential. Extremely cheap and abundant power would be accompanied by sorely needed irrigation water.

An imaginative system of public works could at long last give the country the roads which it lacks so badly, and improved communications in turn would counteract the centrifugal tendencies which have hurled an unnecessarily high proportion of Basutoland's commerce into the hands of South Africa. A good road system would further boost industrial possibilities. A thorough geological survey would finally establish what mineral resources there are, and with the growth of space-age metallurgy, it might well be found that hitherto uneconomical deposits of some minerals might bear exploitation. The diamond mining industry should, as it gets under way, provide useful employment and revenue. The crucial point is that all of these possibilities require immediate and substantial British aid.

Britain's record in Basutoland, however, is even worse than in the other two High Commission Territories. Though Basutoland's population is nearly double that of the other two combined, it has received less than either in development aid and only a third of Bechuanaland's grant-in-aid:

	Basutoland	Swaziland	Bechuanaland
Area	11,716 sq. miles	6,705	222,708
Population (approx.)	900,000–1m.	255,000	350,000
Total U.K. grant-in-aid 48/49–61/62	£1,205,000	£373,000	£3,690,000
Per head per annum	£0 1s. 11d.	£0 2s. 1d.	£0 15s. 1d.

	Basutoland	Swaziland	Bechuanaland
Total C.D.&W.F. expenditure 1946–59/60 inclusive	£2,012,000	£2,967,000	£2,631,000
Per head per annum	£0 3s. 3d.	£0 16s. 7d.	£0 10s. 9d.
Total grant and loan funds from U.K. Government for 1960–64*	£1,232,000	£4,100,000	£1,614,000†
Per head per annum	£0 6s. 9d.	£4 0s. 6d.	£1 3s. 0d.

* £600,000 approximately added for distribution between the three Territories.
† Further £8,000 from C.D.C. Also £1 million from International Development Corporation and £250,000 from the Standard Bank.

It can hardly be said that Britain has been in any danger of bankrupting herself through helping any of the Territories, and least of all Basutoland. In fact, the Territory first received a grant-in-aid in 1960–61.

In that year, Basutoland's total normal revenue was £1·81 million and its total expenditure £2·49 million. The shortfall of £0·68 million was met by Britain through a grant-in-aid and the C.D. & W.F.

But by far the most significant figure in Basutoland's finances is that listed under Revenue as Customs and Excise. In 1960–61 this accounted for fifty-three per cent of Basutoland's normal revenue, of £958,540 out of £1,808,482 – and every penny of it came from the South African Government. This was, for Basutoland, no abnormal year; the Territory has steadily depended for half of its revenue on customs payments made by the hostile Government of encircling South Africa, and continues to do so.

All three High Commission Territories have since 1910 stood in this special customs and excise relation with South Africa, when it was agreed that the new Union would have no internal customs barriers with the High Commission Territories. Instead, South Africa agreed to pay 1·31097 per cent of its own total customs and excise revenue to the High Commission, which passes on a fixed proportion to each Territory: 0·88575 per cent to

Basutoland, 0·276 per cent to Bechuanaland, and 0·149 per cent to Swaziland.

At the time that the overall percentage was fixed, it bore some relation to the comparative imports of the Union and the Territories, and to the relative sizes of their economies. Since then however, South Africa has become the major industrial power in Africa, whilst the Territories have been allowed to stagnate.

The Territories have, on the whole therefore, done well out of the 1910 agreement, and Basutoland has done particularly well. But it has also meant that the Territories have been placed at the mercy of South Africa for a major part of their revenue, and that changes in South African policy, like the imposition of import control, have had disastrous effects on them. In Basutoland, for instance, educational and all other expansion had to be cut back drastically when such import control was imposed in South Africa after the Second World War.

The dangers of this dependence on a source of revenue over which the Territories have no control have become greatest in the case of Basutoland, where in 1959–60 customs and excise receipts from South Africa constituted fifty per cent of total normal revenue, compared with twenty-five per cent in Bechuanaland, and only eleven per cent in Swaziland.

Yet whilst Basutoland is the poorest of the three Territories, it is also far and away the most advanced politically, and South African hostility has increasingly been centred on it. Bechuanaland has also worried Dr Verwoerd seriously, but Swaziland has become more important as a major area for investment by South Africans – including Nationalist cabinet ministers – than as a haven for political refugees. Clearly nothing would please Verwoerd better than to be able to strangle Basutoland economically whilst leaving South African investments in Swaziland untouched. And he has now gained British assent to a revision of the Customs agreement which will enable him to do precisely that.

Mr Eric Louw, South Africa's Foreign Minister, was able to announce in Parliament on 26 February 1962:

As to the future relations between the Republic and the High Commission Territories, it has been agreed in principle that special customs relations between the three Territories and the Republic will be maintained in the form of new agreements between the Republic and *each* of the Territories concerned. ... The South African Government feels that the present proportion of percentages of the Customs and Excise revenue, payable to each of the three High Commission Territories, should be reviewed and incorporated in the proposed *separate agreements*, that is to say, it is not envisaged that the aggregate of the proportion of Customs and Excise revenue be adjusted, but *merely* the proportion of revenue payable to each of the individual Territories. [My italics.]

Nationalist intentions could not be clearer. South Africa will re-allocate the percentages to match the relative degree of economic development in each territory. Related to imports, there is no other 'fair' criterion for re-allocating customs revenue. This will mean simply that Swaziland, which is booming and therefore does not need the revenue so badly, will be given the lion's share, whilst Basutoland, which has been allowed to stagnate and which is desperately in need of monies, will get less even than relatively affluent but still poor Bechuanaland.

The representatives of the British Government felt as one very senior official has explained to me, that 'in principle we could not oppose the idea of reviewing the Territories' individual shares'.

As this is being written, no further details of the Customs agreement revision have been announced, and the old arrangements remain temporarily in force until negotiations are concluded. It will be a major tragedy if, having been forced to concede agreement in principle to a revision of the share-out, the British officials should now allow South Africa to truss Basutoland in the detailed provisions. It is both their political and their moral duty to insist that Britain and the Territories must have the final say in determining the relative needs of the Territories.

But what, it may be asked, can Britain do if the South Africans, holding the economic whip-hand over the Territories, insist upon their own terms? The answer is a great deal, if Britain were willing to stand firm. She has, after all, £1,000,000,000 invested in South Africa, and is, in practice, almost the only 'reliable' friend aside from Portugal that the Republic has left at the United Nations. Her word, if backed by the certainty of action, could count for something yet inside South Africa.

On the official level, it could be made quite clear to South Africa that any unilateral abrogation of its legal Customs agreement obligation towards the Territories would have repercussions on the general Customs arrangements between South Africa and Britain. Here, of course, we come to the wider and fundamental problem of Britain's practical support for, contrasted with its theoretical opposition to, apartheid.

Thus the equivalent of imperial preference trade arrangements have survived South Africa's withdrawal from the Commonwealth, but Commonwealth preferential tariff agreements are currently coming under review, and those with South Africa will have to be re-examined. Here, surely, the British negotiators possess a significant weapon, the mere threatened use of which should have made unnecessary their acceptance of South African dictation on the crucial Customs agreement.

Let us suppose, however, that the worst came to the worst on the Customs front, and South Africa unilaterally renounced all Customs responsibilities towards Basutoland. Further still, let us suppose that South Africa simultaneously put up tariff barriers against the entry of Basutoland produce into the Republic. What could Britain do?

In the immediate result a British Government unprepared to resist would have to make good the nearly £1 million a year which South African customs revenue now brings Basutoland. It need not, in fact, be as much as that, for Basutoland's obvious riposte would be to impose customs duties on the approximately £2½ million worth of South African manufactured goods which enter the Territory, customs-free, every year. But even the full million a year would hardly bankrupt Great Britain.

To drag the other two Territories into the dispute would probably be neither practicable nor popular with their peoples, though, in particular, Swaziland's economic relations with South Africa provide strong grounds for counteraction. With railway construction for booming mine and other development, in which South African interests play by far the major role, Swaziland currently imports something over £4 million a year of South African products. If South Africa retaliated against duties on these goods, there would be strong reaction from Swaziland's British-owned but South-African-connected asbestos mining industry, whose products make up well above £2 million of Swaziland's annual £3½ million exports.

But even on the Basutoland front alone, there is a very definite limit beyond which South Africa dare not go. South Africa could not, for instance, refuse to allow imports from abroad into Basutoland, for this would constitute an economic blockade which would certainly be considered by the United Nations as a hostile act and a threat to peace.

Basutoland's very weakness and encirclement by South Africa is, in the last resort, a source of strength which Verwoerd dare not ignore. For Basutoland is today very much on the world map, with a special committee of the United Nations watching every move affecting it, and with the African world pledged to its political support.

Quite clearly, physical aggression by South Africa against Basutoland is out of the question, both now – when Britain would have to resist it – and after independence, when nothing would better suit South Africa's enemies at the United Nations.

Verwoerd is, despite his theoretical fantasies, too much of a realist to provide over Basutoland the long-sought justification for physical intervention in South Africa. Nor would he wish to produce the final straw which could break the back of Great Power resistance to effective economic sanctions against the apartheid State.

Thus South Africa will not force anything more than a limited show-down with Basutoland inside the limits of international legality. British firmness, even at this late stage, in the negotiations over the revised and separate Customs agreements could certainly ensure that Basutoland's share of the overall percentage is not too drastically reduced.

When Dr Verwoerd threatens 'retaliation', however, the greatest danger to Basutoland looms not in the loss of customs revenue, but in the repatriation of Basuto labour from the Republic.

It is generally agreed that at least 130,000 Basuto are living and working in South Africa. The figure is probably higher, though that of 650,000 given as an estimate recently by one South African cabinet minister can safely be dismissed as a typical flight into fantasy.

The threat to these Basuto falls into two parts: the minor, but still real one to the 55,000 miners, and the major one to the many thousands of farm and urban workers. Of them all, it is the urban workers who are most immediately menaced, for it is against them that Verwoerd could act with greatest impunity.

There seems little chance that the mines will agree to do wholly or even substantially without their Basuto labour. It is true that the supply of Republican mine labour has improved in recent years, in part because drought conditions have forced even more Africans to seek work outside the reserves, and to a lesser, but significant degree because Africans have increasingly been hounded under the 'pass' system which bars their entry to towns in order to force them into work on the farms and in mines. Then, too, the slightly more liberal wage policy now followed by Mr Harry Oppenheimer's vast mining empire must mean, if profits are to be maintained with a fixed gold price, an increasing degree of mechanization, and correspondingly lower labour requirements. The Basuto have already felt the effects of these trends with a temporary ten per cent cut-back in 'their' recruiting quota during the past few years. But it will be a very long time before the mass of Basuto miners are seriously threatened. For one thing, 'influx-control' into South African towns has not stopped their African populations from expanding, and for another the Basuto miners have earned for themselves a unique reputation for hard work, reliability, and such skills as they are permitted to exercise, especially in shaft-sinking.

Nor would there seem to be any major threat to those Basuto who are prepared to work for a couple of shillings a day on farms across the border in the Orange Free State. Conditions on South African farms are notoriously bad and shunned by local men who have any other alternative at all; nearly one third, or some 270,000, of the male labourers on South African farms are foreigners. It is small comfort that the poverty of Basutoland should be such under British rule that many of its citizens find themselves obliged to endure conditions of near serfdom, but it will certainly be a very long time indeed, if ever it comes, before Verwoerd can force sufficient Africans on to the farms of his supporters to make Basuto labourers redundant.

Even the Froneman Report, on which the mass repatriation of

'foreign Bantu' is to be based, 'warns that particularly in mining and agriculture a serious replacement problem could develop. The indigenous Bantu, as he becomes more sophisticated, prefers to seek work in the urban areas.'*

There is little doubt, however, that Verwoerd could hit, and hit hard, at the unknown but large number of Basuto men and women living and working in South African towns. All the machinery for their expulsion exists, and even if some of them were to slip through the net and remain behind, most could be sent home.

Certainly it will be harder from now on for Basuto to enter or leave the Republic legally. With the passing in April 1963 of South Africa's Aliens Control Act, all High Commission Africans automatically became aliens in the Republic, and as such must possess a valid passport or documents to enter the Republic. Work-seekers must report to one of the twelve border control posts now being set up (there are eventually to be eighteen) with a travel document, medical certificate of fitness and freedom from disease, and sets of finger-prints.

Prospective employers in the Republic of other than farm or domestic labour are required to notify the Department of Bantu Administration and Development (suitably abbreviated by its reluctant subjects to BAD), and if applications are approved then, in the words of the official document, 'requisitions will be placed with one or other of the Territories' through their joint Labour Agency in Johannesburg.

Africans from the Territories already employed in South Africa have been given six months' grace to obtain 'valid documents'. If they should lose their employment and be without such documents, they will be sent back at once to a border control post. If they possess the documents, they will be allowed to take another job, provided that no Republican African can be pressurized into taking it instead. Otherwise, valid documents and all, an unemployed Bosuto will be transported to the border.

At least one large detention camp, capable of holding hundreds of Africans, is being established, at Ficksburg on the South African side of the Basutoland border, and a beginning has been made with fencing stretches of the border itself. Any official

* *South African Digest* (a Government propaganda-sheet), 31 January 1963.

connexion between this fence and the new border control, complete with vigilant mobile patrols and helicopters, is blandly denied. The fence, officials allege, is purely for controlling cattle, and similar fences are being built along the borders with Swaziland and Bechuanaland. So are border control posts.

All this, of course, has made the position of Basuto working in South Africa's urban areas very difficult. What is more, Basuto allowed into South Africa to work may do so only for a period of two years. After that, they are to be repatriated, and allowed back into the Republic again only if authorized through a requisition. Persons who move regularly in the course of their employment or business across the border may be exempted from the visa requirements, but they still require valid travel documents.

Indians, as before, remain prohibited immigrants allowed in only on a special visa, and persons of mixed race who want to work in South Africa must obtain from the Secretary of the Interior prior permission, which is not granted without the approval of the Department of Labour.

At the time of writing, it was not yet clear what counter-measures the Basuto authorities intended to take, but Bechuanaland's Legislative Council has set a dubious example by approving a retaliatory demand for passports from all South Africans wanting to enter the Protectorate. In addition, the Bechuanaland authorities have actually asked the South Africans to increase the planned number of border posts!

The clear threat implied in these measures is that Dr Verwoerd can at any time decree that no more Basuto are to be allowed into South Africa. One assumes, of course, that he would except the mines, for it is noticeable that nothing is suggested in the measures so far published which affects *their* recruiting methods. But the more immediate problem is that Verwoerd has started expelling Basuto already working, and long settled, in South African towns.

Very little faith need be placed in the official assurance given by the South Africans to the British authorities, that 'they have no intention gratuitously to disturb the position of those High Commission Territories' Africans who have long been domiciled in the Republic and have come to be regarded almost as Republican subjects'. They have also indicated 'that Africans from the Territories will continue to receive more favourable treatment than those from other foreign countries'.* Similar assurances given over the years to Africans affected by succeeding control measures in the Republic have repeatedly been dishonoured.

South Africa is, of course, quite within her rights in taking such action, and in a free society the Africans of the Republic might reasonably require – if it were necessary – to have their employment opportunities protected. Even if Verwoerd tomorrow repatriated every Basuto in South Africa, he would still be perfectly within his rights. But, not wishing an open breach with Britain, he is not really likely to do that. Nor does it seem likely at present that he will make heavy cuts into mine or farm labour from Basutoland for fear of home repercussions. There is obvious significance in the line taken recently by South Africa's Deputy Minister of Bantu Administration and Development, Mr M. C. Botha, on a request from the Association of Chambers of Commerce of South Africa that the High Commission Territories should, for labour purposes, continue to be regarded as part of South Africa. The association pointed to the dangers of disrupting traditional labour sources. But Mr Botha blandly replied that while the economy was, of course, important, it was 'not the only consideration'.†

It seems likely, therefore, that there will be mass repatriation of at least a section of urban Basuto workers from South Africa. What should Britain do when this happens? The apparent answer would seem to be: nothing much, beyond financing extensive public works into which the repatriates could be temporarily absorbed, and preparing to distribute rations if this proved insufficient. But this clearly is no permanent answer, if indeed it is even a medium-term one. What then?

One progressive chief to whom I put this question did not merely shrug his shoulders in the common reaction. He began to shake with laughter, and then said: 'Well, we'll eat one another. We've done it before, we can do it again.' This chief was no fool, and his facetious reply points the hopelessness which grips any

* Bechuanaland Information Branch Press statement, 1 April 1963.
† The *Star*, Johannesburg, 25 April 1963.

Mosuto when he is forced to face this question. Is there then no solution ?

One possible, if drastic, answer to the problem of Basutoland's excess population is mass transfer to Bechuanaland. Where Basutoland is a tiny overpopulated country, Bechuanaland is the size of France but has only 350,000 people. Only one sixteenth of Bechuanaland's eight million acres of arable land has ever been cultivated, because of a shortage of water and of people. But the water is there, deep under the dry surface of the ground. It could, given a massive programme of well-sinking, be pumped up, and once that were done there would be a crying need for people to farm the land.

The Basuto and Batswana are ethnically related and can understand each others' languages, while tribal interests could be safeguarded by resettling the Basuto only on Bechuanaland's vast stretches of Crown Land unallocated at present to any tribe. Thus there could, in Bechuanaland, be Basuto in the same way as there are Batswana, Batawana or Bakwena, and the agriculture of the whole parched, underdeveloped country could be given an enormous impetus.

It would not, of course, be nearly as simple as it sounds. First, it is very doubtful whether the Basuto would be willing to move before they were literally starving. They are an intensely nationalistic, proud and stubborn people, and pretty conservative to boot. Besides, who would migrate ? The repatriated townsmen would certainly try to insist on their theoretical right to claim land in their native land, and the Basuto as a whole would have to be convinced that Britain had done everything else possible to help them develop their country before they would consider any migration seriously. And even were one or two pilot groups willing to go at the beginning, this would be a long way from mass transfer.

Then there is no reason to assume that the Batswana would agree to such a scheme. They, too, are on the whole conservative, and the delicate inter-tribal balance which today overlays long-standing rivalry between their own major groups would be upset by the influx of large numbers of uprooted, sophisticated Basuto from South Africa's towns. And whilst British maps might show huge chunks of the country as belonging to the Crown, this has never really been accepted by many Batswana.

Such problems and many others were thrown at me when I gingerly broached this idea to Africans both in Basutoland and Bechuanaland last year. To whom, for instance, would the Basuto owe allegiance? Would they want to bring their own chiefs? Or would they come in small groups and ask to be accepted in allegiance by local chiefs? If they were allocated Crown Land, would they then own it in the same way as the tribal groups now own their areas? And would the water table bear this sudden mass drilling of wells and pumping, the more technically minded wanted to know? And why, if the British Government were suddenly able to find the money to drill wells for the Basuto, couldn't it find it instead for the Batswana? And so on and on.

Still, in necessarily limited discussions, I found agreement amongst Basuto that if through sheer hunger they became convinced that there really was no other alternative, the landless and unemployed would go. And amongst those Batswana with whom I spoke, there was at least agreement that small groups of Basuto willing to accept the authority of Batswana chiefs would be accepted. These were only initial reactions to a major new idea. Given correct presentation and time to chew over the scheme, it might well find acceptance within much wider limits than these.

Quite clearly, such a scheme would require careful and tactful preparation, as well as technical exploration. It has been mooted in a desultory and theoretical sort of way in the past, but more recently it has found an active champion in Mr T. F. Betts, Oxfam's very able and energetic field director in southern and east Africa, who is now based in Basutoland. As expected, Mr Betts, who first put the idea to me, has met with considerable official scepticism in his private exploration of its possibilities.

There should be no illusions about the problems involved in its implementation. It would be a major and difficult operation in its beginnings, and would require careful guidance in its later stages if resultant social problems were to be minimized. But in all the many discussions which I had in Basutoland, this was the only suggestion which seemed to offer the gleam of feasibility. It would mean that the British Government would have to shake itself out of its lethargy in the Territories; it would entail the expenditure of large sums of money; it would involve human problems of adjustment and persuasion, of which the need to convince repatriated Basuto to move whilst they still had a few pounds from their South African labours would perhaps be the least, huge as that would be. It might even mean that, to meet the needs of the Basuto, once they had reached the point of desperation at which they were prepared to move, the British Government would have to overrule the objections of some die-hard Batswana. It would be both an expensive and a very difficult project, and it would raise fresh if lesser problems whilst solving that of Basutoland's excess tens of thousands. But no one has put forward any other solution, while the rule of race in South Africa survives.

THE NEW FRAMEWORK

It is against this background that Basutoland is now poised at the beginning of internal self-government and, a year later full independence.

The framework of the new constitution under which these two steps are to be taken was thrashed out at a conference held in London in May and June of 1964, but whilst this conference's conclusions carried the unanimous agreement of all the Basuto and British participants, the extensive powers which Britain will retain until independence were accepted by some of the Basuto only under protest, and the extent of future British economic aid was left unsettled.

The Basuto delegation came to London with a detailed set of proposals from the Constitutional Commission which their National Council had appointed early in 1962. The report of this commission,* consisting of representatives from the main political parties and the chieftainship, had been unanimously accepted by the Basutoland National Council in February 1964. But in order to obtain British agreement on the crucial issue of independence, the Basuto submitted at the 1964 conference to a number of important British conditions for the pre-independence period.

The Basuto made it clear at the outset that they were well aware of the economic difficulties which faced Basutoland, but that, with British economic aid for a limited period, they looked

* Report of the Basutoland Constitutional Commission, 1963 (Maseru, 1963).

to the future with confidence. They also made it clear that they were not asking Britain for any assurance of continued military protection after independence, though they intended to apply for Commonwealth membership.

Britain undertook to make 'every effort' to have the first elections under the new constitution held before the end of 1964, after which the constitution would come into force. The Basuto were unanimous in their demand that full independence should follow automatically one year later, but Mr Duncan Sandys, the Colonial Secretary, insisted that a formal demand for independence would have to be made at that time by resolutions of both Houses of the Basutoland Parliament or, in the event of disagreement between them, by a majority of those voting in a national referendum. It is hard to see why Britain required this procedure, which the Basuto rightly regarded as throwing gratuitous doubt on the strength of their mandate. Even in the event of opposition to independence after a year by the House of Chiefs, there can be no reasonable doubt that a necessarily expensive referendum would overwhelmingly demand independence.

Mr Sandys in fact recognized this, for he declared that the British Government would henceforward base its policy on the 'firm expectation that the request for independence would be confirmed one year after the new elections and take effect as soon as possible thereafter'. It would accordingly at once set in motion the preparations for independence 'on the assumption that, when the time came, conditions in Basutoland would be such as to enable power to be transferred in peace and order'.

But the really crucial issue was the degree of formal power and control to be retained by Britain in the pre-independence period. This issue fell into four parts: whether the Queen or Motlotheli (as the Paramount Chief is now styled) should be the head of State; whether the Basuto should share in the control of defence, external affairs and internal security; what the functions and powers of Britain's senior official in Basutoland should be; and whether Britain, by virtue of giving continued financial aid and protection, should continue to control the public service.

The British Government would not accept Motlotheli as head of State, which would have involved recognizing Basutoland as a Protectorate and not as a Colony. Instead, Motlotheli will, in effect, fulfil the functions of a governor-general in the pre-independence period. He will have the right to be kept informed and to be consulted by his ministers on all matters of government. In his private capacity he will enjoy full immunity from the taxation or the compulsory acquisition of his income and property. He will also be given a civil list of tax-free allowances for his staff. He will have absolute discretionary powers in the appointment of one-third of the thirty-three members of the Senate, which will be the ultimate appeal in disputes over land allocation and deprivation; in certain aspects of disciplinary proceedings against chiefs; and in the approval of appointments to his personal staff and to the National Planning Board.

It has been common practice in British colonies at the stage of internal self-government for defence, external affairs and internal security to remain 'reserved' fields in the hands of the local British governor. The Basuto, however, presented a well-reasoned case that responsibility for these subjects should be shared between themselves and Britain in the pre-independence period, with overriding – but carefully defined – powers of veto and certification in the hands of Great Britain. They put up equally cogent arguments for Basuto control of the public service and of finance.

The crux of their contention was that the one year pre-independence period should be used to give the Basuto as much experience as possible in government, and that to exclude them from these vital fields, in which they have been prohibited from gaining experience in the past, would be likely to make pre-independence preparation 'a hollow and illusory thing'. As they put it:

It is difficult to think of any subject in Lesotho which does not relate to external affairs. Even the milk supply of the township of Maseru is a matter of external affairs, inasmuch as milk still has to be imported from the Republic ... the major part of the revenue of Lesotho is derived from a Customs Agreement negotiated more than fifty years ago between His Majesty's Government and South Africa. If topics of this extent and importance are to continue to be withdrawn from the competence of Basotho authorities it is idle, in our view, to talk of fitting the Basotho for genuine responsibility in government, let alone for independence.

As for the Public Service, the Basuto argued that it was 'essential that the adjustments – necessitated by the early advent of independence – be planned, and what is more, *be made*, *before* independence'. Only thus would 'an atmosphere of indecision' and 'twilight' be avoided. Furthermore, 'no matter how generous and advanced a particular constitution may appear on paper, if it is administered by a public service which is out of sympathy with Basotho aspirations, or maladjusted, it will be worthless'. The pigeons of past paternalism and arrogance were coming home to roost.

The Basuto were 'firmly of the opinion that a proper degree of prudence and responsibility in financial matters' could only be induced if they had complete control of government finance, including that for the fields they proposed to share with the British Government.

The present grant-in-aid system was rightly criticized as 'a guessing game' that involved a double attempt at composing a budget: with a preliminary guess at what the grant-in-aid would be, and then an attempt to transform that guess into real estimates related to what Britain had decided to grant. In place of this system, the Basuto asked for a 'block grant' system, under which a fixed sum would be settled by negotiation as the annual British contribution to the Basutoland budget. This alone would allow for definite planning. There should be one block grant for the Basutoland Government, and another, over which Britain would retain certain ultimate controls, for defence, external affairs and security.

As for the British presence during the pre-independence period, the Basuto, in keeping with their other proposals, wanted this to take the form of a British adviser, whose main functions and powers would be to ensure the effective discharge of British responsibilities in the fields of defence, external affairs and security. With Motlotheli as head of State, the British adviser would represent Her Majesty, in accordance, the Basuto pointed out, with what Moshesh, the Father of the Nation, had had in mind when he had said in 1862:

... What I desire is this – that the Queen should send a man to live with me, who will be her ear and eye and also her hand to work with me in political matters. ... The man whom I ask from the Queen to live with me will guide and direct me. . . . When the agent and I agree as to what is right I shall carry it out.

The Basuto were understandably angered when they learned, during their talks in London, that the British Government had changed the status of the then Resident Commissioner to that of Her Majesty's Commissioner for Basutoland, with direct responsibility to Whitehall; an arrangement which they had specifically rejected in their Constitutional Report and which should at least have been the subject of negotiation with them.

In the event, the British Government not only rejected the proposal that Motlotheli should be head of State and demanded complete control of defence, external affairs, internal security, finance, and the public service, it went even further, and insisted on giving the British Government Representative, as the senior official is to be known, powers which could make him the virtual dictator of Basutoland.

He may refuse to let any Bill passed by the Basutoland Parliament become law, and can demand that the Parliament pass any legislation 'which he considers necessary or expedient in the interests of any of his responsibilities'. If Parliament refuses to pass such legislation, he can himself 'make an order which will have the force of law'. Similarly, he can demand that the Basutoland Government take any executive action which he thinks necessary, and may assume its functions if it refuses to do so. It will also be the British Government Representative who will decide how Motlotheli exercises the prerogative of mercy, who will appoint the Permanent Secretary to the Ministry of Finance, and will exercise for an interim period the powers vested in the Public Service Commission.

The retention of these sweeping powers by the British Government has been accompanied by assurances that they will be devolved upon the Basuto at the earliest possible moment during the pre-independence period, though any such devolution will be revocable. Britain has also promised to take immediate measures to accelerate the localization of the public service, including the retirement of expatriate officers, the creation of additional senior policy-making and administrative jobs in the public service, and the attachment of Basuto officials to British Missions abroad for diplomatic training.

On the issue of finance, the British Government insisted that 'since the Government of Basutoland will be receiving money voted by the British Parliament to meet its budgetary deficit, the British Government Representative will be given responsibility for ensuring proper financial administration'. There is no mention in the Conference Report of development aid either before or after independence, whether in the form of block grants or otherwise, and not even an assurance of any post-independence aid in balancing Basutoland's budget. During the conference, Mr Sandys would not let the Basuto delegation table financial and economic documents, and insisted that the Basuto should trust Britain to do whatever she could to help them.

It was only because they finally won British agreement to elections in 1964 and a subsequent one-year time-table for complete independence that the Basuto accepted the British conditions for the interim period. And, niggling though many of the British-imposed limitations for the short interim period may be, it must be recognized that the Basuto have gained immediately a substantial constitutional advance: fully democratic elections, a Parliament with greatly increased powers, and a wholly elected Executive Council or Cabinet.

Basutoland will now have a bi-cameral legislature, with the National Assembly elected directly by universal adult suffrage, and the Senate, representing the chieftainship, possessing only limited powers of review and delay. The National Assembly will have sixty members, none of whom may be chiefs, while the Senate will consist of the twenty-two principal chiefs and eleven nominees of Motlotheli's. In delimiting the assembly constituencies, a ten per cent weighting in favour of the sparsely populated rural areas will be allowed. Each Parliament will be elected for five years, and there will be a cabinet of not less than eight ministers appointed by the leader of the party or parties commanding majority support in the assembly.

There will be court-enforceable safeguards for human rights, which will be suspended only during a state of emergency, and though this may be proclaimed at any time by the Prime Minister, it must be confirmed within fourteen days by both Houses of Parliament. With such approval, it may be extended for six months at a time. An independent judiciary and public service are to be guaranteed by a Judicial Service Commission and an executive Public Services Commission.

The constitution is to entrench the institution of the chieftainship, but the powers and functions of the chieftainship will be regulated by the Basutoland Parliament. Similarly, the constitution will specifically provide that the land in Basutoland is owned by the Basuto nation and is to be administered in trust for the nation by Motlotheli and the chieftainship, but the principles by which their administration is governed will be laid down by Parliament. Furthermore, the constitution will set up a hierarchy of authorities, in which the chieftainship will be associated with elected advisers, and this will be responsible for the allocation and deprivation of land. The ultimate appeal will lie to Motlotheli, acting in his absolute discretion but assisted by a board of advisers.

A National Planning Board is to be created, responsible in particular for the development of land and other natural resources and for advising the government on land-holding policy. There will also be a College of Chiefs, consisting of the twenty-two principal chiefs and up to three co-opted non-voting members, but its only function will be to determine the succession to the position of Motlotheli in accordance with Basuto law and custom.

This leaves open the ticklish question of land tenure reform for the future Basuto Government. In its own report, the Constitutional Commission had skirted around the issue, declaring that it contemplated no change in the basic legal principles relating to land tenure, but that it was well 'aware of faults within the system' and that 'other faults will be exposed by the very operation of a more effective administration'. Admitting 'it has long been recognized that the system of land tenure and land *use* requires revision', the Commission itself had 'little doubt that the overwhelming majority of Basotho people – for good and sufficient reasons – are neither willing, nor indeed ready, to jettison the fundamental principles of their land law'. After outlining a system of elected advisory boards to assist village headmen in allocating or taking away land, and a simplified system of appeals from the village to the top level in which local government nominees, professional experts and officials would be associated with the chiefs, the Constitutional Commission had commended to the future government 'the urgent need to determine what reforms are required and to see to their implementation'.

After the major crisis regarding the time-table for independence had been surmounted at the London Conference, the Basuto delegates seem to have given up hope of gaining their other points and to have accepted British conditions on the assumption that they would make changes to suit themselves after they had gained independence, which after all would be only one year away. But Britain's refusal to commit herself to post-independence help either for balancing the Basuto budget or for development has raised in its sharpest form the question of independent Basutoland's economic and political viability, neither of which can be separated from its relations with South Africa.

Some significant pointers to Basuto thinking on these questions can be found in the Report of the Constitutional Commission:

No one who has the interests of Lesotho at heart can contemplate, without deep concern, the malnutrition and poverty, the rapidly mounting unemployment and political and economic frustration, which are now scourging the territory. Only too obviously independence itself will be no automatic panacea for these evils. Work and effort and faith and sacrifice are the one hope.

The Basuto stressed their realization that to prepare them for independence 'will involve a heavy financial burden upon Great Britain', but thought it 'perhaps not uncharitable to remark' that Basutoland had financially 'been somewhat left in the cold' over the past eighty years.

They therefore believed that

it would be neither greedy nor extravagant to suggest that Lesotho might expect sympathetic consideration of a request for financial aid, to equip its people to stand on their own feet. No self-respecting Mosotho would wish to live on charity *indefinitely*, and this is certainly not what is here being suggested. What is being asked for is a grant for a *defined* period, sufficient to prepare Lesotho for independence, and [as in the case of Tanganyika and Sierra Leone] to make the necessary adjustments during a comparatively short period after independence ... during the greater part of the present century, while the issue of incorporation in the Republic of South Africa remained unsolved, Lesotho was not given the advantage of participating in the familiar pattern of British Colonial Development. Now that this issue has been put aside ... the barrenness of what have been called Lesotho's 'locust years' calls out for repair.

It is often said that Lesotho is not economically 'self-sufficient', and that this fact should give those who call for independence reason to pause [the Commission noted, adding rather sanguinely that] It may suffice to remark that if this were a relevant consideration there would be few independent States in the world.

It is sometimes said, too, that there is no reasonable prospect of Lesotho being able to balance its budget in the future; and the inference is then sought to be drawn that it must continue to beg a grant-in-aid from Great Britain – the price of which is said to be *indefinite* dependence on Great Britain, *on terms specified by Great Britain.*

The Commission does not regard capacity to balance the national budget as a pre-condition of independence. On the contrary, in Lesotho's case political independence might well make it easier for the country to attain economic health. But, in any event, the Commission does not take the gloomy view of Lesotho's economic future which it is fashionable to propagate in some quarters.

The alert observer pricks up his ears. Have the Basuto something up their sleeves which everyone has missed ? One turns with keen anticipation to the report's chapter on financial implications. Here one finds first a resumé of the current financial position, with a gap of £1·55 million in 1963–4 between an estimated expenditure of £3·65 million and an estimated revenue of £2·1 million (of which Basutoland's Customs and Excise receipts from South Africa make up £0·965 million, or nearly half the total). Approximately thirty-four per cent or £1·2 million of the total budgetary expenditure (excluding Colonial Development and Welfare Fund grants) is at present required to pay 300 expatriate and 2,000 local public servants, and a very small sum is paid to chiefs. The present annual budgetary deficit, which has increased by 138 per cent cumulatively over the past five years due to improved administration and public benefits, is met by a British grant-in-aid. In addition, the Basuto record that during the past three years they have received £1·2 million in C.D. & W.F. grants, and that Basutoland has in recent years raised £0·75 million in Exchequer loans.

Then comes the crucial question: can Basutoland within the

251

foreseeable future expect to balance its budget without permanent or indefinite financial aid from abroad?

The Constitutional Commission answers only that 'with the proper development of Lesotho's water resources, the annual budget *could* be balanced within the foreseeable future, and a reasonable standard of services could be maintained – *without annual grants continuing indefinitely either from Britain or elsewhere*'. (The Commission's italics.)

It then goes on to urge the provision of the £2·12 million needed for the first stage of the Ox-Bow scheme, which would be ready to produce water and power within three years.

This would not only meet all of Lesotho's own needs for electric power and water; it would also prepare the way for the eventual construction of the complete Ox-Bow Scheme at a total cost of some £8·5 million.

Within the foreseeable future we envisage that the need for Lesotho's chemically pure mountain water and hydro-electric power will have made itself insistent in the Republic of South Africa. [My italics.]

The big surplus of water and power available for sale could, in itself, after deducting interest and maintenance costs, and allowing for only a modest profit, go a substantial way towards balancing Lesotho's budget.

Now the contention of the last paragraph is, as has been pointed out earlier in this book, quite true, but its realization depends wholly upon the assumption that South Africa will buy Basutoland's water and electricity. The Basuto correctly claim that 'these commodities can be supplied at very favourable prices', but they themselves go on to note: 'Meanwhile, however, vested interests are being established in other very ambitious, but economically far less attractive, sources of water and power, to the prejudice of Lesotho.' This, of course, refers to South Africa's own gigantic Orange River scheme. But, the Basuto conclude, 'despite the lateness of the hour, Lesotho's natural water resources are still a great asset to exploit'.

Now the Basuto leaders know better than most people that South Africa, under white racialist rule, has in past confidential negotiations refused to guarantee the purchase of the Ox-Bow scheme's cheap water and electricity. If the South Africans were unwilling to help make Basutoland viable whilst it was a British colony, why should they do so when it has become an independent state whose possible government has strong Pan-African connexions?

Are the Basuto naïvely indulging in wishful thinking? Or have they reason to believe that they can change South Africa's attitude? What sort of relationship with South Africa do they, in any case, envisage for independent Lesotho?

On the last question, the Constitutional Commission is quite explicit:

The Commission wishes to record its conviction that the Basotho are ready and willing – given their own government – to trade in friendliness with their neighbours, despite the grave political differences which divide them. *The desire to live and let live is strong among the Basotho. Accordingly* [my italics] the Commission knows of no sufficient reason why the water resources of Lesotho should not be developed for the mutual advantage of Lesotho and her neighbours. Development of the water resources of Lesotho and South Africa need not and should not be mutually exclusive but rather complementary.

This sentiment of good neighbourliness is repeated later in the report, in discussing independence:

We have, in another context, emphasized that the desire to live and let live is strong among the Basotho, *who have no wish to provoke the enmity of any peoples. On the contrary.* [Commission's italics.]

Now, given Basutoland's complete encirclement by South Africa and its dependence on the Republic for revenue, as a labour market and for so much else that has been described earlier, these sort of sentiments could merely be a matter of tactful phrasing, especially since Britain is not being asked to guarantee the protection of an independent Lesotho.

But, unless the Basuto leaders are being wilfully naïve, their confidence that South Africa will buy their water and electric power could suggest a different and rather startling explanation: that they feel confident of doing a deal with Dr Verwoerd. In return for a policy of 'live and let live' pursued by the Basuto, entailing at least a refusal to let Basutoland be used as a base for anti-apartheid propaganda and sabotage, if not as well the closing of its borders to political refugees, Dr Verwoerd might well be

253

prepared to continue letting the Basuto work in the Republic while buying in addition their cheap water and power.

After all, by such a deal Dr Verwoerd's losses would be hugely overshadowed by his gains. He cannot prevent Basutoland from becoming independent, and he must fear the international crisis which would arise if he tried to squeeze it to economic death. On the other hand, Basutoland is a black man's country and not a multi-racial one, and its nominal independence but actual economic dependence on South Africa could be made, in a propaganda exercise, to confirm the sincerity of Dr Verwoerd's frequently proclaimed intention of leading the South African Bantustans to 'independence'. What is more, the sight of an African State, having won its freedom from Britain, living in friendship with South Africa whilst developing socially and politically 'along its own lines', would be invaluable to Verwoerd.

It would, of course, not all be smooth sailing, and there is no hard evidence that the Basuto leaders would contemplate such a deal. In conversation with me during the London conference, Ntsu Mokhehle was as emphatically Pan-Africanist as ever, if not more so. But significantly, straight after Mr Mokhehle had left London at the close of the conference, there appeared in *The Times* a letter, signed by leading non-B.C.P. delegates to the talks, denouncing in the strongest terms proposals to apply economic sanctions against South Africa. This letter not only stressed the suffering which economic sanctions would bring to the people of the High Commission Territories, who opposed apartheid, but went on to describe a policy of economic sanctions as 'stupid and evil' and bound to be 'ineffective'. Apartheid, the Basuto leaders suggested, would 'kill itself', though 'those who believe in it will fight like fanatics'. Dr Verwoerd himself could not have asked for a better endorsement of the 'do-nothing' line in British policy towards South Africa.

Whatever the motivations of this extraordinary letter, which was promptly denounced by Northern Rhodesia's Minister of Justice, Mr Mainza Chona, it is interesting to note that it was followed by an apparently warm welcome for Basutoland's imminent independence by Dr Verwoerd.

POSTSCRIPT – THE 1965 ELECTIONS

In the event, elections were not held until 29 April 1965. The Administration ascribed this to the difficulties of compiling new voters' rolls and delimiting constituencies; Ntsu Mokhehle came to London to allege undue delay and anti-B.C.P. bias in recruiting registration personnel.

Meanwhile, in October 1964, a convoy of B.C.P. vehicles was ambushed at Rothe, a F.M.P. stronghold, and four B.C.P. men killed. Four F.M.P. national executive members were charged with murder. Three were election candidates and, when their trial was postponed until after the elections, they stood from jail. One, Chief Setinane Mapheleba, was elected, but the Rothe ambush, the campaign's only serious incident, harmed the F.M.P.'s reputation widely.

The campaign was intensive, differing from that of 1960 not only in there being adult suffrage but also in there being only four independent candidates and in all three major parties being apparently well-organized and financed. The B.N.P., F.M.P. and B.C.P. contested all sixty seats. Chief Matete's Marema Tlou Party ineffectually contested thirty-seven seats, and the Communist Party of Lesotho none. But of the three major parties only the B.N.P. and F.M.P. put out election manifestoes. Mokhehle, probably avoiding embarrassing specific commitments, claimed that everyone knew the Congress Party's aims and objects. Much inter-party suspicion arose over the arrangements for proxy-voting by Basuto in South Africa. The B.C.P. suspected bias by chiefs and district commissioners in having proxy votes witnessed; the other parties also expressed dissatisfaction; and in March, with the Administration adamant, the leaders of all parties agreed to abandon proxy-voting. Mrs Eirene White, Labour's Colonial Parliamentary Secretary, who was then on a tour of the Territories, which are her special responsibility, accepted their joint decision. Thus only absent Basuto returning on polling day could vote. At most 4,000 did so, thus some 114,000 absent voters were disenfranchized. This probably hurt both the B.N.P. and Congress, for whilst Chief Jonathan was the only Basuto leader permitted by Verwoerd to campaign in the Republic, the

B.C.P. had, despite some branch disaffection, long been organized on the Witwatersrand.

In the event, although 237 Basuto were arrested for carrying arms or 'offensive weapons', policemen were on constant duty and British troops were standing by in Swaziland, the election went off perfectly peacefully. Each party had a campaign symbol: the B.C.P. a knob-kerrie, F.M.P. an open hand (of friendship), B.N.P. a cow and Marema Tlanou an elephant. At the polling booth each voter received a set of discs bearing the symbols of the rival parties, dropped one in an envelope into the ballot box, and then had a finger marked with red dye to prevent double-voting.

The origin of party funds became a vexed issue. Chief Jonathan, who disposed of a South African helicopter, admitted that the B.N.P. received money and vehicles from private South African sympathizers (£10,000 is one estimate). He stressed that Basutoland must do a deal with South Africa to survive – 'think of your stomachs!' he told Basuto workers in the Republic – and that he was the man to do it. The impression that Jonathan was in Verwoerd's pocket was strengthened by the wide circulation of a letter in which he allegedly promised a senior South African official to put Basutoland 'under the wise guidance of South Africa' in all ways in return for the restoration of Caledon valley 'conquered lands'. Another widely circulated letter was supposedly sent to B.C.P. supporters by a Chinese trade-unionist called Tang Chang, mentioning a Chinese gift of £150,000 to the party and reporting thousands of applications daily by Chinese wanting to settle in 'spacious, neglected' Basutoland and transform it into 'a real paradise'. This letter clearly aimed at those voters previously shocked by the disclosure that Ntsu Mokhehle had in fact visited Peking in 1964. Both letters seemed obvious forgeries (Chief Jonathan's even gave a wrong telephone number) but, significantly, appeared to be widely believed. As for the F.M.P., where ex-Congress radicals (as well as traditionalists) had found a home and whose Dr Makotoko had been seen with Mr Joe Matthews, it allegedly received funds from Moscow. But most observers forgot that even, if as alleged, the parties did receive funds from these sources, it does not follow that they necessarily owe them allegiance.

The B.N.P. election manifesto 'rejects incorporation ... *con-*

demns the policy of racial discrimination practiced in South Africa
[my italics] ... however, believes that ... it is in the interests
of the people to cooperate with South Africa on matters of mutual
interest.' *Inter alia*, the party would negotiate for the return of
the 'conquered territories'. Doubtless to counteract reports that
it is still helped also by the Roman Catholics, the B.N.P., while
recognizing 'the sovereignty of Almighty God', supports religious
freedom for all denominations. Conversely, Communism – and
leaders associating with it – are condemned. Independent Lesotho
would join the Commonwealth, the U.N., the I.L.O. as well as the
Organization of African Unity, though it 'must have an army'
for defence.

Internally, the B.N.P. wants a constitutional monarchy and
'upholds the hierarchy of chieftainship as embodied in the present
constitution'; land tenure reform is to be limited to chiefs being
assisted by elected locals. In economics, in view of past British
neglect, the party 'will begin by keeping what we have: jobs in
the Republic, regular money coming in to stay'; it would negotiate for higher wages and easier travel with the Republic. But
the 'bleeding of the nation' through migratory labour is to be
reduced by inviting foreign industrialists, who must, however,
yield Lesotho 'a fair share of profits' and not dominate local
politics. Much is hoped for from thrift and agricultural credit
societies and cooperative marketing through a marketing union
and board. Water, 'our White Gold', and electricity 'can be the
basis of our prosperity', and Ox-Bow negotiations with South
Africa would be undertaken immediately. There is a detailed
and ambitious health policy. Professional, technical and vocational
training is stressed in education. The Declaration of Human
Rights is to become part of the constitution.

The F.M.P. in its manifesto differed mainly in proposing 'to
do all it can to strengthen the institution of Motlotheli within
the framework of a democratic and modern society', reforming
the chieftainship by paying 'regular and adequate allowances,
insisting on Lesotho's international water rights, and supporting
trade unions free from control by political parties'. Apartheid
is not specifically condemned, but Basuto sovereignty is stressed.

B.C.P. speakers in the campaign naturally also promised the
widest range of improvements. They also grew increasingly

critical of the Roman Catholic Church and the chiefs. Mokhehle promised that any chiefs, including Motlotheli, disregarding constitutional limitations of their power would be 'precipitating themselves out'. Denunciations of apartheid sometimes led to a wider anti-white tone, and threats to nationalize trading stores were reported.

Though there were only four women candidates, all parties made a special bid for support from women. Both B.N.P. and F.M.P. manifestoes claimed credit for enfranchizing women, who in Basutoland outnumber men by four to three, and the B.N.P. specifically included women in its promise of equal pay for equal work. Congress made a country-wide push to organize a women's section.

On 29 April, polling was so heavy, with queues of up to 2,000, that it was extended for an extra day. 259,825 votes were cast, representing sixty-two per cent of the 416,952 registered electorate (which included 900 whites and a few Indians). As the poll represented eighty-nine per cent of the resident electorate, some 118,000 voters were in South Africa and effectively debarred. The results were:

	seats	votes	per cent of poll
B.N.P.	31	108,162	41·6
B.C.P.	25	103,050	39·7
F.M.P.	4	42,837	16·5
Others	0	5,776	2·2

As Chief Jonathan was himself defeated, his deputy, Chief Sekhonyana Maseribane, was sworn in as 'interim' Prime Minister until Jonathan arranged to contest a vacated and 'safe' B.N.P. seat. But Chief Jonathan did not wait to lay down Government policy. Political refugees would be welcome provided they did not attempt subversive action against South Africa or interfere in Basuto politics. He wished to meet Dr Verwoerd in Pretoria and establish diplomatic links; similar links with African countries had not yet been considered. He appealed for help

from all friendly countries – but not from Communist ones – for
the Basuto, who were in a parlous state, brought to the verge of
starvation through unemployment and the worst drought in
thirty years. Chief Jonathan castigated chiefs who had been used
as 'tools' by the F.M.P. as lowering 'chieftainship's dignity';
chiefs must stop meddling in politics. This was directed at the
eighteen out of twenty-two senior chiefs who, *ex-officio* members
of the thirty-three strong Senate, are known F.M.P. supporters.

Ntsu Mokhehle was the only party leader to be returned,
though some of his leading lieutenants were defeated. Congress
did best in the 'modern' parts of Basutoland, the lowlands and
the diamond diggings, though B.N.P. also had lowland support.
Mokhehle's brother Shakane won Maseru with an overwhelming
4,669 votes. His four opponents, including Jack Mosiane from
jail (twenty-five votes) and Bennet Khaketla (as an independent),
lost their deposits. Mr Khaketla, who is chairman of the university's senate, has been named to his Privy Council by Motlotheli,
who also included leading defeated political leaders in his eleven
appointments to the National Senate: Mr G. M. Kolisang (general
secretary) and Mr Chakela of the B.C.P.; Dr Makotoko (president)
and Mr J. Mokotso (general secretary) of the F.M.P., Mr C.
Molapo (general secretary) of the B.N.P., and Chief Quobela, who
broke with Mokhehle.

The cabinet formed by the B.N.P. was mostly little known and
inexperienced. Chief Maseribane, the 'interim' Prime Minister,
is forty-seven, a district chief, trader and progressive farmer.
He was a nominated member of the last National Council, has
had official court experience and some association with economic
planning, but is not well known in politics. He is a Roman
Catholic. The other ministers are: Chief Peete Peete (deputy
Prime Minister and justice), Mr Benedict Leseteli (finance), Mr
Setho M. Letsie (public works), Mr Matete Majara (local government), Mr Patrick 'Mota (health), Mr Anthony Manyeli (education) and Mr Selborne Letsie (agriculture). Only the last three
have had relevant education or experience, none were in the last
National Council, and only three served in the largely non-
elective Council before that. Mr Manyeli is the only university
graduate.

Mr Mokhehle was not slow to assert that such a Government

could not command confidence. Its small majority might vanish when, as the B.C.P. intended, several results were legally challenged. (In May Mr L. A. Matooane of the B.C.P. accused the South African and Basutoland Governments of collusion in rigging the election. In Dar-es-Salaam, he asked the U.N. Committee on Colonialism to intervene, alleging that the Administration had purposely left known Congress supporters off the new voters' roll and that ballot boxes had been tampered with whilst being transported in R.A.F. aeroplanes.)

Mr Mokhehle proposed that an interim all-party Government be formed under Chief Maseribane and that fresh elections be held, but this was rejected by the National Party. In his speech from the throne, Motlotheli, now the Queen's representative, announced that the Government would negotiate a new customs agreement and that heavy import duties would be imposed on alcoholic drinks. Chief Maseribane announced top priority for the Ox-Bow scheme, which the Orange Free State Chambers of Commerce had recently urged Verwoerd to discuss with Basutoland. The Minister of Justice promised to destroy trouble-makers and 'the Communist element in the country'.

In white South Africa, the B.N.P. victory was warmly welcomed. Then, on 9 June, Dr Verwoerd announced that Chief Jonathan had appealed, 'as leader of my people and prospective Prime Minister', to him and 'our good neighbour' South Africa for famine relief help, stressing that no other country had responded to his earlier general appeal and that 'my people are in dire distress'. The generous South African response was to donate 100,000 bags of grain, but it seems strange that Dr Verwoerd made the donation not to the Basutoland Government but to Chief Jonathan 'to enable those made responsible by him' to distribute relief. Any party leader with a small and threatened parliamentary majority might well pray for such a gesture.

Two days later, on 11 June, South Africa's Foreign Minister told parliament that the Government would spend £250,000 to improve relations with foreign countries. The money, appropriated for 'secret services', was not intended for subversion but for cases in which it was not in South Africa's best interests to disclose details of requests for aid.

9 'A Very Disreputable Transaction' – Bechuanaland

The Bátswana differ from their Basuto cousins and from the Swazi in having no Paramount Chief. Thus, when Britain did reluctantly take the territory under her protection, there was no central local authority to whom she could turn. Instead, the autocratic chiefs of the eight main tribal divisions were left to get on with the governing of their people

But inevitably, soon enough, what Britain did do, or permit to be done, began to affect the lives of these people, and first amongst these acts was the construction of the railway linking South Africa and the Rhodesias. We have seen that the surrendering of the land for this railway was the price which Khama the Great and his fellow-chiefs had to pay in order to escape being taken over by the British South Africa Company of Cecil Rhodes. That was in 1885, and Britain promised that in return the chiefs would 'continue to rule their people much as at present'. For once, Britain proved as good as her word, and that for almost fifty years. It was only in 1934 that a belated reform began of the chieftainship. Lacking any definition of their powers, some chiefs had abused them, and though Lord Hailey believes that on the whole such abuses were not grave, there was ample cause for concern.

Even so, the chiefs did not let the slow introduction of these reforms go unchallenged. In 1936 Tshekedi Khama of the Bamangwato and Bathoen of the Bangwaketse challenged the legal powers of the British Government in the High Court. The Administration had introduced new measures to define and in some ways limit the hitherto arbitrary powers of the chiefs and to oblige them to consult with new tribal councils. Recognition of chiefs by government was also involved.

Tshekedi, who has played a crucial part in the shaping of modern Bechuanaland, was a highly complex and impressive descendant of Khama the Great, and whilst he was certainly autocratic, he was a man of the greatest personal integrity. He lost the case which he brought together with his life-long friend, Chief Bathoen, who has been a member of the Bechuanaland Executive Council. But they did succeed in showing that the British Government was not acting in accordance with 'native law and custom', as they believed it had originally pledged itself to do. The court ruled that the British Government was obliged only 'to respect' such customs, and being challenged on Britain's legal powers in Bechuanaland, the Crown won the case by invoking the Foreign Jurisdiction Act. The Secretary of State, Mr Malcolm MacDonald, ruled in November 1936 that

His Majesty has unfettered and unlimited power to legislate for the government and administration of justice among the Native Tribes in the Bechuanaland Protectorate, and this power is not limited by Treaty or Agreement.

This *cause célèbre* underlined the failure of preceding British rule, for, as Lord Hailey observed, the chiefs

had some grounds for their protest. That is not because the decision of the Government was arbitrary or unreasonable. But for nearly forty years the Administration had given no sign of its intention to make any material change in the procedure initiated by the Proclamation of 1891, and when the change came, it appeared in consequence to be an unduly abrupt departure from tradition.

Whilst they allowed Bechuanaland to stagnate, the British authorities were not deliberately callous. In fact, they did at times try to launch a project which seemed to them obviously in the interests of the local Africans. But they forgot, or had never bothered sufficiently to understand, that they as tenuous administrators, and the chiefs as both rulers and spokesmen of their peoples, worked and thought within quite different frames of reference.

It is this human hiatus which, as much as outright British stinginess, has bedevilled Bechuanaland's progress. Its best illustration is the life of Tshekedi Khama himself who, during his long Regentship, made the Bamangwato tribe the focus of Bechuanaland affairs.

For the general British public, Bechuanaland has repeatedly

been 'put on the map' through a series of dramatic incidents and disputes. Britain first heard of the territory at all when a Boer commando raided Livingstone's house in the 1850s. World-wide interest – and a good deal of ribaldry as well as indignation – was aroused in 1934 when the British Navy was dispatched into the wastes of the Kalahari to depose Tshekedi, who was accused of having had a white man flogged for molesting African girls.

For the most part, the periodic publicity caused by these events did not extend to the more fundamental and day-to-day problems of Bechuanaland, of which they were the dramatic expression. But the connexion has always been there to see.

Certainly this is true of the two publicized dramas which involved Tshekedi Khama. Tshekedi was called to be Regent of the Bamangwato after the short reign of Khama's successor, Sekgoma. Khama the Great had largely failed to unite his faction-riven tribe; in fact he had exacerbated tension by feuding with his brothers and even with his son. Sekgoma, inheriting these troubles, had done no better, and on his death, the dispute over the succession was resolved only when Seretse Khama, then only four years old, was recognized as heir-apparent or *morwa kgosi* (chief's son). Tshekedi, a younger son of Khama, and then only twenty-one year sold, became Regent, but was plagued from the beginning by inherited family feuds which he in turn sometimes exacerbated.

Tshekedi developed rapidly into a remarkable and controversial figure: strong-willed and autocratic yet deeply imbued with the ideal of service, strongly traditionalist yet eager to absorb and selectively apply progressive ideas, arrogant yet capable of reasonably changing his mind, deeply critical of the local British Administration yet devoted to the British justice which often failed him.

In the Bechuanaland of the twenties and thirties, relations between the strictly hierarchical Administration and the administered were rigorously stratified. Even a chief was expected to respect the white queue of command. Tshekedi, however, repeatedly jumped this queue and, if he obtained no satisfaction in South Africa, was quite prepared to go to London. He was, in fact, prepared to go beyond this and to resort to litigation, all the way up to the Privy Council, against the British Government on the several occasions when he felt that it was not adhering to the agreed terms on which it had become Bechuanaland's protecting power. None of this made Tshekedi popular with the old-fashioned type of administrator, who variously accused him of being truculent, sulky, capricious and obstructive. It seems that he was, in fact, capable of being some or all of these things, but to a large degree they were brought out in him by the frustrations which the current system of administration was bound to breed in a strong-minded, independent and progressive chief.

Ideally, the system of indirect rule which was being practised in Bechuanaland should have involved constant consultation between the administrators and the chiefs to whom the governing of the Africans was left from day to day. Tshekedi's most sympathetic biographer, Mary Benson, points out that when that enlightened British colonial administrator, Sir Charles Arden-Clarke, became Resident Commissioner of Bechuanaland, he got on splendidly with the 'angry young man of the Bamangwato'. It is highly relevant that Arden-Clarke was, when he came to the territory in 1936, the first official ever appointed to it who had had previous experience of colonial administration in Africa.

When Tshekedi became Regent of the Bamangwato in 1926, Bechuanaland possessed an administration of such traditional looseness, peculiar even in British Africa, that only mutual confidence between the administrators and the chiefs could prevent friction. And this required outstanding qualities in the administrators even more than in the chiefs. But the Bechuanaland Administration was bedevilled by second-rateness and cheap South African recruitment. This was, of course, true of all three High Commission Territories, but especially so of Bechuanaland, where there was no Paramount Chief through whom the Administration could work for the whole country. As Leonard Barnes observed after visiting the Protectorate in 1931:

The trouble is that the Bechuanaland Protectorate has never had any first-class minds at work upon its problems. And the local administrative officers, lacking light and leading from above, have hardly been of the calibre to take charge, and frame a constructive policy of their own. Drawn for the most part from the police service, they rejoice, as a group, in the mental habits and range of outlook customary in that walk of life. The passage of some law examination has won them promotion to the rank of Resident Magistrate, but their administrative grounding has been narrow and their training in economics almost non-existent. Thus their general capacity has rested on a lower level than the importance of the task they have been somewhat unfairly saddled with, and they have never risen to an adequate comprehension of what one may call the gravitational field in which their task has to be discharged. If they have failed, failure lies less at their door than at the door of the superior authorities who appointed them.

Tshekedi Khama's series of celebrated clashes with the Administration all had their roots in this situation. The first clash occurred over mining rights. It was believed from early times that Bechuanaland had mineral resources, and the British South Africa Company had in 1893 obtained a mining concession from Tshekedi's father, Khama the Great. Nothing had been done about Khama's subsequent request for the termination of this concession. Now, recognizing the need for something dramatic to relieve Bechuanaland poverty, the Administration plumped for mining development.

Convinced that it was acting in the best interests of the Bamangwato, the Administration only brought Tshekedi into the picture when his signature was needed for a new agreement which had already been negotiated with the British South Africa Company. This alone would have been enough to antagonize Tshekedi, who in any case had seen what mushrooming mines had meant for Africans in South Africa: migratory labour, an influx of whites who scooped the benefits, and, above all, the loss of land by Africans. The tribe, gathered in the traditional *kgotla* or general council, shared these fears, and backed Tshekedi's move to cancel the mining concession altogether. He was prepared to have mining, but on his terms and when he thought the tribe ready for it.

A long and acrimonious legal struggle ensued, which took Tshekedi, against the Administration's wishes, to London, and there he had it clearly acknowledged that he was entitled to terminate the agreement and that nothing could be done without the assent of the tribe, which owned all minerals. Then, having won his point, Tshekedi negotiated a revised agreement with the company, and for those days it was a very favourable one, involving increased compensation, and an undertaking to use Bamangwato instead of outside labour. In an accompanying multiple land deal between the company, the tribe and the Government, the Bamangwato also gained some valuable land. In fact, the company subsequently thought the terms too high for what they believed that they could make, and abandoned the revised concession, so that the Bamangwato got some valuable additional land free.

While this three-year struggle dragged on, Tshekedi was also involved in a tribal dispute which led him to the Privy Council. The Ratshosa faction in the tribe having refused to obey his orders, Tshekedi ordered two of their leaders to be whipped. They broke away from the *kgotla* and, returning with guns, wounded Tshekedi and two other men. This, an attack on the chief in *kgotla*, was the most heinous of all tribal offences, and in the old days it had been punishable by death. The men were arrested, tried by the British for attempted murder, and sentenced to four years' hard labour. Tshekedi, meanwhile, had in *kgotla* ordered the houses of the Ratshosa brothers to be burnt. They sued him for damages and, on appeal from a lower court, won. This Tshekedi felt to be such a slight on his authority that he took the matter to the Privy Council, and in 1931 he won his case. The Judicial Committee found that he had observed native law and custom and had acted with the unanimous approval of his *kgotla*.

At the same time, however, the Privy Council Committee declared that the recognized hut-burning punishment imposed by Tshekedi was not compatible with high standards of 'morality, humanity or natural justice', and suggested that the High Commissioner might revise the traditional chief's powers. Their Lordships' august voices were the first of several that were at this period beginning to call for administrative reforms in the High Commission Territories.

In Bechuanaland there was particular cause for concern. A good deal of attention was focused on the position of the Sarwa, who were, and to some extent today still are, serfs of the Bamangwato and the Batawana. In 1931 the Government appointed a commissioner to inquire into their position, and he reported that while their liberty was controlled, their labour unpaid and their access to the courts difficult, 'their conditions of life are primitive and carefree, though unprogressive'. Yet in 1933, and again in

1937, recognized outside authorities could report that the Sarwa who served Tswana 'masters' could be 'transferred altogether or lent by one man to another, irrespective of their own wishes; if ill-treated they have no remedy than to run away if they can, but are followed up and brought back forcibly'. Clearly white ideas varied even in the thirties on what constituted a 'carefree though unprogressive' life. In 1935 the London Missionary Society published an exposé of the Sarwa conditions; in 1936 the Government outlawed slavery by proclamation; and in 1938 a report was made to the League of Nations. There the matter rested, though then, as now, all that seemed to be needed was an implemented outlawing of serfdom and sufficient funds, as well as guiding administrators, to resettle the Sarwa on Crown Lands. Of these three ingredients, only the Crown Land was, however, available.

Traditionally, a chief was ultimately limited by his symbiotic dependence on the tribe. In the words of a High Court judgment:

A Chief resembles a Saxon King more than a constitutional Monarch. He is a representative Chief, with wide discretionary powers; he is the legislative, executive and final Court of Appeal. In exercising these functions he takes advice from whom he pleases, but he is to some extent controlled by tribal opinions because he has to make his decisions in public in the *kgotla* where he is bound to listen to anyone who cares to speak. In that way he feels the pulse of his tribe, but the decision is his and he can disregard the opinion of the majority. In practice, however, he follows tribal opinion, because the security of his position as Chief to some extent depends upon the character of his rule.

Traditionally, too, the African chiefs seldom had any independent formal machinery with which to impose unpopular decisions on the tribe. But in practice the almost unquestioning support which the administration gave to the chiefs in Bechuanaland had increased their authority far beyond the bounds of tradition. There was no official check on their power to levy taxes, to recruit labour 'regiments' for private as well as public use, or to impose whippings. The latter powers were, according to the personal observations of Leonard Barnes in 1931, 'so commonly and so outrageously abused as to constitute perhaps the most crying scandal in a land of scandals'. And this conclusion was supported by official contemporary investigations.

Being able to rely almost invariably on the support of the Administration, the chiefs not unnaturally tended to discourage criticism from younger and better educated men in *kgotla*, and unlike their equivalents in Basutoland and Swaziland, such men did not have the most rudimentary official contact with the Administration. As it seemed to Barnes, 'in the Bechuanaland Protectorate alone has intelligence been unequivocally regarded as the enemy of the State'.

Even where the chiefs did not seriously abuse their powers, popular suspicion of their stewardship was inevitably aroused after money replaced cattle as the currency of levies and fines. No accounts were kept, and while everyone had been able to see what was done with cattle, no one knew where money went. Some British attention had been focused on the authority of the chiefs by Tshekedi's successful appeal to the Privy Council in the Rat-shosa affair.

In 1933, however, world attention was focused on the ham-handedness, obtuseness, and arrogance of the British Administration itself. Once again the issue revolved around Tshekedi, but this time the racial issue was involved. Two white youths had for some time been misbehaving with African girls, but the Administration did not meet Tshekedi's request that they be removed from the area. When one of them subsequently assaulted a Mong-wato, Tshekedi decided to try him in *kgotla*. This was against the law of the land, which gave African chiefs power only over Afri-cans, but the white youth accepted the trial, and subsequently he refused to lay a charge against Tshekedi. Very much later Tshekedi revealed privately that he had not actually sentenced the youth to be whipped, but that, following a scuffle, the *kgotla* had taken matters into its own hands.* Be that as it may, the fact remained that a white man had been tried and whipped by an African court. An enormous outcry followed.

Tshekedi was already unpopular with the Administration, partly through past disputes and partly because he was by then the leader of opposition to the introduction of administrative reforms which promised both to define the functions of the chiefs

---

* *Tshekedi Kama*, Mary Benson, Faber & Faber, 1960, p. 110. The summaries of Tshekedi's major dramas draw heavily on this very informative book, though not all its evaluations of Tshekedi are shared.

and to introduce tribal councils which they would be obliged to consult. Some officials felt that Tshekedi had too often been 'allowed to get away' with obstruction and cheek, and his most bitter critics included the Resident Commissioner, Colonel Rey. By bad luck, the sympathetic High Commissioner, Sir Herbert Stanley, was then away, and the Acting High Commissioner, Admiral Evans,* was a paternalistic racialist of the old military school who believed that: 'The Negro is a great liar, he is naturally lazy, he loves talking ad infinitum. . . . He understands rough justice, but petting and pampering are considered by the native as signs of weakness.' Such was Britain's proconsul in Southern Africa.

Rough justice was certainly the hallmark of the admiral's actions in Bechuanaland. A warrant was served on Tshekedi to appear for trial, though no details of the charge were given, and meanwhile, in response to an unfounded call for protection from the Magistrate at Serowe, Evans rushed 200 sailors and marines, with three howitzers, from Cape Town to Serowe.

Support for Tshekedi was strong amongst both black and white in the Bamangwato Reserve, and when the trial opened, steel-helmeted marines with fixed bayonets stood on guard, while machine-guns were trained on the Bamangwato assembled to watch. Only on the morning of the trial did Tshekedi learn that he was charged with having unlawfully ordered the flogging of a white man, and that he was suspended from the acting chieftainship. He was refused legal counsel on the excuse that it was an administrative and not a legal inquiry, despite the fact that Mr Douglas Buchanan, K.C., an old friend, had come to represent him at the special request of the Territory's High Court judge. And he was given a rough time at his trial, with an attempt made to introduce fresh supplementary charges when the original case was seen to be doing badly.

The navy's show of force turned into farce when its howitzers nearly bogged down in the Kalahari sand; 'Join the Royal Navy and see the Kalahari', sarcastically suggested one British newspaper. Admiral Evans arrived from the Cape and, in full dress uniform, announced that Tshekedi was suspended from the

* 'Evans of the Broke', later Admiral Lord Mountevans, author of the revealing autobiography, *Adventurous Life*, Hutchinson.

chieftainship, banished to Francistown, and forbidden contact with his tribe. Though acknowledged to be a clean-living man of great intelligence and education, Evans pronounced him guilty (without any proof being produced) of having 'frequently flouted the Administration, of having an overmastering passion for selfishness and personal privilege, and of having undermined the harmony without which the Administration could not function'. With that, the admiral left.

In Douglas Buchanan's words, what followed was

probably unparalleled in African history. The whole white population, including the parents of the boy who had caused the trouble, came forward in a body, each in turn, men, women and children, filed past Tshekedi, shook his hand and told him how sorry they were for what had happened and that they hoped he would soon return as chief,

He did. The tribe refused to appoint a successor. The case had provided marvellous 'colour' material for newspapers everywhere, but the consensus of editorial opinion in Britain was sharply critical of the hamhanded and unfair way in which Evans had handled the case. This opinion was shared even by Afrikaans papers in South Africa, while forty-one local white residents addressed the Secretary of State, deploring as altogether unnecessary the show of force and pointing out that no white woman had ever been maltreated by Africans in Bamangwato territory.

Two weeks later Tshekedi was telegraphically informed by the King of his reinstatement, as he had abandoned any right to try Europeans, had apologized and promised loyally to cooperate. Evans behaved rudely and insensitively to the last, and refused to take back at the public reinstatement any of the unproved accusations he had made publicly earlier, even though Tshekedi had pointed out that allowing them to stand must undermine his chiefly authority.

The whole distasteful affair, which cost the British taxpayer £4,000, foreshadowed the later unjust deposition of Seretse Khama after he had married a white girl. In both cases intimate race relations were involved; in both, the prejudices and anachronistic outlook of the white 'man on the spot' led to justice being seen not to be done; and in both, the cohesion of the tribe, tenuous at the best of times, was undermined.

Tshekedi was no sooner clear of this sorry episode than he was involved in the historic legal fight with the Administration over the proposed chieftainship reforms, and though the Crown won its case, the disputed proclamations were never enforced. Influential officials in Whitehall and Bechuanaland realized that the new laws outraged the traditional forms of tribal life, and that ways had to be found of changing the content of rule without such outrage. Both Tshekedi and Bathoen eventually cooperated in framing fresh reforms, which were proclaimed in 1943.

The British Government, stirred into a new awareness of Bechuanaland and its sister territories, appointed Sir Alan Pim to inquire into the economic affairs of Swaziland and Bechuanaland. What he had to say about Bechuanaland in 1933 was grim, for the chronic plight of the economy had been made acute by a series of events beyond local control.

First, there had been drought, and then an outbreak in part of the Protectorate of the dreaded foot-and-mouth disease, which not only killed off many cattle but caused South Africa to bar Bechuana cattle altogether from its markets. The price of cattle was in any case falling as a result of the deepening world depression, and this also affected revenues from the railway linking South Africa and the Rhodesias. Judged by its balance sheet, Bechuanaland was bankrupt.

Progressive Africans like Tshekedi found little encouragement in the facts revealed by Sir Alan Pim. In education, £1,000 a year was being spent by the Government on 180 white children, and only £100 contributed towards the cost of educating 8,000 African pupils. There was one hospital bed for every 2,800 Africans, and without the earnings of migrant workers in South Africa the situation would have been even worse.

Sir Alan Pim recognized many of the causes of this pathetic situation: the vicious circle of poverty, malnutrition, disease and migratory labour; the lack of capital for water development; the urgent need for properly trained administrators. But the Pim Report only skirted around the main problem, which was how to re-establish the financial stability of the Protectorate whilst providing for expanded social services. It suggested water development, an increase in tax collection, and the improvement of cattle breeding and use, but otherwise left the problems of migratory labour and the raising of additional revenue open.

Both in Bechuanaland and Swaziland, Sir Alan Pim failed to find evidence of a genuine concern on Britain's part for African 'prosperity and advance'. His reports are records of stagnation. The Bechuanaland report's most immediate result was a grant-in-aid of £177,000 by the British Government, but this merely covered the accumulated deficit of the past three years.

Meanwhile, the South Africans renewed their pressure for the incorporation of all three Territories, and General Hertzog, the Prime Minister, began in 1934 to make barely veiled threats of economic sanctions if he did not get his way. This pressure seemed for a time on the verge of proving successful. Though it was recognized that the African people in the Territories were strongly opposed, British ministers agreed with the South Africans to work towards an early hand-over, and even prominent African sympathizers in Britain were so discouraged by the economic weakness of the Territories that they advocated a phased transfer. In 1935 the Protectorate's European Advisory Council, as well as the various white farming blocks which it represented, came out openly for transfer to South Africa, with which their members were intimately connected. The situation seemed desperate.

It was during this time that Tshekedi Khama took the lead in rousing British public opinion. He published three direct appeals, and with the help of a small number of prominent Englishmen and of one woman, Margery Perham, who stubbornly opposed incorporation, they made a considerable impression. General Hertzog then overplayed his hand by publicly stating that the South African Government was lending money, with British agreement, to develop the Territories in the firm expectation of early transfer. The resulting protests in the Territories and in Britain led the British Government to reject the proffered South African money, and to backtrack generally on transfer, and there the issue remained until South African pressures were renewed after the war.

In all this time there had been no move towards creating

in Bechuanaland anything approaching a representative African body with official status. In 1920 the Administration had set up separate councils for Africans and Europeans; but both councils were purely advisory, each met annually under the Presidency of the Resident Commissioner, and while the European Council was elected and had six official, though non-voting, members, the African Council in practice represented only the chiefs and their advisers.

A small hesitant step towards democracy was only taken with the introduction in 1938 of tribal Treasuries, which gave Africans a primary say in how one quarter of their annual £1 tax was to be spent, as well as a public means of checking on its actual use. Under the tribal Treasury system, one source of grievance against the chieftainship was abolished, for chiefs now received a fixed stipend instead of a percentage of their annual tax collection. As we have seen, the Administration's attempt to reform the chieftainship more thoroughly was blocked until it gained chiefly cooperation. But the fixed stipend worked better in Bechuanaland than in Basutoland, probably because, despite the lack of a Paramount Chief, there has been no great proliferation of the lesser chieftainship in the Protectorate.

The African Advisory Council did become a fairly useful form of communication between the chiefs and the Administration, but as a political institution it lagged many years behind even Basutoland's National Council, which itself was many years behind the rest of British Africa. Revenue and rudimentary social services rose fractionally, and after the passing of the Colonial Development and Welfare Act of 1940 there was a significant, though still tragically inadequate, inward trickle of money. But for almost all the Batswana, life changed little until the war, and anything which could be described as modern political development was to wait until nearly the present day.

At the beginning of the war, the Batswana chiefs offered all possible help to the Administration, but they quickly turned down a suggestion by South Africa's General Smuts that their people serve in that country's Native Military Corps. Instead, Tshekedi and his old friend Chief Bathoen pressed for the formation of the special High Commission Territories corps, to which Bechuanaland contributed 10,000 men. As in Basutoland, the war exerted an immeasurable but definite influence on the Batswana, who served far away from their homes, seeing different ways of life. Service also gave men prestige, and it is interesting that one of the present political leaders, Philip Matante of the Bechuanaland People's Party, is still respected for having been a sergeant-major, the highest rank open to a Batswana.

At home, however, the war had little direct impact other than an improving demand for cattle and a slight, though only relative, prosperity. After the war, the demobilization grants helped ex-servicemen and their families, while the Colonial Development and Welfare Fund began to think about ranching development in the Territory.

The world next heard of the Protectorate only in 1948, when Seretse Khama, the heir to the Bamangwato chieftainship, married a white woman, Ruth Williams, in England. The crisis which followed led to the banishment of both Seretse and Tshekedi, and involved both South Africa and the British Labour Government in some very shady trafficking.

The whole episode may well be one of the few to ring a bell with the British public today when the Protectorates are mentioned, and it has been fully described in more than one book.* But it is still of direct relevance to Bechuanaland, where Seretse is now one of the leading political figures. There are many in the British Administration who hope to see him as Bechuanaland's first Prime Minister, and one must therefore look at least in outline at his traumatically formative experience.

In 1944 when Seretse Khama was twenty-three years old and had completed a B.A. at Fort Hare University College in South Africa, he rejected the proposal that he should return home and take over the chieftainship of the Bamangwato. The proposal had come from his uncle Tshekedi, still acting as Regent, and the tribal elders, but they accepted Seretse's counter-proposal that he should go to England and study law. Tshekedi made the necessary arrangements, and Seretse spent first a year at Balliol College, Oxford, and then read law at the Inns of Court. After two years

* *Ruth and Seretse*, John Redfern, Gollancz, 1955; and, from Tshekedi's point of view, *Tshekedi Khama*, Mary Benson. This account draws heavily on both these books.

Tshekedi wrote urging him to come home immediately after he had taken his final examinations that year, whether he passed them or not, since it was urgent that he should take over the chieftainship.

Seretse had, in the meantime, met and fallen in love with Ruth Williams, a City clerk, and they had decided to marry. In September 1948 Tshekedi received a letter from his nephew giving him the news for the first time. Seretse wrote that he would be getting married on 2 October, and said:

I realize that this matter will not please you because the tribe will not like it as the person I am marrying is a white woman. I do not know what the people will say when they hear of this. In spite of what they might do or say I shall still return home whenever you say to serve them in any capacity. I realize that it was my duty to have asked your consent before I had done this thing but I know you would refuse and it would be difficult for me to disregard your advice and that is why I notified you when it was all done. Please forgive me. . . . Please don't try to stop me, father, I want to go through with it.

Seretse, though he had received no detailed instruction in tribal ways, was right in assuming that he should have consulted Tshekedi, and the tribal elders, before choosing a wife. Tshekedi, for his part, was deeply upset, both by Seretse's presenting him with a final decision and by the fact that Ruth Williams was white. The chief's wife is the Mother of the Tribe, and Tshekedi himself could not envisage a white woman in this role. He also foresaw ostracism for Ruth, and possible deposition for Seretse.

Tshekedi tried, through the influence of friends, to prevent Seretse from presenting the tribe with a *fait accompli*, but Seretse married Ruth in a London registry office. Despite Tshekedi's pleas, the Commonwealth Relations Office, under which Bechuanaland then fell, considered that Seretse's private affairs were none of its business.

When Seretse, on his own, returned home in October 1948, all but one of his fifteen most important uncles and cousins of the royal blood were solidly opposed to his marriage, and tried to get him to renounce it. This he refused to do. A *kgotla*, or general tribal gathering, was called to welcome Seretse back. It was strongly against his marriage, with seventy-eight speaking against and only eight in favour. At a second *kgotla* in December, before Seretse returned to England, support for him had substantially increased. This was so especially amongst younger men, but Tshekedi silenced them by ruling that only older, mature men might speak. The majority, however, was still against the marriage.

Seretse returned to England, Ruth, and his law studies. Six months later the Administration confirmed the *kgotla*'s rejection of Ruth as Queen, but it refused to act on Tshekedi's request that she should therefore be barred from coming to the Protectorate. No one had a solution for the problem, and the Administration simply let it drift. Tshekedi himself made it clear throughout the long ensuing dispute that he was not trying to get the chieftainship for himself, and this, from all the evidence, was true. But Tshekedi had ruled the tribe with a very firm hand, and the old internal dynastic and factional disputes still simmered. Thus talk of Tshekedi's own ambitions for the chieftainship began to spread, and support for Seretse gathered strength, both because he was, after all, the hereditary chief, and in opposition to Tshekedi.

Six months later, Seretse returned to Bechuanaland. The issue of tribal procedure had now become inextricably intertwined with a clash between the hard, obstinate will of Tshekedi, and the younger man's determination. A fresh *kgotla* was called, in which first Tshekedi and then Seretse broke with traditional procedures. Tshekedi was blunt, saying at one time: 'I will hand over the chieftainship to him, but if he brings his white wife here I will fight him to the end.' As the *kgotla*, attended by some 4,000 people, dragged on through four days, it became clear that opinion had swung behind Seretse, aided by accusations, now made publicly for the first time, that Tshekedi wanted to usurp Seretse's chieftainship. Tshekedi refuted these accusations, but he handled the *kgotla* arbitrarily and badly.

In a *kgotla*, no vote is taken, but a consensus of opinion is reached through as much discussion as may be needed. Tshekedi made the fatal error of asking his supporters to rise and counting the heads of the senior headmen who opposed the marriage. They numbered nine. Seretse, displaying hitherto unsuspected political astuteness, followed this unprecedented head-counting with one of his own, mustering seventeen. Then Seretse threw the issue to the whole *kgotla*. Only forty-three men stood 'against me and my wife', whilst almost the whole *kgotla* rose for them, with the triumphant acclamation of '*Pula !*' (Rain!)

Tshekedi took it hard. 'If this white woman comes, I go,' he said. 'My nephew has killed us.' Tshekedi had told Seretse months before that if the tribe were divided, he himself would have to leave, and he now did so. Forty-three headmen and other followers joined him in his planned trek to a neighbouring tribe. Tshekedi felt very strongly that only a judicial commission of inquiry could rule on the status of Ruth and her future children, but his request for such an inquiry was refused by the High Commissioner, Sir Evelyn Baring. At the same time, both Seretse and Tshekedi were unofficially given to understand that Seretse would very soon be installed as chief, with Ruth as Queen.

By this time, however, white outrage in neighbouring South Africa and Southern Rhodesia at this 'mixed marriage' had become vociferous and official.

In South Africa, the Afrikaner Nationalists, recently swept to power, were proceeding with the legal prohibition of racial intermarriage, and at least one of their Dutch Reformed Churches protested against Seretse's marriage. On the very day that Tshekedi's request for an inquiry into Ruth's legal position was refused, the Prime Minister of Southern Rhodesia, Sir Godfrey Huggins* told a cheering House that he had written to the British High Commissioner, and would do so again, to say how 'disastrous' it would be if 'this fellow' (Seretse) became chief. On the very next day Sir Evelyn let Tshekedi know that he would, after all, appoint a Commission of Inquiry. Two months later Dr Malan, the Prime Minister of South Africa, revealed that he had sent an unequivocal telegram, opposing Seretse's marriage, to the British Government, and he promptly proceeded to renew his claims to the incorporation of the three Protectorates.

When the Commission of Inquiry was set up under Sir Walter Harrigan, its term of reference ignored the crucial question of Ruth's status, and concentrated instead on Seretse's fitness to be chief. Tshekedi, to clear himself of suspected ambition, wrote officially in October 1949, renouncing all claims to the chieftainship

---

* Later Lord Malvern, first Prime Minister of the ill-fated Federation of Rhodesia and Nyasaland.

for himself and his children. He did not even receive a reply, but he protested before the commission when he found himself cast by officialdom in the role of plaintiff against Seretse. Nevertheless, he argued that Seretse had shown himself unfit to be chief. The commission found him an evasive and unsatisfactory witness, and seemed much to prefer Seretse. The Harrigan Commission's Report went to the Labour Government in London early in 1950.

Quite suddenly, Seretse received an urgent invitation to come to London from Mr Philip Noel-Baker, the Secretary of State for Commonwealth Relations. They were to have informal discussions about the future administration of the tribe. Both Seretse and the *kgotla* were suspicious, but Seretse was verbally assured by the Resident Commissioner that he would freely be allowed to return home, and so he went. Ruth, however, remained behind for safety's sake.

When he got to London, Seretse was asked to relinquish all claims to the chieftainship, in return for which he would receive £1,000 a year tax free. When he refused, he was told that he was banished from Bechuanaland for five years. He sent Ruth a cable:

Tribe and myself tricked by British Government. Am banned from whole Protectorate. Love. Seretse.

Then he angrily gave a Press conference the same news, rightly accusing the British Labour Government of having double-crossed him.

Mr Patrick Gordon Walker, the new Labour Commonwealth Secretary, tried vainly to rebut the widely echoed accusation of trickery, only to be reproached by Mr Churchill with the oft-quoted judgement that it had been 'a very disreputable transaction'. There had not, Mr Gordon Walker stated categorically, been any communication from the South African Government. But in South Africa, the Nationalist paper, *Die Transvaler*, claimed the credit for Seretse's banishment and said:

While trying to prop up with words the whitewashed façade of liberalism, the British Government has had in practice to concede the demands of apartheid.

The British Government 'viewed with grave concern the

danger which recognition would cause to the unity and well-being of the tribe and the administration of the Protectorate', but it would review the position after five years. In the meantime, Tshekedi was banished from Bamangwato territory for five years as well, though no charge had been brought against him.

The Government published a White Paper attempting to justify its actions, but it refused to publish the findings of the Harrigan Commission of Inquiry. These remain secret to the present day, so that neither Seretse nor yet Tshekedi, against whom no accusation was ever officially levelled, knew on what judgement they were banished. The Government did, however, say that the commission had been unanimous in rejecting Seretse's 'placing'.

The White Paper asserts flatly that neither the Southern Rhodesian nor the South African Governments had made any official representations. It has since, however, been revealed that Smuts, then leader of the Opposition in South Africa, had warned the British Government that if Seretse and Ruth were installed Dr Malan would demand the incorporation of the Protectorates. Because of the fanatical emotions involved in South Africa over miscegenation, Smuts warned that he would have to support such a demand.

Without chief or Regent, law and order suffered in the Bamangwato Reserve, worsened by disputes over cattle between Tshekedi's followers, heading for self-imposed exile, and the mass of the tribe, who now used Tshekedi as a scapegoat for all their troubles. In the unsettled atmosphere of the times, this led to attacks on and quarrels with Tshekedi's followers, and culminated in the burning down of Tshekedi's unoccupied house, which his father, Khama the Great, had built.

Then, in 1950, Seretse was allowed back for the birth of his first child – Ruth had remained in the Protectorate – and the two men came close to a solution. They agreed, privately and in principle, that both of them should give up all claims to the chieftainship for themselves and their children, and return to the tribe as private citizens, taking a full part in its affairs.

This agreement in principle was not revealed for some time, though it did ultimately form the basis of the solution towards which the Labour Party's Conservative successors belatedly staggered. Before this happened, however, there was to be a great deal of misunderstanding and suspicion between Seretse and Tshekedi, and hamhanded and unjust dealings by British Governments which two debates in Parliament failed to rectify.

The combined effect was to be seen in divisions within the tribe so strong, as to lead to two serious riots, with police being air-lifted from Southern Rhodesia and Basutoland. Both Seretse and Tshekedi suffered greatly before they were permitted to return home, and the wrong against both of them was never righted nor yet officially recognized. But much as they suffered, their tribe, to which both of them were devoted, suffered almost as greatly, coming near to having the fabric of its life and cohesive institutions destroyed.

The *kgotla* was made a thing to be manipulated or banned by the Administration. Tribal discipline and projects broke down, drunkenness and internecine assault became common, and hatred, persecution, and suspicion became the bitter fruit of frustration.

In this depressing process, the Africans of Bechuanaland lost their faith in British justice, and both the local administration and the party system at Westminster were revealed in their worst light. Against a background of renewed South African demands for incorporation and thinly-veiled threats, there was a glut of abandoned principles and the worst sort of bureaucratic rigidity and evasion.

The Labour Government's shocking record in this dispute was stingingly and rightly criticized by the Liberals and Conservatives when in opposition. But when the Conservatives themselves came to power in 1951, they took an even harsher line towards Seretse than their predecessors had done. Separate requests from Seretse and Tshekedi that each be allowed to return home as a private individual were refused, and Seretse was now told that he would *never* be allowed to return. He was considered a danger to the peace and good government of Bechuanaland. Yet in the same breath he was offered a post in Jamaica as a member of the Colonial Service!

Seretse, who steadily grew in dignity and determination, spurned this sorry sop which served only to reinforce the widespread belief that his continued persecution was dictated by the desire to appease the South Africans. In 1952 the Conservative Government issued an Order-in-Council stripping Seretse and his children of all rights to the chieftainship, and barring him, as well as Tshekedi, from any post or authority connected with the chieftainship. The worst riots in Bechuanaland's history followed, with three African policemen killed by a mob demanding Seretse's return. But Seretse remained banished.

Tshekedi was allowed to return home late in 1952 where, contrary to official prognostications, he met with no violence. The Labour Party, now in opposition, changed its views, but the Conservatives persisted in attempts to have the tribe select a new chief. But the tribe knew only one chief, Seretse, and in the face of their determination an 'African Authority' had to be appointed. Clumsy attempts, bedevilled by the basic disputes, were made to create local councils to replace the debarred chief and *kgotla*.

Life assumed an appearance of normality, but the sore of Seretse's absence and of the dispute with Tshekedi festered. Progress was held up, and without Tshekedi and Seretse nothing could really be done. Certainly there could be no progress without them on schemes for mining development, and it may be that in the end this weighed very heavily with the British Government.

In any event, a solution of sorts was reached in 1956. Seretse had been deeply disturbed by the deterioration which the seemingly endless dispute and his absence had caused. He finally saw that the only way out was to return as a private individual, and to work for new patterns. He and Tshekedi became reconciled for the good of the tribe, and they took a joint initiative in presenting the British Government with a renunciation of all claims to the chieftainship. In return they asked that both should be allowed to return home and play a full part in public life. They pledged themselves to cooperate with the appointed African Authority and the British Administration, and the British Government agreed to their proposal. It was a splendid gesture by Seretse, and one which served to emphasize how truly 'disreputable' had been transactions by both Labour and Conservative Governments.

SLOW MOTION

If the outside world heard about Bechuanaland between the

twenties and the forties mainly through the troubles of the Bamangwato and of Tshekedi, this was not only because Tshekedi was a big man with the courage to challenge authority. The long silence in which Bechuanaland appeared to be wrapped was matched by the reality within the Protectorate.

While the Basuto were beginning to stir politically, the people of Bechuanaland lived apparently placid lives. This did not, however, mean prosperous or expanding lives. On the contrary, the lives of most Batswana were, by any outside standards, marked by an unrelieved poverty, with health and education services which could hardly be said to exist. Scattered through this vast territory and engaged chiefly in cattle herding, successive generations of young Africans grew up illiterate, under conservative chiefs, who were themselves for long well satisfied with the Advisory Council system created by the Administration in 1920.

In that year both a Native and a European Advisory Council had – as noted before – been formed, both with authority only to advise, but each from the beginning constituted differently, and differently treated by the Administration. While the European Council was elected, the members of the African Council were nominated, 'according to their custom', by the main tribes. This meant that the chiefs were automatically members, and though in theory the *kgotla* of each tribe would nominate the other members, in practice the chief usually selected one or two headmen and nominated them. Not all the chiefs, however, welcomed the creation of the Advisory Council. Khama the Great thought that the Bamangwato, the largest tribe, would be better off on their own, and this policy was continued after his death, with the Bamangwato, represented by Tshekedi as Regent, only attending regularly after 1938.

A place was found on the Council for one or two outstanding commoners as 'councillors', but there were very few of these and there was never any likelihood that the African Advisory Council would become a popular or representative institution. In a situation where the Administration was more than content to leave the chiefs alone to get on with their business, this suited both sides well enough. The chiefs thus remained, on the Council as outside it, the main link and contact between the Administration and the people. The Council's original mandate was 'to discuss with the Resident Commissioner all matters affecting Native interests which the members desired to bring forward, especially the administration of the Native Fund'. Its members met once a year under the presidency of the Resident Commissioner, and their sessions were observed by senior Government officials.

With hardly any popular pressure upon it, the African Advisory Council, as it was renamed in 1940, devoted itself in the main to the chieftainship and the administrative reforms put forward by the Administration in the thirties. It also played, however, a vital role in voicing African opposition to the continuing South African pressures for incorporation, and made clear Batswana unease when Britain seemed to be weakening on this issue. It is notable too, that it was the more progressive members of the African Council, like Chiefs Tshekedi and Bathoen II, who took the lead in pressing for the formation of a Joint Advisory Council, and, after the war, for a Legislative Council.

The European Advisory Council early exercised more influence on the Administration, though its formal powers were no greater than its African counterpart. It became the practice to submit the Protectorate's Estimates to the council, as well as to discuss proposed legislation with its members. But where the African Council's discussions were on the whole circumspect, the European Council became a platform for blistering attacks on the inadequacy of services for whites. Most of its members made no bones about their desire to have the country placed under South African rule. At various times the council members suggested closer association with South Africa, and on at least two occasions they demanded that their blocks of farms be incorporated. All this, of course, was hardly surprising, for most of the whites were South Africans, many of them of the poorly educated Afrikaner farming sort, and the Protectorate, until fairly recently, did not really differ much from South Africa except in its poverty and stagnation.

In 1950 the Administration finally agreed to the creation of a Joint Advisory Council, which consisted of eight Europeans and eight Africans, chosen by their respective councils, with four senior officials. This was an advance, as it meant that black and white worked formally together, but the power of the new body did not extend beyond mere consultation.

The real need, for a Legislative Council, was not met for another ten years, despite repeated requests by the Batswana, who were told time and again by the British authorities that they were 'not ready' for this step. They noted, however, that countries like Northern Rhodesia and Nyasaland, which had gained Advisory Councils long after the Bechuana, already had Legislative Councils, and they wondered whether it was not fear of South African reaction that was blocking their own progress.

By 1958, however, when the Nationalists had been in power for a decade in South Africa, it had become clear that there would be no incorporation and that therefore something had to be done about the Territories. Thus when white and black members of the Joint Advisory Council called yet again in 1958 for the creation of a Legislative Council, the Administration at last decided to give way, and the Protectorate's first Legislative Council met in 1961.

This again, in the context of Bechuanaland's time-lag, was a major step forward, but the composition of the Legislative Council itself left it open to severe criticism. In many ways it was modelled on the previous Joint Advisory Council. In the first place, the Protectorate's 3,200 whites and 317,000 Africans were given the same representation, with ten elected members each, plus two appointed members of each race. Then there were three *ex officio* official members, and seven nominated officials as members. With the ten officials all inevitably white (there being no Africans of remotely sufficient seniority), the resultant composition looked like racial stacking with a vengeance: not twelve and twelve, but twelve Africans and twenty-two whites, plus the Resident Commissioner as president. The small Asian community, which numbered 250, was allowed to elect one Asian member.

African fears of racial stacking wrongly presupposed that white officials could not be impartial; but there were certainly good grounds for criticism of the indirect system by which the Legislative Council's African, but not white, members were elected. This system had been recommended by a committee of black and white members of the old Joint Advisory Council who, together with officials, had considered that 'the time was not yet ripe' for direct African elections, though in the process at least one important failing of the old African Council election system had been partially remedied. The creation of the Legislative Council had been linked with the establishment of largely elective tribal councils, and these gave the ordinary people more say. Thus, in the first round of elections, which were to the area or village councils, it became more difficult for a local sub-chief to ignore or override popular opinion. The area councils then acted as electoral colleges to the tribal or district councils, and these in turn elected the African Council. This last succeeded the old African Advisory Council, but it remained a stronghold of the chieftainship, and it was this African Council which elected the ten African members of the Legislative Council.

In the only elections which have been held for the Legislative Council, the actual voting procedure adopted in the final elections of Legco members was also open to just criticism. Names of candidates were chalked up in random order on a blackboard, and it seems that the names at the top of the list were usually elected. Of such small details is significant bitterness born.

It is a mark of the newness of modern politics in Bechuanaland that the first elections to the Legislative Council, held in 1961, were not contested by today's major political parties. The Bechuanaland Democratic Party did not yet exist, and the Bechuanaland People's Party had been formed only shortly before the elections.

The Protectorate's first political party, the Bechuanaland Protectorate Federal Party, was formed only in 1959, following the publication of draft proposals for a Legislative Council. After a year, however, it claimed only a very small membership – the days of competitive estimates still lying ahead – and had not issued a programme. When finally it did issue its programme, it listed as its first object 'the enhancement of the institution of chieftainship' whilst also calling for 'the removal of the chiefs from party politics'. The party called for the establishment of a chamber of chiefs with considerable powers and the entrenchment of 'tribal autonomy' within Bechuanaland 'as a federal unit'. In conservative vein, the programme condemned calls for a black majority in the Legislative Council as conflicting with multi-racial unity, and even more modestly, it denounced as 'dangerous' calls for independence in 1963 or 'at the shortest possible time', considering the nation to be 'still politically immature and economically unsound'. Finally, the Federal Party called, like all other parties later, for general uplift and improvement, the recognition of multi-racialism and the improvement of taxation.

The founder and president of the Federal Party, Leetile Disang Ratidladi, is one of the tiny handful of well-educated Africans in Bechuanaland. He was born at Serowe in 1910 and, after attending tribal school, took his Junior Certificate at Tiger Kloof High School in South Africa; through London Missionary Society connexions, most of those Bechuana of the pre-war generations who gained any secondary education went to Tiger Kloof. Ratidladi then matriculated at Lovedale College in Natal, and went on to Fort Hare University College.

He belongs to the dissident house of the Bamangwato royal family which opposed the Khamas, and in 1937, after a much discussed fight with Tshekedi, he and his father were banished from the Bamangwato Reserve. Having settled in Francistown, where he worked as a clerk in the Administration, he later became tribal secretary to the Queen of Ngamiland and, after he was allowed to return to the Bamangwato, became secretary of their tribal council. He thus had by descent and latterly by function, strong links with the chieftainship, as well as considerable administrative experience.

Despite this, the Federal Party, with its highly conservative programme, made very little headway. Mr Ratidladi did gain a seat in the Legislative Council, reputedly with chiefly backing, but, following unsuccessful attempts to join with Seretse Khama's Bechuanaland Democratic Party, the Federal Party has effectively ceased to exist, and it was not represented in the 1963 discussions leading to the new constitution. Mr Ratidladi himself, however, now holds office as a vice-president in the B.D.P.

Politics of a more serious sort came to the Protectorate with the founding, on 6 December 1960, of the Bechuanaland People's Party, which was also stimulated by the arrangements, announced on the same date, for Bechuanaland's first Legislative Council. But unlike its solitary predecessor, the People's Party has had from the beginning a modern, nationalist outlook. It organized itself on lines similar to those of South Africa's African National Congress, and rapidly established itself on the Pan-African map.

Its programme was, however, a relatively general document, calling, aside from the usual generalities, for 'compulsory military training on modern lines at some time' for all young men. This was an oblique reaction to the threats from South Africa. A common 'national unity and solidarity' was urged for all 'Bechuanalanders' without exception, and the non-racialism of the party stressed. Membership was open to all. The party called for 'localization' of the Administration; and promised to defend the interests of Bechuanalanders 'against foreigners and immigrants'.

It was strongly anti-tribalist, and politely critical of the chieftainship: 'The Party is fully appreciative of the good and opportune service rendered by the ancient institution of the chieftainship ... as a focal and rallying point in socialization' but in present Bechuanaland, 'when deference to a chief is almost tantamount to deification, very great caution and circumspection must be exercised' in nominating any chief or subchief for party office. Tribalism was denounced as promoting 'a narrow, exclusive, totalitarian outlook, communal chauvinism, stagnating conservatism, nepotism, patronage, belief in a mythical hereditary divine right of precedence, etc.' The party demanded that merit alone should count. Finally, it called for cooperation with the authorities, whilst reserving the right to 'expose, criticize and protest against' bad measures, and pledged itself to achieve its objectives, including independence for Bechuanaland, by constitutional and non-violent means.

The high-flown language of the party's constitution revealed the drafting hand of its first president, Mr K. T. Motsete, whose educational achievements must be the most remarkable in Bechuanaland. Kgaleman Motsete was born around the turn of the century at Serowe, where he had his early education. He then went to Tiger Kloof in South Africa, where he took his Junior Certificate in 1918, and subsequently matriculated. Breaking new ground, he then went, with missionary help, to London University, where he took four degrees: Bachelor of Divinity, Bachelor of Divinity (Honours), B.A. (Honours) and an M.A. in philosophy. After this he qualified in London as a music teacher. These great achievements made him, when he returned to Bechuanaland, by far the best-educated person of any race in the Protectorate, and immediately complicated his relationship with the largely unimaginative and none-too-brilliantly educated members of the Administration.

In 1932 Motsete founded in Bechuanaland a primary-cum-secondary school known as the Tati Training Institute, supported by grants from the Carnegie Corporation in America and the local Administration, but this closed during the war, when the Carnegie Grant was not renewed in 1941. In his own Bamangwato tribe, Motsete was a major supporter of Seretse Khama in the chieftain-ship dispute, and was one of the main speakers before a committee of three observers sent from Britain to assess opinion in 1951. He was also the first secretary of the Bamangwato tribal council.

Motsete is well read and politically knowledgeable. Not one of the new school of demagogues, he is, rather, a soft-spoken and rather self-effacing man, an intellectual and educationalist turned politician. This impression has been borne out by his role in the internal troubles which have lately plagued the People's Party.

In its early days, the People's Party made impressive progress. In February 1961 it held what is claimed to be the first open-air meeting by a political party in Bechuanaland, and Mr Motsete kicked off with a strong denunciation of colour bars in the Pro-tectorate, against which the Administration had begun to move. Demands for the reform of the projected Legislative Council on a non-tribal, directly elected basis of 'one man – one vote' set the pattern for a series of further meetings. This was something new in the Protectorate's experience, and the B.P.P. drew increasing audiences despite the hostility of some African chiefs, who found themselves under increasing attack.

For all that, the B.P.P. did not contest the indirect elections held to select the African members of the first Legislative Council, and bitterly criticized the refusal of the Administration to provide for postal voting by the several thousand Batswana working outside the Territory, mainly in South Africa. This sort of activity and talk immediately aroused the interest of the Pan-African world, which was strengthened by the close connexions of the B.P.P.'s secretary-general, Mr Motsamai Mpho, with the African National Congress Alliance in South Africa.

Motsamai Mpho was born in Ngamiland, a tribal reserve in northern Bechuanaland, on 3 February 1921. He is a member of the Bayei tribe, which has traditionally 'served' the local Batawana; though the Bayei have not been serfs, they did pay tribute to the Batawana and, until they were permitted to set up their own Bayei village in 1948, came directly under Batawana headmen. This background of belonging to a subject tribe is probably a hindrance to Mpho in politics, as tribal prestige and descent count for much with many Batswana.

Mpho obtained his primary education at Maun and then, like most other leading Bechuana figures, went on to Tiger Kloof in South Africa, where he took his Junior Certificate. He was employed for five years as a welfare worker at Crown Mines, a Johannesburg gold mine, during which time he attended part-time courses at the Jan Hofmeyer School for Social Work. Later he worked for two years as personal clerk to Arthur Blaxall, the saintly Anglican clergyman who has done magnificent work for the African blind in South Africa and who was then secretary of the Christian Council of South Africa.

In 1952 Motsamai Mpho joined the African Congress in Johannesburg, moved to join, he declares, by the contrast which the daily humiliations of Africans under apartheid offered with the relative freedom of Bechuanaland. He was soon well thought of by important people in the Congress movement, and in 1956 was taken on as a part-time reporter by *New Age*, the Congress-line weekly. In the same year he was one of the 156 put on trial for high treason, and though he was discharged in 1958, was re-arrested in the round-ups which accompanied the declaration of a State of Emergency in South Africa after the mass shootings of Africans by the police at Sharpeville in March 1961. He was detained in Pretoria jail for four months, and both in prison and during the Treason Trial he formed close ties with the leading figures in the South African Congress movement. On being released from Pretoria jail in 1960 he was deported to Bechuanaland, where he soon afterwards became a key figure in the formation of the Bechuanaland People's Party. He has since been at least twice to Pan-African conferences at Accra and once to Addis Ababa.

Within three months of the party's formation, it had obtained a gift of three jeeps from the All African People's Conference in Accra, and with this transport its leaders enjoyed a head start in the huge spaces of Bechuanaland. Understandably, both the chiefs and the Administration became increasingly worried by such outside support, and by the significant, though still limited, local response which the B.P.P. was evoking. For the first time, too, the white traders who dominate the Protectorate's commerce began to hear threats of boycotts if complaints about racial discrimination and unfair trading were not heeded. Modern African politics inevitably brought with it a challenge to the established ways of both black and white.

The B.P.P.'s organization was modelled very closely on that of South Africa's A.N.C., with colours and uniforms of black, gold and green and the adaptation of South African freedom songs and greetings. Other Batswana who had been active politically in South Africa became prominent in the party, amongst them Mr Fish Keitsing, another former treason trialist, and Batswana working in the Transvaal formed a branch of the party. At its first conference, held at Lobatsi in January 1962, fourteen branches with a membership of 3,000 were claimed, while 500 members attended. Mr Mpho, fresh from an Accra meeting of the Pan-African Freedom Movement for East, Central and South Africa (PAFMECSA), demanded independence for Bechuanaland by 1963, and Mr Motsete looked forward to a planned common front of the three High Commission Territories.

Within six months, however, the party had split, with Mr Mpho on one side, Mr Motsete and his vice-president, Mr Philip Matante, on the other, and – as is usual in such splits – accusations of corruption and outside influence were freely proclaimed. The Motsete–Matante group suspended Mpho and six other members of the national executive, accusing them of planning a South African Communist-inspired *coup* to take over the party. The Mpho faction alleged that Matante had failed to account for £9,000 given to him from Pan-African sources for the party, and that he had put two South African refugees back across the border. Both the latter accusations became the subject of court actions. The second was flatly disbelieved by a magistrate, and the first apparently remained unproved. Matante in turn accused Mpho of misusing money intended for political refugees, but again there was no proof of this.

The bitterness generated by the split was fanned by the alignment of outside groups, and especially by two South African newspapers: the weekly Congress-supporting *New Age* for Mpho, and *Contact*, the liberal fortnightly, for Matante.* These alignments have echoed the South African split between the multi-racial Congress Alliance and the Pan-Africanist Congress. In the dispute, Motsete and Matante have strongly attacked the Mpho faction's South African connexions, smearing them as Communist, and have accused them of planning a take-over similar to that which Mokhehle alleged had been tried in Basutoland. Both factions have tried to obtain support and recognition from the independent African States and nationalist movements in other African countries. While the situation is still relatively fluid, it was significant that the Motsete–Matante faction had, at their first national conference, held in 1963, as guests Mr G. M. Kolisang, then Secretary-General of the Basutoland Congress Party and Mr Victor Zaza of Northern Rhodesia's United National Independence Party.

In the course of the split, Matante emerged as the dominant influence on the one side, rather than K. T. Motsete. Philip Matante is a large, well-built man in his forties, who has had a varied background in which religion has played a large part. He belongs to a Bamangwato commoner family, but gained considerable standing during the war when he reached the rank of sergeant-major with the Bechuana troops, the highest allowed them under the colour-bar conditions of their service. He has been a wandering evangelist for various sects, and it is probably from this time in his life that he has his passionate, almost revivalist, platform manner, which makes him a very effective speaker. Shortly before the split, he was chosen by Mr Motsete to go to New York to petition the United Nations, and he has also been to Accra. But in 1963–4 Matante and Motsete split in turn, with allegations of misuse of money by Matante one of the issues between them. Matante has since spent a good deal of time in Lusaka, trying to obtain support from Dr Kenneth Kaunda.

The split into three factions appears to have become a permanent one, with Mpho's faction renamed the Botswana Independence Party in 1964. It has been difficult to evaluate their rival claims to mass following, and probably the first elections to take place under Bechuanaland's new constitution, which are

* *New Age* has since been banned by the South African Government.

to be on the basis of 'one man – one vote', will be the only way to settle the argument. Both Mpho and the Motsete–Matante group, before they split, were represented at the constitutional discussions, and agreed to the proposals.

In these elections, however, the three groups will come up against the Bechuanaland Democratic Party, which was formally founded by Seretse Khama at the beginning of 1962. After his return to Bechuanaland, Seretse had, on Tshekedi's nomination, been unanimously elected vice-chairman of the Bamangwato tribal council (Tshekedi later became, on Seretse's nomination, the council's secretary, despite opposition from the Bechuanaland Administration). But Seretse otherwise kept out of political life until the 1961 Constitution was proclaimed. He then agreed to be a candidate for the new Legislative Council, topped the final poll, and was appointed to the Executive Council.

The formation of the Bechuanaland Democratic Party has been seen by its opponents as a reaction to the increasing impact being made by the then still unified People's Party, and it is true that both its programme and its approach were more moderate than its rivals'. This moderation of approach lay originally in the time-table adopted by the Democratic Party at its inaugural congress in January 1962:

'To attain one man one vote and an African majority in the Legislative Council by the next elections' (which were due in 1965); 'to attain full self-government based on a proper ministerial system by the following elections' (which presumably would take place only in 1970); and 'to attain an economically viable and fully independent State thereafter'. By contrast, the People's Party was demanding independence by 1963.

Similarly, the B.D.P. fully supports the controversial Prevention of Violence Abroad Proclamation, which makes it an offence for anyone in Bechuanaland to plot or invite violent subversion of the South African régime, though the party agrees in principle that political refuge should be given to opponents of apartheid.

For the rest, the programme of the B.D.P. is noteworthy for two reasons: first, the party calls for specific measures to achieve 'the substitution of constitutional rule for the exercise of arbitrary powers by the Chiefs', advocating directly elected tribal councils, to elect in their turn and control Executive Committees; secondly, the party pledges itself 'to strengthen labour and the trade-union movement, so that no man may be exploited by his employer'.

It would, of course, be a mistake to judge parties in Bechuanaland – as elsewhere – chiefly by their formal programmes. Thus the fact that the Democratic Party alone mentions trade-unions does not make it more radical in outlook than its rivals, as is testified by the support which it alone is receiving from some white traders.

In founding his party, Seretse in fact played his cards shrewdly. With the chiefs, the Administration and the traders alarmed at the shrill militancy and growing support of the People's Party, Seretse first canvassed the idea of his B.D.P. at the end of 1961, and recruited ten of the twelve African members in the Legislative Council.

With Seretse a member of the Executive Council, the Democratic Party thus became at one stroke a major force, and although the Democratic Party as such had no mandate from the electorate, it has to the Administration assumed almost the character of a party in power. Certainly, the Administration, whilst maintaining formal impartiality, now thinks highly of Seretse Khama and the B.D.P.

In April 1962, a sort of 'trainee-minister' arrangement was announced, under which the four unofficial members of the Executive Council became 'associated with' Government departments. Seretse Khama himself was given the senior of these posts, being associated with the Government Secretary's work, mainly on the political side, while Chief Bathoen II was associated with Administration, Mr Russel England with Development, and Mr D. Morgan with Townships, Works and Communications. This was seen in the Protectorate as a grooming of Seretse Khama as a future Prime Minister, and it is clear that whites will feel less unhappy with him in the top job than with any of the other African political leaders.

In September 1963, some 300 white farmers from the Tuli Block and the Tati Concession met and proposed to set these regions up as independent areas in close association with South Africa. But when Mr van Gass, the Tuli Block's ultra-conservative representative in the Legislative Council, died a short time later, only those farmers who had opted for British citizenship could vote in selecting his successor. This reduced the electorate from about 130 to some twenty, who significantly chose a veteran white trader member of Seretse's B.D.P., a Mr Steinberg.

The B.D.P. has, in fact, a small number of active white sympathizers and one or two white members among the traders of the Bamangwato Reserve. Within the Reserve, too, Seretse Khama's prestige and popularity as the rightful hereditary chief is heavily exploited by his party, though Seretse himself formally insists that he is only a private individual.

Again only the next elections can show what support the B.D.P. commands. It has a considerable asset in Mr Quet Masire, a young, intelligent and energetic member of the Legislative Council with progressive views. But in a modern political context, the main question mark remains Seretse himself.

Seretse is considerably occupied with the administration of his large personal wealth, mainly in the form of vast herds of cattle. Although it is said that he is not a particularly progressive employer, he is supporting the cooperative farming project of the Bamangwato Development Association, started under the guidance of Guy and Molly Clutton-Brock, and he has recently visited Israel, where he learnt more about cooperative work. He is keenly aware, too, of the appalling state of education in Bechuanaland, as well as of its health services. Nevertheless, Seretse Khama's wider activities and political interest frequently seem sporadic, and even his admirers often doubt his political judgement. Thus he has antagonized young militants along 'the line of rail', where the modern life of Bechuanaland lies, by repeatedly breaking boycotts of shopkeepers who had aroused resentment by offensive racialistic practices and behaviour.

Moreover, he has embarrassed himself and his supporters by pronouncements on possible links between Bechuanaland and the late Federation of Rhodesia and Nyasaland, although he explained that these would depend on federal changes. In wholly modern African politics, Seretse Khama would be a conservative figure. It remains to be seen how he will develop in Bechuanaland, though it seems certain that he will in any event play a large part in the country's future affairs.

An attempt was made late in 1962 to form a Bechuanaland

Liberal Party, but its support seems to have been limited to a small number of white and African businessmen. They announced proposals for a qualified franchise and intended to ask Chief Bathoen II of the Bangwaketse to lead them, but little more has been heard of them.

It will, therefore, be the two factions of the Bechuanaland People's Party, the Botswana Independence Party and the Bechuanaland Democratic Party who will be the main contenders for power under the Protectorate's new constitution. This was announced in November 1963, and accepted by the British Government in 1964, following consultations between the Resident Commissioner and representatives of the three major parties, the European and Asian communities, and the chiefs. It was no small achievement that unanimous agreement should have been reached, especially as it takes Bechuanaland forward to the penultimate stage of internal self-government.

Significantly, Bechuanaland is to avoid the complicated systems of dual or multiple voters' rolls which have marked this stage of constitutional advance in other British African territories with a settled white population. Instead, there is to be a common voters' roll on the basis of universal adult suffrage, electing directly a Legislative Assembly of some thirty-two members, who will then choose an additional four as representing special knowledge or interests. Anyone will qualify for the franchise if he is over twenty-one, is a British subject or British protected person, has resided in Bechuanaland for a year before registration, or was born in Bechuanaland, and is domiciled there on the date of registration. This means that, in contrast with Swaziland, those whites in Bechuanaland who retain their South African nationality will not be able to vote. There is to be no postal registration or voting, but there is a provision which would allow migrant workers who have maintained their principal home in the Protectorate to register and vote, provided that they do both in Bechuanaland.

The absence of postal voting is a very serious and presumably deliberate omission, whose purpose can only be to avoid giving offence to the South African Government by importing demo-cratic processes for black men into the apartheid State. There are at any given time about 20,000 Bechuana employed in South

Africa,* or over twenty-five per cent of the adult male population, and it must prove practically impossible for them to obtain leave first to go home and register and then again to vote. Thus one-eighth of the electorate has effectively been disfranchised in order to appease Dr Verwoerd.

Under the new constitution, the leader of the majority party will become Prime Minister, choosing five other ministers and, initially, three parliamentary secretaries. The Minister of Finance will, for the time being, remain an official. The Prime Minister will be able to request at any time that this portfolio too should go to an elected minister, but he will be able to do nothing about the extensive powers retained by Her Majesty's Commissioner, as the Resident Commissioner is now known.

The commissioner himself will retain exclusive control over external affairs and defence, internal security (including the organization, use and operational control of the police), and the public service. He will also have extensive reserve powers. This is roughly the usual colonial arrangement at this constitutional stage.

Chiefs, however, are to be barred from the Legislative Assembly. Instead, there is to be a House of Chiefs, consisting of the Protectorate's eight principal and four senior sub-chiefs. Significantly, this House of Chiefs is to be only consultative, with no power to block legislation. Organizing elections under such a new constitution will be, for the small staff available, a major operation, though they will be helped by the publication of last-year's new census, the first to be considered relatively reliable. An effort is to be made to have elections in September or October 1964, 'but in any case not later than the first quarter of 1965'.

Although, as is usual, nothing is said in the proposals for Bechuanaland's new constitution about its expected length of life, it seems certain that it will stimulate further pressure for complete political independence. Thus Bechuanaland today presents a picture of accelerating, though belated, political progress.

Such progress must arouse the hostility of the South African Government even more in the case of Bechuanaland than in the other two High Commission Territories. For Bechuanaland alone

* Bechuanaland Protectorate Development Plan, 1963-8.

has direct access to black-ruled Africa, and with Northern Rhodesia gaining its independence in October 1964, this could become a very real threat to Dr Verwoerd's régime. Then, too, Bechuanaland's long common border with South West Africa could prove of great importance if the United Nations took action to remove that territory from South African rule.

Any popular Bechuanaland Government moving towards independence must therefore reckon on at least the possibility of hostile pressures from South Africa, and must look to the state of the Bechuanaland economy and of its social services. Both present great problems.

SPACE AND CATTLE

The fundamental facts about the economy of Bechuanaland could be gloomily put something like this: In an area of 225,000 square miles, most of the 350,000 people subsist on ranching some 1½ million poor-grade cattle. There is a chronic shortage of water, and when the rains fail, which happens frequently, finding work in neighbouring territories is for many Batswana the only alternative to starvation. Pasture is in danger of rapid deterioration, while tsetse-fly and foot-and-mouth disease constantly threaten the cattle. Land husbandry is largely primitive and limited by the scarcity of water, with only five per cent of arable land under any sort of cultivation. Communications and marketing services are poor, as are health services, and education is so inadequate that a literate and skilled labour force would be hard to build up even if it were required. Yet even at this low standard of services, Bechuanaland cannot balance its budget, and is heavily dependent on financial aid from Britain and on cooperation from South Africa.

Nor can any of the problems listed be easily solved, for the state of the Protectorate, like that of Basutoland, is largely a result of long neglect by Britain and the conservatism of the local people. But in Bechuanaland, unlike Basutoland, there is at least plenty of land, and the pioneer work, both of some devoted officials and the Batswana themselves, has shown that, if only money and training staff were made available, many of Bechuanaland's chronic difficulties could largely be eased.

The Economic Survey Mission led by Professor Morse reported in 1960 that the additional expenditure of only £2·8 million in the next five years would 'set in motion in the Protectorate a series of processes that will gradually enable it to stand on its own feet'. Not a quarter of this amount has, however, been made available by the British Government.

Because of the natural features of the Protectorate, some eighty per cent of the population live in its eastern part, on either side of the 'line-of-rail' which links South Africa with Southern Rhodesia. Bechuanaland, like the other two Territories, has no reliable statistics. Even the size of its population will not be reliably established until the results of a full scale census, which was started early in 1964 with assistance from U.N.E.P.T.A., become known.

But a census taken in 1956 showed a population as follows (the 1963 estimates are given in brackets):*

African	316,578	(435,000)
Asian	248	(300)
Coloured	676	(1,000)
European	3,173	(3,000)

There is also a substantial number of Bushmen, making their home in the Kalahari, estimated at between two and ten thousand.

The distribution of the people and the way they live particularly affects development plans, for the Bechuanaland tribes have evolved a traditional type of centralized town living, in a pattern that resembles a series of concentric circles, with the village or town at the centre, the arable lands in a band around it, and the cattle posts and grazing lands on the outside. Traditionally, the men are required to be in the central, residential section for a substantial part of the year, so that they may be available for tribal affairs, and it is part of the chief's prerogative to say when ploughing of the arable lands and harvesting should begin, and to permit departure for the cattle-posts.

This centralized pattern of living has led to the development of large towns in the eastern and north-western part of the Protector-

* As all but one of the available reports use the 1956 figures, these are used also in this book.

ate, with four towns having a population of over 10,000. Such large populations also means that ploughing lands may be as far as ten miles from the village or town, and cattle posts as far as thirty miles away.

In the tribal Reserves, where most of the African population lives, land is communally held, and – put very simply – each family is entitled to an allocation of arable land and a share of communal grazing. If a family abandons a land holding, it reverts to the chief and the tribe and is re-allocated by the chief. If, on the other hand, the chief decides, theoretically after discussion in a *kgotla*, that a family's holding is required for some other purpose, the family has to move but is entitled to some other allocation.

Cattle in Bechuanaland are, on the other hand, owned individually and, as in many parts of Africa, are by tradition regarded as symbols of wealth and prestige, rather than as commodities for marketing. The beauty of a Botswana's cattle are a source of great pride to him, and the language has many more words for beautiful cattle than for beautiful women.

In recent years, however, there has been growing evidence that this traditional attitude is beginning to break down. Inducements for sale are provided by the gradually increasing demand for consumer goods, as well as by taxation. But probably the most crucial impact has been made by improved marketing facilities, centred on the abbatoir which was erected through the Colonial Development Corporation at Lobatsi in 1954.

Until this abbatoir was opened, all cattle from Bechuanaland had to be exported on the hoof, involving treks through parched scrub-country of hundreds of miles, with consequent deterioration. Indeed, such treks are still necessary for cattle coming from the north-eastern part of the territory, which must be driven along a cattle route of some 400 miles to the abbatoir, and this has given rise to repeated demands for the erection of a second abbatoir in the north-east, at Francistown. After much discussion the Administration agreed in 1962 to investigate the possibilities.

The pressure for a second abbatoir shows how marked an effect the one at Lobatsi has had on the cattle industry, which has been and still is the lifeblood of the Bechuanaland economy. Though there has been a good deal of justified criticism levelled at the detailed operation of the abbatoir, including the low level of wages paid to its workers, it has proved an undoubted economic success. It has provided a stable and accessible market for cattle in at least the southern part of the territory, and in 1960 representatives of the producers acquired a quarter share in the issued capital of a limited liability company which took the abbatoir over. The Bechuanaland Government has a further quarter share of the issued capital, and the C.D.C. a half share. Certainly the capital cost of erecting the Lobatsi abbatoir, at just under £700,000, was a low investment for the benefit it has brought, even when reckoned together with the cost of improving associated services, such as disease control, stock routes, etc.

There is a very strong case for the erection of a second abbatoir. But if the cattle industry is to develop fully, even more will have to be done than to persuade increasing numbers of African owners to part with their cattle. Owners already show a keen appreciation of the facilities offered, and more and more of them are selling directly to the abbatoir, by-passing the speculators and middle-man traders. Between 1954 and 1962 the number of registered African suppliers increased from twelve to 1,500. What worries expert observers is the need to improve the *quality* of the cattle offered. At present, most owners offer old rather than prime cattle, and under the traditional grazing system, in far-flung cattle posts with little if any breeding control, most of the cattle eventually sold are of poor quality.

Furthermore, Bechuanaland's cattle industry must maintain and if possible increase exports to Britain. This was first attempted in 1958 by a Mr Cyril Hurwitz, who in 1959 sold nearly 27,000 head abroad, and in 1961 a subsidiary of the abbatoir company was formed, known as the Export and Canning Company, which now handles all export of beef and which has erected a medium-size cannery at Lobatsi. The importance of the British market, of course, is that it will enable Bechuanaland to diminish its dependence on the traditional but declining markets in South Africa, the Congo and the Rhodesias.

In 1959, which was a peak year, the distribution of beef exports was:

To	Number (in carcasses and on the hoof)
South Africa	56,000
Federation (Rhodesia)	11,400
Congo	3,000
Overseas	26,600
	97,000

The South African Meat Board will accept only a fixed monthly quantity of Bechuanaland beef, and this, in recent years, has generally been 4,000 carcasses a month. But the Lobatsi abbatoir slaughters perhaps 10,000 head during what is known as the 'flush season', when grazing conditions have been good. A good deal of the balance used to go to the Cold Storage Commission in Southern Rhodesia, but since 1960 this will accept only live cattle, and while there were once also substantial exports to the Congo, these have been disturbed by political unrest in recent years. Hence the importance of the British market, increased by the suspicion that the South African authorities tend to be harsher than they need in the length of the bans they promptly place on Bechuanaland cattle as soon as any outbreak of the dreaded foot-and-mouth disease occurs in the Protectorate. Fortunately, good progress seems to have been made in enlarging the British market, and exports to it increased from nearly 27,000 carcasses in 1959 to over 52,000 in 1961.

With a second abbatoir, and with the expansion of the British market, the problem of holding over cattle could be eased, and with the cannery in operation, it will be possible to market some beef even during foot-and-mouth disease outbreaks.

The cattle industry as a whole, however, will only become really profitable if the off-take, or percentage of total herds sold annually, is increased, and if the quality of cattle is improved. At present off-take has seldom risen above five per cent for African-owned herds, whereas with well-managed European-owned herds it is generally as high as fifteen per cent.

Both improved off-take and quality depend, however, on a change in the habits and customs of many of the cattle owners in the tribal Reserves, and since such changes would be social as well as economic, they cannot reasonably be expected to take place overnight or by decree. It will, for instance, be impossible to improve the breed of cattle unless fencing of at least some grazing lands is undertaken, since it is useless to introduce a good bull if cows are left roaming where they continue to be served by local scrub bulls. The influential tribal elders would certainly oppose any kind of fencing, actively if necessary, for they regard it as the beginning of an end to tribal land. But if the Administration had the money and trained staff, there is a great deal that it could do, or finance local councils to do, to encourage improvements.

Conditions for the whole cattle industry can be improved through expanded research in pasture management, through the provision of more watering points once the safe yields of under-ground water from boreholes has been established, and through supervising the number of cattle allowed around any watering point, so that neighbouring pasture will not be destroyed. There is a great need to instruct farmers in good land and animal husbandry, and if cattle quality is to be improved there must be funds for such instruction, for loans and for the control of disease.

The present Administration of Bechuanaland is keenly aware of the need to do these and many other necessary things to improve the cattle industry. It has had the benefit of expert outside advice, the latest coming at the end of 1963 from a two-man commission of inquiry invited through the U.N.'s Food and Agricultural Organization. This commission was very critical of the present operation of the abbatoir. But the Government has been starved of funds, and fresh advice will help relatively little without fresh funds.

If the reform and development of the cattle industry are inter-woven with both social and economic problems, the development of agriculture is in some ways even more involved. For where cattle-ranching development comes partially up against the problem of land tenure, agricultural development must meet it head-on.

Agriculture in Bechuanaland is at present so underdeveloped that even in relatively good years maize, which is the country's staple food, has to be imported. In a year of bad or no rains, famine relief has to be organized, as it was again in 1963. In a good year such as 1955, Bechuanaland imported nearly 14,000 bags of maize and maize meal at a cost of some £26,000.

The 'blocks' of European settlement at Tuli, Ghanzi, Lobatsi, and Gaberones comprise some of the best agricultural land in the Protectorate, and farmers in the Tuli Block have practically unlimited water for irrigation from its river frontage. These farmers make an important contribution to the overall economy of Bechuanaland, but the great bulk of crop production, valued at about £1 million a year, comes from African dryland farms.

The Morse Report declares that in the eastern region, where most of the crop production takes place, economic yields can be produced under dryland conditions if the standard of husbandry is sufficiently high, but that it is not easy to achieve such a standard in the face of both natural and social obstacles. The natural obstacles include:

(a) uncertainty of amount and distribution of rainfall;

(b) an inherent infertility of the soil coupled with loss of fertility through unsound cropping practices and failure to restore soil nutrients;

(c) the ever-present threat of pests and disease;

(d) wind erosion in the lands to the west and water erosion in the east where the soils are more compact but rainfall is heavier and gradients are steeper.

These natural difficulties are aggravated in the tribal areas by social obstacles, like:

(a) the practice of living in villages and cultivating lands that are often at a great distance;

(b) the communal form of land ownership, which means that lands improved by one man may be reallocated to another (though this is not often done in practice), and which also discourages the permanent fencing of lands for protection of crops against animals;

(c) the rule that ploughing and harvesting cannot begin until the chief gives the word (though this practice is now being relaxed in some tribal areas);

(d) the tradition that, except for the barest essential ploughing, planting, and reaping, nature need not be aided;

303

(e) the subsistence character of traditional consumer wants, and the consequent lack of interest in increasing the yield of what, to be enjoyed, must be in part a cash crop; and

(f) the lack of good storage and marketing facilities.

Arable farming is still done largely by the Batswana women. Seed is scattered, ploughed or hoed in, and the rest left to nature. With uncertain rains, it is not surprising that yields of maize and kaffir-corn have averaged less than one bag of 200 pounds weight per acre.

But as the Government's Development Plan for 1963–8 proclaims:

During the past seven years abundant proof has been provided to support the belief that, even without the introduction of large amounts of capital, the productivity of peasant farmers can be doubled and tripled by sympathetic extension work and help in the application of modern techniques. Agricultural training facilities are, however, at present limited. . . .

Increasing numbers of farmers have come forward to enrol under the Department of Agriculture's pupil-farmer or 'co-operator' scheme, and it is the training of demonstrators which is the key to the problem. Each demonstrator 'adopts' five farmers, who in turn must have enrolled the support of ten neighbours. On very meagre funds, the number of demonstrators has jumped from seventeen in 1952–3 to ninety-four in 1961–2, and this has meant that the number of pupil farmers could increase from eighty-four to 663. In 1962 another 269 applicants had to be turned away for lack of trained demonstrators to supervise them.

These are, of course, tiny figures, but their importance lies in the impact of their achievements. The pupil progressive farmers average about thirty acres of ground each, and on these they have been obtaining average yields of £7 instead of their previous £1 per acre. Thus even the small number of progressive farmers had, by 1961, added something between £150,000 and £200,000 to the value of arable output. They have made an increasing impression, too, by being the only ones in several areas to raise crops in years of rain-failure.

Bechuanaland's pupil-farmer scheme resembles that of

Basutoland in its rationale and approach, but it has not until now been able to look for marketing and credit to a real cooperative movement. For a long time, there even seemed to be actual distrust of cooperatives in the Administration, where the concept was linked with 'socialism' or worse. This attitude, however, changed in official circles, once pressure for cooperative societies began to come from groups of progressive farmers and from some officials within the Administration itself. But it is typical of Bechuanaland's financial straits that the Government had no money with which it felt that it could finance cooperative development. A cooperative officer is to be appointed, and the relevant legislation drafted, only because of a £9,000 grant from the Oxford Committee for Famine Relief.

It would seem that in Bechuanaland, as in Basutoland, cooperative societies hold out the greatest promise of progress. They can provide credit against the standing of the individual member, they can decrease costs and rationalize marketing, and above all they give people the framework within which to help themselves. In Bechuanaland, cooperative marketing could also eliminate one of the main potential sources of racial friction: the resentment felt against the white traders who have long acted as market agents. In the absence of other agencies, these traders have fulfilled a necessary function; but this side of their activities has necessarily been speculative, and whilst there is no readily available proof of their making excessive profits, the belief that they do so is almost universal amongst Africans. When, during a drought, an African has to buy back at inflated prices the grain that he sold to the white trader cheaply before, there is obvious ground for racial mistrust. The primary attraction of cooperatives lies, of course, in their direct economic benefits to members, but it is encouraging in a wider sense to find that both white and black farmers are becoming interested in multi-racial marketing, credit and supply cooperatives in which all members, irrespective of their wealth, enjoy equal status.

But even now that there is a popular demand for cooperatives and official support for their establishment, a shortage of finance may cripple their development. Thus the Government in its development plan says that it needs £40,500 for cooperatives between 1963–8. Of this it can allocate only £18,000, and in the years 1963–6 it does not know where it will get an immediately essential £3,500.

Long years of conditioning have more or less guaranteed that the financial requests of the Bechuanaland Administration to London are pared down very near to the bone. The Administration must, of course, consider that the amount of money which it can efficiently spend is in any case limited by the size and expert knowledge of its authorized staff. But even where it could, with existing staff, use a great deal more money than it does in fact request, it does not ask for more because it knows from past experience that it hasn't any chance of getting it. In fact, the Administration has a great deal of trouble in getting anything near what it regards as absolutely essential.

What is more, it is only since 1954 that the British Government has been prepared to give some budgetary aid in order that the appallingly low standard of social services might be improved. The small amounts of development funds which were allocated to Bechuanaland in the first post-war decade were, in the Administration's own words, 'insufficient to make any substantial impact on the Territory's financial position'. This is hardly surprising: the amount allocated in 1946 for development was £1 million for the next ten years, or £100,000 a year.

In these first ten post-war years, Bechuanaland actually balanced its annual budget, but it did this only by keeping it to less than £1 million, by allowing social services to remain at a vestigial level, and at the expense of development. By 1954, this had caused such stagnation that there were Africans advocating Bechuanaland's association with the neighbouring Federation of Rhodesia and Nyasaland, whilst the whites were almost solidly in favour of incorporation into South Africa.

It was only then that Britain decided to grant aid to Bechuanaland so that services could be improved, and this aid has risen from £140,000 in 1956–7 to an estimated £1·1 million in 1962–3. At the same time the rate of development expenditure after 1956 was stepped up to about £600,000 a year.

These figures must be seen against Bechuanaland's general financial position. The size of the Budget has grown from £1·2 million in 1956–7 to an estimated £3·19 million in 1962–3, of which C.D. & W.F. expenditure accounts for nearly £500,000.

Like the other two Territories, Bechuanaland obtains a fixed share of South Africa's customs revenue, in its case 0·276222 per cent. With the growing size of Bechuanaland's budget, the relative importance of these receipts from South Africa has lessened, but in 1962–3 they still amounted to approximately ten per cent of its ordinary revenue (excluding C.D. & W.F. monies).

Even more importantly, the earnings of migratory workers in South Africa are relatively substantial, helping significantly to redress the negative balance of trade which occurs in drought years. In 1960, when the loss was a trifle under £600,000, migrant workers brought £356,000 into Bechuanaland in deferred pay and remittances. During 1962, 25,315 workers left Bechuanaland to work in South Africa.

For those who seek employment in Bechuanaland, the opportunities and rewards are small. With an estimated ninety per cent of the population engaged in stock raising and agriculture, the Government has become the biggest single employer in the country. No reliable statistics exist, but the official estimate of employment and monthly wages for 1960 was:

Employment	Number	Average monthly wage
Government service (includes 1,700 casual labourers)	3,300	£5–£94
Agriculture	3,500	£4
Building	500	£6
Trade & Industry	3,500	£6
Domestic Service	2,000	£4

Whilst increased grants-in-aid and C.D. & W.F. expenditure have led to a relative improvement, they have barely made an impression on the combination of past neglect and the increasing demand for social services. Nowhere is this better illustrated than in Bechuanaland's educational system.

THIRSTS

Educationally, the Batswana are probably more backward than any other people in Africa which has been under British rule; they are challenged only by the Swazi for this dubious distinction.

Certainly in Bechuanaland as a whole the schools are, in the opinion of experts, worse housed and worse equipped than any in British-administered Africa.

Until 1961 the whole cost of African primary education has been borne by the Africans themselves, through their tribal Treasuries (since then the Government has helped to raise teachers' salaries), though the Treasuries do receive fifty per cent of the African tax paid initially to the central Government. The Government, moreover, has until now built for Africans only one classroom block, a trades school and two teacher training colleges in the whole Protectorate. All the existing schools have been built by missions, the tribes themselves, or by a few private bodies or individuals, and it is only in very recent years that the Government has even provided grants towards school upkeep and teachers' salaries.

The appetite of the Batswana for education is illustrated by the fact that most tribes spend up to seventy per cent of their Treasury funds on it, while, in addition, African parents have to find money for school fees. Amongst the Bakgatla, for example, each child in the lower primary classes has to pay 5s. a year and as much again for books and stationery, while in the higher classes fees rise to £1 a year. This, let alone the £7 10s. 0d. for fees in the secondary schools, plus money for books and stationery, is more then the poor parents can usually manage.

It would be difficult to find anywhere in the world such over-crowding. Classes of seventy or more children are common, and frequently a beginners' class of some 100 pupils will be taught by one *unqualified* teacher. Of 432 primary school teachers in 1960, only 139, or thirty-two per cent, were qualified in any formal way.

Nevertheless, probably at most one half of the African children of school age attend school at all, and most of these drop out after a year or two. This fantastic wastage can best be shown by the primary school enrolment figures for Bechuanaland in 1958:

Sub A:	9,113
Sub B:	6,653
Std I:	4,812
Std II:	3,507
Std III:	2,654

Std IV:	1,706
Std V:	840
Std VI:	639

In fact, only six per cent of the first year primary school pupils complete the seven-year primary school course and only three per cent of those who started schooling in 1957 actually entered a secondary school in 1964. Part of the reason for this has been that parents have traditionally sent their young sons out to herd cattle at distant posts shortly after they started school. But more and more parents are today anxious to keep their children in school, as is shown by the dramatic rise in school enrolment over the past ten years. Between 1953 and 1960 the number of children in primary schools doubled from about 18,000 to 36,000, and by 1962 it had reached 48,000.

The Bechuanaland Education Department estimates that at least 1,000 additional classrooms will be needed in the next decade. This increased demand for facilities has eaten up the small additional sums made available for education, and have left the lack of accommodation and equipment, but above all the lack of qualified teachers, as acute as ever, if not more so.

Thus whilst the school population rose by fifty-five per cent between 1960 and 1964, school buildings have risen by twenty per cent and the teaching force by only eighteen per cent. This means, of course, that the already shocking pupil:teacher ratio is becoming worse yet. In 1960 the figure was 32:1; in 1963 it was 42:1. But these are average figures, and despite the recently introduced shift system classes of seventy, eighty and even more remain common.

Because of poor teaching and lack of places, children are commonly forced to repeat classes in the primary schools. One third of the total school population are in the first year of the course, and two thirds in the first three years. This chokes up classes and discourages the pupils. The very high proportion who complete less than four years of primary school tend to lapse into illiteracy, which means that their years at school serve neither to widen their own horizons nor to make them more useful citizens.

The system of recruiting teachers is simply one of appointing such as may apply and, while conditions vary, it is common to find a blackboard as the only 'educational equipment'. There is, generally speaking, an enormous dearth of materials of all kinds – and especially of books – which might provide even the most rudimentary stimuli to intellectual curiosity and educational growth.

Expenditure on education from all sources, local and central, totalled only £28,000 in 1940. By 1950 this had increased to £67,000 and by 1960, as a result of grant-in-aid, to £320,000, of which tribal Treasuries contributed £115,000 and missions £25,000.

The real inadequacy of even the 1960 figure, however, becomes clear only when one splits up expenditure into that for white and that for African children. In 1960 £55,152 was spent on the education of 411 white children, or £134·2 per white child per year, while by contrast £268,683 was spent on the education of 36,273 African children, or £7·4 per African child per year. The point here is not only that *eighteen times as much was being spent on the education of every white child enrolled as on every black one*, but that it is hard to think of a worthwhile education which could be given on only £7·4 per head per year. It is little wonder that most African schools have no lavatories, and that racial integration bristles with problems.

A considerable building programme was undertaken after Britain finally made some funds available in 1954, yet by 1959 the overcrowding difficulties seemed no different; the new schools had barely managed to keep up with the increase in enrolment. The need for a crash programme in primary education was realized in 1959, but by 1962 only £25,000 had been found towards it. The African schools are run by local committees and financed from the tribal treasuries, which obtain from the Administration half of the £2 annual tax paid by all African men. This system of school management encourages local interest and trains people in local government, but it is also administratively complicated, wasteful and confused. The hitherto extremely low salaries of teachers have been raised in all three Territories, but the real need remains for greatly increased finance to provide class-rooms, equipment and additional teaching staff, as well as for the training or substitution of present untrained staff. Until these needs are met, it will help little to drop the school entrance age to eleven, as has been done, or to seven, as is planned.

What is more, preliminary census figures indicate that Bechuanaland's population has 'exploded' in recent years, so that there may well be more than 500,000 Batswana, and not the 317,000 on which all calculations of needs and *per capita* expenditure have been based. The average age of this population appears to be remarkably low at between eighteen and twenty years. This may partly be due to short life expectancy, but it also indicates that children probably outnumber adults by two or three to one. If this is so, the size of Bechuanaland's educational problem is far, far greater than has hitherto been supposed.

Bad as the position is in primary education, it is pitiful in secondary schooling. Bechuanaland has taken an inordinately long time to approach the stage of internal self-government. Yet despite this delay, or more probably because of it, the country cannot begin to provide educated men and women even for the medium range of present administrative posts, let alone for executive positions. In 1960 there were only 561 children in Bechuanaland secondary schools, and half of these were in the first year of their five-year course. Only eighteen pupils were preparing to sit for the matriculation examination. There were only two schools in the whole country which offered a full secondary course, and only one of these led to the academic matriculation examination. Three other schools took pupils for three years to Junior Certificate level, with another three offering such courses in 1962. Between 1956 and 1960 only seven Bechuana students passed the Senior Certificate (at non-matriculation level) and only five the full matriculation.

With the shifting of the Government headquarters from Mafeking, in South Africa, to the new township of Gaberones within the Protectorate, the first attempt at racial integration in schools is to be made. There are to be two primary schools in Gaberones, one English-medium and one Tswana-medium, with identical facilities and staffs of equal standard. Beyond this, there is to be one multi-racial secondary school, which is planned as something of a showpiece.

The Bechuanaland Administration has worked out quite detailed plans for tackling education on a 'crash programme' basis. A further secondary school is planned for Serowe, and the idea is to concentrate secondary education at these two schools, which it is hoped to equip and staff at a high level. Both schools will be built and run by the Government.

This concentration of scarce secondary education resources makes sense from an administrative point of view. But its corollary is the stopping of subsidies to all tribal secondary schools, including Moeng College, which was Tshekedi Khama's great venture. This announced withdrawal of subsidies is causing bitter resentment among the Batswana, who have sacrificed much to establish their tribal secondary schools. They realize that this decision has been forced on the local Administration by the meanness of Whitehall, and some of them, led by the Bakgatla, are determined to carry on somehow. The Administration's decision could also cripple the imaginative effort being made by Patrick van Rensburg, the South African refugee, to build up a new secondary school near Serowe. So, modest as the Administration's plans are for lack of finance, they bristle with difficulties, not the least of which will be the removal of the stimulating social influence of secondary education in the tribal areas.

The magnitude of the educational challenge facing Bechuanaland is staggering for so poor and underdeveloped a country. A conservative expert estimate of educational needs is for expenditure to rise to £900,000 by 1969 by Government and the tribal Treasuries, compared with £535,000 in 1964. But even if this money were found, it would allow the primary school population to expand only from the present 55,000 to 72,000 and would leave the pupil : teacher ratio at 45 : 1. And whilst this increased expenditure envisages an increase in secondary education, it looks forward to a 1974 target of only 150 people leaving secondary schools with the School Certificate or equivalent qualifications.

Where is this sort of money to come from ? Official thinking is that aside from massive self-help in the building of schools the tribal Treasuries must by 1969 find £350,000 of the £900,000 required (their estimated 1964 expenditure was £257,000). This would leave an estimated Government expenditure in 1969 of some £555,000 (against £386,000 in 1963). It is hard to know where the tribal Treasuries are to find this sort of money, but even if they succeeded in doing so it would mean that the Government would have to spend twenty-nine per cent of its estimated ordinary revenue on education. As no country can afford to do this assistance will clearly have to be found from outside if even a minimally reasonable educational system is to operate.

Quite aside from any other consideration, it will be impossible to press ahead with localization or Africanization of the Bechuanaland civil service if the educational system is not rapidly and radically improved. In 1962 there were only three Batswana in the service's 155 professional and administrative (or senior) grades, seventeen out of 260 in the technical (or medium) grades, and twenty-two out of 182 in the executive (or lower) grade. This situation is, of course, partly due to racial attitudes, discrimination and lack of in-job training for promotion in the past. But today, with 'localization' the official policy and the structure of the service recently reformed, it is largely the lack of sufficiently educated candidates which is holding up African advancement in the general service. In 1960 there were only eight known Bechuana university students: five at Pius XII in Basutoland, and three in Britain.

Lack of educated men is also a hindrance in beginning the Africanization of the Bechuanaland Protectorate police, though not the only one. This small force, with an establishment of just under 500 men to police 220,000 square miles, has until recently observed the colour bar of southern Africa in reserving commissioned officerships to whites. Africans have been able to rise to the rank of warrant-officer, whilst whites have been recruited at the inspectorate level, from which gazetted officers have been drawn. With the Administration committed to a policy of 'localization', Africans reached the inspectorate for the first time in 1962. Four African warrant-officers became inspectors, and four African non-commissioned officers became sub-inspectors. In time, one of the Africans may become a gazetted officer, and if there were more Africans available with the necessary educational qualifications to attend police courses in Britain, much faster progress would no doubt be made.

In the Development Plan for 1963–8, the Bechuanaland Government has proposed that £1·6 million should be spent on education, or only 15·7 per cent of the £10¼ million total. It would mean spending only a trifle more than £320,000 a year, or less than £1 per head of population. Yet the Government had itself previously calculated that it needed a minimum of £2½ million for education. If £2½ million were to be spent in these five years instead of £1·6 million, the results would at best be modest enough: by 1965 there could have been 135 students passing the Junior Certificate with eighty passing the final School Certificate, and by 1970 there could have been 230 Junior and 165 Senior passes. This, at a very optimistic estimate, could have meant that eight to ten graduates a year might have become available by 1970. But the Administration, knowing what it is likely to get from London, finally asked for only £1·6 million, so that even these very modest targets will not be reached. There is surely a clear case here for substantially increased aid.

The health of Bechuanaland is impossible to measure statistically, as not even records of African births and deaths are kept. In a country having pastoral communities scattered over vast distances, the Administration is obviously hampered by the lack of statistics in all spheres, but there can be no doubt of the grave shortage of medical services. A medical practitioner in the Protectorate believes that perhaps half the children die at birth and a third of the remainder in their first year.

The whole medical service, responsible for over 350,000 people in so great an area, had only sixteen doctors in 1959 and sixty-eight qualified nurses. The shortage of hospitals means that most parts of the country must make do with health centres, which do not have operating facilities, or with dispensaries, which in many cases are only visited periodically.

Missions of various denominations make a relatively large contribution to the health services, and are partly helped by Government finance. But there were, in 1960, still only thirty-eight beds for paying patients, 792 for free patients, and 191 cots in Bechuanaland's hospitals and health centres. Certainly this leaves a great deal of room for improvement, especially as the beds and better facilities are concentrated along the line of rail. Even here ante- and post-natal clinics exist only at the larger centres.

There are still areas like Sefhope, in the eastern spur of the Protectorate, where something like 14,000 people are served only by one dispenser, who has no transport. And there were in 1962 still pockets of up to 10,000 people who have no facilities at all in their area. At a very rough estimate, not much more than half the people are reached by medical services.

Recently, both the World Health Organization and U.N.I.C.E.F. have been helping in a survey on the incidence and control of diseases in Bechuanaland, but in general even the staff in the field, despite a limited 'flying-doctor' service, know about the ill only when they come to health centres and dispensaries.

Trachoma, enteritis, tick-bite and other fevers, including malaria, are common, and bilharzia is rife in the eastern part of the country, though it is said not to be a problem in the Okavango swamps. A major source of disease is the migrant labour system. A good deal of the Health Department's time is taken up by examining recruits for the mines, and in trying to care for those who return with tuberculosis. More than two per cent of the population is believed to be suffering from tuberculosis, and more than six per cent from venereal disease.

In the absence of any proper survey, it is hard to say what proportion of Bechuana are undernourished, but it would be surprising if the proportion were not high in a country where meat, despite cattle ranching, is not much eaten; where fresh vegetables and fruit do not form part of the common diet; and where the staple maize may fail for three or four drought years in succession. Anyone who has seen African school children queueing up for their plates of 'emergency feeding' mealie (maize) meal during a drought, or who has visited the villages at such times, will think conservative the opinion of one medical observer that 'most of the Bechuana people are undernourished most of the time'.

With funds from the British Government so limited, and the problems of raising productivity internally so large, any chance of mineral development in Bechuanaland is, of course, of great interest.

Bechuanaland has a long history of mining concessions and a fairly long history of actual small-scale mining. Small quantities of gold, silver, and copper have long been known to exist; asbestos was found in the twenties; and manganese and very large coal deposits have been explored recently. At present, however, mining is confined to two small manganese mines, one small asbestos mine, and an insignificant amount of gold and silver.

Both the manganese and the asbestos are mined in Tribal Reserves: asbestos and manganese in the Bangwaketse Reserve by the Marlime Company, a South African concern, and manganese in the Bamalete Reserve by the Bechuana and Protectorate Mining Corporation. But only 45,787 short tons of manganese ore, valued at £341,093, had been exported by 1963 from Bangwaketsi territory since active mining began in 1957, with even smaller quantities in the Bamalete reserve. Asbestos development has been hit by the drop in world prices, and since 1951 production has totalled just under 14,500 short tons valued at slightly over £1½ million. A new asbestos mill, which can increase production by forty per cent, was installed in 1962, but it seems clear that mining, if confined to these minerals, will not reach much more than its present 5·5 per cent of Bechuanaland's exports.

If mining is not very significant at present, however, it could become so in the near future. Over the past six or seven years, an increasing interest has been shown in Bechuanaland's mineral potential by large South African and Rhodesian firms, and important work has been done by the Protectorate's own Geological Survey Department.

The most exciting of present schemes is the exploitation of the sodium carbonate-bearing brines of the Makarikari pans, which lie in the Kalahari on the edge of the Bamangwato Reserve. The Makarikari salt pans cover a vast area, stretching to the horizon in a greyish white haze of heat, and their sodium carbonate content seems ideal for use in producing soda ash, which has wide industrial use and high grade salt. Such a project has been thoroughly investigated by a subsidiary of the American-dominated Rhodesian Selection Trust, which shares control of the Northern Rhodesian copper industry with South Africa's Anglo-American Corporation. R.S.T. plan to pump concentrated brine 100 miles through the shrub country to the nearest railhead at Shashi, where the company is to establish a chemical plant capable of producing 60,000 tons of soda ash and 180,000 tons of common salt a year. The idea is to supply the soda ash needs of South Africa, which has been importing 60,000 tons a year from Kenya through Imperial Chemical Industries Ltd, and to provide the Rhodesias, parts of the Congo and perhaps the Northern Transvaal with high grade salt. The Rhodesias have no salt supplies of their own, and with Kenya now committed to boycotting trade with South Africa, Bechuanaland supplies of soda ash will be welcomed in the Republic.

The Morse Mission pointed out that such a plant should be profitable on demand from the Rhodesias and Nyasaland alone, which have been importing 35,000 tons of salt a year, paying a great deal for freight. The whole Makarikari salt project involves a capital investment of about £3 million, but it should produce exports valued at £1–2 million a year. It should also provide some badly needed local employment, and give a general boost to the area.

Rhodesian Selection Trust also has a concession to prospect for minerals in the whole of the Bamangwato Reserve. This work has been carried out through a subsidiary company, Bamangwato Concessions Ltd, and there have been recent reports of major copper finds. Diamond prospecting is being carried out over wide areas of Crown and tribal land by the De Beers Anglo-American Group.

There would seem to be some chance of oil, too, for the Vacuum Oil Company of South Africa, after carrying out an exploratory survey over an extensive area, was sufficiently interested to apply for a renewal of its prospecting grant. This is now being handled by Mobiloil.

Prospecting and the possibility of substantial mining raises the crucial question of how far they will benefit the local Africans. Under Bechuanaland law, mineral rights in all tribal areas are vested in the people, through the chief, and if a prospecting or mining agreement is made, any money due must be paid to the tribal Treasury. In the Tati Concession, the mineral rights are owned by the Tati Company, and in the Lobatsi, Gaberones, and Tuli blocks they are owned by the British South Africa Company. In the rest of the territory, mineral rights are vested in the Crown, which can give grants for prospecting and mining without consulting local opinion. But as the Crown is administering or holding these Crown Lands on behalf of the people of the Protectorate, it should consider their interests before granting any concessions.

We have seen how strongly Tshekedi Khama and the Bamangwato fought against the well-meant but autocratic attempt of the

Government to push them into mining agreements with the British South Africa Company in the late twenties. The Bamang-wato feared that through mining agreements they might lose some of their land, that there would be an influx of unwanted whites, and that the profits would go to outsiders. This issue came up again in 1956, when the Anglo-American Corporation of South Africa became interested in gaining a concession. The Government was keen that it should be granted, but the then raging dispute over Seretse Khama's position had sharpened African suspicions. Once the dispute was settled, Tshekedi, who was in any case suspicious of bringing in a South African company, arranged to meet Sir Ronald Prain, the head of Rhodesian Selection Trust. From this successful meeting, at which the two men took a liking to one another, there grew the first of the concession agreements under which R.S.T. today operates in Bamangwato territory. These agreements have been much praised because they give the Bamangwato token representation on the board of directors and a 'free' shareholding in the company, instead of a mere receipt of royalties.

As part of its prospecting agreement, R.S.T. has considered the economic possibilities of the very substantial coal deposits which Bechuanaland is now known to possess. There are two major deposits, both of them adjacent to the railway line running through the Territory. Borings have proved reserves of 150 million and over 400 million tons, and there may well be more than this. The difficulty is that, whilst the coal is of good medium South African quality, it would have to be raised so cheaply that, after the necessary treatment, it could compete with the very low-priced South African and Rhodesian coal. At present there seems every chance of its doing so in the Protectorate, in South West Africa and parts of South Africa more distant from other coal-fields. R.S.T. has, however, concluded that it does not wish to take up its option to mine the Bamangwato coal, and so far no other company has come forward. It is estimated that it would cost about £1½ million to open a large open-cast colliery, and that this would have to sell 500,000 tons a year to be profitable.

The Morse Mission, however, makes two suggestions that do not require a straightforward full-scale mining project. First, if an appreciable local demand could be established for run-of-mine coal, it would be practicable to mine an existing shallow, easily-won seam on a small scale. The Mission urges that this less ambitious possibility should be investigated, and with the establishment of the new Government headquarters in Gaberones this might well become possible. Then, too, the Mission appends to its report some notes on gas turbines, compiled by Sir Alexander Gibb and Partners, the eminent consulting engineers, which strongly suggest that it would be a practicable proposition to generate electricity in Bechuanaland by using the local coal deposits.

There are also other lines of approach which might be tried, such as negotiating with Rhodesian railways to take a fixed percentage of low grade Bechuanaland coal for its operations within the territory. The difficulty here, as with many other projects in Bechuanaland, is that the Government itself has no monies with which to initiate, let alone subsidize, development capable of paying off after a time and meanwhile providing employment and boosting the economy.

Indeed, the lack of finance threatens today to block the one project which, more than any other, could transform Bechuanaland: the tapping of the abundant waters of the Okavango swamps for the parched but arable lands in the rest of the country.

Water, or the lack of it, is what ultimately limits every kind of economic development in Bechuanaland, and it has infuriated more than one planner to think how the abundant, clear waters of the Okavango River are lost in the swamps in the north-west corner of the country. Clearly, if these waters could be brought to other parts of the country, the benefits would be enormous. Several plans have been put forward over the years for doing this, but they have either been dismissed out of hand as impracticable or pigeonholed because they involved large sums of money.

But a plan for utilizing the waters of the Okavango was judged to be quite feasible by the Morse Mission. The fundamental idea would be to tap the waters of the Okavango River, which rises in Angola and passes through the Caprivi Strip, shortly after it enters Bechuanaland. It would then be led in a canal around the outer, western side of the swamps, providing both irrigation water and a means of barge transport. Such a canal, says the

Morse Mission 'would be easy to maintain and control', and though no estimate of costs could be given because no ground contours are available, the Mission thought that £75,000 'would probably suffice for its construction (without lining) to carry 500 cusecs'.

The Mission also discussed plans to extend the canal from Toteng, near Maun, to Rakops in the Kalahari, and then to pump water (possibly with pumps powered by Bechuanaland coal) over the intervening flat lands all the way to the Francistown and the Serowe–Mahalapye areas.

Were this done, the water requirements for all conceivable development of these two population centres ... would be catered for. In addition, supplies for cattle watering and for irrigation of both arable lands and pasture would be available along the route.

Water means life in Bechuanaland. For the Batswana, excluded from the river frontages of the white farming blocks, water is the main subject of their thoughts and talk, and their most enthusiastic acclamation of a good speech or event is '*Pula ! Pula !*' – Rain! Rain! Every year they wait and pray for rain, but only too often their crops wither and their cattle die in drought.

The Administration has encouraged the formation of syndicates to which it loans money for sinking new boreholes, but no one knows what boreholes are doing to the water tables. What is certain is that it has sunk over 100 feet in some areas within living memory, and it may even be that new boreholes will use up irreplaceable fossil water. A good deal could be done with small dams to catch the flash floods when the rains do come, but again the Government lacks money, and the tribes are too poor to raise it on their own. The few dams which have been built recently have been made possible only because Oxfam has made funds available, which is a sad reflection on how official Britain is meeting the basic needs of the people under its protection.

So poor is the available hydrological information in Bechuanaland that in 1960 the Morse Mission placed the need for a proper survey amongst its most urgent recommendations. Lacking this sort of information, as well as much else, the Mission could make no estimate of the costs of the full Okavango water project, but it did stress strongly its great importance and intrinsic feasibility.

Following the Mission's advice, the Government has successfully applied to the United Nations Expanded Technical Assistance Programme (U.N.E.P.T.A.) for help in making a more detailed preliminary investigation. This report was not yet available at the time of writing, and it can only be hoped that this is the reason why the Okavango scheme is not mentioned at all in the Administration's 1963–8 development plan.

But whatever the reason for the omission, the Government, both in Bechuanaland and in London, should be pressed to act on the Okavango project. It represents Bechuanaland's only major water concentration, and its exploitation will become essential if this land of drought and sand is to undergo major development.

The Morse Mission has stressed that there is an attitude and spirit in Bechuanaland, and in the other two Territories, of people wanting help in order to help themselves, and that this is obviously an invaluable asset.

One of the difficulties in stimulating social development in underdeveloped countries is that they lack the sort of educated people with leisure and means who have furthered many voluntary associations in a country like Britain. Most people in Bechuanaland live on a subsistence standard, or less, and even if they club together they do not command much capital in cash or even in kind. But many Batswana and their leaders are keen to have advice from outside, provided it is given in an acceptable way, to act on it and to learn from example.

This is the importance of the Bamangwato Development Association, which is an attempt to make this sort of advice and example, as well as some capital, available to a group of people who want to cooperate in helping themselves and their community.

The idea of this informal association to foster social and economic development came originally from Tshekedi Khama, who had seen similar work being done at St Faith's Mission in Southern Rhodesia under the guidance of Guy and Molly Clutton-Brock. Tshekedi invited the Clutton-Brocks to come and work amongst the Bamangwato, which they eventually did (after Guy had been arbitrarily imprisoned in Southern Rhodesia and Tshekedi had died) with the support of Seretse Khama.

The B.D.A. is run under the aegis of a committee appointed by the Pelikwe *kgotla*, or tribal general meeting, and this makes it at least an extension of the local community. Its general policy is to tackle local development as widely as possible, and by providing social facilities it aims at raising the social horizon of the community, halting the drift from the land. This should be stimulated by and stimulate greater production, though it is accepted that in a poor country like Bechuanaland this presently implies heavy subsidy from abroad.

The B.D.A. has therefore tackled a wide range of local needs as it found them: a farm, a cattle ranch project, a trading store, grain milling and storage, and a vegetable garden; a community centre, a clinic and local credit; and the development of water supplies. The work of the association is not done communally, since it employs local people under small B.D.A. staff. But it seems to be generally accepted by the employees that the farm and other B.D.A. projects are in the interests of the local *kgotla* members and that, in the long run, wages will depend on their productivity. The idea that they are all engaged in *joint* labour seems to have been established.

It is hard to judge just how 'successful' the B.D.A. is, especially when it comes to the strict requirements of normal accountancy. Most of its projects are still in the early stages of development, and it will probably transpire that some are uneconomic. But the B.D.A. has certainly aroused the enthusiasm of its local African staff, and it seems to be having a catalytic effect in the whole area. Even if, as seems certain, it were found that some of its work could be done more 'economically' by orthodox methods, this would leave out of account the impact which it makes on ordinary people's lives. It is by its success as an 'agent of change' that the B.D.A. will have to be judged.

Another interesting, and highly promising, community development is the Swaneng Hill School project near Serowe. This was inspired by Patrick van Rensburg, a young white South African who, after spending some time as a political refugee in Britain, returned to Bechuanaland together with his wife in order to start a self-help secondary school. The van Rensburgs have since been joined by three other expatriate couples, and have gained the confidence of the local Bamangwato to such an extent that the school project, which is now in operation, has been expanded to include the country's first registered cooperative – a consumer one with some 500 members – and agricultural education.

On the official level, the Government has in 1964 at long last decided to sponsor cooperatives, of which six agricultural, two consumer and two for borehole maintenance were scheduled in 1964 under a five-year British grant.

It seems clear that the future of most people in Bechuanaland lies in ranching and farming, but that mining, with its ancillary services, could bring about a quite dramatic change in the Territory's financial position. There is, as we have seen, a great deal to be done in developing agriculture, and progress must depend both on the pumping in of funds from outside and on the people themselves.

But for development in all these spheres, the Government will have above all to tackle the key problems of water and of communications. The Public Works Department has, like most other departments, been limited by a very inadequate budget, but now the Agency for International Development is prepared to consider large-scale investment in developing the Territory's roads. The figure involved is believed to be £2·5 million over five years, though the whole project may be endangered or lost because the British Government feels that it cannot find a matching £500,000.

What roads mean to Bechuanaland was emphasized by a Food and Agricultural Mission which recently investigated the livestock industry: 'An integrated road system is an urgent need as a first prerequisite for real expansion and development. This condition for expansion cannot be over-emphasized.'

If such a road system were developed, improved distribution could also do something to stimulate some industrial development. What little industry exists at the moment is almost all connected with cattle. Aside from the abbatoir and cannery, there is one independently-owned small soap factory and one small bone-meal factory, a marginal creamery, a recently opened maize mill and a new tannery, which processes the tough game hide of wildebeest for making mining boots. One sees the point of the official summary that 'industrial development is in its infancy'.

In Bechuanaland's present position, with the vast mass of Africans at subsistence level and with trade and commerce largely in the hands of prospering whites, it is surprising that race relations are apparently very good. There has been no racial riot in Bechuanaland, and in the dusty hotels white and black can be seen drinking in the same bars.

But for almost everybody, black and white, that is about as far as it goes. The Government does, it is true, hold parties on official occasions to which black and white come, but for the most part there is no other social contact. Nor does one gain the impression that such contact is much wanted, especially by the whites, and certainly not by those who farm in the various white 'blocks'. Their attitudes are very much those of racialist Afrikaners, and in fact farms in the Tuli Block are owned by two South African Cabinet Ministers: Mr J. J. Serfontein and Mr P. M. K. le Roux.

One of the leading elected representatives of these white farmers, the late 'Oom Hendrik' van Gass, summed up the feelings of the die-hards for me over lunch during a recent session of the Legislative Council. Within easy hearing distance of African members whom he had a few minutes earlier been addressing as 'The honourable,' Oom Hendrik told me in Afrikaans, which many Africans understand: 'Well, yes, education is all very well, and you can educate these people. But education is not civilization, man. For us, a kaffir remains a kaffir. You put *that* in your book.'

Mr van Gass was, of course, known as something of a die-hard, and tried to have the borders of Bechuanaland changed so as to incorporate at least the Ghanzi Block in South Africa. There are other whites with much more moderate attitudes, but there is a danger in the two racial groups merely tolerating each other's separate presence, especially where whites are so clearly identified with wealth made from ranching and trading with Africans. Certainly non-racialism was not helped when Afrikaans farmers in the Ghanzi Block withdrew their children from its primary school in 1963 because a few non-white pupils were admitted. The school had to close down.

For many years, too, really bitter resentment has been built up in Francistown by the operations of the Tati Company, which owns most of the Francistown area under a concession originally given by the Matabele King Lobengula. The concession has passed through many hands, but for a good number of years now the company has been controlled by the Glazer brothers, two Johannesburg property tycoons, of whom only Mr B. Glazer is still alive.

On the outskirts of the little town of Francistown, the company set aside an area for Africans, which in the usual South African manner was known as the 'location'. There some 5,000 Africans paid between 2s. 6d. and 5s. for the ground rent on which to put up shelters, with only two water points and no sewerage among the lot of them. The result, not surprisingly, was a suppurating slum. The company itself was able to make its own regulations for the township, and erected a company beer hall after prohibiting home brewing and enforcing the ban with its own tiny police force.

This situation was permitted to exist until 1963, when the relevant legislation was amended to allow the creation of a statutory, elected township board, which is taking over an increasing range of powers and functions. The Government has considered buying Mr Glazer out, but felt that his price was unrealistic, and it is true that until the law was changed there was little it could do. But even if the ordinary township inhabitant understood this, which is extremely improbable, he would have wondered why it took so long to change the law. Certainly, by the time that reform was introduced, the issue had, of course, been taken up by African politicians. A great deal of suspicion and bitterness had been created, and much of it had distinctly racial overtones. Such tardiness in Government action is dangerous, especially when ordinary people are left with the feeling that the Government is powerless in the face of vested white interests, or – worse – is in cahoots with them.

Communication is a real problem in Bechuanaland, and it should be said that the Government is making as energetic an effort as funds allow to build up an Information Department, which is already far ahead of similar attempts in Swaziland and Basutoland. A special effort is being made through daily summaries to let people know what the Legislative Council is doing, and a monthly magazine, partly written in the vernacular, has become Bechuanaland's only 'newspaper'. But this excellent work is limited not only by lack of funds but also by the territory's high rate of illiteracy. It has now been decided to set up a broadcasting station which, as in other parts of Africa, is by far the most effective way of reaching the mass of people.

But even broadcasting is a one-way method of communication, and it is unlikely that it will provide the answer to the two main charges which African politicians are justifiably laying against the British Administration: its failure to tackle the educational problem, and its failure to develop the Territory economically so as to provide alternative forms of employment to those in South Africa. These charges are, today, only partly to be brought against the local Administration, because it is up to the British Government to provide the funds without which the 'men on the spot' are hamstrung.

That the local Administration has come to realize the gravity of the economic situation is shown by a passage from its Development Plan for 1963–8:

Bechuanaland is at present precariously balanced in a situation from which it would either sink backwards into a state of almost permanent insolvency or move forward to a more prosperous future. To tip the balance on the right side the Territory needs a much more ambitious development plan than it has had in the past, and the most determined efforts must be made to implement it.

It seems certain that Bechuanaland faces a troubled future, especially in its relations with South Africa. The sorest point is, of course, Bechuanaland's inescapable role as a route of flight and as a sanctuary for anti-apartheid refugees.

Though it is impractical to police the whole of Bechuanaland's vast borders, the South Africans have set up a number of control posts, and so, towards the end of 1963, have the Southern Rhodesian police. Under South African law, travel documents are being demanded from people coming from Bechuanaland, and the Protectorate Legislative Council has imposed similar conditions on immigrants from South Africa.

As with the other Territories, aircraft flying between Bechuanaland and the Republic must now be checked into and out of South Africa at designated South African police points. The Bechuanaland authorities have made it clear that they will continue to grant political refuge, and that South Africans wanted for political offences which are not crimes in Bechuanaland will not be extradited, though they must abstain from politics whilst in the Protectorate.

South African resentment flared up afresh in October 1962, when a secret but widely publicized conference of the banned African National Congress was held in Lobatsi, with exiled leaders from various parts of the world meeting underground leaders from the Republic behind locked doors. And tension mounted further in November 1962, when the Bechuanaland police boarded a train passing through the Territory and freed three South West African refugees who were being escorted back to South Africa after having been arrested in the Rhodesias. Sir John Maud, the then High Commissioner, took the unchallengeable line that these men were being illegally detained in Bechuanaland, and personally ordered their release.

Relations between Bechuanaland and South Africa then reached a point of unprecedented crisis, as we have seen, in 1963, when Dr Abrahams, the Coloured South West African leader, was kidnapped by South Africans within the territory and when Arthur Goldreich and Harold Wolpe, the two South African escapees, found temporary asylum there. In both cases, the British authorities stood firm against what must have been enormous South African pressures. Public dismay was therefore all the greater when a little while later they seemed to be 'cutting' the escape line in sending back to Basutoland a small group of refugees who had flown into Bechuanaland without proper papers.

Dr Abrahams's case was, for Bechuanaland, not directly connected with the issue of South West Africa, although his kidnappers came from there. But if international action against South Africa's illegal administration of South West Africa became a reality, Bechuanaland could easily become embroiled. For the Protectorate has a long common border with South West and particularly with the Caprivi Strip, a narrow finger of land jutting out from South West Africa to the point on the Zambesi where Bechuanaland meets Northern and Southern Rhodesia. This Caprivi Strip was administered by Bechuanaland from

1922–9, and then again came under South African authority by an arrangement which some members of the Protectorate's Legislative Council would like to see challenged even at this late date.

Against this background of certain tension, it might seem sanguine for Bechuanaland to launch a programme of economic expansion which seems to require South African cooperation at least for markets. It may reasonably be supposed that unless Bechuanaland submits to South African pressures over refugees, Dr Verwoerd's Government will pursue a policy of economic hostility, rather than cooperation. Alternative markets for Bechuanaland's cattle and potential agriculture crops should therefore be urgently explored.

But this line of speculation ignores the strength which Bechuanaland possesses precisely by virtue of its being so great a potential source of trouble for South Africa. The British authorities, whilst they have stood firm on the international conventions of refuge, are also making strenuous efforts to limit the activities of refugees, and are determined to prevent the Protectorate from becoming a base for any physical action against South Africa. This policy will continue under Bechuanaland's new constitution, and it seems to be supported at least by the Democratic Party. It would seem in South Africa's interest to maintain this position as the least of the evils open to it in relation to Bechuanaland, rather than to precipitate a situation of open hostility.

POSTSCRIPT – THE 1965 ELECTIONS

The general elections held on 1 March 1965 were remarkable for the high percentage poll, their complete peacefulness, and for the overwhelming victory won by Seretse Khama's B.D.P.

Twelve seats are in the Bamangwato Reserve, which loyally follows Seretse, and in three seats the B.D.P. was unopposed. But the results demonstrated massive B.D.P. support throughout the country. With a total poll of 140,789, or about seventy-five per cent, the results were:

	contested	won	votes	per cent of poll
B.D.P.	31	28	113,168	80
B.P.P. (Matante)	26	3	19,964	14
B.I.P.	24	0	6,491	5
Independent	1	0	789	—
B.P.P. (Motsete)	1	0	377	—

Only in five contested constituencies was the B.D.P. convincingly challenged while itself challenging all three seats won by the B.P.P.; twenty-three non-B.D.P. candidates lost their deposits.

The three major parties apparently disposed of significant election funds. It was widely accepted that Bechuanaland whites, including Afrikaners, donated funds to Seretse Khama's B.D.P., regarding him as the least of alternative evils. B.D.P. speakers stressed that both Matante and Mpho had recently visited Communist countries, and it was widely alleged that they received funds originating either from Peking or Moscow. In any event, loudspeaker vans became a familiar sight, though only the B.D.P. organized an aircraft drop of leaflets on isolated Kalahari villages.

With a largely illiterate electorate, the Administration allocated a different colour to each party. In the polling booth each voter received a disc or 'button' for each competing party, dropped the coloured button he favoured in a sealed envelope into the ballot box, and threw away the other buttons. The percentage of spoilt ballots was small. More revealingly, each party chose a campaign symbol: Matante a Ghana-type black star, underlining the B.P.P.'s Pan-African orientation; Mpho a black cow on a green field, stressing the B.I.P.'s emphasis on the land issue. 'Democratic' apparently meant little to ordinary voters and was popularly rendered as '*Domkrag*', which is Afrikaans for 'brute force'. Seretse therefore chose an ox-wagon jack: the B.D.P. would jack Bechuanaland up.

But the B.D.P.'s only radical election plank was that the Government should take over, by negotiation, all mineral rights from tribal authorities and private companies. Pledged to democracy, non-racialism and a multi-party State, the B.D.P. also stood 'for a *gradual* but *sure* evolution of a national State', to which

329

tribal interests and institutions will become secondary. But, important for tribalists and white farmers, both communal and individual land-ownership will be respected. The cattle industry, agriculture, water conservation and utilization, education, technical training, medical services and civil-service localization are to be boosted. Economic planning and an industrial finance corporation are promised, but outside investment 'from whatever country' will be sought provided that 'as far as conditions permit local labour will be trained and used'; *equal pay for equal work*, or equal qualifications, and what is more important, *for equal productivity*' is promised. Rural community development will forestall the evils of excessive urbanization; indigent rural Batswana will be found employment. The planks are good and sensible, but there is no indication of how the building will be financed.

Full independence 'within the shortest possible time' is the aim (Seretse now speaks of September 1966), with non-alignment combined with membership of the Commonwealth, the U.N. and the Organization of African Unity.

The B.P.P. manifesto is often less specific, but differs only in demanding free education until fifteen, opposing nationalization of mines, stressing cooperatives and calling both for an African Common Market and protective Bechuanaland tariffs.

Most voters were probably more impressed by differences in slogans, the candidates' local standing, their chief's attitude and the past image of the parties and leaders. The B.D.P. fielded a strong team under Seretse, alone had parliamentary experience, had ample funds and, with a moderate image, was favoured by some important chiefs.

Seretse Khama stood on his home ground at Serowe, Matante in urban Francistown-Tati East (a lieutenant took Tati West), Mpho on Baye tribal home ground in remote Okavango, and Motsete on urban-rural home ground in Lobatsi-Barolong. They polled: Khama: 5,909 (B.P.P. 39, B.I.P. 53), Matante 4,415 (B.D.P. 1,214, B.I.P. 85), Mpho 1,666 (B.D.P. 1,929), Motsete 377 (B.D.P. 4,655, B.P.P. 604, B.I.P. 165).

There were three women candidates, all B.I.P. and unsuccessful. The only white candidate, Mr Benny Steinberg, gained 5,451 B.D.P. votes (ninety-seven per cent of poll), including many from

Bushmen. Though elsewhere candidates' speeches could have meant libel actions, there was no overt anti-white-ism. But the B.I.P. election demand that all privately- or foreign-owned land should, with compensation, be nationalized (whites who stay should become 'White Bechuana', grazing cattle communally) deeply alarmed white farmers, most of whom are Afrikaners. In the Tuli block the old idea of joining neighbouring Southern Rhodesia was revived. Tati concession farmers, led by Mr L. Beyers, a Pretoria advocate and local land-owner, began a campaign for Tati independence. But the Administration refused to entertain their petition, as has the new Government.

In the event, Seretse's landslide victory reassured most whites, as did the inclusion of a white man in his Government. Mr David James Morgan is one of four special members whom the legislature can elect. A Francistown businessman and farmer, in Bechuanaland since 1928, he was unofficially responsible for Works and Communications in the last Legco. He is now minister in these crucial fields, which include the completion of the new capital at Gaberones, to which the Government moved from Mafeking in South Africa in February 1965.

As Prime Minister, Mr Khama appointed as ministers: deputy Prime Minister – Quet Masire; Agriculture – M. Nwako; Labour and Social Services – B. Thema; Mines, Commerce and Industry – A. Dambe; Works and Communications – D. Morgan; Parliamentary Secretary, ministry of Finance – E. Kgabo.

With Seretse troubled by ill-health, Mr Quet Masire's post may be crucially important. Intelligent, capable and sophisticated, only thirty-nine years old, he matriculated from Tigerkloof in South Africa, obtained a teaching diploma, was a journalist, and has been a very successful progressive farmer and secretary-general of the B.D.P. Several of his fellow ministers have been school headmasters. A British official remains Minister of Finance, and the Queen's Commissioner, retaining sweeping powers, presides over the cabinet and not the Prime Minister. It is unfortunate that Sir Peter Fawcus, widely respected and trusted, retired after the elections. His successor is Mr H. S. Norman-Walker, previously Secretary to the Treasury in Malawi.

Before the elections, Seretse Khama objected strongly to some 30,000 Batswana working in South Africa being treated as 'third-class citizens' and said that he would not attempt to establish diplomatic relations with the Republic. But since taking office he has stressed that, while condemning apartheid, Bechuanaland would foster trade with and investment from South Africa. 'I am certain that other African countries realize that it is in our interests to trade with whoever will trade with us.' After the elections Dr Verwoerd claimed that Seretse had ceased to be a Prohibited Immigrant in South Africa in October 1964. But this was the first that Seretse, the Bechuanaland Administration or the British Embassy in Cape Town had heard of it. Seretse in any case does not wish to visit the Republic without his wife Ruth. The ban resulted from their marriage; now she is the only white first lady in African government.

In the event, the new Prime Minister's first foreign trip was to Zambia, at President Kaunda's invitation. Though he again stressed Bechuanaland's dependence on South Africa, he was fêted as a sincere – if realistic – African nationalist. In Zambia, dependent on Southern Rhodesia and Moçambique, his problem is understood. Indeed, an eventual federation of Bechuanaland and Zambia, though linked physically only by their tiny common border at the Zambesi, is being mooted privately in the Protectorate. Seretse, whilst wanting increased trade with the North, is said to be cool to the idea, chiefly because existing links are so sketchy and most Batswana live along the line of rail, 300 miles from Zambia. But the completion of the Francistown–Maun road, financed by £1 million from America's International Development Agency, could open up the neglected North, and mining activities might even lead R.S.T. to support railway building northwards.

In the meantime, the very scale of the B.D.P.'s victory raises two major problems. How will the other parties accept their defeat, especially the unrepresented B.I.P.? Perhaps more seriously, lack of an effective opposition could strengthen the B.D.P.'s essentially conservative character. A lack of badly needed dynamism, let alone radicalism, could result, with Seretse and his ministers relying too heavily on conservatively minded white expatriate officials. Equally, much will depend on how senior British officials exercise their large remaining direct powers, and on British financial support.

10 The Mouth that Speaks no Lies – Swaziland

If it took the British Government a very long time to arrive at any definite policy in its administration of Basutoland and Bechuanaland, this took even longer in Swaziland. The High Commissioner under whom Swaziland came in 1903 was instructed 'to respect any native laws by which the civil relations of any native chiefs, tribes or populations under His Majesty's protection are now governed', provided that they did not conflict with British sovereignty or were not 'clearly injurious to the welfare of the said natives'. It was only in 1944 that an attempt was made to place 'Native administration' on a formal basis, and even then Swazi opposition frustrated any effective reform until 1950.

In the intervening years, the Swazi chiefs were largely left to their own devices. Land, however, provided a constant source of friction and dissatisfaction, and, together with the ownership of mineral rights, remains a burning issue today. It is, in fact, the question of mineral rights which has bedevilled the negotiations for political advance under a new Swaziland constitution in the past few years, and which has marked the main clashes with the Administration ever since Swaziland came under British protection.

Swaziland today is a jumble of areas either reserved for or owned by the Swazi or by Europeans, and this patchwork pattern resulted from early attempts by the British to sort out the fantastic confusion which had been created, before they took over, by the lavish grants of multiple concessions by the ruler Mbandzeni. The way out taken by Britain was to review all the concessions, and to partition the land involved between the Swazi and Europeans. One third of the land was set aside for the exclusive use of the Swazi, who were ordered to leave the other two-thirds unless they made agreements with the concessionaires to remain, and in return for 'giving up' that third to the Swazi, many concessionaires were given freehold instead of terminable leasehold title. These arrangements were formalized in the Concessions Partition Proclamation of 1907, and under an Order-in-Council of 1908, the rights of all expired mineral and land concessions were to revert to the Crown.

The Swazi chiefs felt that they had been permanently deprived of two-thirds of their land, and sent a delegation of five to protest, unsuccessfully, in London. Swaziland was not greatly affected by the First World War, and to the chiefs the main anxiety of the era following the war was that the Government sold or leased Crown Lands to Europeans. The Chief Regent and her advisers felt that the only way in which they could regain the lost Swazi lands was to challenge the legality of the original partition and of the measures which went with it.

In 1922 Sobhuza II, who had by then reached his majority, was installed as Paramount Chief, and in that year he challenged in the courts the validity of the original partition, of the concessions, and of the Orders-in-Council which defined Crown Lands.

This case, which was fought all the way to the Privy Council, failed, however, and the Swazi have gone on chafing under what they see as an enforced and unfair partition.

The British, having confirmed the legality of their right to rule in Swaziland, did very little actual ruling. In almost all important respects, day-to-day life was left to be run by the chiefs, who commonly exceeded and abused their powers. There was hardly any money available to the Government, and no official attempts to provide social services. The administrators were concerned mainly with their magisterial functions in criminal cases and with the affairs of the white community, which was given a European Advisory Council in 1921. This had nine elected members, and received statutory recognition in 1949.

It was two chance events which saved Swaziland from stagnating altogether in the inter-war years. The first was the visit in 1927 of Mr L. Amery, then Secretary of State for Dominions. What he saw must have shaken him considerably, for in the very next year Swaziland was for the first time given a grant-in-aid by the British Parliament. The second event, at the same time, was the extension of the South African railway system to Gollel on the Swaziland border, which suddenly ended the territory's physical isolation.

A few years later, in 1931, Sir Alan Pim was appointed to look into the financial and economic position of Swaziland, and he delivered himself of a scathing report. He thought poorly of what little economic development there had been, including both mining and agriculture, and observed that there was no money to provide the social services necessary if African agriculture in particular was to improve. Hardly anything had been done by the Administration for African education, and what little facilities existed had mainly been the work of missions or of the Africans themselves. Even the Native Tax was collected only sketchily, and officials gave little thought to the future of the territory. Lord Hailey, in summarizing this period, quotes the opinion of one expert visitor who in the early thirties described Swaziland as 'the least reputable and most neglected of British dependencies'.

Some changes were made after the Pim Report was published in 1932, and the financial situation improved through continued small annual grants-in-aid and some funds for Colonial Development. More substantial, though still relatively small, aid for social services had to await the C.D. & W.F. Act of 1940. In the administrative field the Pim Report showed the urgent need to change the attitude which regarded the tribal administration as a sort of separate régime, pretty well free to go its own way if social services and better government were to affect the lives of the ordinary Swazi. But the Second World War came and went without any basic reform in Swaziland. The Territory remained a nearly forgotten backwater, although 4,000 Swazi enlisted and served in the Royal Pioneer Corps in north Africa, Sicily, Italy and the Middle East. As with African volunteers from Basutoland and Bechuanaland, they were white-officered and initially denied any training in arms, though they were to distinguish themselves in the fiercely fought landings at Salerno and Anzio.

The traditional structure of Swazi organization is extremely complex and deeply rooted, with an aristocratic hierarchy headed by the Ngwenyama, whose role and powers are semi-religious and connected with the fertility of the land and his people. In this he is closely dependent upon his mother, the Ndlovukasi or Lady Elephant, who annually renews his powers in an important ceremony, and who enjoys a crucial position.

This traditional structure, with its web of privilege and obligation, has long governed the day-to-day life of most Swazi, including the allocation and use of land, which is held by the chief for the people, and the raising of 'regiments' according to age groups for communal works. The whole system has been exceptionally well described in anthropological works,* and a great deal of it has been retained in the modern form of the Swazi National Administration. The Ngwenyama occupies, in theory, the position of a constitutional monarch; he is advised by two councils, is supposed to be bound by their advice, and should not initiate any formal action without their approval.

Ultimate authority lies with the National Council, or Libandla, which theoretically includes the head of every Swazi household. It meets once a year, usually in the winter, and remains in session for about a month, but in modern conditions it has lost much of its character as a national gathering and is attended mainly by chiefs and a number of senior commoners. There is also an inner or Privy Council, called the Liqoqo, which consists of the Ngwenyama's most important relatives and other advisers chosen by him. Since the Government reforms of 1950, this traditional ruling system has had added to it a Swazi National Treasury and formally constituted African courts, from which appeal lies ultimately to the High Court of Swaziland.

In practice, the most important part of the Swazi National Administration has been the Standing Committee, which is appointed by the Ngwenyama-in-Libandla, has had regular weekly meetings with Government, and has been the channel along which all business affecting the Swazi people has flowed. It consists of a chairman, the treasurer of the Swazi National Treasury, the secretary to the nation, and six members, representing the six administrative districts. All the members of the Standing Committee are paid from the Swazi National Treasury, and whilst those representing districts have considerable influence

* See especially *An African Aristocracy*, Hilda Kuper, O.U.P., 1947, and *The Swazi*, B. A. Marwick, C.U.P., 1940.

in them, more and more effective power has in fact devolved upon the full-time paid officials of the Swazi Administration. The Standing Committee has in fact taken over many of the functions of the Liqoqo, and its full-time officials, especially the secretary to the nation, have become key figures. In practice, too, the position of the Ngwenyama has changed during the long rule of Sobhuza II, for in over forty years his authority and formally recognized position have given him a very great influence over the National Council.

In all this time, Sobhuza II has never been personally touched by the persistent rumours of corruption which have surrounded some of his advisers and officials. The Ngwenyama, the Ndlovukasi or Queen-Mother, the chiefs and the officers of the Swazi Administration are all paid from the National Treasury, which has a revenue of some £70,000 a year, from a share of certain Government taxes, and from the proceeds of all fees and fines in the Swazi courts.

Below this central structure there are 172 chiefs, each of whom has his own Liqoqo and Libandla, and exercises considerable powers. They are, for the most part, very conservative and even reactionary, and have succeeded in stifling an attempt to bring groups of them together in the establishment of rural district councils. There is therefore no local government machinery.

Thus the modernization of the traditional Swazi system, which the British authorities belatedly attempted in 1944 and only implemented, with Swazi agreement, in 1950, has not in practice provided increased scope for the small but growing number of progressive Swazi. It has, rather, created a new centre of conservative power in the Swazi National Administration, whose senior officials realize that their careers and power depend on the warding off of modern democratic practices. This realization is shared by the chiefs, whose main source of authority remains the allocation of lands. And both the officials of the Swazi National Council and the chiefs realize that their future is bound up with the power of Sobhuza II, who, even before he formed the party which won the recent elections, had in practice become very much more than a constitutional ruler.

Probably the most impressive achievement of Swazi national organization has been the buying back, for the nation, of lands held by Europeans. This process began as a reaction to the partition of the territory, when the Queen Regent encouraged young men to find work and earn money in South Africa so that the lost Swazi lands could be recovered, and over the years bits of land were bought back with money raised from local levies. In 1945 there came the opportunity to buy a large ranch, and this was achieved by a general collection of cattle. The success of this scheme increased the desire of the Swazi to purchase more land, especially since the area available to them had become heavily overstocked and European owners were trying to get rid of Swazi who had 'squatted' on their farms.

In 1946 a general levy was organized to buy land, and in 1950 the Lifa, or Inheritance, Fund was formally established. All Swazi are obliged to contribute to it regularly in cattle or cash, and by the end of 1960 a little over a quarter of a million acres had been purchased from its resources, bringing the proportion of land available for occupation by the Swazi to 51·6 per cent of the country's total area. 45·9 per cent of the territory is owned by individual Europeans, some Eurafricans and a small number of individual Africans, by missions and by mining groups, while the remainder is a small amount of Government-owned freehold land and unallocated Crown Land. One of Swaziland's perennial problems is that a considerable proportion of European-owned land belongs to sheep farmers from the neighbouring Transvaal, who use their Swaziland holdings only as winter feeding grounds, tend to erode the land, and make no contribution to the Swaziland economy. Critics of the Lifa Fund rightly allege that it has been laxly administered and even abused through corruption, but it remains an impressive demonstration of Swazi national effort.

With the post-war development of Swaziland's mining industries, and a growing Swazi population pressing harder and harder upon the land, both land and minerals concessions have remained very live issues. Over the years, Sobhuza continued to take them up with the British Government, and it was from discussion of one such petition in 1960 that the question of a Legislative Council for Swaziland emerged.

Proposals for a joint council of Swazi and Europeans, having legislative functions, came first from the European Advisory

Council, which had been formally reconstituted in 1949 'to advise the Resident Commissioner on matters directly affecting the European residents of the Territory and on any matter specifically referred to the Council by the Resident Commissioner'. The European population in 1949 was estimated at only 3,400, and it was they who elected ten members of the council, to join six official but non-voting members. Every European British subject – including at that time South Africans – who was over twenty-one and had lived in Swaziland for five years was entitled to vote.

This European Advisory Council has always been a highly conservative body, reflecting the strong South African sympathies and connexions of most Swaziland whites. At the latest count, in April–May 1962, there were 8,040 whites in Swaziland, and today there are probably 10,000. Over half of these whites are South African citizens, and Afrikaans is the home language of thirty-one per cent; indeed, in the southern half of Swaziland, sixty-seven per cent of whites speak Afrikaans amongst themselves. White South Africans today constitute an estimated sixty per cent of the European voters' roll.

Many whites divide their residence between Swaziland and South Africa, as some leading members of the now superceded European Advisory Council have done. Thus Mr Carl Todd, the chairman of the elected members of the council, is a senior partner in a leading Johannesburg law firm and a director of over thirty South African companies, including major enterprises like African Explosives and Chemical Industries Ltd (part of the Anglo-American group and connected with Imperial Chemical Industries), the American–South African Investment Co. Ltd, the Netherlands Bank of South Africa Ltd, and the National Industrial Credit Corporation Ltd.

Mr Todd, who has dominated white politics in Swaziland, is on close personal terms with leading Afrikaner Nationalist politicians, and has been host in Swaziland to Dr Dönges, South Africa's Minister of Finance. It has been under Mr Todd's leadership that members of the European Advisory Council have committed themselves to the closest cooperation with Sobhuza and the traditionalists of the Swazi National Council, seeing in this the best way of perpetuating their own privileged position.

339

As a result, Todd has led a long and bitter fight against the introduction of a common voters' roll in Swaziland. When in February 1963 he seemed about to lose this fight against the British Government, he denounced the proposed new constitution over South Africa's Government-dominated national broadcasting system. This led the Swaziland Democratic Party, amongst others, to condemn him for using South African facilities 'for propaganda undermining real freedom and race equality in Swaziland, an act of direct interference in Swaziland's domestic affairs'. Earlier in 1962, Todd had welcomed a plan of Dr Verwoerd's under which South Africa would have acquired a section of Swaziland due to be flooded by one of the Republic's irrigation schemes.

Representative, though perhaps the most outspoken, of Todd's colleagues in the European Advisory Council has been Mr R. P. Stephens, who favoured federation with South Africa as recently as 1963 in a British television interview, and who warned in October 1963 that the new constitution would plunge Swaziland 'into the perhaps pinkish stewpot of boiling African democracy'.

Another of its members, Mr Sidney Gaiger, who is a local hotelier, has travelled at his own expense to Rhodesia to seek advice from Sir Roy Welensky, then Prime Minister of the now defunct Federation of Rhodesia and Nyasaland.

In January 1960 the European Advisory Council took the initiative with a memorandum to the Secretary of State in which it gave its views on his reply to a petition by the Ngwenyama on land and mineral concessions. This memorandum ended by stating the Council's belief that the time had been reached 'for the examination of a multi-racial council in which both European and Swazi interests will be represented . . . the Swazi National Council should nominate its Swazi representatives to such a legislative body' (which would subsequently be created).

The Ngwenyama then, in April 1960, declared his views on political development to a select audience; he too felt that there was room for a much closer community of interests in Swaziland. In order to make both white and black feel secure in Swaziland, they should come together 'on a basis of equality' in a joint council; but, as the Swazi National Council already had legislative and executive powers which the European Council lacked, the best solution lay in the establishment of a Legislative Council. To such a council, the Europeans should send their representatives under their own system of election, while the Swazi would choose men in their traditional way. He had in mind a sort of 'federation' in which the precise number of representatives from each group would not matter, and he spoke very strongly against 'one man – one vote'. Thus from the outset the conservative whites and blacks opposed any common voters' roll.

By the time that a Constitutional Committee was set up at the end of 1960, the Swaziland Progressive Party had been formed, and though the Ngwenyama opposed the existence of political parties amongst the Swazi, he included three leading members of the party in the Constitutional Committee, to serve in their personal capacities. They were Mr J. J. Nquku, the party's president, Dr A. P. Zwane, its general secretary, and Mr O. M. Mabuza, a member of its Executive Committee. But it was not long before a conflict developed between these Progressive Party leaders on the one hand and the Swazi traditionalists, headed by the Paramount Chief, and the representative of the white settlers on the other.

The clash centred on the limitations that the committee tried to impose on the Progressive Party members. It was made clear to them that they were not free to express their party's views, nor to press for free political organization so that the views of the Swazi might be determined in a modern way. Above all, they were told that the Constitutional Committee's discussions were to take place 'within the framework of the Paramount Chief's proposals'. This prevented the discussion of any alternative arrangements, such as a common roll system or adult suffrage. They were reminded that the Paramount Chief had said: 'If only we could extricate Africa from this idea of one man, one vote, I am sure we would have achieved our objectives.'

Mr Nquku was suspended from the committee, and his two colleagues resigned in protest. Dr Zwane protested to the Resident Commissioner that they were expected to suppress their convictions and to defer to the traditionalists. If they remained on the committee whilst being forbidden to express their views, they would be 'giving the public the misleading impression that the Swaziland Progressive Party is having a hand in the shaping of the new constitution'. The party then requested formal representation on the committee, but this was refused on the grounds that the Swazi National Council was the only body properly representative of the Swazi people. Thus the Constitutional Committee represented only the traditionalists, the white settlers and officials, and in the event the officials dissociated themselves from its main proposals.

These proposals, which were styled a plan for racial 'federation', offered a fifty-fifty division of the Legislative Council between the Swazi traditionalists and the whites, with land and minerals excluded from the control of the council and placed under the Ngwenyama. There was to be no common roll, and no direct elections amongst the Swazi. Their members would be selected in the traditional way, which in effect meant they would be chosen by the Ngwenyama and his close circle of advisers. The Europeans were to elect their own representatives by the ordinary democratic processes.

This cosy arrangement was, it is significant, strongly opposed by the Resident Commissioner and the other officials on the committee. They pointed out that once a start was made with 'racial federation' it would be 'virtually impossible to turn onto a non-racial path'; that expression must be given to those Swazi who wanted to take part in modern democracy, and that therefore a common roll was needed. The officials also declared that equal representation for less than 10,000 whites and approximately 270,000 Africans could not really be justified, and that the whites in their own interests should agree to a Swazi majority. Finally, the officials felt that it should be left to the Legislative Council to determine the powers and functions of the Ngwenyama and the traditional Swazi National Council.

Throughout these negotiations the European Advisory Council, led by Mr Carl Todd, played a crucial role. The Ngwenyama took no personal part in them and appointed special negotiators, but though these traditionalists enjoyed a considerable amount of discretion, they had to refer back for any final authority to the Ngwenyama. What soon emerged clearly was that the main aim of Sobhuza and his men was to retain control of Swazi lands and to regain control of minerals. The Europeans, for their part, were satisfied to support these aims, if in turn they could reinforce the continuance of their dominant economic position with political power and keep out the modern political parties which threatened both them and the traditionalists. It is with the question of land and minerals that we come to the nub of the constitutional negotiations which for almost three years defeated all efforts to reach an agreed solution. In the end, as we shall see, the British Government has had to impose a formula.

The plan of the conservative Swazi–European alliance looked like succeeding in the early part of the negotiations. The Ngwenyama's position of wanting black and white to meet 'on a basis of equality' was converted under the persuasion of the Europeans into the formula for fifty:fifty representation, split between the whites and the traditionalists. Political parties were excluded, and land and mineral rights were to come under the Ngwenyama. But in private the British officials put their objections even more strongly than in their official minority report, and this carried much weight in London. What was more, ordinary tribesmen and councillors were disturbed by the proposals to give such heavy representation to the tiny white minority, and so reinforced the criticisms made by the Progressive Party. These feelings were so strongly put in the annual Libandla that by May 1962 Sobhuza felt obliged to explain that he did not necessarily support the fifty:fifty arrangement. He spoke of meeting 'on a basis of equality', but did not explain precisely what this meant.

In the meantime, two new political parties had arisen in the Territory, the Swaziland Democratic Party (S.D.P.) and the Mbandzeni National Convention. The Administration saw these new parties as reinforcing the need to find expression for modern Swazi in the new constitution, and therefore as strengthening the case for a common roll to be introduced.

With agreement on the spot blocked, a constitutional conference was convened at London in January 1963. To this were invited six representatives of the Swazi National Council, four of the European Advisory Council, one each of the three political parties, a representative of the Eurafrican Welfare Association, and one independent delegate. The Administration itself was represented by two delegates.

The representation of the political parties, however, was complicated by a split which had divided the Progressive Party into rival factions led by Mr Nquku and Dr A. P. Zwane. The Administration was not prepared to recognize both, and seated Mr Nquku. Though not himself admitted to the conference, Dr Zwane gave his support to the Alliance of Political Organizations which was formed under the leadership of Mr Simon Nxumalo of the Democratic Party.

When the conference commenced, the protagonists of the fifty:fifty arrangement found the British Government insistent that control of minerals and land should fall under the new Legislative Council, and it was around this point that the conference really revolved. Clearly no viable modern State can be created in Swaziland if its main source of wealth is outside the control of its legislature.

This British insistence came as a shock to the traditionalists. Whether there was a cut-and-dried agreement, as the political parties allege, between the traditionalists and the Europeans cannot be proved. But the understanding which they had was based on the assumption that European support would be decisive in gaining Sobhuza's control of land and minerals. When British opposition showed this assumption to be false, the traditionalists changed their stand. They showed during the conference that they were prepared to abandon the fifty:fifty arrangement and possibly even their European allies, provided that they got the land and minerals.

The British Government, for its part, went so far at one stage as to propose a substantially non-racial scheme, providing for a majority of common-roll representation. But, under influential lobbying and pressure, it shifted its ground. In fact, the British Government was presented with the very difficult problem of deciding between the claims of rival groups to speak for Swaziland. Clearly no one group spoke for the whole country. The past and much of the present lay with Sobhuza and the Europeans, but a significant part of the present and the future lay with the political parties.

In this situation, the British Government tried to have a compromise arrangement accepted, which would make a small beginning with common-roll suffrage, would leave the Swazi traditionalists and the Europeans heavily represented, but would give the legislature so created all control of minerals. This was rejected by all groups, with the traditionalists rejecting especially the mineral arrangement, and the conference broke up without any agreement in February 1963. Nor did the Government get any further with the continuing consultations it asked the Resident Commissioner to hold in Swaziland.

Finally, in May 1963, with agreement as far away as ever, Mr Duncan Sandys, the Secretary of State for the Colonies, proclaimed his own solution. His decisions, which were embodied in a new constitution, published as an Order-in-Council at the end of 1963, give the Legislative Council the power of legislation over minerals, though not over Swazi land. Mineral ownership is formally vested in the Ngwenyama on behalf of the Swazi nation, and he is to be consulted before mineral rights are granted. But, after consultation with him and with the Executive Council, the actual granting or refusing of rights and concessions is left in the hands of Her Majesty's Commissioner for Swaziland, which is the name given to the up-graded former Resident Commissioner. Formally, this commissioner has been given extremely wide reserve and discretionary powers which, if exercised, could make both the Legislative and the Executive Councils merely advisory.

In practice, much must depend on the character and force of the Legislative Council, and here only a very small beginning has been made with non-racial and popular representation. The new body has twenty-four elected members, divided as follows: eight Swazi chosen through the traditional tribal methods; four Europeans elected on a purely European roll; four Europeans elected on a national or common roll; and eight members of any race elected on the national roll.

This has been criticized as being in effect a new fifty:fifty arrangement, with the division between the black and the white 'tribalists' on the one hand and the politicians on the other. The people whom it leaves in the middle are Swaziland's 2,500 Eurafrican or Coloured people, who must opt to be regarded either as Swazi or as Europeans. This, as Professor Denis Cowen has pointed out in a lucid report,* is unjust if racial divisions are to be maintained at all.

Under the new constitution, whites and Coloured people who

---

* *Swaziland: Report on Constitutional Reform*, Professor D. V. Cowen, Swaziland Progressive Party, Mbabane.

are South African citizens are able to vote on the European roll until the end of 1965, but Africans from South Africa have no franchise at all. This means that some 1,700 white South Africans, who form a majority of the present white electorate, can ensure its conservative character, while some 6,700 Africans from the Republic – containing a large proportion of teachers, better-educated and semi-skilled workers – will have no say in the Swazi or national-roll elections, thus eliminating one of the potentially most progressive sections of the African electorate. It was also made difficult for progressive whites or Coloured to be nominated for the racially reserved national-roll seats. The constitution requires at least twenty-five white or Coloured nominators, which represents something like five per cent of the potential electorate of those races in each constituency.

In effect, elections under the new constitution, if contested by all the major groups, were almost certain to give a majority to a coalition of black and white traditionalists. The Ngwenyama nonetheless, perhaps hoping for an even better deal, delayed his acceptance of the constitution, and early in 1964 unsuccessfully petitioned the British Parliament against its promulgation. This petition put forward complicated alternative arrangements under cover of which he still fought for control of minerals and the enhancement of traditional powers.

But it was clear that if Sobhuza should decide to boycott the constitution, the Legislative Council could still function through the commissioner's powers to appoint any number of extra members. Sobhuza was advised by his South African lawyer, who is closely connected with Dr Verwoerd's National Party, that as a last resort and if he did not wish to be by-passed in this way, he should form his own party, since this would practically guarantee to him and his European allies a majority in the new legislature. He had eight traditionalist seats to start off with, for there could be no doubt that these will be filled by his men. The traditional Swazi method of 'election' is by acclamation in public, and the chief's nominees were thus certain to be chosen. It was equally certain, given the attitudes of most Swaziland whites, that the four seats reserved for them on their own roll would be filled from the conservatives who had comprised the European Advisory Council. Thus the white and black conservatives would have half the elected seats, and needed to win only one more to command a majority. With four national roll seats reserved for Europeans or Coloured opting as such, and with the mass of rural, illiterate Swazi almost certain to vote for their King's men, this presented no difficulty.

The new constitution is open to serious criticism, for it presents only a small beginning towards non-racial voting. In its racial division of the electorate it conflicts with the British Government's announced policy of non-racialism. And whilst the mere creation of a Legislative Council must be an advance on none at all, the new constitution leaves sweepingly wide and arbitrary powers in the hands of Her Majesty's Commissioner, powers that could be used both to overrule the Legislative Council and to by-pass the Ngwenyama.

Thus the new constitution satisfies no one. At the beginning of 1964, the Ngwenyama organized what he called a referendum amongst the Swazi, in which they were supposedly asked to say whether they supported his petition to the House of Commons. The results were some 10,000 in support, and less than 100 against, but it is certain that hardly any of those taking part knew much about the petition. The issue was presented as a choice between supporting Sobhuza or the Resident Commissioner, and in such a choice, the result was predictable.

As the elections approached, the formation of two new political groups added further colours to Swaziland's political spectrum. Where before 1960 there were no political parties at all, no less than eight contested the elections.

Swaziland has the unusual distinction of being able to claim that its modern political parties are directly descended from a body formed by its British Resident Commissioner and blessed by its feudal tribal King. In January 1929 the then Resident Commissioner presided at the inaugural meeting of the Swaziland Progressive Association, founded to provide a social and discussion forum for the small number of educated Swazi, who found little outlet for their interests in the tribal councils and who had no access to the Administration. The association's establishment was supported by the then young Ngwenyama, Sobhuza II.

There the seed of modern political life remained buried, until

347

August 1960, when the Swaziland Progressive Association changed itself into the Swaziland Progressive Party (S.P.P.), the first political party in the country's history.

It was clear that there would soon be constitutional talks, and the initiative to transform the S.P.A. was taken by its president, Mr J. J. Nquku, who achieved agreement by the annual general meeting and so, without the bother of fresh elections, remained in the presidential chair which he had occupied since 1942. The party issued a manifesto containing as its main points:

(a) a non-racial policy with full democratic rights for all persons in Swaziland, irrespective of race, colour or creed;

(b) the strongest opposition to the incorporation of Swaziland by South Africa;

(c) early self-determination for Swaziland;

(d) complete racial integration in every walk of life and the ending of racial discrimination in all its forms; and

(e) the adoption of the United Nations Declaration of Human Rights.

John June Nquku, who issued this manifesto, had for many years been the nearest thing to a politician in Swaziland, though himself not a Swazi. Born in Pietermaritzburg in South Africa of Zulu parents in 1899, he was educated in that town and at the Pholela Institute in Natal, after which he trained as a teacher at St Chad's Training College in Ladysmith. He made a very successful career in teaching, becoming principal of two African schools near his home town, and in 1930 earned the distinction of being appointed the first African Inspector of Education in Swaziland, which started his varied career in the country. In 1934 he started what seems to have been Swaziland's first vernacular newspaper, *Izwi Lama Swazi* (The Voice of the Swazi), which he edited until it was taken over by the large South African Bantu Press group.

Nquku has always had a strong religious streak and became a leading figure in Swaziland's Zionist separatist churches. Indeed, when he joined the Swazi National Council staff in 1940 after resigning as school inspector, the Ngwenyama assigned him to religious and educational duties, and through this he is believed to have strengthened his own religious following.

In 1955 he founded another newspaper, *The Swazilander*, and in 1957 he visited America, Britain and western Europe. By the time that he presided over the birth of the S.P.P., he was thus a veteran in education, administration and public writing, a combination rare in then sleepy Swaziland. A small man, with a strong belief in the rightness of his own outlook he is not an impressive public speaker, and his showing as a petitioner to the United Nations was disappointing.

But Nquku and his party, filling a vacuum in the Pan-African map, were rapidly welcomed by other African countries and leaders, several of whom Nquku visited and from whom he received financial aid.

In February 1962, however, the Progressive Party split wide open, in a rift more personal than ideological. There had for some time been complaints about Nquku's running of the party; it was alleged that he was dictatorial in his attitude towards the executive, that he kept everything, including the allocation of Pan-African scholarships, in his own hands, and there were accusations – which he met with counter-accusations – about the financial affairs of the party. At last a substantial group, under the leadership of Dr Zwane rebelled, and this, pulling rapidly ahead in popularity, renamed itself the Ngwane National Liberatory Congress (N.N.L.C.) in 1963.

Nquku's following and standing have declined since this split, though he did outsmart Dr Zwane over the constitutional talks held in London in early 1963. The Administration decided to recognize only one Progressive Party for the talks, and Nquku gained this recognition. He did not join the alliance formed by the other political organizations at the conference, though he supported their general line.

Nquku's political strength is tiny, even though he seems to confuse it with his religious adherents, but partly because of his political experience and partly because of his contacts in Africa, Nquku himself remains a public figure in Swaziland's young political life, if no longer a major one. In November 1963 he issued a joint statement with Dr Allen Nxumalo, leader of the Swaziland Democratic Party, declaring that 'in all matters affecting the general interest of Swaziland we shall act together, but we shall maintain different parties'. This declaration, however, was not followed up by any action, except that the two leaders went together to the Kenya independence celebrations. In 1964 some 200 people, described as delegates, attended a pre-election conference of Nquku's S.P.P., and the party subsequently put up seven outstandingly unsuccessful candidates to contest the eight unreserved national roll seats, as well as one to contest a national roll seat reserved for Europeans. But it made it clear that it was participating only under protest, and that it disapproved vehemently of the racialistic nature of the new constitution. Nquku himself remains violently opposed to any closer association with South Africa, favours asylum for South African political refugees 'in accordance with international concept', and demands better conditions for Swazi workers. He also 'condemns most vehemently the protectorate government for allowing the establishment of a gambling Casino in Swaziland and demands from the British Government as a protector the cancellation of this corruptive establishment'.

Since the 1962 split with Zwane, Nquku has been weakened by a further split, which has resulted in the existence of another Swaziland Progressive Party, led by Mr O. M. Mabuza. This is a splinter of a splinter group, but it put up seven national-roll candidates for the elections, in which it also participated only under protest.

While the Nquku–Zwane split originally involved personal and not ideological differences, Dr Zwane's Ngwane National Liberatory Congress has since become far more militant than its parent ever was.

Dr Ambrose Pesheya Zwane, one of the tiny handful of Swazi doctors (there are thought to be only four), resigned from the health service to become the S.P.P.'s general secretary on its formation. Born in 1924 at Bremersdorp (now Manzini) in Swaziland, he had received his early education in local Roman Catholic schools – he remains a Roman Catholic today – and at the Inkama High School in Zululand, South Africa. Then, having graduated from Fort Hare University College, he had gone on to qualify in medicine at the University of the Witwatersrand in Johannesburg and after graduation to join the Swaziland Health Service as a Government medical officer. But after seven years in the post, he had found his work stultifying, with the need to hurdle everyday barriers of racial discrimination and with all prospect of promotion blocked. He says today that it was this personal frustration, the despair of ever achieving real progress from within that brought him to politics. Certainly at first sight he does not seem to be cut out for his new profession. Rather shy, though friendly, Dr Zwane is an intelligent man who is a very diffident public speaker. He is an admirer of both Dr Nkrumah and Jomo Kenyatta, has attended a number of Pan-African gatherings – the most recent being the 1964 Lagos conference of African leaders – and has also visited Ghana, Egypt and Kenya.

Dr Zwane's chief lieutenant in the N.N.L.C. is a very different sort of man, for young Dumisa Dlamini is a crowd-rousing orator who resembles the late Patrice Lumumba somewhat in appearance. He is a nephew of Sobhuza II, which stands him in good stead with the status-conscious Swazi in public life, and it is believed that the Ngwenyama paid for his fees when he went to study at Basutoland's Pius XII University College in 1960. Dlamini, however, left after his first year in order to devote himself to the S.P.P., which he had joined on its formation. He started a youth wing for the party, and produced its short-lived journal, the *Swaziland Freedom Star*. In 1961 he attended a World Assembly of Youth conference in Tanganyika, and went with Nquku and Zwane to represent Swaziland at that year's Accra conference of African non-self-governing territories.

Dlamini probably proves a frequent source of embarrassment to Zwane, if not politically then because of his violent temper and personal life. He has recently completed a jail sentence for indecent assault. But he showed himself to be an effective mass leader when he played the leading role in two major Swaziland strikes. As a result of the second strike in 1963, which came near to being a general strike and led to the flying in of British troops, Dlamini has a suspended sentence of five months' imprisonment for public violence hanging over him. Despite his connexions with the Swazi royal family, he has on a recent occasion thrown a gathering in the royal kraal, presided over by Sobhuza himself, into uproar by challenging, without permission, political moves by the King. All this has won him both notoriety and a personal following. He has even succeeded in drawing Sobhuza's eldest daughter, Princess Bethusila, into the N.N.L.C., which has taken on some tribal overtones.

In its election manifesto, however, the N.N.L.C. stressed that it opposed 'tribalism, racialism, colonialism, imperialism and neo-colonialism', and that it stood for 'a nationalist democratic, socialist and Pan-African state within the fraternity of African states and the British Commonwealth'. More specifically, it called for independence by the end of 1965, an equitable redistribution of land, the communalizing of owned but unused land, and the nationalization of all major industries, the railways and passenger aircraft. For the rest, the congress called for free trade-unions, a minimum wage, and the improvement of all social services and of agriculture – though it promised that 'destocking will be discouraged'. The chiefs would be 'accorded a position of honour in the new Ngwane Nation' and paid salaries. 'Such unbalanced and irregular taxes as the Lifa Fund shall be abolished.'

It is a programme based on Swazi grievances, with a sop to the chiefs and the whites, and plenty of Pan-Africanist flourishes to stress its militancy and, presumably, to keep support flowing from outside. In his travels abroad, Dr Zwane has seemed to align himself with South Africa's Pan-Africanist Congress, which opposes that country's multi-racial African National Congress Alliance, though this does not seem to have become an issue in Swaziland. The N.N.L.C. has consistently denounced the Territory's new constitution, from whose negotiation it was excluded, but though it stands for 'one man – one vote' and the scrapping of the constitution, finally decided to participate in the elections 'under protest'.

The N.N.L.C.'s only serious rival is the Swaziland Democratic Party, which was formed in 1962 by Mr Simon Nxumalo, and which then revealed differences of approach from other parties, especially over the franchise issue. The initial party programme recognized universal suffrage as only the final aim to be achieved, and believed that it should be introduced after a phased advance so that the people might acquire more political experience. Thus the party's first call was for a qualified franchise on a common voters' roll, and its resultant reputation as a moderate grouping was reinforced by its selection of objective as 'a non-racial, stable, democratic government endowed with checks and balances guaranteeing freedom of opposition and criticism' and the protection of minority groups. In starting the Democratic Party, Simon Nxumalo was advised by Major V. Rozwadowski, a talented emigré Pole turned farmer who is strongly anti-Communist, and his participation gave the party, of which he is now vice-president, a multi-racial slant, though it has never attracted more than half a dozen other whites from the almost wholly conservative, racially hidebound and often wealthy white community.

Simon Nxumalo is a determined but modest man in his early thirties with no previous experience in politics, a trained primary school teacher who worked as such in the civil service for some years in Swaziland. He has written Swazi primers for schools, and together with Major Rozwadowski and Mrs Nell Green, a former member of the South African women's Black Sash protest movement, started the now flourishing *Sebenta* adult education society. He thus came to politics through education, in which his experiences persuaded him that only a change of Government could really tackle the country's needs.

At the London constitutional talks in February 1963, Nxumalo did very well, emerging as the leader of the alliance of political organizations which successfully opposed the straight racial carve-up on a 'fifty:fifty' basis. But in Swaziland itself, he was thought somewhat young and lacking in public prestige, despite his connexion with a house of the royal family, and in 1963 he stood down from the party's presidency, to become its executive secretary.

The new president of the Swaziland Democratic Party is Dr Allen Nxumalo, who is no relative of Simon's. Like his rival Dr Zwane, he is one of the tiny group of Swazi medical practitioners and, again like his rival, he resigned from government service in order to enter politics.

Allen Mkaulo Nxumalo, also known by the name Malabane which Sobhuza gave him as an infant, was born on 14 February 1921 at Manzini in Swaziland. His father, Benjamin Nxumalo, was a brother of Sobhuza's mother, the Ndlovukasi, and the family is thus a very important one in the tribal hierarchy. Mr Benjamin Nxumalo himself played a leading part for many years in Swazi affairs, serving as an intimate adviser and as secretary to the

Ngwenyama, as well as being president of the Swaziland Progressive Association from its inception in 1929 until his death in 1942. In the early years of the century, he founded the first Swazi school, Zombode, after having obtained permission to do so from Kitchener, and also established the A.M.E. Church in Swaziland.

With a father so distinguished in public affairs, Allen Nxumalo was almost bound to enter politics and public life himself. He was educated first at the A.M.E. primary school in Manzini – he is today a senior Church member – and then took his Junior Certificate at the Swazi National School. The Swazi Administration then granted him a scholarship to Fort Hare College in South Africa, where he matriculated in 1942, and when his father died in that year, he returned to Swaziland, where he taught in a primary school for a year. But he was keen to study medicine, and made his way to Johannesburg, there to work first in a correspondence college for a year, correcting Zulu scripts at a salary of £6 a month, and then, in order to earn more money, finding work as an unskilled factory hand, at £8 a month. He worked under semi-literate white men 'who detested the idea of a matriculated kaffir', and was delighted when the late Professor Vilakasi obtained a post for him as an assistant in the library of the University of the Witwatersrand. He had come to Johannesburg in the hope of finding someone to help him undertake medical studies, and he was lucky enough to acquire a benefactor. Through his two student sons, Mr Joe Glasser, a Jewish clothing manufacturer, met Allen Nxumalo and took him unostentatiously under his wing. He paid his fees for a three-year B.Sc. course at Fort Hare, clothed him and gave him pocket money, and this highly unusual, discreet generosity has left an enduring impression on Nxumalo.

Nevertheless, Allen Nxumalo had in Johannesburg come under the influence of black nationalism through the legendary Lembede, and when the African National Congress Youth League was formed, Nxumalo was elected to its executive. He was active in Youth League and student politics at Fort Hare, where he became vice-president of the Students' Representative Council and met other future African leaders. Then, from 1949 to 1951, he taught at an African secondary school in Johannesburg, becoming chairman of the A.N.C. Youth League in Johannesburg's Western Areas. At this time, he says, he taught his pupils to hate all white men, but he subsequently 'came to see that Africanism is the other side of the apartheid coin', so that today he is the leading exponent of non-racialism in Swaziland.

Obtaining a scholarship from the Swaziland Government, which obliged him to quit active politics, he finally studied medicine at the University of the Witwatersrand from 1952–7, failing one year. Then, after serving his housemanship at Baragwanath Hospital, he returned to Swaziland and entered the medical service, which he found 'pretty stuffy'. As a civil servant, he took no part in politics, but was appointed to the Constitutional Commission, from which he resigned in protest against the fifty:fifty racial proposals shortly before the London conference.

Dr Nxumalo is both intelligent and articulate, and he has brought to the leadership of the S.D.P. a much greater political sophistication than Simon Nxumalo possessed. At first he appeared to share the obsessive anti-Communism of his vice-president, Major Rozwadowski, but today believes, as do the leaders of the A.N.C. in South Africa, that witch-hunting amongst those who sincerely oppose apartheid is futile and dangerous. It was under his leadership that the S.D.P. adopted in 1964 the Freedom Charter of the A.N.C. and its allies as the new party programme.

The S.D.P. had previously changed to support of universal adult suffrage and to a demand for Swaziland's early independence, but it has been at pains to stress its loyalty to Sobhuza – as a constitutional monarch. Thus while its slogan is 'social justice in a non-racial society', its motto, based on the S.D.P. initials, is Sobhuza II for Democracy and Progress. The party has been unofficially looked upon with approval by the Administration, and this has obliged it to counter the gibe of its opponents that it was 'Marwick's party'. Having led the opposition to the fifty:fifty proposals at the London constitutional conference, the S.D.P. has also opposed the new constitution, and participated in the elections only under protest. Its membership claims are probably more accurate than those of its rivals, for at the beginning of 1963 it had a lawyer check its books, and these showed an audited membership of 2,200, which it says has since increased.

Faced with this array of small but growing political parties, and the certainty that an election would have to be fought under a new constitution, Swaziland's conservative white community felt impelled likewise to organize itself along party-political lines. The United Swaziland Association (U.S.A.) was accordingly formed in 1963. It opened its membership to Europeans and Eurafricans and, in a rambling policy circular, came out for what amounts to a policy which approximated to the theory of apartheid: cooperation between racial groups which are to be kept separate. Thus it promised 'Respect of each group for the other's culture and tradition' and set itself to 'promote and defend the institutions of each group'. Dr Verwoerd could not have put it more smoothly. The association backed Sobhuza's stand on land and minerals, and in return, demanded European representation in the Legislative Council 'due and proper' for those 'carrying the major burden of responsibility in the economic and social development of the nation'. In addition, foreign investment was to be encouraged and protected.

As Mr Willie van Rensburg, the association's secretary, subsequently elucidated: 'Let me add that should any political issues arise where we have to choose, our backing goes to the Ngwenyama-in-Council and the Swazi Nation.'

The association claims a membership of 4,000 residents, from which it says that civil servants, missionaries, and temporary residents are excluded. If this is true, then it can indeed claim to speak for Swaziland's whites, since with the listed exclusions there are probably less than 4,000 white adults in the whole Territory.

The association threatened to sue for £10,000 any persons alleging that it or any of its members was in collusion with the Republic of South Africa to bring Swaziland under its domination. But its openly uncritical backing of Sobhuza against the Administration and the political parties, with its ultra-conservatism, clearly went too far for a more liberal, or perhaps merely conservative, element in the white population.

In April 1964, a group of white farmers and businessmen formed the Swaziland Independent Front, which endorsed the much debated new constitution and issued a policy statement that was, by white lights, 'realistic'. While backing the Ngwenyama's claim to have the allegiance of most Swazi for traditional institutions, it recognized that political parties had come to stay: 'This natural evolution cannot, and should not, be retarded, nor should it be hastened.' The front opposed political ties with South Africa or the inclusion of Swaziland in any Bantustan scheme, though it promised to strive for 'close economic cooperation and good neighbourliness with the Republic'. It envisaged a slow political evolution which would let Europeans 'gain confidence as to their future under an African majority', and in the meantime claimed that separate racial representation was necessary. For the rest, the front's programme had a 'progressive business' outlook. It approved of trade-unions, provided that they were not exploited for political ends, and called for increased education, to help swell the number of skilled workers, better medical and social services, a sound agricultural policy, and the encouragement of investment and all forms of commercial development.

The Swaziland Independent Front anticipated that it would gain some support from the followers of the Ngwenyama, but any such hopes were soon shattered. For, also in April, the King decided to enter politics on his own account. At a meeting of some 2,500 tribesmen in the royal cattle kraal, Sobhuza announced that he had accepted a recommendation by the Swazi National Council that he and his supporters should contest the Legislative Council elections in June. Party leaders who attended were not given a chance to speak, and Prince Makhosini Dlamini was appointed to head the election campaign, in which candidates were to be appointed by a show of hands at further tribal gatherings. Sobhuza named the new political group 'Imbokodo', which means a grindstone which is hard, compact and difficult to break, and suggested that its candidates stand for four main objectives: the continuance of the monarchy, Swazi customs, mineral and land rights, and the prerogative of the Ngwenyama. Both the timing of the party's formation, after it had become clear that Sobhuza could not stop the new constitution, and its aims tallied exactly with the advice previously given by his South African Nationalist lawyer, Mr van Wyk de Vries, who is a member of the secret and sinister Broederbond Society dominating all aspects of South African Government.

In fact, the advice of this lawyer, who has since been elevated to the South African Bench, has been followed closely by Sobhuza and the S.N.C. at every stage of the constitutional controversy. The advice given was more political than legal, and it is worth while examining it closely, for there are grounds for believing that Sobhuza and the Swazi National Council are attracted by South African offers to take over the 'protection' of their tribal privileges and life. The document fell into hostile hands, and received sufficient publicity for the Administration to rebut some of its assertions.

It is certainly calculated to fan the worst fears of Sobhuza and his men into flame, as in its statement that

No one in his sound senses can deny that this constitution is a decisive step towards the extermination [sic] of the Ngwenyama, the Swazi Nation as an organic entity, the Swazi language, culture, law and customs. ... The Ngwenyama is being told by the British Government: 'Ngwenyama, you are not King of Swaziland, we do not concede that you are King of the Swazi. But we are putting you into a little kraal with a few privileges and some nominal powers and we will pay you an emolument, but if you do not behave and obey the Commissioner, this will all be taken away from you.'

This sort of language is more appropriate to rabble-rousing than to a legal opinion, and clearly fanned the traditionalists' fear of political parties of any Swazi who spoke up for themselves, and of losing control over the allocation of land and of minerals.

The document advises Sobhuza to press for explicit recognition of Swaziland as a Protectorate, which would make easier his own recognition as King of Swaziland, and that Swazi land and minerals must primarily be used for the development of the Swazi nation and vested in the Ngwenyama. 'It would be of great assistance to have the support of the Europeans on these three issues.'

Then the document goes on to itemize the enormous powers left to the Queen's Commissioner. Here Sobhuza's lawyer was on firm ground; for if the commissioner were to use his powers fully, he would, as is claimed, be 'the virtual dictator of Swaziland'. The British reply to this is that such powers are 'normal' in the early stages of transition to self-government, and that the new constitution will be reviewed in three years' time, to be replaced by others, under which the commissioner's powers will be progressively reduced until full internal self-government and independence are achieved.

Open to criticism as this answer is – for the enormously over-due first step could and should, in Africa today, have been much more·extensive – its good faith can be accepted, especially since Basutoland and Bechuanaland have both been advanced nearer to independence. If Sobhuza is tempted to look to South Africa rather than Britain for protection, he should remember that the white commissioner of a Bantustan has as much power as the Queen's Commissioner, with no likelihood that these powers will – under apartheid – *ever* be diminished.

Sobhuza's Broederbond lawyer saw that it would be suicidal for the Ngwenyama alone flatly to reject the new constitution, and advised a process of procrastination, counter-proposals and petition, all of which were duly tried. Then, advised the lawyer, when the constitution was proclaimed and accepted by Sobhuza under protest, he should launch his own political party, for which careful preparation had to be made beforehand. And this, once again, is precisely what Sobhuza did. The lawyer predicted that Sobhuza's men would win a majority in the Legislative Council and that 'the Ngwenyama's men will then go to London as the strongest political force in Swaziland to call for the removal of all colonial rule in Swaziland, which is one of the principles of the Labour Party in the United Kingdom (which might by then be in power)'.

Sobhuza's decision to enter politics when it came (exactly according to plan), raised a storm of protest from the leaders of all existing political parties. It aroused unease even amongst some whites, though Mr Carl Todd issued a strong appeal to whites to back the Imbokodo, since Legislative Council members 'who can be trusted to support Ngwenyama and his Council' were the best hope for whites against the threat of universal suffrage.

No apology was made by Imbokodo for the participation of the King and his council in politics. On the contrary, Imbokodo proclaimed that 'in Africa Kings are Leaders as well as Kings'. Imbokodo made it clear, too, that it would not tolerate trade-unions which participated in politics, and that since 'so far the [other political] parties have used despicable methods of bribery, intimidation, calumny, defamation', there was no need to permit them to put their case to Swazi living in the Swazi areas. Imbokodo claimed that the record of the Swazi National Council was a progressive one, and denounced the British Administration for having signed away rights to the huge Bomvu Ridge iron ore deposits 'without our consultation'.

The most telling comments made on the formation of the King's Imbokodo came in a remarkable farewell message in April from Sir Brian Marwick, retiring as Her Majesty's Commissioner for Swaziland. Sir Brian had served in Swaziland for some thirty years; he had in 1940 published *The Swazi*, an anthropological account of their customs which is still a standard work; he speaks Siswati better than many Swazi do; and his service as Resident Commissioner and Her Majesty's Commissioner had been widely admired for its relatively progressive and humane outlook. Unsatisfactory as the new Swaziland constitution is, it was Marwick who had been the key figure in persuading the British Government to provide at least some form of common-roll representation, while attempting to keep on good terms with the Swazi traditionalists.

Now, in his farewell message, he allowed himself the luxury of some straight talking. Looking back at the remarkable progress which had been made in economic, health and other fields, he was sadly forced to conclude that these developments

owed little or nothing to the Swazi National Council, which for the most part was content to contemplate the imagined wrongs of the past and to be critical of the Government's efforts to bring progress and stability to the people of Swaziland

The Swazi National Council had disregarded recommendations for the improvement of its functioning. Recognizing the then complete reliance of the Swazi nation on one man and one man only – the Ngwenyama – Marwick declared that he had tried to develop and encourage advisory and executive talent within the traditional Swazi system.

Nevertheless [he said] I leave Swaziland dissatisfied with the results of my efforts to produce leaders amongst the Swazi people capable of supporting their King with sound, objective and fearless advice, or capable of removing from his shoulders the heavy burden which he has carried for so long.

The word 'corruption' was not mentioned, but it hung clearly in the Swaziland air.

As for labour relations, Marwick said that improved legislation had been so 'strenuously opposed' that improvements came too late to prevent the 1963 strikes. Though the Swazi National Council assumed that it was being blamed here, Marwick may equally have had the employers in mind when he declared that 'Few people in Swaziland who are not themselves workers even now realize that it is wrong and dangerous to deny workers the right to organize themselves to secure adequate wages and conditions of work'.

In part, of course, Marwick's strictures were disingenuous, for he ignored the fact that his Administration, in possession of sweeping powers, could have paid less heed to the strenuous objections of vested interests to various overdue reforms. Then, too, his speech was, for all its progressive notes, paternalistic in tone, and papered over the faults which both traditionalists and the modern political parties could point out in the new constitution. As if sensing this, he stressed the quite genuine and 'enormously complicated' difficulties of advancing Swaziland towards multi-racialism and independence if full weight were given to 'the desires, history, traditions and sophistication of its various population groups'. The answer to this, of course, is that too much weight has for far too long been given to the conservative vested interests.

But Sir Brian was on solid ground when he warned of the dangers of the King entering into politics through Imbokodo.

If that particular political group [i.e. one controlled by the King] obtains control of the government, the King is in a powerful and safe position – for the time being – but if at a later date that political group should be replaced by a rival, the King is likely to find himself cast aside as well.

The stabilizing value of the Kingship would vanish, and the King would, under the new constitution, be unable to carry out impartially his functions to delay or initiate legislation.

As for the Swazi National Council, Marwick said:

I put it to you gentlemen that by identifying the Ngwenyama with S.N.C. or 'Imbokodo' political thinking and by misusing your staff and machinery for electioneering purposes as I have no doubt you intend to do, you will do more to put Swazi against Swazi and to bring the kingship into disrepute than by any other act.

The S.N.C. machinery was paid for by the tax-payers of Swaziland, many of whom supported other political parties, and there was thus 'a strong argument for withholding the salaries of the S.N.C.'s officials'.

Realizing, too, too late, that the use of the King's name could easily give his party a majority or even all the seats on the common roll, Marwick warned the traditionalists that this, far from eliminating other parties, would make them more embittered and extreme, and that these parties had the backing of large numbers of the educated Swazi on whom future progress depended. The progress of political parties could not be stifled, said Marwick, and he called for an unequivocal declaration by the Ngwenyama-in-Council that all parties would be permitted to put their case freely to the voters in the Swazi areas (where chiefs and headmen can prevent meetings).

'I feel it my duty to tell you on this final visit,' he warned Sobhuza, 'that the course you are taking is full of grave dangers and pitfalls.'

It was in many ways a sad farewell, and its bang became an almost inaudible whimper for the ordinary tribal Swazi when Marwick, instead of speaking it publicly to the Swazi National Council as he had planned, was deprived of the chance by Sobhuza, and chose merely to hand his written text to the King. Very few of the still overwhelmingly illiterate Swazi tribesmen will have been reached by its subsequent local newspaper publication. It would have been salutary, too, for the Swazi whites who thus read it, if Marwick had gone on record with an equally outspoken farewell criticism of them. As it is, making one of his last public speeches before leaving Swaziland, Sir Brian Marwick did say in April 1964

There is, I fear, evidence in some quarters of an impenetrable conceit, a clutching at crutches to support limping traditions, a Canutism in the face of the rising tides of new thoughts and experiences which are flooding our Swaziland backwater. There is a lack of awareness and perception which reminds me of the questioning complaint 'O fat white woman whom nobody loves, why do you walk through the fields in gloves, missing so much and so much'.

Sir Brian retired shortly before the elections, and was succeeded as Queen's Commissioner by Mr Francis A. Lloyd, C.M.G., O.B.E., who had been a permanent secretary in Kenya. Born in 1916 and educated at Eton and Trinity College, Oxford, Mr Lloyd had joined the Kenya Colonial Service in 1939 and, except for two years of war service, remained in that country until his transfer to Swaziland. He has so far shown himself an old-style colonial administrator, and has quickly earned the mistrust of Swaziland's African-led political parties.

In May an unprecedented political meeting of 2,000–3,000 at Lobombo, the royal seat, heard Dumisa Dlamini of the N.N.L.C. and Allen Nxumalo of the S.D.P. warn that the King's actions might even lead to civil war. A joint delegation from the Swaziland Democratic Party, the Ngwane National Liberatory Congress and the two Swaziland Progressive Parties also presented the new commissioner with a memorandum for the Colonial Secretary. In this, the parties wished

to put on record their deep concern about the conditions under which the elections in Swaziland are going to take place. They humbly submit that the continuation of these conditions will make it impossible for the elections to be genuinely democratic, thus defeating the very spirit of the constitution. They further submit that the direct involvement in party politics of the King and the Swazi National Council may in due course threaten peace and order in the territory.

The memorandum went on to point out that Ngwenyama had

asked the Swazi people to give the Imbokodo full support as to a national movement of all the Swazis. Directed against the political parties, the Imbokodo is for all practical purposes a new incarnation of the Swazi National Council. Through the people involved in it the Imbokodo combines the prestige of the Swazi monarchy, the statutory privileges of the Swazi National Council, and the traditional powers of the chiefs.

The new party is in a position to use directly or indirectly the financial resources of the various organs of the tribal authority and to exert on our predominantly rural population various forms of pressure and intimidation stemming from the control of land allocation by the chiefs.

The parties stressed that six of the Imbokodo's eight candidates were members of the S.N.C., and that 'to the voter they are people who have power over him in their capacity as tribal civil servants'. One of these candidates, Mr A. K. Hlophe, who was also information officer of the s.n.c. and private secretary to the Ngwenyama, had even said at a public meeting that

the Imbokodo is the ruling party of the Swazi Tribal Government and has as such full right to use public funds for its own aims.

Through the s.n.c. the Imbokodo exercises full control over the chiefs who – whatever the denials – have become the Imbokodo's electoral agents.

The chiefs control the allocation of land to the Swazi people and exercise wide jurisdiction over the people in their areas. These powers of the chiefs are now being abused to force the people to vote for the Imbokodo candidates under threat of ejection from land holdings and banishment from the chief's area.

All over the country these powers are used to obstruct or prevent the activities of the political parties in the chiefs' areas.

Our accusations of abuse of power by the s.n.c., the chiefs and the Imbokodo – all in blatant breach of democratic principles – can be substantiated by numerous sworn affidavits.

The parties ended their joint memorandum with an appeal to the British Government 'to create conditions under which truly free elections can take place', failing which they might be forced to have the elections invalidated in the courts, creating 'conditions of acute friction in the Territory'.

The Swaziland Democratic Party followed up this memorandum with a lengthy letter to the King, in which it said that

In the King's name our people are subjected to pressure and intimidation by the chiefs. They are threatened with fines in cattle, dispossession and bodily harm unless they align themselves behind 'the King's Party' and vote for the Imbokodo. This makes a mockery out of Swaziland's first democratic elections.

The s.d.p. alleged that a 'reed curtain' had been erected around the King by certain members of the Swazi National Council 'to prevent him from hearing the views of the best sons of Swaziland'. It appealed to the King to return to the position of a strictly non-partisan constitutional monarch, to whom the s.d.p. and all in Swaziland would always be loyal, asked him to nullify any secret agreements he may have entered into with South Africa, and demanded the creation of a new Swazi National Council.

Both the joint appeal to the British Government and the S.D.F. petition to Sobhuza fell on deaf ears, and when the elections took place in the latter half of June they resulted in an overwhelming victory for the Imbokodo and, in the European seats, for its allied United Swaziland Association. Between them these two captured every contested seat.

The elections for the four European roll seats took place first, with the whole of Swaziland treated as one constituency. 2,209 voters, or sixty per cent of the potential European and Eurafrican total, had registered, and of these eighty-five per cent went to the polls. All four seats went to the ultra-conservative United Swaziland Association, which gained 59·3 per cent of the votes cast, while the moderate Swaziland Independent Front's four candidates gained only thirty-one per cent of the votes, and two independents between them gained 9·7 per cent. None of the African-led political parties bothered to contest these seats.

Enrolment on the national roll was 70,809 or eighty-eight per cent of the potential, mainly in consequence of an order by Sobhuza to all qualified Swazi to register. The country was treated as four constituencies, each of which returned two candidates of any race (which effectively made these eight Swazi seats) and one European or Eurafrican.

As most of the Swazi electorate is illiterate, candidates were each allocated a symbol which, together with their photograph, identified them at the polls, and voters were told to spike their papers on to a six-inch nail next to the symbol of their favoured candidates. In order to circumvent the traditional identification of the lion with Sobhuza which Imbokodo wanted to exploit, symbols were of inanimate objects. The range went from agricultural tools like a plough through a comb and a pair of spectacles to the pair of trousers which was drawn by the only woman candidate, a Mrs Twala, who stood for the N.N.L.C. on the national roll.

Nevertheless, the S.D.P. was forced a few days before the elections to obtain a court interdict against three Imbokodo candidates in a vain attempt to prevent them from making use of handbills and pamphlets on which a lion symbol was prominently displayed.

In the event, all eight unreserved seats were won by Imbokodo candidates with crushing majorities over their opponents. In a

73·8 per cent poll, 16·4 per cent of the ballot papers were spoilt.

The eight Imbokodo candidates gained 85·45 per cent of the valid votes (79,683); the eight official N.N.L.C. candidates, 12·3 per cent (11,364); the eight S.D.P. candidates only 1·4 per cent (1,271); Nquku's seven S.P.P. candidates 0·6 per cent (589); and Mabuza's S.P.P., 0·25 per cent (247). With individual Imbokodo candidates polling from 8,799 to 13,561 votes, the N.N.L.C.'s president, Dr Ambrose Zwane, gained only 2,438 and his deputy-president, Mr McDonald Maseko, only 923 votes. The S.D.P.'s President, Dr Allen Nxumalo (who contested the same constituency as Dr Zwane), gained only 237, and his secretary-general, Simon Nxumalo (who joined battle with Mr Maseko) only 147 votes. As for John June Nquku of the S.P.P., he polled exactly fifty-six votes, and the leader of the rival S.P.P., Mr O. M. Mabuza, thirty-four, both of them losing their deposits.

Of the four nation-roll seats reserved for European or Eurafrican candidates, one was unopposed. The U.S.A. candidates annihilated their opponents in the two seats they contested, gaining 62·5 per cent (20,093) of the votes cast in all three contested constituencies. Mr Carl Todd, standing as the Imbokodo's only white candidate, romped home with 19·8 per cent (6,385) of the total poll. The S.D.P., contesting all three constituencies, gained only 14·7 per cent (4,717) of the votes. Its vice-president, Major Vincent Rozwadowski, who did far and away the best of his party's defeated candidates, went down with only 2,601 votes to his U.S.A. opponent's 8,947. As for the solitary white candidate put up by Nquku's S.P.P., he polled 981 votes, in the only three-cornered contest, to his S.D.P. opponent's 161 and the winning U.S.A. man's 11,146.

Thus of the new Legislative Council's twenty-four members, six are whites belonging to the United Swaziland Association, one is a white belonging to Sobhuza's Imbokodo, one is a white independent, eight are elected members of Imbokodo and eight more Sobhuza's tribal representatives. With the solitary white independent almost certain to back the U.S.A. line, this represents a clean sweep for the alliance of white and black ultra-conservatives.

Even when one has given full weight to the crippling conditions under which the political parties were prevented from campaigning by the S.N.C. and the chiefs, the national-roll results are an impressive demonstration of the awe in which Sobhuza is held by the illiterate rural Swazi, and of the power of the tribal machine. Amongst the political parties, Dr Zwane's N.N.L.C. has clearly emerged as the only one with substantial following among the Swazi, obtaining its votes almost wholly from the urban areas. The S.D.P., realizing that its record in the big strike some time earlier had discredited it in those areas, had concentrated on more rural areas and had vainly tried to repair its image with a pre-election call for immediate independence.

It remains to be seen what policy Sobhuza's men will follow towards the political parties, but both Sobhuza and the S.N.C. have made their hostility clear. If they should now ignore the interests of the urban Swazi, the bitterness and friction of which Sir Brian Marwick warned the King will become real. It seems more than likely, too, that the triumphant white ultra-conservatives, having proved that they represent the overwhelming mass of Swaziland's white population, will use their alliance with Sobhuza to restrict the growth of trade-unions, especially in agriculture. The split between urban and rural Swazi would then be complete, with the former having no voice in the country's councils and the latter held down, more firmly than ever, by the tribal machine.

The Ngwenyama has thus emerged as the crucial figure in Swaziland. His influence had already been strengthened before the elections, when Her Majesty's Commissioner gave up his power to control or request the revocation or suspension of a chief by the Ngwenyama, so leaving Sobhuza in unfettered control of the tribal machine. Now his men, even without their white allies, have a majority in the new Legislative Council.

Sobhuza II was born in 1898 into the Dlamini house through which the Swazi ruling family traces back its genealogy for some 200 years. He received his primary education at Zombodze School and his junior secondary education at Lovedale College in the Eastern Cape of South Africa. Since becoming Ngwenyama in 1921, he has travelled abroad only twice, once to England in 1922, and again to England for the coronation of Queen Elizabeth II. Traditionalist and patriarchal in outlook, he pays much attention to his ritualistic duties. But he has proved himself a shrewd and stubborn operator in his protracted and continuing political fight to control directly mineral and land rights and to stultify Swaziland's young political parties. His religious position as the nation's rain-maker and the guardian of its land and fertility give his directives on almost any subject great weight with the rural Swazi. About forty-three per cent of all adult Swazi hold traditional beliefs, but a good many of the estimated 73,400 Christians are still influenced by the old animistic ways. And it is interesting to note that 34,400 of Swazi Christians are members of Zionist or other African separatist Churches. Sobhuza's word carries much weight with them too.

But today, at the age of seventy-five, Sobhuza is probably out of touch even with the problems of the rural Swazi, for in the forty-three years of his reign the broad popular base of national participation in the Libandla, or national council gathering, has withered away. He has increasingly been surrounded by self-interested and often venal sycophants, and has developed the obsessive conviction that his assassination is continually being attempted, a conviction only strengthened by successive official proofs that his suspicions and accusations have been groundless. He has repeatedly promised to deliver an historic speech to the world, in which he will set all of its major problems right, and when he favours new suggestions which are made to him he promptly plans to incorporate them in this speech. This magnified idea of his own importance has been reinforced by most of Swaziland's whites, who have built Sobhuza up into almost a mystical demigod because they believe that he knows both how to rule the Swazi and to prevent them from effectively challenging white privileges. Yet very few Swazilanders, as the whites call themselves in distinction from the Swazi, have had any contact with Sobhuza, and probably not one in five would even recognize him in Swazi dress.

While it is not clear to what extent Sobhuza has become captive to the controlling inner clique of the Swazi National Council, there is good reason to believe that he firmly plays his own game while leaving his councillors plenty of rope. The men around him have gained and kept their positions by flattery and a show of obedience, but they have on many occasions acted in his name without referring to him. Many corrupt ones amongst them may have hidden their operations from Sobhuza, but there have been some cases in which he has been reluctant to recognize or punish even blatant corruption. He himself is avaricious, reputedly owning trading stores through straw men, and whilst he makes good use with simple Swazi of the Ngwenyama's traditional title as 'the mouth that speaks no lies', others think he is better described by one of the names his father gave him: *Mona*, which means 'jealousy'.

The man to be watched within Sobhuza's inner circle is Polycarp Ka-Lazarus Dlamini, the veteran secretary of the Swazi National Council who was given a tribal seat in the Legislative Council by Sobhuza. As S.N.C. secretary, Polycarp Dlamini has been the council's most influential official, and in the royal kraal he is often seated at the King's side. But while he has an undoubted mastery of tribal ways, he is by no means at a loss in the white man's world. On the contrary, he is an astute and polished operator, a master of obfuscation, a confident public speaker with an excellent command of English and, like many other short men, a considerable conceit. Mr Dlamini was the Ngwenyama's chief representative throughout the constitutional talks in Swaziland and London. If any secret deals have been done with Swaziland's whites, Dr Verwoerd, or anyone else, it is certain that Polycarp Dlamini played a crucial role in them, and he is certain to be at the centre of any deals which may yet be done.

STRIKE!

Whilst the country was in the grip of constitutional uncertainty in 1963, it also underwent a major series of strikes which, taking on strong political overtones, in turn influenced its political life.

Swaziland today is thick with signs of industrial and commercial development. It is being traversed from west to east, from South Africa to Moçambique, by a splendid tarred highway of international standard, for which the International Development Association, an off-shoot of the World Bank, has lent £1 million. This was Swaziland's first loan from an international body and the I.D.A.'s first investment in Africa.

An airfield of medium capacity is in operation, and a 137-mile railway was completed last year, giving the territory its first direct link with the sea in the Portuguese colony of Moçambique. Along this railway there have begun to move millions of tons of high grade iron ore, which are to be hewn out of phenomenally rich iron ore mountains where mining commenced in 1964. The country's first hydroelectric scheme will also soon be in operation. In its gigantic forest plantations, the Usutu Pulp Mill is turning out 100,000 tons of pulp for paper every year, while boxes and plywood veneer are produced nearby. And from the Havelock asbestos mine, one of the world's five largest, over 30,000 tons a year go to South Africa, Britain, France and other parts of the world. Huge deposits of coal may soon be exploited, and high grade deposits of kaolin are already being mined and exported.

In the midst of lush agricultural lands, a modern fruit and vegetable canning factory is in full operation, building up a useful international export market. Sugar plantations and milling are prosperous. There is a modern maize milling plant, and a substantial printing and publishing company in the columns of whose weekly newspaper is reflected the boom in land prices. Mbabane, the miniscule capital, affectionately known to its British expatriates as 'the village', has woken from its long sleep with a rash of new buildings. The tourist trade is booming, too. £17½ million have been spent or committed in Swaziland by the Commonwealth (formerly Colonial) Development Corporation since 1948, and even larger sums by South African and British interests over the years. This very real economic progress, which far outstrips anything achieved or even planned in Bechuanaland and Basutoland, makes it difficult to remember that it was once Swaziland which was regarded as the ugly duckling of the High Commission Territories, subsidized for a time by Basutoland revenues.

But behind Swaziland's present development lies the question of how much it is benefiting the ordinary Swazi, and here a very different and disturbing picture emerges.

Swaziland's larger employers of labour have strongly resisted the introduction of trade-unions, and during 1963 the country's two major political parties began to interest themselves actively in the conditions of most workers. Contrary to what most local whites believed, Swazi workers had, however, been dissatisfied long before politicians vocalized their grievances. Indeed, until 1963, labour relations in Swaziland were reminiscent of the early industrial revolution in England. When, in 1948, there had occurred a major strike at the highly profitable Havelock asbestos mine, it had been sharply broken. Then, in 1962, there took place at the C.D.C.–Courtaulds Usutu Pulp Company mill the first strike to centre on trade-union organization. In a short, sharp but total strike, the workers gained the reinstatement of men dismissed because of their part in trying, quite legally, to form a trade-union, and also achieved a hearing at last for their grievances about pay and living conditions. Later in 1962, and early in 1963, short but total strikes took place in the forestry industry at Peak Timbers and amongst workers building Swaziland's new railway.

Conditions were particularly poor on the sugar plantations in the Big Bend area of Swaziland, of which the most important is known as Ubombo Ranches. This company is registered in Swaziland, but is controlled by British and South African directors. Its labour practices, and those of other sugar estates, have been modelled on those in the South African sugar industry, where conditions for workers are notoriously poor, but those in Swaziland did not even reach South African standards.

An official board of inquiry subsequently found that in March 1963 most workers of the Ubombo Ranches group still had to 'house' themselves in self-erected hovels, with no sanitation, and to use water unfit for human consumption. Wages were even lower than those in South Africa. The basic wage for an unskilled recruit was 2s. 1d. a day plus rations, with a complicated system of tiny attendance, and later incentive bonuses. Irrigation workers, who worked twelve-hour day or night shifts, earned a basic wage of only £4 7s. od. a month, with rations, housing and medical attention which the company valued at another £4 8s. od. Where incentive bonuses operated for semi-skilled work, these earnings could be increased, but labour relations and management were so poor that the bonus and quota fixing system generated more hostility than satisfaction. Very strict and often arbitrary discipline operated, assaults by supervisors on workers occurred, and any failure to perform a set task was penalized by pay deductions or stoppage of rations.

The sugar workers' grievances were taken up by the militant wing of the Progressive Party led by Dr A.P. Zwane and Mr Dumisa Dlamini. Through them, the workers demanded £15 a month, and complained about food, water, housing and the high-handedness of white company officials. These demands were flatly rejected, and workers arbitrarily dismissed. There then followed a totally effective strike of 2,500 men at Ubombo Ranches and three neighbouring estates, which – marked by an absence of violence, but accompanied by arrests for alleged intimidation – lasted for nine days in March 1963, ended when the Government appointed a board of inquiry. As a result the companies speeded up some minor improvements though basically conditions remained extremely poor, and the Government rushed through a proclamation of regulations to cover labour disputes, which came into force shortly before the biggest strike in the country's history took place in May 1963.

By that time, the unrest caused by the protracted constitutional negotiations was becoming obvious. In April, Lord Lansdowne, the Minister of State for Colonial Affairs, had visited Swaziland in connexion with the constitution, and when leaders of the three main political parties had marched with 400 orderly followers to make representations to him at the residency in Mbabane, they had been dispersed by police using tear gas. This had been an ominous new departure, and the protest of the parties against the proposed new constitution had remained undelivered.

The May strike began at the Havelock mine, which produces the asbestos that is Swaziland's chief source of revenue and export earnings. Owned by the British group of Turner, Newall and Co., it is one of the five largest producers of chrysotile asbestos in the world, and in 1961 it produced 30·8 million short tons, valued at slightly over £2½ million. This constituted ninety-eight per cent by value of Swaziland's total mineral production, and so indicates that the mine was responsible for almost the whole of the £508,000 tax paid by mining companies in 1960–61. Given the favourable rate of Swaziland tax for mining companies, this suggests a profit *after* taxation in the region of £1 million. It is hard to understand why, in return for such lush pickings, Havelock should not be obliged to process its asbestos in Swaziland instead of taking it by cable hoist for processing in South Africa.

Wages at the Havelock mine have been anything but princely. Before the strike, the management showed a marked reluctance to reveal figures of its profits and wage structure, but the report of the commission of inquiry into the strike is somewhat more helpful. The lowest wage drawn by an adult employee is 5s. 3d. per day worked, or £6 17s. 9d. a month, plus normal rations, 10s. worth of free food a month, housing valued by the company at £2 10s. 0d., medical attention and some schooling for children.

But even this low basic wage of 5s. 3d. a day is a substantial advance on the pre-strike figure of 3s. 9d., and was offered by the mine management in a last-minute attempt to ward off the strike. The miners, however, stuck to their demand for £1 a day, and some 1,350 men, constituting ninety-five per cent of the labour force, stopped work. The mine management waived for a time a court interdict which it had obtained to prevent Mr Dumisa Dlamini of the Ngwane National Liberatory Congress from entering mine property, and he spoke for the strikers in abortive negotiations. The men remained unmoved when, after a week, the Government appointed a one-man commission of inquiry into the strike, wages and labour conditions at Havelock.

Ripples of their militancy spread to Mbabane, where the Democratic Party held a mass meeting of domestic workers and labourers. The meeting demanded that the Resident Commissioner institute a general inquiry into Swazi wages, improve 'intolerable working conditions', and fix a national minimum wage. In passing on these requests to the Resident Commissioner, Dr Allen Nxumalo of the Democratic Party pointed out that domestic servants earned between £2–£5 10s. 0d. a month, worked unlimited hours and had to find their own accommodation. He referred to widespread malnutrition of children, to 'poverty, low wages, bad and unhygienic accommodation, poor food' as 'inflammable material' and declared 'it is imperative that immediate steps should be taken to effect reforms before the present mood of the people gets out of control and paralyses the economy'.

His warning was timely. The Havelock strike, which had begun on 20 May, remained peaceful until the police arrested twelve alleged ringleaders on 8 June. These men were almost all members of the Ngwane National Liberatory Congress (N.N.L.C.), the new name adopted by the Zwane–Dlamini faction of the old Progressive Party. Some 2,000 strikers demonstrated against the police, who dispersed them with tear gas.

On the following day, a Saturday, a mass meeting of over 3,500 in Mbabane's slummy African township protested against the arrests and, under Dumisa Dlamini's leadership, gave the strike a political twist by protesting also against the country's new constitution. A call for a general strike in Mbabane was issued and the town was brought to a standstill on Monday. There was some intimidation, undoubtedly, but popular support must have been deep and widespread for most domestic servants and all other workers to stay away from work.

Scenes just as unprecedented were to follow. Over 3,000 orderly marchers, led by Dumisa Dlamini, demanded to see the Resident Commissioner, who agreed to receive a deputation of fifteen. Led by Dlamini and Macdonald Maseko, the N.N.L.C.'s deputy-president (who had fled to Swaziland from house arrest in South Africa), the deputation demanded the release of the twelve arrested strike leaders, a minimum wage of £1 a day, and the rejection of the new constitution. News of such events travels fast, and that night the prisoners in Mbabane's antiquated and over-crowded jail rioted. Despite the use of tear gas and the firing of shots, ten escaped.

The general strike in Mbabane held solid, ignoring a representative whom the Ngwenyama had sent to urge the striking men and women back to work. The weekly *Times of Swaziland* came out only in a one-page edition, produced by the two white men on its staff. The Havelock men were joined by workers at Ubombo Ranches in the Big Bend area, by 300 men of the neighbouring Swaziland Plantations, by the Bar Circle Ranch, and by cotton pickers on a farm on the other side of the territory.

In Mbabane, meetings of strikers were banned, and whites in the territory's main centres were enlisted as special constables, to patrol the streets day and night. The carrying of sticks, which to many Swazi is habitual, and of 'other dangerous weapons' was pronounced illegal. Then, in rapid succession, the Government announced that it would institute a general inquiry into wages and conditions of employment; took emergency powers which, *inter alia*, raised the penalty for intimidation from three months' to three years' imprisonment; and brought in police reinforcements from Bechuanaland.

Hard on the heels of these thirty-seven police, came the most dramatic move of all: the air-lifting into the Territory of a whole battalion of Gordon Highlanders from the British troops in Kenya. The wisest course would have been to use these troops to prevent intimidation, whilst the employers were persuaded to negotiate with the strikers. Instead, the Gordons went into immediate action with the Swaziland police to *break* first the Havelock and then other strikes. Strike areas were sealed off by army cordons, the workers rounded up and, in 'screening', given the choice between returning to work or remaining in custody and having charges brought against them.

Troops and police, aided by a spotter plane, scoured the bush into which groups of strikers, reportedly armed with sugar cane knives, had fled. Within a week, the *Times of Swaziland* announced 'Strikers go back to work – Swaziland returns to normal'. It may have seemed so on the spot, but the strike and the flying in of troops to break it had irrevocably changed the meaning of 'normal'. Swaziland had at last been put on the world map of colonial unrest and protests against the Government's handling of the strike promptly came from African leaders, with Mr Tom Mboya demanding that British troops quit Kenya, which Britain was using as a base 'to oppose our brothers'.

The Swaziland Government explained that the troops had been summoned because the 350-strong Swaziland police had been unable to cope with widespread flouting of the law. As the Government Secretary saw it:

The disturbances in Swaziland, which included illegal strikes, illegal gatherings and processions, illegal carrying of weapons, assaults and intimidation, were brought about by leaders and organizations which appeared to have as their main aim the standstill of the whole economy of the country. It is the first duty of any government to ensure that law and order is maintained. . . .

It seems, the Government Secretary said, that there had been some organizing behind the strike, for the strikers in Mbabane had had food, for which money must have come from somewhere. There was no sign that it came from outside. 'The strikes,' he concluded, 'seem to be political demonstrations wedded to genuine local grievances.'

With the leaders of the Liberatory Congress, including Mr Dlamini and Dr Zwane (who had been out of the country when the strike began), either in custody or about to be arrested, the rival Democratic Party accused them of 'having betrayed the poor and exploited people of Swaziland in throwing the country into a series of sudden strikes without adequate preparation'. The Democratic Party echoed current rumours of South African troop movements when it alleged that chaos in Swaziland 'is precisely the excuse Dr Verwoerd needs to march into the Protectorate in the interests of white South Africans'.

The Democratic Party, whilst pressing for higher wages to relieve 'the crushing poverty of the masses of the Swazi people', had in fact, together with trade-unions where these existed, opposed the strike. It was highly significant, indeed, that the strike succeeded precisely where employers had used vigorous, and sometimes violent, methods to prevent the formation of unions. In the affected industries the employers had actually expelled any trade-union workers found on the premises, and had threatened any worker joining a trade-union with dismissal. In place of trade-unionism, these employers had attempted to invoke the old tribal structure by appointing an Induna, or head-man, as a sort of tribal representative in the workers' compound, to act as spokesman and go-between. In fact, until the troops arrived, the political parties and the trade-unions emerged as the crucial groups in the labour force of the Territory, with one party leading the strike and the other, supported by its trade-union allies, opposing it.

Thus the strike not only revealed a crisis of authority in Swaziland, in which both the Ngwenyama and the Administration were shown to be out of touch and unable to deal with modern reality. It also established the prime importance of the young political parties which were being given so small a role in Swaziland's new constitution. The Administration, having waited far too long before beginning to tackle the improvement of labour conditions, found imported force the only answer.

Certainly the state of the small Swaziland police, as revealed in its commissioner's report for 1963, was far from happy.

The inhabitants of the Territory are gradually becoming more politically conscious and the marked increase in political activity during the year has resulted in more work devolving upon the already strained resources of the Force.

The Public Works Department had been too busy elsewhere to improve police buildings for which money had been approved, and housing conditions for junior ranks were so poor that their loyalty was in danger of being impaired. Pay was so bad that better-educated recruits could not be attracted even with a direct entry sub-inspection scheme. The morale of subordinate (white) officers was so low that five inspectors, representing almost twelve per cent of the establishment for subordinate officers, had resigned. 'The inadequate financial rewards for the onerous duties and responsibilities combined with diminishing prospects of a permanent career were the principal reasons for the resignation and for the low morale.' There was, however, a brighter side to the strike picture. As the commissioner added with unconscious irony, 'The morale of the junior [i.e. African] ranks improved as the opportunities for a worthwhile career became more apparent.' A £400,000 Police College is now being built by the Swaziland subsidiary of a leading South African firm.

The Ngwenyama proved ineffectual both with the strikers and the Administration. The practice had been for his representative to reside at the mine, in order to provide liaison between workers and management, but the strike proved this liaison to be illusory. When the strike spread, the Administration vainly asked the Ngwenyama to provide men from his royal 'regiments' to protect workers against intimidation. And when the British troops arrived, the workers appealed just as vainly to the Ngwenyama to intercede with the authorities on their behalf.

The troops were employed, after breaking the main strike, in a series of raids on African townships to help the police round up some hundreds of alleged tax defaulters and illegal immigrants. Several hundred Africans were arrested as a result of the strike itself, with 244 in custody a fortnight after the troops arrived, and of these, a majority were convicted on charges of striking illegally, holding illegal meetings or possessing dangerous weapons. The main and considerably protracted trial, was that of fifteen leading members of the Liberatory Congress on charges of public violence. In this, brilliantly defended by Mr David Soggot, a young Johannesburg barrister, Dr Zwane was acquitted but seven others, including Dumisa Dlamini, were convicted. In sentencing them to three to six months' imprisonment, suspended in all but one case, the Chief Justice accepted that nothing had been done 'for many years' to improve the 'generally very low' wages in Swaziland, and that Dumisa Dlamini and the other two main accused 'did not want this strike to be accompanied with acts of physical violence and they did their utmost to stop it'. But they had organized groups of young men, known as *malindane*, to stop people from going to work, and these *malindane* had carried sticks which inspired fear.

The number of actual cases of intimidation cited in the judgment is small and, whilst intimidation is notoriously hard to prove, this does underline the general restraint and peacefulness of the strike. No life was lost, and no significant damage to property reported.

The Resident Commissioner subsequently reduced the six months' sentences, which would have disqualified their recipients from candidature in the new Legislative Council elections until their sentences had been served, to five months. This was seen as political appeasement by a white correspondent in the local weekly paper, though it may prove to be a farsighted action. Leaders who could organize such a strike and such disciplined demonstrations are better included in an elected legislature than otherwise.

Until energetic efforts to build up the Swaziland police bear fruit a battalion of British troops will remain in the country, where permanent barracks are being built for them. In one probably unforeseen way, their presence has given all three Territories a new insurance against South African aggression. For if British troops can be flown in to break a strike, world opinion would never again accept the argument that they could not be flown in to meet any South African threat.

The strike permanently shattered the image of the urban Swazi as a happy, complacent lot of people, satisfied to let their lives be run by their King, the British Administration and white employers.

This new situation has its roots in the changing conditions of Swaziland, where poor wages, high unemployment and a general sense of frustration are all common to the Swazi at a time when the country is visibly booming for the whites.

It can hardly be said that the Swaziland Administration acted with excessive speed in tackling the wage and employment crisis which the strikes of 1962 and early 1963 signalled and which the big strike in May and June 1963 starkly underlined. The general commission of inquiry promised at the end of the strikes only began its work seven months later. It consisted of Mr H. A. Whitson, and the 'Whitson Report' was delivered in March 1964. Yet in February 1964 an official spokesman stressed that 'For two years Her Majesty's Commissioner has urged that more be done for the under-privileged. He has often spoken in public of the unjustified difference between the haves and the have-nots.'

As a liberal white resident commented in the local Press: 'Two years is a long time to be hungry ... but Government has not promulgated a law which enforces every employer to pay a minimum rate of wages for unskilled labour, nor has it done anything to stop the spiralling cost of living, which is as important a factor as the actual wage rates.'

The Government's only move in the meantime was to create a purely voluntary, non-statutory National Joint Consultative Council, composed of representatives of employers, registered trade-unions, the Government and the Swazi National Council. This was Swaziland's first attempt to bring the various parties concerned with wages and work conditions together nationally, and characteristically it was no more than a talking shop.

When the Whitson Report into regulating wages and conditions of employment in Swaziland finally appeared in March 1964, it underlined the massive need for action, but side-stepped some of the major problems. Thus Mr Whitson recommended that there should be no general statutory minimum wage for the whole country 'because it would have to be fixed at such a low figure that it would be of little benefit to most workers and it would be extremely difficult to enforce'. For roughly similar reasons, he found that it would be impossible to establish wage-fixing machinery for domestic service, although he expressed concern at conditions in this field, which is the main outlet for Swazi women seeking employment. At present, the average monthly wage of a domestic servant is £2 18s. 0d., with food, but frequently without quarters, provided.

The Government, in accepting the Whitson Report's

recommendations, undertook to look at these two questions again at a later date, and announced that it would meanwhile proceed with the establishment of wages councils for agriculture (excluding the sugar and forestry mills), hotels and catering and retail distribution. Statutory procedures for the fixing of minimum wages had hitherto remained unused since 1937.

Action in these fields is certainly needed. In agriculture the average wage for an African labourer has been £3 a month, with rations and quarters (while a white farm assistant gets £50 together with quarters), and there has been no limit to the number of hours worked. Agriculture is the largest employer of labour in Swaziland, accounting for some 10,000 or more than forty-four per cent* of Africans in local employment, and two-thirds of this total are engaged in the sugar industry.

In forestry, which together with timber processing has accounted for twenty-two per cent of locally employed Africans, an African labourer has been earning from £3 to £6 5s. 0d. a month, with rations and quarters. A white forest foreman has been earning £40, and a forester £54 with quarters.

The third largest field of employment in 1962 was construction, in which the wage for an African labourer ranged from £4 6s. 0d. to £6 a month, with neither food nor quarters provided, while the white road foreman under whom such Africans worked received £60 a month. The normal working week in construction and quarrying is from forty-seven to fifty-eight hours. An African building worker received from £8 10s. 0d. to £25 a month, while a white artisan received £62 basic. Between them, private contractors and the Government employed nearly 3,000 African construction workers, or thirteen per cent of Africans locally employed.

In promising speedy action on the Whitson Report, the Government undertook to establish a representative joint body to negotiate conditions for its own daily paid workmen, preferably with representatives of a properly constituted trade-union. Meanwhile, it proposed to pay its own workers 4s. a nine-hour day, or £5 8s. 0d. a month of six-day weeks, together with rations, from 1 April 1964.

* Figures from Swaziland Annual Report, 1962, which refers only to employers of fifty or more Africans. Many white farmers employ smaller numbers.

In retail distribution, the average wage of an African store assistant has been £7 10s. 0d. a month with quarters, while a white store assistant has received £41 10s. 0d. together with quarters. The working week in urban areas is supposedly forty-five to forty-eight hours, but in many places, especially stores, it is longer.

The gross wage disparity between white and black needs no underlining, and it is cold comfort to the Swazi that it is because of past educational neglect and lack of training facilities that very few of them are equipped to undertake skilled jobs. In fact, most of the semi-skilled and skilled African workers in Swaziland are South Africans. Employers claim that these foreign workers are more sophisticated and responsible, and there is a great deal of bitterness felt by the Swazi at being left at the bottom of the employment pile. Nor are labour relations helped by the fact that almost all white artisans are South African or Portuguese.

There is only one Trade Training Centre in Swaziland, where twenty-four Swazi and Coloured pupils a year can take courses in bricklaying, carpentry, motor-mechanics, and electrical wiring. Semi-skilled workers, such as drivers and operatives, are trained on the job by employers. In 1962 the Government introduced a new, short apprenticeship system with supervision in industry and also aptitude tests for semi-skilled workers, and it placed twenty-six apprentices in the following year. There were also sixteen apprentices being trained by employers under the conventional five-year scheme. Yet Swaziland's total population at the end of 1962 was about 280,700, of whom some 270,000 were Africans.

The Government has accepted the Whitson Report's conclusion that in only two fields is trade-union organization advanced enough to make joint voluntary wage-fixing machinery effective, and thus workers in railways and mining are being left to work out their own wage levels.

What this is likely to mean in practice is shown by the agreement reached in March 1964 between the South African consortium building Swaziland's new multi-million-pound railway and the Swaziland Railway Workers' and Railway Construction Workers' Union. This is believed to be the first agreement on recognition and wages negotiated in Swaziland, and the union gained the important concession of having its dues collected by the company from the workers' pay. It also gained an advance of nearly twenty per cent in unskilled wages, but even *with* the increase, labourers on this highly profitable railway project are earning only 5s. 4d. a day, with rations and quarters.

There are now eight registered trade-unions in Swaziland, though the first of them was only established in September 1962. They have been helped by visits from representatives of the International Confederation of Free Trade Unions (I.C.F.T.U.) and of the Miners' International Federation, but by March 1964 only two of them had gained recognition from the employers.

The Whitson Report stressed the desirability of trade-unions being formed, of their receiving help from the I.C.F.T.U., and the urgent need for wage regulation. Until now, the report pointed out, wages in Swaziland have been determined solely by the employers, or in other words simply by the law of supply and demand, and with too many workers seeking the few jobs available, extremely low wages have been the result. There were, Mr Whitson declared in 1964, 'at present no adequate arrangements whereby the workers' claims can be submitted and considered. At present the only forum for the statement of workers' claims appears to be the political meeting.' So much for the belief of most Swaziland whites that strikes have resulted from irrelevant political incitement.

The Swaziland Government accepted the report's view that wages had to be raised even if this resulted in fewer workers being employed, and it pledged itself to attract new industries to provide more jobs and also to make agriculture more attractive for peasant farmers.

In considering the difficulties facing trade-union organization in Swaziland, the Whitson Report stressed that the suspicions both of some illiterate workers and employers had to be overcome, though 'employers generally whom I have met have shown no opposition to trade-unions as such and indeed some have given encouragement'. Other sources suggest that such employers must be very few in number, but Mr Whitson reserved his main criticism for the opposition of the Swazi National Council to the formation of trade-unions. Clearly the S.N.C. knows that trade-unions, just like political parties, must expose the archaic sham of the council as the best body to speak for and defend Swazi interests.

But the fundamental difficulty against which trade-unions must battle is that Swaziland, even with recent industrial advances, simply does not supply remotely enough jobs for the thousands of Swazi who must periodically find work in order to pay their taxes and support their families. Swaziland has a working age group (aged fifteen to sixty-four) of 138,000, of whom 65,800 are males. Of this group, only 38,200 can presently find employment in Swaziland, and even with a continued economic boom this total is not likely to be much increased in the next few years. Fifty-seven per cent of present wage earners draw from £3–£6 a month, though Swaziland's first nutritional survey* recently noted that one 180-lb. bag of maize meal, which is the Swazi's staple food, costs £2 8s. 1d.; at $1\frac{1}{4}$ lb. per person per day, such a bag could at most last an average homestead of six people twenty-four days. As the survey concludes, 'the average earnings of the majority of Swazi (in employment) would be insufficient to purchase more than two bags of maize meal per month *if all the earnings were devoted to maize meal*'. (My italics.) What of all the other necessities of life ?

As in South Africa, Swaziland employers, and amongst them the Government, apparently assume that wage earners are single men, or that where they have families these are supported by work on their own farms. Even if this were true, the resulting 'bachelor' wages decree that the married urban worker must be separated from his family. But, in fact, the women and children cannot support themselves on their patches of land. In 1960, for example, wages constituted an average twenty per cent of the income of Swazi homesteads from all sources, including the subsistence element. And, as an official report coolly puts it, 'the average Swazi homestead is becoming more dependent on wage earnings as a source of income'.

Meanwhile, the Swazi population is increasing by approximately 2·7 per cent every year, and with the reduction in the infant mortality rate the population increase may soon be 5,000 a year. Since Swaziland is unable to provide adequate employment, and unable under present conditions even to meet its present food

* *A Study of Swazi Nutrition*, Sonya M. Jones, Institute for Social Research, University of Natal, for the Swaziland Administration, 1963.

needs, there has inevitably been a continued dependence on labour migrating temporarily to South Africa, with all the attendant social evils of such a system.

In 1962, some 9,400 Swazi men (comprising twenty-eight per cent of the African male labour force) and 800 women were employed in South Africa, with the South African gold mines recruiting 8,800 of the men and the Natal coal mines 400. The rest found work mainly on South African farms and in small mines bordering on Swaziland, being barred by South African law from urban areas.

These migrant workers inject money into the Swaziland economy at an annual rate of £198,000 in the form of deferred pay and family allowances, and £225,000 in the value of goods and money brought home by returning recruits. In addition, more than £14,000 of tax money is deducted from the migrant mine workers' pay and handed over to the Swaziland Government. The resultant total of nearly £440,000 is clearly important to a territory whose ordinary revenue in 1961–2 was only £4,326,052.

Although Swaziland's dependence on migratory labour is far smaller than Basutoland's, it is still a major factor in its economy. And this lends bitter irony to the fact that African immigration *into* Swaziland has increased as its economic boom has developed. There were in 1962 over 14,000 Africans from the Republic in Swaziland, and approximately 5,600 Africans from other territories, mainly Moçambique.

For the most part, Africans from the Republic come to Swaziland in order to do skilled or semi-skilled work. Many of them leave again when the work on which they have been employed is completed, but the net African immigration gain from 1955–62 was 1,200. This was double the rate for the preceding decade, and it has increased further since 1962 with the construction of the railway line on which Swaziland's newly mined iron ore is to be carried to Lourenço Marques for export.

Although the railway line, which is Swaziland's first, runs to the Portuguese colony of Moçambique rather than to South Africa, both its construction and the mining of iron ore illustrate the domination which foreign, and especially South African, capital has established in Swaziland.

We have already noted that the Havelock asbestos mine, which was for many years the Territory's only industry, is owned by the British firm of Turner and Newall Ltd, which has been making a profit after taxation of something like £1 million a year. These profits have not, however, been even partly ploughed back into Swaziland development. Swaziland itself remains in currency union with South Africa, and certainly contibutes more to the common pool of foreign currency than it draws, thus helping to strengthen South Africa's currency. In return, although Swaziland in general applies South African exchange control regulations, the funds of Swaziland residents and companies may be freely transferred within the sterling area, provided that they have not been earned in the Republic. Thus the profits of Turner and Newall flow freely abroad.

The same seems certain to happen with the exploitation of the high grade iron ore deposits at Ngwenya in north-western Swaziland, which are so rich that Ngwenya fully justifies its alternative name of 'iron mountain'. The concession for mining this ore, which will be done by the simple and cheap 'open-cast' method, has been given by the Swaziland Administration to a combination of South African and British capital. South Africa's giant Anglo-American Corporation, which dominates South African mining and controls the world diamond market through De Beers, has joined with the British industrial combine of Guest, Keen and Nettlefolds to form the Swaziland Iron Ore Development Company, with a minimum authorized capital of £3 million. The Colonial Development Corporation subscribed £500,000 to this company, which negotiated a ten-year contract to supply twelve million tons of ore to a Japanese consortium headed by the Yawata and Fuji iron and steel groups. This contract at £3 10s. od. a ton, is valued at £41 million, but this will exhaust hardly the beginning of the mine's life. The 'iron mountain' is divided into three blocks, which thirsty geologists named castle, lion, and stag after three popular South African beers. Preliminary and shallow exploration of only two of these blocks indicate ore reserves of forty-seven million short tons.

So profitable is the 'iron mountain' certain to be that it has justified the construction of a 137-mile railway line from Ngwenya to the port of Lourenço Marques in the Portuguese colony of Moçambique, an outlet chosen after the South African Railway authorities had turned down approaches to link Ngwenya with their own system, since this would have involved fresh railway extensions in South Africa. The contract for building this £8 million railway went after open tendering to a consortium of three South African firms, Roberts Construction, Murray and Stewart, and Rand Earthworks, which together registered a Swaziland company known as R.M.R. (Swaziland) Limited. Anglo-American provided £1 million towards financing the operation, the Colonial Development Corporation supplied £4 million, and £2·9 million was raised by the South African Mutual Life Assurance Society, which itself provided £1·36 million of the loan. Interest is at seven per cent.

The construction of the new railway will, of course, improve Swaziland's communications. But critics of its route point out that while it will suit South African iron ore and coal mining concessionaires, it will not fit in with the pattern of other necessary development in Swaziland. One leading South African industrial consultant has gone so far as to say that in fifty years' time Swaziland will find itself with a big hole in the ground and a badly sited railway. The Government, however, plans to create a new industrial area on the railway route.

The British Government could, of course, have raised the funds for the development of the iron ore mine and for the construction of the railway, leaving both, after amortization, as the nationalized property of the people of Swaziland. International bodies such as the World Bank might well have been interested in such a venture. The British Government, however, did not take the proper action and South African finance houses and construction firms were quick to take advantage. South African concerns, highly competitive because of their geographical proximity, are supplying the rails, plant and spares valued at £$\frac{1}{2}$ million, reinforcing steel, cement, explosives, rock-drill equipment and prefabricated housing units, signalling equipment and probably all of the 475 railway trucks.

What is most disturbing is the cheapness of the mining lease, the absence of Swazi participation in the directorship and shareholding of the mining company, the lack of effective guarantees for the training of Swazi in skilled work by the concessionaires and contractors, and the failure of the Administration to ensure that those who will exploit the wasting asset of minerals should create compensatory assets.

The lease negotiated between the mining company and the Swaziland Administration is for twenty-one years, renewable for another twenty-one, and gives the company exclusive rights not only to mining but also to the possible processing of the iron ore. The erection of a plant to produce pig iron from the ore would certainly seem feasible, and though it might cost around £10 million, the price of pig iron is more than double that of iron ore. Swaziland's huge but untapped deposits of coal or anthracite could be used, and the limestone required is abundant not far from the border in Moçambique. A steel-making plant could well follow. What remains to be seen is whether South African capital, in whose hands the decision has now been placed, will wish to proceed with such projects, which might antagonize South Africa's State-owned iron- and steel-producing industry.

For its blanket concession the Swaziland Iron Ore Development Company will pay a derisory annual rental of just over £200, plus a very modest 2½ per cent of the value of the mineral production in tax. Its only obligation towards the Swazi themselves is to do its 'best' to train local people for skilled and responsible posts and to appoint them when the opportunity arises. The company alone will be the judge of these criteria.

The responsibility of the major construction contractors is even less binding. They have merely undertaken to engage and train as many Swazi as they can profitably use. As tunnelling and other railway construction jobs are carried out in the main by trained teams and supervisors, it is more profitable for the contractors to bring in their own men, who have been working together for years. The Swazi have once again been left at the bottom of the labour pile.

The mining concession was, significantly, negotiated and signed by Her Majesty's Commissioner, and not by the Swazi. Sobhuza probably postponed giving it his approval as part of his campaign to have all mineral rights recognized as belonging to the Swazi nation; but he also objected to specific aspects of the agreement, and the responsibility for not obtaining Swazi shareholding and training guarantees thus rests squarely with the British Administration.

That some such participation and guarantees can be obtained was shown by the late Tshekedi Khama in Bechuanaland. Equally important in the long run is the obvious fact, already noted, that minerals, once their exploitation has begun, are a wasting asset. Thus, as even the orthodox Morse Economic Survey Mission warned, profits and taxes from mineral exploitation should not be regarded simply as income. The mission urged that the Government, through taxation or in other ways, should see to it that part of the gross value of mineral production is allocated and used to create fresh capital assets in the country, against the time when its minerals are exhausted. An orthodox way to do this would be to allocate part of mining tax revenue to a development fund. Nothing is known of any such plan by the Swaziland Administration. In fact, the tax it will levy on the Swaziland Iron Ore Development Company is so low that anticipated receipts are only £99,000 a year. One third of this is to be paid to the Swazi National Council, and half to the Swaziland Railway Board until the railway loans have been amortized.

The same criticisms apply to the other crucial Swaziland mineral concessions. Thus the building of the railway promises to give a boost to plans for exploiting Swaziland's very considerable coal resources, which have been proved at 250 million tons, though they are almost certainly much larger, with at least 5 million tons of high-grade anthracite in addition; but the mining rights have already been given to South African firms, Rand Mines Ltd and the Johannesburg Consolidated Investment Company, without any guarantees for Swazi training or participation.

Industrial development in Swaziland will, of course, lead to an increase in local employment opportunities for the Swazi, but these are likely to be mainly for unskilled labour, whilst profits from the exploitation of Swaziland's mineral resources will flow, after gentle taxation, out of the country into South Africa and Britain.

THE TWO NATIONS

For a country of its small size, Swaziland is remarkably rich in base minerals. The vastly profitable asbestos ore-body at Havelock is now known to extend into adjacent concession areas, with an additional 750,000 tons likely to be proved in one of them and further high-grade deposits in another. On a very much smaller scale, but still of significance for a small country, is the mining of pyrophyllite and kaolin. Swaziland's extensive deposits of kaolin, which is a type of china clay highly prized in ceramic manufacture, are of particularly high quality, and are the only such known in southern Africa. In the area proved so far, 500,000 tons should be mineable by open-cast methods at shallow depths, and production to date has been eagerly taken up by the ceramics industry in South Africa, which has no deposits of comparable quality. Certainly, there seems no reason why overseas manufacture should not establish in Swaziland factories for crockery and tableware. But once again it is to be South Africa which will make the money out of a Swaziland mineral resource. The mineral rights to Swaziland's kaolin were acquired early in 1963 by a South African registered company, Pinata Finance and Development Corporation Ltd, which has also acquired the 10,500-acre Pinata Ranch in Swaziland, one of the largest cotton-producing areas in southern Africa, as well as two butcheries. The company's directors show the level at which South African businessmen are climbing into Swaziland: its managing director is a former South African Secretary for Mines, and another director is chairman of the South African Railways Tender Board. Tin, barytes, diaspore, beryl, and gola are also mined, though in very small quantities, in the Territory.

Industry in Swaziland has until now been concerned with processing local production, as with a modern maize mill and a creamery. The latter produces some half million pounds of butter annually, almost all of which is sold in South Africa. For the rest, there are several small concerns providing services such as motor-car repairs and tyre retreading, the manufacture of mineral waters, and the High Commission Printing and Publishing Company Ltd in Mbabane. This last has a trained African staff of forty who, under European supervision, do general printing, produce Government Gazettes for the High Commission Territories, and print Swaziland's only newspaper, the weekly *Times of Swaziland*. A vernacular weekly ceased publication in 1964. All of Swaziland's industries are white-owned and run, with Swazi 'enterprises' confined to hand-made products for the tourist trade, sold at colourful markets in the main townships.

The Morse Economic Survey Mission, looking to plausible future industrial development, suggested the establishment of a distillery to produce alcohol from the surplus molasses of the established sugar industry. Such alcohol could be used as a supplement to imported motor fuel or, perhaps more profitably, in the manufacture of plastics.

With coal so cheaply and readily available to the sugar mills, it might pay them to turn to coal as a fuel and to sell the bagasse, which they now burn, for the manufacture of paper, with Usutu pulp added, where necessary, to give strength and finish to the higher grades. These and other industrial developments would require electricity supplies, and since the iron ore mine and the railway were decided upon, the first substantial step has been taken towards exploiting Swaziland's abundant hydroelectric potential. Before, industries such as the Usutu Pulp Mill had to generate their own electricity, and Mbabane was served by a diesel generator. In 1962 the Swaziland Electricity Board was formed, and contracts were let for a £1·7 million hydroelectric scheme on the Little Usutu River. The initial installed generating capacity will be 5MW, with provision for quadrupling this capacity before the much higher potential of the Great Usutu River is tapped.

The only large-scale venture in which the Swazi have obtained a shareholding is the Usutu Pulp Company, the largest of the three major forestry concerns in the country. Swaziland's Highveld, with its generous rainfall, is an ideal forestry region, in which the rate of growth of conifers and eucalyptus is amongst the highest in the world. Pulpwood, for example, can be grown on a fifteen-year rotation, compared with forty to fifty years in the Scandinavian countries and Germany. The planting of the 119,000-acre Usutu forest itself was initiated by the Colonial Development Corporation in 1948, which in the following year went into a £5 million fifty:fifty partnership with Courtaulds Ltd, the huge British synthetic fibres concern. The resultant Usutu Pulp Company now has a mill in operation capable of producing 100,000 tons of unbleached sulphate pulp a year, and this, used for paper making, is exported through Lourenço Marques. The C.D.C. initially afforested two small areas for the Swazi nation, which Usutu Pulp bought in 1962, and in return, the Swazi nation acquired a £50,000 interest in the company.

No such Swazi participation exists in Peak Timbers Ltd, a wholly-owned subsidiary of South Africa's Anglo-American group, which has afforested over 65,000 acres, and has a sawmill and a chipboard manufacturing plant in operation. Swaziland Plantations, which has afforested 9,500 of its 11,000 acres, is a private company which is an offshoot of a larger South African concern and which operates a small box-mill on its property.

Aside from its investment in forestry and pulp-making, the C.D.C. has also played an important part in developing irrigation farming and sugar production in Swaziland. It launched the Swaziland irrigation scheme, whose biggest customer today is the Mhlume (Swaziland) Sugar Company, in which the C.D.C. and the South African firm of Sir J. L. Hulett and Sons are partners. Mhlume is second in importance as a sugar producer only to Ubombo Ranches in the Big Bend area, which is registered in Swaziland but controlled by South African and British interests. Prominent amongst its directors is Mr Geoffrey Lloyd, the Conservative M.P. There are also several smaller producers, including a very small Swazi national estate, which depend on the sugar mills which the two giants have built, but the whole highly promising industry is dependent on the production quotas fixed for it by the South African Sugar Association.

Commonwealth sugar marketing is controlled by national quotas in which South Africa, though she has left the Commonwealth, continues to have a share. In return for marketing Swaziland sugar, the South African Sugar Association pegged the Territory's production at 80,000 tons a year. This total was very nearly reached in 1961–2, and a new agreement was then negotiated with the South African Government, under which Swaziland was allowed to produce 8½ per cent of the combined sales of South Africa and Swaziland, entailing an increase in

Swaziland's quota from 80,000 to roughly 90,000 tons. But the Territory could produce much more than that, since because of favourable soil, water and climate, its average sugar yield per acre is over fifty tons, compared with thirty-five in Natal, and even its existing two mills could handle much more than 90,000 tons. From 1965, however, the agreements between South Africa, Britain and Swaziland will end, and Swaziland will market its own sugar, probably joining the Commonwealth Sugar Agreement.

Ways might also be considered of marketing Swaziland's increasing citrus and fruit crop, which is grown largely by white farmers, independently, instead of through South African marketing boards. 414,000 citrus trees had been planted by 1962 in Swaziland's three major irrigation scheme areas, and it is conservatively estimated that by 1967–8 Swaziland will produce 500,000 cases of export citrus fruit.

One way in which some of Swaziland's increasing citrus production will be independently marketed is through Swaziland Canners, situated in the Malkerns valley and prospering under the family ownership and management of an American, Mr J. W. Allen, and his two sons. Modern Italian plant has been installed and pineapple, tomatoes and citrus are being exported under the brand name of 'Malkerns', carefully labelled 'Produced in the British Protectorate of Swaziland' to escape the effects of anti-South African boycotts. 'Swaziland could be a second Hawaii in the production of pineapples', according to a former head of the Pineapple Research Institute of Hawaii, and its high rainfall means that this might be done without irrigation. It remains to be seen how far Swazi farmers will be drawn into pineapple growing. At present the growing of fruit and vegetables for canning is still an almost wholly white affair, except for the labourers employed by Swaziland Canners, who have been waging a hard struggle to gain recognition for a trade-union.

In Swaziland's sub-tropical climate, avocados and bananas flourish, but the danger of complete dependence for agricultural marketing on South Africa was illustrated in 1962, when decrees by the Republic's Banana Industry Control Board led to nearly half of Swaziland's banana plantations being ploughed under as no longer economic because of a South African glut.

Meanwhile maize, which is a dry-land crop and the staple of Swazi agriculture, continues to occupy the largest acreage, its 200,000 acres representing sixty-seven per cent of all cultivated cropland. Sorghum occupies 24,000 acres, sugar cane 22,000 irrigated acres, cotton 17,000 acres, and rice 6,000 irrigated acres.

Tobacco, butter, hides, and skins are all exported in small quantities to South Africa, as is rice valued at some £300,000 a year. The number of cattle exported for slaughter to South Africa has been increasing, and in 1962 was valued at £636,000.

Aside from cattle and a small amount of legumes, hardly any of the crops from Swazi lands are marketed. The maize, groundnuts, and various kinds of beans grown are consumed by the growers. Yet in a bad year such as 1961, 170,000 bags of maize had to be imported from South Africa, and Oxfam had urgently to provide £10,000 to subsidize the cost of seed maize to Swazi farmers and to help feed paupers unable to meet the cost of imported South African grain. Even in a good year like 1960, some 64,000 bags of maize had to be imported.

As he travels through Swaziland, the tourist can admire a range of scenic contrasts amazing in so small a country. He can pass in a few hours from lush, sub-tropical valleys to the rocky heights of the Lebombo plateau, and from pineapple to pine forests. But if he is reasonably observant, the tourist can note even from his car other contrasts: thriving plains of sugar cane and patches of stunted maize, modern industrial plants and open-air handicraft markets, luxury hotels and mud huts, tarred highway and poor tracks leading off towards Swazi villages.

Swaziland's contrasts are more than scenic, for they reflect two starkly different economies. In the one, white men and outside capital are forging profitably ahead, employing more Swazi but at a mere subsistence wage, or even less. In the other economy, the overwhelming majority of the Swazi scratch ineffectually for a living on fragmented bits of land, following traditional paths, using primitive methods, illiterate, poor, and touched by white prosperity at home and in South Africa only to the degree that it offers migrant labourers a chance to earn a little money.

Only thirteen per cent of Swazi are urbanized; the other

eighty-seven per cent, or 221,000 people, live and have their home in what are officially known as the Swazi areas, the fifty-two per cent of the country which is officially 'theirs'. On this land they do no more than eke out a living, or rather the women do, for at any given time forty per cent of the able-bodied men are away working and another forty-five per cent resting at home between periods of employment. Thus in 1962 there were 9,400 Swazi men, or twenty-eight per cent of all African male workers, temporarily outside Swaziland. And, as the Territory's annual report for that year put it, 'this high proportion of absentee labourers has been a feature of Swaziland's economy since 1887'. During the whole period of British rule, therefore, nothing has occurred to make life on the land viable, let alone attractive.

The reliance on supplementing income from the land by out-side employment is so great that a social survey,* commendably commissioned by the Administration, showed that in 1960 only one man in six in the rural areas had never been in wage-earning employment. Moreover, even with the added production of the recently much more efficient white farmers, Swaziland has, as we have seen, been unable to feed itself. When the weather is bad, as in 1962, Swazi planting yielded only the pitifully low figure of 1·9 bags of maize per acre.

This poor state of Swazi farming can be traced to several causes, which between them have created a vicious circle. The amount of land available to the Swazi is insufficient to enable them to make a living from it, except perhaps by modern tech-niques for which they lack the knowledge, equipment and capital. What land there is is almost all held in the traditional form of communal ownership, with the local chief allocating agricultural and residential plots to the rural households. Inevitably, there-fore, these plots are usually fragmented, and fencing them against grazing cattle is frowned upon, since it is construed as an attempt to stake permanent claims. Cattle are regarded, as in other parts of Africa, as status symbols or a sort of insurance policy, with numbers more important than quality, and though there is an increasing awareness of their cash value, there is also heavy over-stocking. As the grazing areas are communal, there is marked

* *Experiment in Swaziland*, ed. Professor J. F. Holleman, Institute for Social Research, University of Natal, for the Swaziland Administration, 1962.

resistance by any particular owner to culling his cattle unless his neighbours do so as well. Furthermore, there is no abbatoir in the whole territory, and propaganda for marketing cattle is making slow progress. Goats and sheep add to the problem. As for farming, this is traditionally regarded as women's work, and very many Swazi fail to see why they should bind themselves to continuous work when they can survive on periodic bursts.

Attempts to establish improved farming techniques are hampered, aside from anything else, by the lack of security of tenure under the communal system, though in many areas the authority of the chiefs is so far from what it once was that even if a chief agrees to improvement measures, he may not be able to enforce them.

With periodic employment in South Africa or Swaziland more or less available, most rural households have come to rely on wage income to make ends meet. In the words of a recent Government statement,

the possibility of making a career on the land has been all but neglected by the Swazi people. In the past, lack of agricultural credit and ignorance of modern methods have successfully prevented the improvement of the rural economy.

Optimistically, the Government says that

it has now been possible to seek provision for agricultural loans under the new development plan and this, together with the accumulated knowledge of the agricultural research stations and improved services, will make the farming of the Swazi areas a much more profitable occupation than it has been in the past.

But credit and services will have to increase far beyond the still very meagre provisons of belated Government plans to make an impact on the mass of rural Swazi. The Government's principal agricultural officer estimates that an enterprising Swazi farmer, cultivating a developed holding of about twelve acres, could reasonably hope for an annual net income of £90–100. This, however, assumes that the farmer would have assured markets for his produce – which he does not have today because of the lack of rural feeder roads and adequate marketing arrangements – and that he would employ techniques far in advance of those at present common.

These conditions could not be met with the small sums that the Government plans to spend at this late date on improving techniques, marketing and agricultural credit. But even if they could be, the prospect of becoming a full-time cultivator would not at present seriously tempt many Swazi. Over a quarter of rural homesteads in some areas already have, through migratory labour, annual cash incomes of £85 or more, and so the possibility of earning £90–100 a year, with food for his family, as a full-time cultivator would seem to offer little in the way of inducement to a Swazi in this group.

Most Swazi today find themselves in an in-between position. Through periodic wage earning they have started on the journey from a purely subsistence economy to a monetized one, but only a small minority have reached or passed even the half-way mark.

Historically, the present state of Swazi agriculture has many similarities with farming in England before the Enclosure Acts, with Swazi society experiencing new economic, sociological, industrial and population pressures. In Swaziland, quasi-industrial development is taking place rapidly, a few progressive farmers have made a start with fencing of land (which the white farmers, owning nearly half the country, have long completed), the population is increasing, and education is bringing about expectations of higher living standards which cannot be met within the traditional feudal framework.

If left unchecked, these pressures could lead either to the emergence of a relatively huge landless class or, as is already happening, to a dangerously uneconomic fragmentation of holdings. The official view is that the solution lies in the development of individual land tenure, leading to the emergence of a class of property-owning, productive farmers whose land can be registered, transferred by deed of sale and bonded for the raising of credit. This would deprive very many tribesmen of even the breadline security of the present system, and explosions could only be avoided if there were sufficient permanent employment, security of domicile and pensions available for those who would be displaced.

But there is no reason to believe that the British Administration, whilst it remains, could create such conditions nor, committed as it is to development by outside capital, that it would seriously try to achieve them. Such objectives stand any chance of accomplishment only in a socialist society, and for all the phrases which some Swazi politicians use about African socialism, Swaziland will not be within sight of that even when it gets its independence.

Thus the policy of promoting individual land tenure, attractive as it may seem to the orthodox planner, must under present conditions lead to rootlessness and misery for many of those it displaces. Yet between the present outmoded system of tribal ownership vested in the chief and individual tenure there is the third choice of public ownership of land, which could combine the best features of the old traditions and the new ways. If the Swazi, or for that matter the Batswana or the Basuto, could skip the stage of individual ownership and go straight to public ownership of land, they could have lessons to teach even to Britain.

Today, rural development in the Swazi tribal areas is at the cross-roads. There must either be fundamental reforms and a new approach, particularly to land tenure, or the Swazi will continue to stagnate while the other forty-eight per cent of the country progresses under white enterprise. With such stagnation, the already gross disparity in wealth between black and white will increase, and the chances of harmonious non-racial political development will vanish.

Many Swazi have been led to believe that education will provide the panacea for closing the cultural and economic racial gaps. But whilst greatly increased education is urgently required and may indeed narrow the cultural gap, it will do little about the economic one if it is not accompanied by drastic economic reform. Education on its own will merely enable its graduates to earn better wages in a white or foreign-controlled economy, while the rural Swazi continue to eke out a subsistence living augmented by low wage earning. In between will be the half-educated who, unwilling to fit any longer into the old society and insufficiently skilled to win a relatively well-paid job in the new one, already plague many African countries. And all this will take place within a context of increasing population and decreasing soil fertility, with family incomes from the land shrinking and the dependence on wage earnings, however meagre, in the 'white' economy expanding. It would be hard to imagine a more unsatisfactory basis for the development of a non-racial society.

But even if a British Administration is unlikely to promote a planned economy – though there is no reason why under a Labour Government some start should not be made – there are many improvements and reforms which could be achieved today if only funds and trained men were available. Even under present conditions, when Swazi land users are almost all mere crop cultivators and communal graziers, properly organized rural credit facilities for the purchase of fertilizers, carts, grain bags, fencing, grain storage, and the irrigation facilities would have a marked effect in increasing productivity. Irrigation, which has changed the face of white-owned farms in a few years, has left the rural Swazi untouched, while the small beginning made some years ago with subsidizing implements and supplies for Swazi farmers was dropped in 1963.

Basutoland has shown that progressive farming can be promoted and rural credit established even without a change-over to permanent private ownership of land, and the intermediate device of giving individual farmers the right to improvements they make on the land allocated to them has not even been tried as yet.

But in Swaziland a start was made only in 1962 with a 'master farmer' training scheme, and none has yet been made with co-operatives. The conservative Morse Mission recommended in 1960 as a matter of urgency that the absurdly small sum of £50,000 be provided by the British Government for the establishment of a Land and Agricultural Loan Fund, but nothing emerged from the British Treasury, and a start with a revolving fund for Swazi farmers was made possible only by a grant of £20,000 from the International Cooperation Administration of America.

The Morse Mission, which limited itself to recommending only the most obvious and urgently needed additional expenditure, also urged in 1960 that some £224,000 be spent immediately on farm planning, additional field services, animal husbandry and cattle breeding. But the British Government felt itself unable to find any of this money, and this time no international aid agency came to the rescue.

With maize the staple Swazi food, it is obviously important to improve the quality of seed available to Swazi farmers. Yet in 1962 it had to be left to Oxfam to make such progress possible with a subsidy of £2,000.

Getting technical 'know-how' to Swazi farmers is of the greatest importance, yet once again it was left to Oxfam in 1962 to provide the Department of Land Utilization with a Landrover equipped for showing films and slides and with a loudspeaker recording system.

Similarly, the establishment of a sorely needed Agricultural College and Short Course Centre is being made possible only because the U.K. committee of the Freedom from Hunger campaign is making a gift of £270,000 to cover the costs for the first three years.

Again it was left to Oxfam to finance the erection of a few simple buildings as meeting centres and field staff accommodation for the Swazi Women's Associations, though these could well spark off important agricultural development. It is surely encouraging that 1,200 Swazi women have formed themselves into eighty associations and that, in the words of an official report, 'there is no doubt that Swazi women are showing a keener interest in the advisory work of the Department of Land Utilization'.

This sort of list could be extended, with, amongst other examples, the Government unable to find £150,000 for simple rural feeder roads, without which most Swazi farmers are cut off from marketing.

That anything at all has been done to meet this last need is due to Swazi farmers themselves, who in many areas have realized the need for better communications and have proceeded to construct roads. With some assistance from Government departments, local Swazi have laid many miles of roads and tracks to open up hitherto inaccessible rural areas, contributing voluntary labour and some materials for the building of bridges, dams, and storerooms.

Similarly, whilst apathy and backwardness are still dominant, some 4,000 Swazi farmers have banded together in twenty-two farmers' associations, to order their farming requirements through them or direct from the trade.

The importance of progress in Swazi agriculture is obvious. Swazi lands constitute fifty-two per cent of the country. The

Swazi constitute over ninety-five per cent of the country's population, and only thirteen per cent of them can be said to be urbanized. Yet during the past decades, in which increased development funds have become available to the Swaziland Government, Swazi agriculture has remained sadly neglected.

This has not been for lack of officials deeply aware of the urgent need for developing Swazi agriculture. The Department of Land Utilization, under its excellent director, Mr Jock King (now retired), has done splendid work and laid well thought-out plans, but it has been crippled by the lack of funds and trained personnel.

This has been the result of deliberate Government policy, which saw the prime need during the past decade as being the development of an infra-structure of roads and communications likely to attract large scale industrial and quasi-industrial enterprises into the Territory. Thus whilst the Administration could not find £150,000 for rural feeder roads, it readily committed itself to spending £500,000 to construct the tarred road which Usutu Pulp demanded from its site to the nearest railhead before it would commit itself to establishing its pulp mill. The Public Works Department alone has built up an efficient planning section, which in turn has enabled it to obtain international credits for well-prepared schemes.

Despite the urging of the Morse Mission and other experts, the Administration has failed to appoint a Secretary for Development, who would be responsible for overall economic planning. Instead, development has remained the responsibility for the Secretary for Finance, who has understandably welcomed the ability of the Public Works Department to produce specific and internationally attractive projects. Inevitably, everything has been overshadowed by road-building and the expansion of the Public Works Department, which today is itself housed in expensive new headquarters.

Thus agriculture, including white farming, was allocated only 11·1 per cent of the £2·886 million development funds spent from 1955–60, whilst public works received 76·5 per cent. Similarly, agriculture received only 5·8 per cent of the £5·267 million spent on development from 1960–63, whilst public works took 73·8 per cent.

If agricultural production has nevertheless advanced, it has been because of the major strides made in its white-owned sector, and especially in the establishment of sugar and cotton growing. In 1962 exports of farm and forest produce exceeded £5 million for the first time in Swaziland's history, whilst mineral production was valued at slightly more than £2½ million.

One does not envy the Swaziland Administration its task of deciding on priorities for development expenditure, with available funds limited and every sector of the country having its own crying needs. It was not until 1945 that Swaziland received any significant sum for development, and then its allocation under the Colonial Development and Welfare Act was only slightly above £1 million.

There was no dearth of problems for the Administration to tackle in 1945. Revenue and expenditure each totalled £380,000 for a total population of 185,000, and aside from the Havelock asbestos mine the economy showed little sign of life. Afforestation had not yet begun, and the few existing irrigation projects were designed solely to meet the small-scale needs of individual farmers.

In the Swazi areas, conservation farming was unknown, ploughing was carried on up and down hill and extended to sponges and the very banks of streams, seed was planted only by broadcast methods, cattle manure was regarded as a saleable commodity, and virtually no use of artificial fertilizer was made.

The school population numbered no more than 11,073 Africans, 539 whites and 195 Eurafricans. Education to matriculation standard was conducted at one white school but at no African or Eurafrican school; it was not until 1951 that the first Swazi student wrote the matriculation examination at school in his own country. There were no facilities whatsoever for trade training.

There were only ten Government-subsidized doctors for the population of 185,000, and no private practitioners. There were only 214 beds in Government and mission hospitals, and sixteen outlying clinics. Malaria, tuberculosis, bilharzia, and malnutrition were rife.

The road system was primitive, and with the onset of the summer large stretches became impassable; the territory could not boast a single foot of black-topped road. Bridges were lacking even over some of the most important rivers, and travelling at all times of the year was hazardous.

Even in the townships life was uncomfortable, since there was no Government-owned electricity or sewerage scheme, and a piped water supply was the exception rather than the rule. The postal system was in no better state. And apart from the existence of the Havelock asbestos mine, little or nothing was known about the rest of the Territory's mineral resources.

On expert advice from Britain, it was decided that the most urgent problem was to stabilize and improve the use of the soil in the Swazi areas, and by 1955, when the development plan period ended, a minor revolution had been achieved: the greater proportion of Swazi arable lands had been protected against erosion by the establishment of grass filter strips and the construction of major contour furrows.

The percentage allocation of development funds from 1945 to 1966 shows some sharp changes in priorities:

	1945–55 (£1m.)	1955–60 (£2·886m.)	1960–63 (£5·267m.) incl. £1·5m. from I.D.A. for roads	1963–66 (£13·4m.) incl. £7m. private S. African and £1·5m. from I.D.A. for railway and electricity and £0·6m. from U.K. charities	1963–66* (£4·14m.) U.K. Govt only incl. £1m. loan for railway, C.D. & W.F. £2·3m.
Agriculture	40·3	11·1	5·8	8·6	2·1
Education	23·7	3·5	11·3	5·8	18·8
Medical	17·4	2·8	3·3	3·2	6·9
Mineral Works	13·0	2·7	0·3	1·2	1·0
Public Works	5·6	76·5	73·5	76·6	45·1
Telecommunications	—	3·4	5·5	1·1	3·6

* The figures in this column show the percentage allocation per sector of the total funds from the U.K. (composed of a C.D. & W.F. grant of £2·59m. and a railway loan of £1m.). They do not therefore reflect the total sums channelled into each sector. These are reflected in the previous column.

The dramatic switch after 1955 to road-building and public-works was triggered off by investments which the Colonial Development Corporation and private groups had begun to make in Swaziland, and it has certainly shown results in the booming European sector of the economy. But the change in emphasis has been carried too far, to the grave danger point of creating two economies, with the Swazi one backward and stagnating.

The European section of Swaziland's population has made an undeniable contribution to the country's economic growth since 1945, and the privately-inspired development which has taken place could bring important benefits to the whole Territory. But the gap between rich and poor in Swaziland has grown no less with the economic development of the Territory, and in several sectors, such as agriculture, it has widened frighteningly.

New firms entering Swaziland are only too ready to believe that they are doing the Territory a favour. But this is arguable. Indeed, unless they do more than is minimally necessary to look after the welfare of their employees, their activities in the Territory are little better than exploitation.

There have been a few men in the Swaziland Government who realize this truth, but they have achieved practically nothing in making employers provide high wages and good welfare service (which lead in any case to greater efficiency and output), employ a minimum percentage of local labour and ensure its training in skills.

Having served as the handmaiden of *laissez faire* growth for the past decade, during which most development funds have gone into providing the communications and other facilities that private enterprise demanded before doing Swaziland such favours as exploiting its mineral riches, the Administration has announced it is now at long last turning its attention to Swazi agriculture.

But the figures, both absolutely and relatively, in the so-called 1963–6 Development Plan sharply temper the enthusiasm which this announced switch of Government priorities may have aroused. Total expenditure under the plan is to be £13·4 million, and of this agriculture (including extension work and an agricultural college) has been allocated precisely £1·056 million.

Even when one recognizes that of the development plan total the British Government and the Commonwealth Development

Corporation are finding only £4·14 million (the rest is coming from private South African capital and the World Bank for the railway and hydroelectric scheme), one also has to note that of agriculture's £1 million, Oxfam and the Freedom from Hunger campaign, who are after all charities, are contributing £270,000 and United Nations agencies another £19,000.

Proudly, the plan announces that 'in the agricultural development programme the highest priority is being given to a scheme to expand agricultural credit facilities'. Elsewhere, it rightly notes that this is one of the most promising ways towards creating popular support for the reform of land tenure. The allocation for agricultural credit is £105,000 over the three years, representing something like 2s. 10d. per Swazi per year.

Social services as a whole receive a welcome though inadequate increase, but the health services are left much as they are and the verbal recognition that education is of great importance is very inadequately backed financially. 'Self-help' is to remain the key to more schools for the Swazi. Even allowing for the completion of the railway, the overall picture remains an unhealthy one for a country which has for ten years come close to subsidizing the private investors who are exploiting irreplacable natural resources.

	per cent
Infra-structure	76·8
Economic	10·9
Social Services	10·4
Administrative	1·9

There is, moreover, the same failure in this development 'plan' as in its predecessors to relate activity in any particular sector to the development of the economy as a whole. There is, similarly, the same blind assumption that if only sufficient outsiders will invest in Swaziland all will be well.

It is, of course, not possible to do any plan in the strict sense of the word in the absence of statistics, but it is equally clear that more than a statistical service will be needed to alter the thinking of the men deputed by Britain to plan Swaziland's economic future.

As the health of a people depends not only on how much they eat but also on what kinds of food they eat, it is clearly connected with agriculture and with education as well as with their incomes and the medical services available to them.

In Swaziland these medical services, though better than in several underdeveloped African countries, are still very poor when viewed by the higher standards which the Territory's booming economy and over half a century of British administration should justify. What is more, half of the hospital and clinic facilities available today have been created by religious missions, who continue to run their institutions with only a partial Government subsidy.

Hospitals and other facilities are concentrated in the larger centres, where the state of public health hardly justifies the official euphemism of 'fairly satisfactory', while primitive conditions characterize the rural areas, in which the vast majority of the population lives. Despite the smallness of the country, there are still areas without ready access to medical care, where sanitation is at best primitive and usually absent altogether, and where water supplies are commonly polluted. Were it not for the healthy climate of the Territory, the picture would be even more disturbing, for with widespread malnutrition and tuberculosis, the resistance of most Swazi to disease cannot be high.

The first study of Swazi nutrition was made during 1960–63 by Miss Sonya Jones, and published in 1963.* In his foreword, Swaziland's director of medical services declares:

In the field of clinical medicine in Swaziland, malnutrition has assumed a progressively more important place over the past years and has become one of the leading causes of mortality and morbidity amongst young children, while there can be little doubt that, in view of the large number of cases of frank malnutrition seen, the condition is also a factor of great importance in such conditions as gastro-enteritis, broncho-pneumonia, tuberculosis and other infections. The incidence of pellagra also seems to be on the increase.

Such health statistics as Swaziland can furnish concern only patients treated in hospitals, and these are alarming enough.

* *A Study of Swazi Nutrition*, Sonya M. Jones, Institute for Social Research, University of Natal, for the Swaziland Administration, 1963.

From 1958 to 1962 the number of recorded cases of malnutrition rose by 229 per cent – from 1,411 to 3,240 – whilst resulting deaths rose from fifty-three to 101. And these sharply increased figures can be only marginally attributed to an increase in the number of patients seen because of the slight expansion of hospital and medical services during this period.

Miss Jones reported in 1963 that 'eighty-seven per cent of the food consumption groups [investigated] failed to meet the recommended allowances in the majority of the nutrients under study'.

She found that in general the Swazi diet, which consists chiefly of maize, is deficient in calories, animal protein, calcium, and certain essential vitamins. The position seems to be worst in the peri-urban areas, where the Swazi have adopted a more sophisticated diet but lack the money to buy those foods essential for a balanced one.

Within families, the younger children show the greatest incidence of malnutrition, with children aged 1–4 and 7–12, pregnant women, and the mothers of infants the most vulnerable everywhere, while the infant mortality rate is estimated at 147 per thousand for the whole Territory (against twenty-two per thousand in England and Wales). It was the obvious plight of young Swazi children which led U.N.I.C.E.F. in 1961 to donate thirty tons of dried skimmed milk for free distribution, and this generous gesture has had to be repeated annually since then. The problem is even *increased* by improvements in other social services. Thus spreading education has now begun to reach under-nourished rural children, who consequently walk long distances to school, often without a meal before setting out, and who miss another meal at midday.

Maize plays an unrivalled part in the Swazi diet, and during poor harvest years the community, farming at subsistence level, is exposed to the peril of famine. Even in good years, many homes experience a shortage. [With the diet thus deficient even in calories, Miss Jones found that] the population has no reserves on which to draw; this situation is aggravated by the fact that, at the end of the winter when the shortages are greatest, the seasonal activities are most demanding. . . . In the Lowveld area, during the winter months, particularly after a bad harvest, there is often semi-starvation.

An improvement in nutrition demands action in many inter-related fields, from the provision of more guidance and facilities to farmers, and the encouragement of new types of crops and better marketing, to an increase in wages and the education of Swazi women in the principles of nutrition. Much is often made of the dietary taboos which tribal tradition prescribes, but many of these have their roots in the practice of men reserving scarce foods for themselves. Thus Miss Jones, having worked for over two years in the field, feels that the taboo on girls and women eating eggs (which are supposed to affect childbearing), would probably vanish if eggs were more plentiful, and certainly Swazi women already accept eggs in cakes.

A pilot campaign against malnutrition in Swaziland is now to be launched by the Swaziland Government with the help of two United Nations agencies, the F.A.O. and U.N.I.C.E.F. It aims at encouraging the production of vegetables, poultry and eggs by Swazi farmers, and their produce is to be delivered to schools, where groups of Swazi women will be shown by domestic science demonstrators how to cook it properly. The meals so prepared will be eaten by the children attending schools.

Malnutrition is, of course, due to a shortage of food among subsistence level farmers, but it often results as well from ignorance of healthy food and its preparation. Some Swazi vege-table growers who sell their produce on local markets themselves have undernourished children because they do not appreciate the value of vegetables as food.

Seven areas where improved land use has already been initiated have been chosen for the new pilot campaign. The F.A.O. will give loans to selected Swazi to help them set themselves up as poultry farmers or market gardeners, while the Government will train them in improved farming methods and will teach women the value of food and the best way to cook it. Farmers will pay off their F.A.O. loans by supplying food to the schools, and the children will pay a nominal amount for the meals they receive.

The F.A.O. will provide an expert in nutrition and an expert in extension methods to start the scheme, and local staff will be trained to carry on the project and extend it to other areas. The F.A.O. has already provided fellowships for overseas training in nutrition and home economics, horticulture, poultry management, public relations, and audio-visual aids, and on their return to Swaziland the recipients will help to train local field staff employed in the chosen areas of the scheme before it is launched in the field. The local planning committee has representatives from the Department of Education and from the Swazi National Council.

Other taboos affecting nutrition are already breaking down under the pressure of empty bellies. Thus the Swazi are not supposed to eat new crops until the Ngwenyama gives the signal during the Incwala festival, the most important of the Swazi year, when new crops reach fruition; on the fourth day, the King ceremoniously 'bites' the new season's crops, followed by the royal family and important officials. Only when this has happened should the people eat the new crops, but this ban is increasingly being disregarded.

These are thus signs that in health, as in agriculture, traditional practices can be changed, but it would be a mistake to underestimate their strength. A great deal of educational work, for instance, will be needed to change the rural Swazi's almost total ignorance of sanitation and hygiene.

In the meantime, excellent work has been done by the Medical Department in almost eradicating malaria, while the problem of bilharzia, with which thirty per cent of the Swazis are infected and which is directly connected with water-supplies, is slowly being tackled. But this is about as far as the Swaziland Medical Department has been able to go in preventive medicine with the limited staff and funds available to it.

Swaziland today has 680 hospital beds – just under half of them in mission hospitals – or 2·4 beds per 1,000 people, compared with the western European average of 4–5 beds per 1,000, and the south of the Sahara figure of two. There is a small mission-run leper hospital which is adequate for the Territory's needs, but there is no mental hospital at all, and violent mental patients are lodged in primitive conditions in the jails, which are in any event in a scandalous state of overcrowding.

Worst of all, there is no tuberculosis hospital, although tuberculosis is Swaziland's most serious disease. Three of the general hospitals have tuberculosis wards, but this is hardly adequate when over 1,000 new cases are diagnosed and an average of sixty-six deaths are recorded every year. Most cases have to be treated as out-patients, and there are no follow-up facilities. The World Health Organization and U.N.I.C.E.F. have joined forces to conduct a tuberculosis control project which is now under way, and if one remembers that the official figures of cases and deaths reflect only those who have actually sought treatment at a hospital or clinic, one can anticipate that a thorough survey will show the incidence of tuberculosis to be very much higher.

In addition to the hospitals, there are twenty-nine clinics in the outlying districts of Swaziland – staffed by trained nurses – seventeen of which are run by missions, only nine by the Government, and two by the Swazi National Treasury. There are maternity and child welfare centres and venereal disease clinics at all hospitals and clinics. The Havelock mine has its own hospital, four other large industrial concerns provide some medical facilities for their employees, and the Red Cross runs several small infant welfare clinics.

There were thirty-eight medical practitioners working in Swaziland in 1962, which is one doctor per 7,368 people. This compares poorly with the western European standard of one doctor per 1,000 persons, though more favourably with the average of one doctor per 10,000 persons south of the Sahara. But for most Swazi, as for Africans in other multi-racial countries the significant figure is the number of doctors *not* in private practice, which most Africans cannot afford and which does not touch rural African areas. Here Swaziland's total comes down to only nineteen doctors, or half of those registered, serving over eighty per cent of the total population.

Swaziland trains its own nurses, and nursing has become, as in South Africa and the Rhodesias, a sought after profession despite relatively poor pay and conditions. Earlier last year, Swazi nurses successfully established their own association to press for improved conditions.

The diseases causing most attendances at Swaziland hospitals are those of the digestive and genito-urinary systems and acute upper respiratory tract infections. But amongst the infectious diseases, enteric fever and infantile gastro-enteritis are increasing yearly. Both are due to primitive or non-existent sanitation, the flies which this attracts, and polluted water.

It is supposed to be one function of the Health and Sanitary Department to check and control such conditions, but the task has not even been attempted in the Swazi areas. Even in the towns they have not been controlled, as the festering slum of Msunduza African township, a stone's throw away from the centre of Mbabane, illustrates.

One reason for this is that there have been no local authorities in Swaziland, so that the prosperous white householders of Mbabane and Manzini have paid neither rates nor municipal taxes, and no one has felt responsible for the conditions under which Africans live. The Government has had other priorities. The commissioner now has powers to create local authorities and relevant officials have been appointed, but there is a great deal to be done in Swaziland's towns and an enormous amount in the country before health services can be considered even 'fairly satisfactory'.

Education in Swaziland has made considerable progress in recent years, but the legacy of past neglect is such that there is still a crying need for improvement. The Government continues to rely for most African education on the missions which have pioneered and supported it for so long, while, despite the official acceptance in 1962 of a policy of racial integration in education, resentment continues to be stirred by the gross inequalities in educational opportunity and finance for black and white children. With constitutional advance, the acute shortage of secondary education in particular becomes more dangerous by the month. Because they have not been and are not being given the facilities to produce sufficient educated men and women, the Swazi already cannot fill the increasing number of responsible positions in government opening up for them.

It is estimated that the present primary school enrolment of 40,000 Swazi children represents about sixty-three per cent of the potential, and this, on the face of it, seems to justify the official description of 'a not altogether unreasonable figure for an "underdeveloped" and financially dependent Territory'.

The trouble is, however, that whilst these 40,000 children are receiving *some* primary education, the overwhelming majority drop out of school after the first three or four years, during which they are taught no English, while most of the remainder leave before completing the eight-year primary course, which at best confers only a functional literacy in English.

The small number completing primary school is nevertheless too large to be accommodated in the twenty-five schools offering or developing the three-year junior secondary school course, and from here only a tiny number filter through to the three schools offering the further two years to matriculation.

The Swazi school enrolment pyramid in 1962 looked like this:

Elementary Vernacular		Primary		Secondary	
Sub A	9,642	Std III	4,020	Std VII	1,083
Sub B	7,158	Std IV	2,904	Std VIII	548
Std I	6,245	Std V	2,469	Junior Certificates	293
Std II	4,860	Std VI	1,965	Matric. I	57
				Matric. II	18

Thus seventy-one per cent of Swazi children enrolled in primary schools are in the elementary vernacular classes; eighteen per cent in Standards III and IV; and only eleven per cent in the final two years of the primary course, Standards V and VI. Yet present percentages for the holding power of the middle and upper primary classes represent a marked increase over 1957.

It speaks for itself that more than eighty years after the first missions established education for the Swazi, and fifty-six years after Swaziland came under direct British rule, only eighteen pupils should in 1962 have been preparing to write the matriculation examination. And the shortage of secondary school places has been made more serious since 1955, when the South African authorities refused to take any more secondary school pupils from Swaziland.

Only twenty of Swaziland's 292 African primary schools and five of its twenty-four secondary schools were government schools in 1962. The Swazi National Treasury, aided by a small Government grant, provided three primary and secondary schools. For the rest, voluntary agencies, mainly missions, provided 233 primary schools (of which only 129 received Government aid) and eighteen aided secondary schools, while tribal schools numbered thirty-six. Thus government primary schools accounted for only thirteen per cent of total enrolment.

Nor is the proportional share of Government expenditure impressive. Of the total £567,176 spent on African education in 1962, missions provided no less than twenty-two per cent, and the Swazi National Treasury another one per cent.

By contrast, the Government provided practically all of the £190,802 spent on the education of white children, 1,555 of whom were at school. Attendance is compulsory only for white children, who in 1962 had eleven government primary schools and two aided secondary schools. It is, indeed, when one compares Government expenditure on children of different races that the cause of much Swazi bitterness becomes plain. With almost 100 per cent potential enrolment amongst white children, but only sixty-five per cent of primary enrolment and a derisory percentage of secondary enrolment for African children, the *Government in 1962 spent 9·7 times as much on every white child as on every African child at school, and 4·3 as much as on every Eurafrican child.* (African: £10 7s. 0d. Eurafrican: £44 12s. 0d. European: £100 19s. 0d.) And even this disgraceful disparity represented a great improvement on the position in 1960, when the African : Eurafrican : European ratios were 1:4·4:16·5 (£4 7s. 0d. : £19 3s. 3d. : £71 12s. 0d.). It will be noted, however, that the cash difference between expenditure on the African and the white child has actually *increased*. Even South Africa, which uses education to maintain master-servant relationships, had in 1959 only a 1:8 cash ratio on black : white schooling.

Swaziland's gross disparity in educational expenditure is, even with the substantial contribution of the missions, reflected in both teacher : pupil ratios and in the quality of teaching provided. The average African teacher : pupil ratio is 1:35, but in many primary schools between 50 and 150 pupils are found in one classroom. The decrepit state of most African schools is alarming, as is their paucity of teaching equipment. What is more, of 1,131 African primary school teachers, only thirteen had themselves completed the full course of secondary education, and 368 had received no teaching training whatsoever by 1962. Even amongst the 101 African secondary school teachers, only seventy had themselves completed a secondary course, though these included forty-three graduates and all had had teacher training.

In 1962 only 135 Swazi teachers were being trained, and of these forty-seven had themselves had no secondary education; forty-seven teachers qualified in the same year. Part, but only part, of the desperate need for more Swazi teachers is now being met by the Swaziland Teacher Training College which, built at a cost of £110,000 from C.D. & W.F. sources, is now producing forty extra teachers a year.

That it has been possible to maintain an educational system at all under these conditions has been due to the initiative of the missions, the Swazi nation, and – more recently – a number of chiefs; to the underpaid and poorly housed teachers; and to African parents who have taxed themselves to provide buildings, school fees, private teachers, books and stationery.

At African schools self-help is the rule. Fees are collected to help meet the cost of domestic science classes, building levies are paid by parents at many of the grant-aided schools, and contributions are collected from those attending unaided schools to help pay the teachers' salaries. It seems that under the current development plan an increasing amount of equipment will have to be provided from the contributions of pupils themselves.

Until 1962 schooling, books and stationery were free for white children, but since then they have also had to pay for their books and stationery, and the money thus saved is being used to buy equipment for African schools. Also since 1962, the white school committees have agreed to levy 'subscriptions' on their pupils ranging from £3–12 a year, and this brings in an annual £9,000.

But this sort of adjustment is clearly trifling, for if the Swaziland – or British – Government were to equalize standards by spending as much on every black child in school as it does on every white, it would, on 1962 figures, have to spend an additional £3,735,000 a year. In 1961–2 the Territory's total normal revenue was only £2,163,000, of which 18·5 per cent was spent on education, and this, in absolute terms, was some forty-five per cent more than had been spent in 1959–60.

It seems unrealistic to expect the British Government to find this amount of money for education in Swaziland, since if it did so it would have, in equity, to make similar grants to Basutoland and

Bechuanaland as well. Yet something must be done, and done quickly, to improve Swazi education and to narrow the enormous gap between facilities for white and black. The now officially adopted policy of racial integration from the beginning of primary school is admirable in principle, but it will have little effect in practice because of the conditions with which it has been laden. African or Eurafrican pupils may now be admitted as day scholars to the Grade I, or first, primary class of European schools 'provided that accommodation is available and that:

(a) the applicant's age does not exceed seven years at 1 January;
(b) the headmaster is satisfied that the applicant has sufficient command of English to enable him/her to follow the teaching;
(c) the headmaster is satisfied that the child is in a position to observe all the school rules.'

This must mean that only a tiny handful of African children will enter the white schools. Few would suggest, however, that any useful purpose would be served by either swamping beyond their absorptive capacity the handful of white schools with African pupils, or by lowering the standards of the white schools to those of the African.

The answer would seem to lie rather in raising the level of African primary schools and teaching as rapidly as possible, and in ensuring that discrimination in public funds ceases at once by limiting Government expenditure per head to the minimum able to provide for *all* children in the foreseeable future. Any extra primary facilities above this minimum might then be supplied by a special education level on the communities concerned.

At the same time, entry to secondary schooling should be opened to children of all races on the basis of merit, measured perhaps through intelligence tests. The secondary schools constitute the bottle-neck in education and must, in the painful choice between urgent needs, receive priority. It took the authorities in Swaziland much longer than those in Basutoland and Bechuanaland to accept this, and it only became official policy in 1963. No doubt the Territory's long political stagnation and belated constitutional progress reinforced official myopia. But the fact that there are so few secondary schools in existence can now be turned to the advantage of integration. Raising facilities and standards in existing Swazi secondary schools to the high level of the existing two white schools would involve a relatively modest expenditure, and this would apply also to badly needed additional secondary schools. This being done, all government or government-aided secondary schools should become non-racial.

A stimulating example of what can be achieved in non-racial education is being provided in Swaziland, through private initiative, at Waterford School near Mbabane. Opened in 1963, Waterford plans to provide a first-class, integrated, residential education on a Christian foundation for boys of all races and creeds from the primary level to university entrance. Under the headmastership of Mr Michael Stern, who previously ran schools for the Community of the Resurrection in Johannesburg, it has attracted distinguished liberal patronage in South Africa and Swaziland, and the boys of all races enrolled from both countries in its first three years have been helping with the construction of the school. Fees are relatively high, but bursary funds have been secured to allow African pupils to be selected on merit, and the school already has a long waiting list, mainly because so many liberal white parents in South Africa see in it the only chance of providing their children with a sane, non-racial education. An excellent African secondary school, St Christopher's, has also been built up, largely with private funds, over recent years.

A useful start is being made towards a single school system by revising primary school syllabuses to make them the same for all schools, but the need for more far-reaching action is urgent.

For until now the educational systems in Swaziland have been leading to increasing cleavage between the races, a sense of grievance on the part of Africans and Eurafricans, a perpetuation of the social occupational colour bars which their recent legal abolition will not fundamentally affect, and a vicious spiral of ignorance and poverty which vitiates the attempts of other Government departments to raise the standard of health and agriculture.

The shortage of educated Swazi to take on skilled work has meant that such posts are filled by white migrant labourers from South Africa or Moçambique, who bring social problems in their train and who export money from the Territory.

Immediate and substantial action is needed also in increasing technical training, which is at present confined to one trades school with a yearly capacity of some twenty-four men trained in motor mechanics, general building, carpentry, and joining. Courses more directly connected with the needs of modern industry are necessary, and it should not be beyond the resources of the Swaziland Government to set up a proper technical high school leading to matriculation level. In addition, industries should be obliged to establish their own training schemes.

A splendid example of what local enthusiasm can do to attract outside help has been provided in the field of mass literacy by the Sabenta Society, which was started a few years ago by a small group of Europeans and Swazi, financing their efforts from local subscriptions. Sir Brian Marwick, the Resident Commissioner, became the patron, and as a result of the publicity which its efforts received the Sabenta Society has now been given substantial grants by the Gulbenkian Foundation and smaller grants by the Anglo-American Corporation and other firms. The demand for classes is extremely large, and the society plans to add English literacy classes to its present vernacular ones.

What remains to be begun is the provision of adult education, through which Swazi would be given a chance to continue whatever education they have managed to pick up as children.

Finally, of course, there must be a rapid expansion and improvement of teacher training facilities. Not only are present teaching standards disturbingly low, but a considerable proportion of the qualified teaching staff in African schools has had to be imported from South Africa.

The whole country has well below 100 African graduates, and in 1962 only forty-two Swazi were studying at institutions outside the Territory, many of them below university level; only £6,188 was spent in 1962 by the Government on bursaries and scholarships of all kinds. With the increasing interest of many countries in accommodating African students, and the British Government committed to developing the University College of Basutoland, Bechuanaland, and Swaziland at Roma in Basutoland, these figures could and should be dramatically increased.

The Swazi have shown beyond doubt that they are prepared to make sacrifices for education. It is the responsibility of the British

Government to provide the funds to make rapid expansion possible. Not the least of the consequences of its failure to do so would be that Swazi will continue to be almost wholly excluded from intermediate and senior positions in their country's civil service.

The economic dependence of Swaziland on South Africa extends, as has already been indicated, far beyond the field of agricultural marketing, and as this dependence is the most crucial element in the relations between the two countries, it may be useful briefly to summarize its various aspects.

The most important leverage which South Africa can use against Swaziland, as against Basutoland and Bechuanaland, would seem to be the customs agreement. Swaziland's share of customs and excise revenue collected by South Africa was fixed in 1910 at 0·149 per cent, and in 1961–2 this amounted to £140,000, or seven per cent of Swaziland's territorial revenue. By contrast, South African customs payments made up approximately half of Basutoland's territorial revenue. Thus Swaziland is at present not significantly dependent on revenue from the common customs agreement, but it clearly receives less than its fair share of customs revenue, and its percentage should be raised to 0·53 per cent if the present economic state of the three High Commission Territories is to be accurately reflected in the share-out of total receipts which South Africa passes on to them. Swazi officials are pressing this point in the negotiations for a revised agreement. If they gain their point, Swaziland's receipts will be more than trebled, but so will its dependence on South Africa.

It would be dangerous for Basutoland in particular if the three Territories, now going their separate ways, were not to maintain a common front in the customs arrangements with South Africa, but Swaziland would have the least to fear from their possible breakdown. With current development in Swaziland making such heavy use of South African materials, and with the Territory in any case importing more from South Africa than it exports, any breakdown of common customs agreement would mean a clear – if minor – blow to South Africa. Moreover, Swaziland's borders, unlike Bechuanaland's or Basutoland's, are for the most part policeable, so that its own customs service could prevent mass smuggling, while its rail-link to the sea through Moçambique will provide an alternative line of export and import.

For Swaziland, the most important provision of the customs agreement is that which provides for the 'free interchange' of products and manufactures, since this ensures access to an adjacent and profitable market for a wide range of agricultural produce which it might be difficult to sell elsewhere at the prices now realized.

The production of many agricultural commodities is controlled by marketing organizations in the Republic with which corresponding Swaziland organizations are either integrated or associated, and in such cases Swaziland and Rrepublican producers are accorded parity of treatment, so that when there is mutual over-production, this is a valuable facility. But whilst it would be expensive for Swaziland, with its relatively small volume of production, to operate its own marketing organization, it could do so if it ever became necessary.

Certainly the advantage of present arrangements does not lie entirely with Swaziland, which provides a significant outlet for South African manufacturers. On the whole, these articles are of good quality, and are competitive in price with equivalents which could be imported from elsewhere. But with its new railway outlet to the sea, Swaziland could, if it ran its own customs services, encourage or discourage certain imports through tariff adjustments which are presently beyond its control. The 1962 import–export position was as follows:

Imports
From South Africa: £6,390,000   From other countries: £811,500

Exports
To South Africa: £4,721,000   To other countries: £2,853,000

The main items imported from South Africa were machinery and equipment (£924,750), textiles (£647,500), motor cars and heavy vehicles (£606,850), fertilizers (£302,850) and maize products (£375,150). Machinery, textiles and vehicles could be competitively obtained from other sources and railed from Lourenço Marques; fertilizers could probably be manufactured more cheaply in Swaziland itself by exploiting abundant local materials; and maize imports could be eliminated if Swazi farmers could increase their present yield of 3½ bags per acre to only four bags.

Of exports to South Africa, the chief items in 1962 were sugar (£2,516,000), asbestos (£503,250), timber (£244,400), slaughter cattle (£636,500), rice (£305,000) and seed cotton (£206,300). If Swaziland were allocated its own quota under the Commonwealth Sugar Agreement, its sugar industry could be expanded and the produce railed to Lourenço Marques. Only good could come of obliging the Havelock mine to prepare its asbestos for export in Swaziland, instead of in South Africa as at present, and sending it along the new railway to the sea. If Swaziland had an abattoir and its beef production were increased, there seems no reason why it should not follow Bechuanaland's example and export frozen meat to Britain, or sell it in Portuguese territory. Rice could be similarly exported – current prices in Europe would still make it profitable for Swaziland exports – and again it could only do good if Swaziland established its own cotton ginnery. Exports to Moçambique in 1962 totalled only £7,850, and with the completion of the railway, much could be done dramatically to increase this figure. The Portuguese, of course, are not ideal partners either, but they seem to place business before politics, and the régime in Moçambique may well change before South Africa's does.

Until recently, not only railway feeder road services but also the majority of internal public road transport services in Swaziland were provided by South African Railways. The dangers of such dependence were shown when, in 1963, the S.A.R. withdrew all its road services in Swaziland with the exception of certain trunk routes, leaving them with an effective monopoly of all scheduled trans-border road traffic. There is no reason whatever why the Swaziland Government should not appoint its own national carrier. If South Africa refused this carrier reciprocal rights with the S.A.R. on trans-border services, this would necessitate a costly transfer at the border which would decrease the competitiveness of South African manufactures.

At present all external mail, telephone and telegraph services operate through South Africa, and the local Post Office Savings Bank and Postal Order Service are operated on Swaziland's behalf by the South African authorities. Though the initial running costs might be high, Swaziland should follow Bechuanaland's lead and introduce its own Post Office Savings Bank and Postal Order Service. Africans make extensive use of Post Office savings, and it is absurd that such monies should strengthen South Africa's economy rather than Swaziland's. If South Africa attempted reprisals through cutting the telephone and postal services, overseas calls could be re-routed through Nairobi, at substantial if not prohibitive extra cost, while overseas mail could be re-routed with only a slight loss in convenience.

The common currency union with South Africa is on the whole of more value to the Republic than to Swaziland. It might, as an investigation by British experts has shown, be expensive initially for the High Commission Territories to establish their own currency, but in the long run a country can lay little claim to independence whilst its banking is wholly controlled from outside.

The trickiest aspect of Swaziland's present dependence on South Africa is in the labour field, with nearly 12,000 Swazi employed in the Republic's mines and farms. Their earnings, as we have seen earlier, are of great importance to Swaziland, but even here real independence need present no insuperable problem. Much could be done to increase the profitability and therefore attraction of Swazi agriculture, especially if this were accompanied by an imaginative, and not necessarily very expensive, programme of bringing social facilities such as cinema shows and mobile shops to the rural areas. Then, too, there are at present some 2,000 Republican Africans and 3,000 Moçambique Africans employed in Swaziland. If employers were obliged to train Swazi for the semi-skilled jobs which many of these foreigners do, they would no longer be needed in Swaziland. And as for the 7,200 Swazi who were in 1962 working in South African mines, it is unlikely that the South African Government would exclude them whilst Republican Africans remain reluctant, despite all sorts of pressures, to do the same work.

Bechuanaland will face some serious problems in cutting adrift from South Africa, and for Basutoland – unaided – the problem could seem insuperable. But Swaziland, if it wished to, could stand quite well on its own.

Meanwhile, as repression in South Africa has increased, Swaziland has once more been sharply faced with the problem of political refugees. Still following the course which it took during the South African Emergency in 1960, the Administration had been granting refugees temporary asylum on condition that they do not take part in the politics of Swaziland or of any neighbouring States. As recently as March 1964, the Swaziland Refugee Committee described these conditions as 'vague, embarrassing and humiliating', and 'regretfully and respectfully' returned to the Queen's Commissioner special permits which he had issued to Dr J. Meidlinger, a former member of South Africa's banned, all-white Congress of Democrats, Mr Reg September, a South African Coloured who had been a leading trade-unionist and politician in the Republic's banned Congress Alliance, and to Mrs H. September. At the same time, the commissioner was informed that eight other refugees whose permits had expired would not apply for renewal if similar conditions of asylum were applied.

In a letter to the commissioner, the Swaziland Refugee Committee described the three-month validity of the permits as 'an act of grace granted with as little grace as possible. If asylum is granted, it should be until it is safe for us to return to our homes in South Africa.' As for the ban on political activity, the refugees pointed out that 'if we were prepared to lead non-political lives we could have done so in our own country'. The Administration's conditions themselves were vague, for the refugees could not know whether local trade-union work, in which some of them were participating, was included. They asserted that the trade-union movement 'has no national barriers, yet regards politics as part of its business'.

The refugees served notice on the commissioner that they were about to launch a campaign for the release of political prisoners in South Africa, in the course of which they hoped 'to cement an alliance between the people of Swaziland and the opponents of Dr Verwoerd at home and abroad'. This alliance seemed to be achieved almost immediately, with an Anti-Apartheid Committee formed under the leadership of Mr Maseko, vice-president of the N.N.L.C., Dr Allen Nxumalo, leader of the Swaziland Democratic Party, and Mr Seperepere of the Refugees Committee. It called for the release of political prisoners in South Africa, the abolition of residence permits for refugees, and a stop to Britain's 'collaborating with the Government of the Republic of South Africa'.

The Anti-Apartheid Committee also announced that it would hold a mass meeting at which refugees would speak. Before this took place, however, Dr Nxumalo dissociated himself and his party from the committee, which he called 'suspicious and Communist-inspired', and he alleged that he had not been consulted about statements and plans. Dr Zwane, the leader of the N.N.L.C., also declared himself unhappy. Mr Seperepere, the Committee's chairman, denounced Dr Nxumalo's accusations as a smear. He had some Communists on the committee, just as the African National Congress had had in South Africa, but this was irrelevant to its purposes.

The refugees went ahead on their own with the planned political meeting, at which they denounced apartheid as a threat to Swaziland, and five of them were subsequently charged with being in Swaziland without a permit, of having illegally addressed a political meeting, and of having taken part in the politics of a neighbouring territory. They were acquitted, on the charge of having illegally addressed a political meeting, by a technicality, and subsequently Mr September was aquitted on the charge of having taken part in the politics of a neighbouring territory. The magistrate, in what may prove to be an important ruling, declared:

I cannot for the life of me see that he was taking part in the politics of South Africa. It seems to me that a political meeting in the heart of Swaziland, fifty miles from the border of the Republic, with the object of warning people of Swaziland (against the danger of becoming dominated by South Africa, where the speaker had said that freedom of speech and political organization had been suppressed) cannot by any stretch of imagination be called taking part in the politics of South Africa.

The magistrate also rejected the Crown's submission that Press reporters at the meeting might have brought September's statements to the notice of the Republic's Africans, who might then have been swayed by them. The charge against Dr Meidlinger was withdrawn, and an African refugee from Moçambique was also acquitted.

Thus for the moment the situation eased once more, but it is likely to blow up again at any time. One can see the difficulties in which refugee activity might place the Swaziland Administration, but it seems that the present Administration is unduly considerate of official South African feelings. Thus, whilst it was announced in April 1964 that Swaziland is to have its own Government-run broadcasting station, its broadcasts will reportedly not be beamed to South Africa. Clearly Dr Verwoerd would not like Africans in the Republic to have such easy access to, say, the B.B.C. news; but need the Swaziland Government oblige him? It is bad enough that Swaziland, like the other two Territories, should have the Prevention of Violence Abroad Proclamation, which makes it an offence to plan in Swaziland any action against the South African Government which would also be an offence in Swaziland.

POSTSCRIPT

Dr Meidlinger, who was refused employment in a Swaziland government hospital, and Mr and Mrs September have since made their way through South Africa to Bechuanaland via what seems to have become an established 'underground' route. So has Mr Oswald Dennis, a bricklayer expelled from Swaziland after leading two strikes. Mr Seperepere was caught in South Africa *en route* from Swaziland to Bechuanaland and imprisoned for twelve months for planning to leave without a passport. Mr Sidney Kitching, a wealthy farmer and active socialist, was also expelled from Swaziland.

Then Mrs Rosemary Wentzel vanished from Swaziland on 10 August 1964. An active member of the South African Liberal Party, she had fled to Swaziland without a passport, fearing arrest under the notorious Ninety-Day law. She was granted political asylum together with one of her young children and worked as a government teacher. After 10 August she was next heard from in a South African prison. There can be no doubting the account which she subsequently gave to her lawyer of how three unknown men kidnapped her at night from her house, drove her across the border, released her and left her to be arrested by security police at a road-block as she tried to return to Swaziland. The *prima facie* evidence of a violation of British sovereignty was overwhelming and the story was splashed in the

South African Press. But so unwilling were the British Ambassador, Sir Hugh Stephenson, and his staff to interest themselves publicly in the case that Johannesburg's *Rand Daily Mail* had bitterly to ask. Are the British authorities content that she should simply vanish into thin air and be heard of next in a South African jail? Repeated inquiries have brought only evasiveness, glib rationalizations and some depressing buck-passing . . . none of which has reflected any credit on the British foreign service.

In 1965 large numbers of Moçambique Africans, members of the Frelimo freedom movement, fled to Swaziland to escape increased Portuguese police activities. Nearly 100 were granted asylum, though their homes were later raided by the Swaziland police. In May, ninety of them attempted to make their way to Bechuanaland, but only twenty-five are known to have arrived, going on to Tanzania via Zambia. The others are believed to have been returned to Moçambique by the South African police.

Predictably, attacks on the granting of political refuge have been made in the Legislative Assembly since it first met in September 1964. Prince Makhosini, the Imbokodo leader, in stating his party's policy, denounced South African refugees as subverting the Ngwenyama and Imbokodo, supporting Swazi politicians and taking work from the Swazi. 'Always they have brought us problems and trouble,' he said. 'Why should we tolerate this position?' For the U.S.A., Imbokodo's white partners, Dr T. Brocklehurst has suggested in the Press that *bona fide* refugees be housed and fed in Nissen huts surrounded by a 12-ft barbed-wire fence with armed guards, 'thus ensuring them against being kidnapped . . . [and] also protect them against any temptation to abuse our hospitality'. Meanwhile, in South Africa, the anonymous leader of a refugee-kidnapping organization informed the Press that they were operating in the High Commission Territories and specifically threatened refugees in Swaziland. The Swaziland Government reacted by stating that 'any offences against individual persons . . . will be dealt with according to the law'.

Two African and two European M.L.C.s have been appointed to the Executive Council, which also has four officials and the Queen's Commissioner as chairman. Mr Polycarp Dlamini is 'associated' with education and health, Mr A. K. Hlope with local government and social services, Mr Carl Todd with natural resources and Mr H. Fitzpatrick with public works and communications. Mr Frances Mbelu, a young and very capable Swazi graduate, was nominated to the Assembly and has been its only progressive voice.

Mr Hlope and Mr Todd were amongst the fourteen elected candidates whom members of the defeated political parties tried to unseat through petitions to the Swaziland High Court, alleging intimidation by chiefs, the illegal use of the lion symbol and the absence of the printer's name on election literature. The case dragged on from June 1964 to March 1965. Under a provision of the Electoral Proclamation, the judge made an order allowing as an exception the lion symbol and lack of printer's particulars. The charges of undue influence and corrupt practice he dismissed.

Keeping to its plan, the Imbokodo, supported by the U.S.A., has begun a drive for independence in the Assembly. Early in 1965 Prince Makhosini and Dr George Msibi, Imbokodo's general secretary, visited several independent African countries and Formosa, reportedly financed by Chiang Kai-shek. They claimed support from Dr Nkrumah and other leaders, as well as 100 scholarships from Kenya, Ethiopia, Ghana, Nigeria, India, Nationalist China and America. Reportedly they also tried to persuade African countries to withdraw aid from Swaziland's political parties. In April 1965, Imbokodo demanded 'independence *now*'.

The Swaziland Democratic Party, previously weakened by internal conflict, thereupon joined the Imbokodo. The S.D.P.'s founder and secretary-general, Mr Simon Nxumalo, had resigned on the eve of the party's national congress in October 1964 in order to work for 'wider national unity'. The Ngwenyama subsequently gave him a senior S.N.C. appointment. At the conference, two white members were expelled: Mr Vincent Rozwadowski, a vice-president, for allegedly acting without executive committee authorization, and Dr V. S. Leibrandt, an election candidate who absented himself on nomination day. Dr Allen Nxumalo, still president, announced in March that the S.D.P. felt that any opposition to the Imbokodo was meaningless and that maximum unity would lead to earliest independence.

Part Four

Outlook

11 The Final Challenge

The ever present danger that South Africa would incorporate the High Commission Territories seemed to have been formally laid in 1961, when Dr Verwoerd publicly told his followers that, in view of Britain's changed policies and South Africa's withdrawal from the Commonwealth, the Territories were legally lost for ever to the Republic. Relations with them were henceforth to be placed on the basis of relations with foreign States.

This historic admission by the most fanatical of all South African Prime Ministers ironically brought him under attack from his supposedly more enlightened constitutional opposition, the United Party, which accused him of surrendering crucial South African interests. But he failed to set at rest the fears of the United Nations Committee on Colonialism. In June 1962 the Afro-Asian and Soviet block majority on this committee recommended that the General Assembly declare any attempt to annex Basutoland, Bechuanaland or Swaziland, or to encroach upon their territory in any way, an act of aggression violating the United Nations Charter. The committee also called for the return to the Territories of all lands taken from them, whatever the form or pretext of such alienation; for the immediate introduction of 'one man – one vote'; and for immediate constitutional talks leading to independence.

Dr Verwoerd reiterated his new position in September 1962. Opening a congress of his party in Pretoria, he said of the High Commission Territories:

If they wish to cooperate with us, we are prepared to do so in the best interests of both parties. But we do not aspire to incorporation, which is clearly not practical politics.*

* *Rhodesia Herald*, Salisbury, 7 September 1962.

When petitioners before the General Assembly's Trusteeship Committee nevertheless continued to allege that the aim of South African and British policy was the incorporation of the High Commission Territories into South Africa, both countries went on formal record with categorical denials in December 1962.

In the meantime, however, the South African Government was becoming increasingly disturbed by the use which opponents of apartheid were making of their safe havens in the Territories. The overseas and South African underground leaders of the banned African National Congress held a 'secret', but inevitably highly publicized, conference at Lobatsi in Bechuanaland towards the end of 1962 to plan 'the liberation of South Africa', and a little later publicity was given to the mass escape through Bechuanaland of fifty-four Africans from the Republic.

This added fresh point and delicacy to the private negotiations, in which the South African and Republican authorities were at the time engaged, over the new extradition treaties made necessary by South Africa's departure from the Commonwealth. Britain, however, made it clear that she was not prepared to surrender the traditional right of asylum in the Territories for genuine political refugees. She also resisted South African pressures for the separation of the Offices of Ambassador to the Republic and High Commissioner for Basutoland, the Bechuanaland Protectorate and Swaziland. Dr Verwoerd, in an unprecedented parliamentary statement earlier in 1962, had urged this separation, stressing that the interests of the two posts were bound to conflict, but when Britain announced that Sir Hugh Stephenson was to succeed Sir John Maud in South Africa, it was in both capacities.

The negotiations underlined that the Republic would henceforth treat the Territories as foreign States, beginning with control of the hitherto practically unhampered movement across their common borders. In fact, Dr Verwoerd began to treat the Territories almost as though they were *dangerous* foreign States. In January 1963, the commissioner of the South African police announced that the twenty armed posts planned on the borders of the Territories were only the forerunners of a system of 'several hundred' posts to protect the Republic's thousands of miles of border, including that with Rhodesia and Moçambique. The commissioner denied, of course, that these hundreds of posts were aimed at checking the movement of political refugees and members of underground organizations.

In the same month, the Froneman Commission appointed by Dr Verwoerd to examine the position of foreign Africans in the Republic reported, with recommendations that boded ill for all three Territories, and especially for Basutoland. The commission estimated the number of foreign Africans in the Republic as over 800,000, of whom 650,000 were men; of these, it estimated that 441,000 come from the High Commission Territories, with the overwhelming majority from Basutoland. The commission urged the elimination of all such Africans from the Republic, and proposed that their places should be taken by unemployed local Africans, Asians and Coloured people. Initially, an exception should be made for foreign workers on farms and mines; but as the mines are a wasting asset, the commission anticipated that their labour needs would in time decrease, and foreign mine workers could then be sent back to their homes. In the meantime, there should be an annual quota for admission, in which the Territories would receive preference.

The commission further called for the immediate repatriation of foreign African women and children; the institution of special 'passes' to be shown on entry into the Republic; the establishment of detention 'depots' at strategic points near the border where foreign Africans could be held for 'screening' and, if necessary, punishment; and recommended that schools should bar foreign African children, even if they at present lived in the Republic.

The South African Government accepted the Froneman recommendations with alacrity, and began establishing its border control posts, which are, of course, also useful for screening and holding Africans suspected of being political refugees or sabotage trainees. Mobile patrols on the ground and aerial patrols by helicopter have been introduced between armed border posts, and the erection of barbed-wire fencing, ostensibly to control cattle and game, is being pushed ahead on crucial stretches of the borders with the Territories.

By February, 1963, Sir Roy Welensky, Prime Minister of the then still extant Federation of Rhodesia and Nyasaland, tightened up immigration and repatriation arrangements on the border which Southern Rhodesia shares with Bechuanaland. In March 1963, a new system under which permits would be required for entry to the Republic was announced, with labour influx control due to become operative by July and the general travel requirements to be fully in force by the beginning of 1964. The Bechuanaland Government announced that it would in turn take steps to control the entry of South African subjects, and though this sounded like a defiant tit-for-tat, it effectively promised to play into Dr Verwoerd's hands by discouraging those refugees who did not know that they would still be admitted if they claimed political asylum.

The United Nations Committee on Colonialism continued to concern itself with the possibility of annexation. In July 1963, it called for observation teams to be sent to each Territory in order to establish an effective United Nations presence, which could get information about 'possible infractions against the territorial integrity of these areas', or – in plain words – any attempt at annexation. In fact, however, the Republic and the Territories seemed to be drifting further apart, and a new high in tension between them was reached with the escape through Swaziland and Bechuanaland of Goldreich and Wolpe and the kidnapping in Bechuanaland of Dr Abrahams.

Then, in September 1963, Dr Verwoerd exploded an unexpected bombshell. In a public speech,* he declared that

if South Africa were to be, or to become, the guardian, the protector or the helper of these adjacent Territories, instead of the United Kingdom, we could lead them far better and much more quickly to independence and economic prosperity than Great Britain can do

and he challenged Britain to let him put this case to the people of the Territories themselves. Though he carefully added: 'I have most clearly stated on behalf of my Government that South Africa has no territorial ambitions with regard to these areas', he brought back at one stroke all the worst fears of incorporation which have haunted the Territories since 1910.

The good doctor wrapped his 'offer' up handsomely. 'We respect,' he said, 'the principle of territorial integrity; we also honour the dictates and demands of international law.' He even

---

* *The Road to Freedom for Basutoland, Bechuanaland, Swaziland*, Dr H. F. Verwoerd, Fact Paper 107, S.A. Department of Information, 1963.

claimed blandly that the Ganyile affair in Basutoland and the recent return of Dr Abrahams to Bechuanaland 'proved our sincerity'.

He appealed to private South African citizens not to take personal action, adding: 'I must admit that the part played by the High Commission Territories can become very trying at times, for example when our air-space is violated by aircraft transporting fugitives and offenders from South Africa between such territories. . . . Since we have to suffer abuse on our policies even within the United Kingdom Parliament', he felt called upon 'to discuss in public – though dispassionately' relations between the Republic and the High Commission Territories.

Britain was mistakenly

trying to transform these historically black areas into multi-racial territories . . . it is common knowledge that these Territories are nevertheless economically dependent upon South Africa. Great Britain might guide them to political freedom, but she is almost powerless to regulate the ultimate economic situation or to achieve the economic viability of these areas for their peoples.

South Africa was greatly concerned about their future: 'We have a very direct interest, because our advantage lies in having good, prosperous and trustworthy neighbours.'

South Africa's apartheid policy had been sadly misunderstood: in reality independence for black territories was part of its aim. Thus, if these Territories were South Africa's responsibility and not Britain's, they would enjoy several advantages.

First, we would aim at making them democratic states in which the masses would not be dominated by small groups of authoritarians. [Instead there would be rule by] natural native democracy and its leaders, coupled with representative democracy – as in the Transkei. Secondly, we would steer away from the principle of multi-racialism. [Those whites who would be needed for a time in the Territories would exercise their political rights in the Republic's white areas.] Thirdly, wherever it might be necessary, we would repurchase or exchange areas now wrongly [sic] occupied in order either to include them in the white areas or the black.

This must have gladdened the hearts of Bechuanaland's

Afrikaner farmers but not those of the Basuto. For, as Verwoerd made clear in a later statement, he certainly did not mean that he would restore to the Basuto the conquered territories of the Orange Free State. Nor did he intend to return 'British Bechuanaland' in the Cape Province to the Batswana. He did envisage a 'greater Basutoland, Swaziland and Bechuanaland', but only by joining them with the obviously enviable 'Bantustan' areas allocated to Africans 'of the same ethnic groups within the Republic'.

Thus he could overcome an internal political difficulty, for as he candidly admitted:

We are often asked when the Transkei plan is going to be applied to other (black) groups in South Africa . . . were it possible for them to be joined to those High Commission Territories to which their people are ethnically linked, then the present difficulty of establishing one big Tswana area, or one large Sotho or Swazi area in Southern Africa would fall away.

Finally, South Africa would help the Territories economically by setting up industries on their borders (naturally, as with existing 'border industries', dispensing with unAfrican devices like a minimum wage) and by including them 'in future planning on the basis of a common market'.

'These are great ideals' claimed the doctor blandly. And he added with uncustomary directness: 'In stating them we are motivated by a desire, on the one hand, to solve our own problems, and on the other, to ensure that we have good and friendly neighbours.' All he wanted was 'to prevent possible enmity from growing' through tragic misunderstandings about the noble and disinterested nature of apartheid.

For these reasons I am now making an offer to Great Britain – I might almost call it a challenge – to allow us to put the essentials of our policies before the inhabitants of these Territories [he declared. And in the tail came his sting.] If they decide to go their own way, *in growing isolation* from South Africa, so well and good [my italics]. . . . Surely this is little enough to ask?

Since he was at that very time engaged in delicate negotiations with the British authorities on future relations with the Territories, Dr Verwoerd can hardly have believed that this 'challenge' thrown out at a Nationalist Party Congress and addressed over Britain's head to the people of the Territories, was asking 'little enough'. But whatever he may have believed, the speed and hostility of public and private reaction in the Territories, Britain and the United Nations were unmistakable.

Verwoerd's 'offer' was seen as a take-over bid, and condemned by the major Africa-led political parties in all three Territories and by the British Press. A few Afrikaner farmers in Bechuanaland and Mr Carl Todd in Swaziland welcomed it. Sobhuza and his S.N.C. in Swaziland, who were widely thought to have made private approaches to Verwoerd and so to have encouraged him to make his offer, tacitly supported him by their silence. In Basutoland the Freedom–Marema Tlou party said that it was prepared to discuss problems of mutual interest – but *not* on the basis of 'separate development'. But for the rest so strong was the general reaction that Verwoerd felt obliged, only two days later, to issue another statement denying that any 'offer was made to the United Kingdom to "annex" or "take-over" or "incorporate" or "administer" these territories'.

Despite Dr Verwoerd's airs of injured innocence, most observers had understood him perfectly well. He was suggesting that the Territories abandon their present form of political advancement and adopt instead the Bantu Authorities system; that – in other words – the modern system of political parties should be scrapped and the powers of the chiefs, under white control, restored. As the *Evening Post* of Port Elizabeth remarked: 'The audacity of the scheme is breath-taking. Is this an attempt to provoke conflict between tribalists and non-tribalists in the Protectorates?'

Yet Dr Verwoerd was aware that in Basutoland and Bechuanaland the chiefs and politicians had forged a certain understanding of each other's aims, and that he was unlikely to stir them up against each other now. Swaziland, of course, was a different case, but Swaziland, least of all the Territories, could physically be turned into a Bantustan, because of its patch-work pattern of white and black land-holdings.

He might, of course, have been trying to create a division of loyalties between black and white in Bechuanaland and even

Swaziland, for his speech inevitably had the effect of encouraging Afrikaners there to look to Pretoria for their salvation. But this could hardly have compensated him for the free ammunition which he was giving to his enemies at the United Nations by stirring up all the old fears of South African territorial ambitions, nor for the justified resentment of the British Government at having him make 'offers' over its head. Besides, it is difficult to understand why he needed British permission at all to put his case to Africans in the Territories, unless he wanted to send agents into them. The public platform, the radio, normal printing and distribution have always been open to him, and copies of his speech were, in fact, distributed, without charge, on the borders of Swaziland.

Some observers thought that Verwoerd was merely 'flying a kite'. But he is not given to kite-flying, and a major policy statement at a monolithic party congress means the laying down of a firm political line. What, then, did he intend? Stripping away all the propaganda and verbiage about the nobility of apartheid, Dr Verwoerd was, in effect, threatening the Territories with an economic 'squeeze'. Deeply disturbed by the use of the Territories as escape routes and humiliated by the fiasco of Dr Abrahams's kidnapping, he was telling the Territories that if they continued on their present paths, they would do so 'in growing isolation from South Africa', and that it was 'in their interests' not to have this happen.

If this is not a 'take-over' bid, it is hard to know what is. For the Territories, if they did agree to develop on Bantustan lines, would never be able to stand alone. Industries might be established just across their borders in South Africa, but that would only increase the dependence of the Territories on the apartheid State.

Britain did not react officially to Dr Verwoerd's 'offer', and within months of its having been made was in a position to announce new constitutions for all three Territories, with Basutoland scheduled for independence in 1966. And so Dr Verwoerd felt it necessary to speak again.

I want to challenge [he told the South African Senate on 5 June 1964], the supposition that once these Territories become independent, it must necessarily be accompanied by hostility. . . . I personally believe that their becoming independent will perhaps afford us a better opportunity not for a hostile relationship, but the contrary.

The independence of these High Commission Territories will mean that the people themselves will become responsible for their future existence and they will have to consider what is in their interests. As long as Britain was the overlord they could even be hostile towards us and reckon that anything they lose here in the form of employment or revenue will be made up by Britain. The father must look after the children!

But as this fatherly hand disappears more and more and they become more and more responsible for their own future existence and collect their own funds and see to it themselves that their own people have work, then they must consider their neighbour.

If this is their place of employment, if this is the source of their revenue, if our cooperation in connexion with customs revenue is in their interest, then any individual government that is established there must maintain friendship with its neighbour in the interests of its own people. [My italics.]

Let me state the following as clear policy, to see to it that the friendship with the High Commission Territories be maintained after independence.

The gradual process of independence in these Territories may cause difficulties – and it will be a pity – but the chances are better that the difficulties will rather be less than more. I cannot say that the presence of Britain as overlord there helped to engender better relations between the people in the Territories and South Africa . . . in the present situation it was no longer in the interest of South Africa to bring about incorporation. At the same time it was no longer practical to do so.

Beneath the semi-diplomatic gloss, Dr Verwoerd's message to the Territories was painfully plain. They were to play it his way, or they were to face the economic consequences.

There is, especially for Basutoland, a chilling realism in Verwoerd's threat which no amount of Pan-African fervour can dispel. After all, even African States more 'viable' than Basutoland feel themselves obliged to tailor their work-a-day clothes to their economic cloth.

Thus, when the Heads of African States called at their Cairo meeting in July 1964 for a boycott of Portugal in order to liberate Angola and Moçambique, Malawi and Northern Rhodesia found themselves in a very difficult position. All of Northern

Rhodesia's copper is exported through these Portuguese colonies, and a great proportion of imports for Malawi and Northern Rhodesia comes through the Moçambique port of Beira.

The Prime Minister of newly independent Malawi, Dr Banda, felt obliged to tell the Cairo conference that whilst he fervently believed in the complete independence of Africa, he could not 'commit economic suicide to be a loyal Organization of African Unity member'. He said that compliance with the resolution demanding severance of diplomatic and economic ties with Portugal 'would mean economic strangulation' for Malawi, and he would not be a hypocrite and promise what he could not do.

Similarly, Northern Rhodesia's Dr Kenneth Kaunda, about to become the first President of an independent Zambia, felt obliged to explain his difficulties in being largely surrounded by hostile countries.

If such problems are to hinder Pan-African action by Zambia, which possesses great copper riches, and by Malawi, which even on the worst reckoning could always at least feed its population, what is independent Lesotho, as Basutoland will be called, to do against South Africa?

If the international campaign for the imposition of economic sanctions against South Africa succeeds, this problem would be raised in starkest form for Basutoland, Bechuanaland, and Swaziland.

Such sanctions, to be effective, would at least have to cut off South Africa's oil supplies, and at most would have to be total. In either event they would have to involve a naval blockade not only of South Africa's ports but also of the Moçambique port of Lourenço Marques, which, with the completion of the new railway, will increasingly provide Swaziland with an alternative to South Africa for its imports and exports. Bechuanaland, of course, has its rail connexion with Southern and thence with Northern Rhodesia, though it is by no means clear how the former country's white minority Government would behave in a sanctions situation.

None of the three Territories is itself in a position to take part in any international sanctions by refusing to trade with South Africa. On the contrary, they are all, as we have seen, heavily dependent on the Republic for the importation of maize and other basic foodstuffs as well as capital and manufactured goods, petrol, medicines, and almost anything else which they need. South Africa, moreover, provides them with the only market for their surplus labour, on whose earnings they significantly depend, and with crucial communications and other services such as banking. For Basutoland, revenue from the common customs union is equalled in importance only by South African absorption of labour, and both constitute a significant part of the budget in Bechuanaland and even in Swaziland. Furthermore, South Africa at present provides their main market, and marketing arrangements are very closely integrated.

Something could and should be done to decrease this dependence on South Africa by Bechuanaland and Swaziland; but Basutoland, completely surrounded by the Republic, must substantially remain dependent upon its Big Brother.

Certainly, even if the sort of development which is urged in this book is rapidly undertaken, it would be unrealistic to expect the Territories actively to take part in economic sanctions against South Africa.

Their fate during any sanctions period would, however, be little affected by their neutrality, or even by any friendship that they might bring themselves to show for South Africa. It would depend on what the Republic itself decided to do about the Territories, and on what effective measures the organizers of sanctions could take to alleviate the hardship which their action against South Africa must inevitably cause the Territories.

Economic action against South Africa would doubtless lead Dr Verwoerd to bring the Territories into play as hostages, but it is unlikely that he would invade them, despite the fact that a physical take-over would present little immediate practical difficulty once British troops were withdrawn from Swaziland.

During a sanctions period there would, moreover, presumably be much increased internal unrest within South Africa and increased attempts to smuggle arms and trained men into the country, especially through Bechuanaland. Thus there would be an enhanced temptation for Verwoerd to send in troops. But, quite aside from the consequent difficulties of policing fresh hostile populations and enormous areas at a time when his resources would already be strained, Verwoerd must realize that if international opinion had already reached the pitch and unanimity required for sanctions, physical aggression against the Territories would provoke counter-intervention and escalate sanctions into war.

The much more likely South African reaction to international economic action would be to apply a total economic squeeze in turn on the Territories, in the hope that the resulting suffering, especially in Basutoland, and dislocation in Bechuanaland and Swaziland would lead to a lifting of international sanctions.

No one can doubt that the purpose of international sanctions would effectively be the overthrow of South Africa's racialist Government, and at such a time Verwoerd would hardly worry about the minor niceties of international contracts. Even so, except for the arbitrary cancellation of the customs agreement, the other measures he could take are all domestic matters within South Africa's normal and proper competence: the closing of the frontiers with the Territories; the repatriation of their labourers and nationals from South Africa; the withdrawal of all South African services, including communications; the prohibition of all trade with the Territories or, less drastically, the placing of prohibitive duties on all exports from or to them.

Of these measures, the total repatriation of their migrant workers to the Territories would seem to be the only one likely to cause South Africa any serious inconvenience. Certainly it would be difficult, if not impossible, for the mines to replace their highly prized Basuto labourers, or those from Bechuanaland and Swaziland, during international sanctions which would surely include a ban by African States on the export of any migrant labour to South Africa. But even the repatriation of non-mine labour would suffice to precipitate a major crisis in Basutoland, whilst the other measures outlined would have the same effect.

Thus international sanctions against South Africa would have to include plans for alleviating distress in the Territories and, at the very least, for preventing mass starvation and economic breakdown in Basutoland, together with provision for the rehabilitation of the Territories once sanctions themselves had achieved their objective. Specifically, this would mean the provision of relatively large amounts of maize for Basutoland, as well as medical supplies, petrol, and other crucial, if small-scale, needs.

Bechuanaland has imported maize in bulk from the Rhodesias in the past, and could probably meet its needs again in this way during a boycott. Swaziland could probably substitute its own rice production for the maize it presently imports from South Africa, though the change might not be popular with the ordinary tribesmen. Both countries could also, as has been noted earlier, do a great deal to improve their present production of maize, so that, given an intensive and adequately financed agricultural programme in the period before sanctions were instituted, they could even reach the point of self-sufficiency.

In Basutoland, the Department of Agriculture believes that in no single crop now grown are yields per acre more than half the possible ones, and that maize yields could be trebled from the present 'efficient' level of three bags per acre (one bag per acre is common). If even half this increase in maize production were achieved, Basutoland would, outside of drought years, be self-sufficient in maize, for present production is roughly estimated at 70,000 bags* and imports in a moderately bad climatic year run at approximately 25,000 bags.

But if plans for sanctions against South Africa are to consider the three Territories, allowance will have to be made for drought conditions, with even a complete crop failure, during the whole period of international action. In that event, Basutoland's food needs under sanctions could be met in only one of two ways: by previous stockpiling, or by flying in maize once sanctions began.

If funds and trained demonstrators were made available at once for increasing agricultural production in Basutoland, and if sanctions did not occur for two or three years, it might be possible for Basutoland to stock-pile the major part of the maize reserves she would need to survive a full year's economic siege. The sums and training facilities needed for such a crash agricultural programme are relatively small, though beyond Basutoland's own resources, and in providing them now the African and other countries working for sanctions against South Africa could both strengthen their case and give badly needed aid.

* *Report and Recommendations on a Nutrition Survey conducted in Basutoland*, Dr J. A. Munoz and Miss M. M. Anderson, World Health Organization Regional Office for Africa South of the Sahara, 1960.

If a crash agricultural programme were not successfully and speedily implemented, stockpiling could normally take place by purchase of maize from South Africa, though in a drought year the Republic must herself restrict maize exports, as she did in 1964.

In 1960, which was a moderately bad year, Basutoland imported 231,301 bags of maize, weighing 200 lb. each, from South Africa, and on this basis an annual shortfall of 25,000 tons can be taken as a rough estimate of import needs.

If the South Africans decided to hamper stockpiling by refusing to sell available supplies to Basutoland, maize could be imported from the U.S.A. or Argentina, though South Africa could make this very expensive by raising its already high import duty on maize.

It has been calculated* that, at 1964 prices, the c.i.f. cost of importing maize from the U.S.A. or Argentina would be in the region of £20–25 per ton, to which must be added present import duties of £2·24 per ton (which South Africa might raise) and storage costs of £8–10 per ton (for a system of aluminium crittal bins). On this basis, it would cost £30–40 a ton to import and store maize in Basutoland, and in a moderately bad year, when 25,000 tons would be needed, the total cost would be between £750,000 and £1,200,000. In a really bad drought year, the need could even reach 40,000 tons, which would raise the cost to the region of £1,600,000, and if, in addition, Basuto now working in South Africa were repatriated, the total would rise much higher. This proper stockpiling against the possibility of prolonged sanctions – in a drought year, and allowing for the repatriation of Basuto by South Africa – could involve *an expenditure of £2,000,000 prior to the actual imposition of sanctions* – a substantial sum but not, considering the stakes involved, by any means a prohibitive one.

If prior stockpiling were not undertaken, maize supplies would have to be flown into Basutoland, and even assuming that South Africa would permit such flights, which would have to pass over its territory, the nearest suitable airport would be Lusaka, some 1,000 miles away. The additional cost of air-lifting maize would thus be considerable. Certainly, whichever method were adopted

---

* *Sanctions and the High Commission Territories*, R. M. Bostock. A paper presented to the International Conference on Sanctions Against South Africa, held at London in 1964, and published in *Sanctions Against South Africa*, Penguin, 1964.

to enable Basutoland to survive sanctions against South Africa, substantial sums of money would have to be made available either by Britain or by the international group sponsoring and supervising such action. And clearly the rapid increase of Basutoland's own agricultural production would be the cheapest and generally the most positive course of action. The same applies – if to a lesser extent – to Swaziland and Bechuanaland.

If the plight of the Territories as South Africa's hostages is most starkly revealed by the possibility of economic sanctions against the Republic itself, it also affects them in their day-to-day life. Dr Verwoerd's thinly-veiled threats of economic pressure against any Territory which, after independence, does not act as South Africa wishes, presents Britain inescapably with her final challenge.

Quite clearly, every additional million which Britain spends on furthering the economic and social development of the Territories will make them much less dependent on South Africa. To give them, after many decades of gross neglect, political independence without economic backing would be a final betrayal of trust.

Economically and socially, the three Territories have many needs in common. All of them urgently require development in African agriculture and stock-raising, with special emphasis on the fostering of cooperatives and agricultural credit; better marketing and transport facilities; drastically improved educational services, especially in the secondary, vocational and technical fields and the training of administrators; better preventive and curative health services and the elimination of malnutrition; thorough mineral and hydrological surveys; fuller utilization of water resources; improved soil conservation; the creation of statistical services; and the substitution of economic planning for the present system of emergency 'shopping lists'.

Fundamentally, each Territory needs to undertake and successfully complete an agricultural revolution if its political and social evolution is to be securely grounded.* And such a revolution can

* See in this connexion 'Africa's Other Revolution', by T. F. Betts, *New Statesman*, 10 September 1960.

only be undertaken with any prospect of success if African farmers acquire the means for maintaining or enhancing the fertility of the soil, principally through the provision of subsidized artificial fertilizers and more efficient equipment. If these needs are met, Basutoland and Bechuanaland may in one way be fortunate in lacking the possibility of rapid industrialization, which in other parts of Africa has entailed the narrow concentration of available development funds on the provision of industrial ancilliary services to the neglect of indigenous agriculture. This neglect can bring, in basically agricultural countries, the threat of famine and the necessity to import food. Swaziland, whose industries are basically extractive and repatriate their profits, illustrates this process in its most dangerous form. Rural income, and therefore the purchasing power of the great majority of its population, has remained frighteningly low, and glaring differences in income and social advancement are being created both between races and, increasingly, between urban and rural dwellers.

The British Government still maintains its faith in private investment as the main instrument of overseas development, but it is clear that peasant agriculture will never attract sufficient funds from such a source. The grants made for colonial agriculture by Britain from the Colonial (now Commonwealth) Development and Welfare Fund have been totally inadequate, and where Exhequer and Commonwealth Assistance loans have been made these are unsuitable because their terms are rigid and their interest rates too high.

What the Territories need is *grant* aid to help pay for fertilizer, tractors and major capital works like irrigation services, together with *cheap* loan aid which can be passed on to the cultivator at a reasonable cost. At the same time an intensive survey of fertilizer sources within the Territories is necessary, with special attention paid to the utilization of coal deposits and the possibilities of afforestation. In denuded Basutoland, for instance, the provision of wood or coal fuel could put an end to the present use of animal manure instead, while in Bechuanaland utilization of the extensive coal deposits could provide a basis for the mass production of fertilizers.

But even if funds for these purposes are found, there remains the problem of their distribution and the recovery of loans. If progress is to be achieved, then the bulk of loan funds must be fed to the cultivator at the small-holding level, and this involves the fundamental problems of credit-worthiness and land tenure.

As the African farmer has no individual title to his land, he cannot obtain conventional credit, and so the officially favoured solution is to introduce such title. This, in theory, would give the peasant farmer acceptable security for cultivation loans. But in many underdeveloped countries, especially in the Far East, long-established private land tenure has merely resulted in a burden of private debt which has become the main block to rural development.

In the Territories, moreover, the overwhelming majority of Africans are deeply suspicious of attempts by a foreign Government to tamper with land tenure, especially where, as in Swaziland and Bechuanaland, there are settled white communities. To succeed, an agricultural revolution must have the active support of the ordinary African farmer, and thus land tenure reform cannot be made a prerequisite of farm improvement. Land tenure may indeed change once improvements in cultivation and rural life generally have been promoted, but to insist on private tenure first is to put the cart before the horse.

Private tenure is, in any event, neither the sole nor even the best method of reform. If Africans could find a way of by-passing private ownership of land and moving from the present communal system to public ownership, they might well have a few lessons to teach Britain and the world.

In the meantime, however, the African farmer *does* have one crucial asset which can be used as security for agricultural credit: his standing within his own community. We have seen in Basutoland that groups of farmers, banding together in cooperatives, can organize credit on the basis of their collective crop expectations, and that this credit can be passed on to individual members whose reputation and past application warrant the trust of their peers. Until political interference bedevilled the Basutoland Cooperative Banking Union, the Territory's cooperative movement was making impressive progress, all the more valuable for springing from the ordinary African farmer's initiative and desire to improve himself and his community.

The sums required for launching cooperative credit are small in relation to the results it can achieve, and if they were provided the cooperative movement could contribute to the present small-holder system the benefits of estate production without the latter's inevitable pattern of economic inequality.

The pressing need of each Territory for education has already been examined; but before the present copying of British-type methods is continued on a much expanded scale, the people and administrators of the Territories themselves should pause and consider what types of schools and schooling are really needed in Africa today.

It is clear* that those responsible for African education until now have not properly examined its relation to the real needs of the Territories, but have merely imported patterns developed in Britain to suit Britain's needs. In the Territories, as in the rest of Africa, the vast majority of the population live in villages and depend on agriculture and other pastoral activity. Only if they produce more can they hope to prosper. Thus what is needed is primarily, though by no means exclusively, a rural and technical education programme. The elementary schools should become the adjunct of a farm, and the farm the adjunct of a school. Teachers should be trained so that they do not become alienated from their original rural environment, and are fitted to improve not only knowledge but technique.

At the secondary level, the emphasis should be on vocational and technical training related to the economic needs of the Territories, and to producing the many junior officials who could perform their jobs perfectly well without the high level of formal education and pay established by the era of the expatriate official. At the post-secondary level, it would be a tragic waste of scarce resources if Swaziland and Bechuanaland, on attaining independence, should feel compelled by national pride to erect universities of their own; the existing university for all three Territories in Basutoland, adequately expanded and allied with scholarships to other universities, can more than meet their combined needs for an élite with high formal qualifications.

At both elementary and secondary levels, moreover, there is an

* In this connexion, see 'What Schools for Africa?', by Thomas Balogh, *New Statesman*, 23 March 1962.

urgent need to revise the syllabuses and textbooks used in subjects like history, which are still taught from a purely European and out-dated point of view, and which too often give a distorted picture of Africa's past.

Such reforms in educational structure and content will, of course, meet with formidable opposition, not least from those Africans who have been educated in the old colonial ways and who, together with the politicians, will distrust anything that looks like an 'inferior' article. In the Territories, with their proximity to South Africa, suspicions of anything that smacks of Dr Verwoerd's racialist and inferior Bantu Education are rightly acute. Certainly no educational reform could be justified which would merely turn out semi-skilled or skilled black labour for white-owned extractive industries to exploit. In the Territories, too, present facilities for secondary education are so limited that the products of foreseeable expansion could be fully absorbed into a localized administration as independence nears.

The social structure and economy of both Swaziland and Bechuanaland have been distorted by the concentration of wealth and privilege in the hands of the local white communities, leaving the indigenous Africans, almost untouched, in rural poverty. It will be harder for these countries, if they are to aim at the promotion of non-racial democracy, to rationalize their educational systems than for an all-African country like Basutoland, but the attempt will have to be made if rural African poverty is to be overcome. And even where, as in Basutoland, no racial problem exists, the mere displacement of the expatriate élite by a local African equivalent living at the same inflated standards can hardly fail to perpetuate the division between rulers and ruled.

12 Go Well – Stay Well

Politically, Basutoland's immediate future is now clearly marked, with an agreed time-table for independence by the end of 1966. But Britain, by insisting on retaining control of external affairs, defence, internal security, the public service and finance in the intervening period of internal self-government, has the responsibility during that year of defending and promoting Basutoland's legitimate interest. This will include the conclusion of the already long drawn out negotiations with South Africa over a revision of the Customs agreement; and if Basutoland's Customs receipts, which constitute half of her annual revenue, are in strict fairness decreased, Britain should help her to obtain alternative funds. Furthermore, there is the international piracy which the South Africans are proposing to practice by arrogating to themselves 97·5 per cent of the waters of the Orange River, half of which rises in Basutoland and which, since it borders the Republic, can therefore only be disposed of in international law by agreement between Basutoland and South Africa.

The Basuto will, of course, want Britain to keep the written pledges, given by Mr Duncan Sandys, that in the pre-independence period 'it would be the intention of the British Government to delegate powers in regard to external affairs and internal security as fully and as quickly as circumstances allowed'. They will be acutely interested, too, in how soon the British Government Representative is instructed to relinquish responsibility for the public service to the Public Service Commission, and will remember that in May 1964 'the Secretary of State assured the conference that arrangements would be made forthwith to accelerate the localization of the public service'. The Secretary of State also gave an assurance that 'whenever practicable the British Government Representative would consult Motlotheli and the

Prime Minister of Basutoland before exercising the powers conferred upon him'.

The Basuto accepted the present arrangements because they will, after all, last only for one year, and in the long run they will attach the greatest importance of all to what Britain does now and later to help them economically. There was no reference to this in the report of the London conference, because Mr Sandys refused to enter into financial and economic discussions. He said instead that Britain was fully aware of the position, and that the Basuto must trust her to do what is right.

But a most disturbing indication that Britain's Commonwealth and Colonial Secretary still fails to grasp or respect what is right in the view of the Basuto themselves has come since the conference. With the Basuto forced to accept the presence and wide powers of a British Government Representative, much must clearly depend during the months before independence on how well this official gets on personally with the Basuto and their leaders.

At the London conference itself, the Basuto leaders made it clear that they wanted the then Resident Commissioner, Mr A. F. Giles, replaced. Mr Ntsu Mokhehle, voicing the general feeling, declared:

Mr Giles has not kept contact with the African people. It is true that he has said that his door is always open to us, but we think that more than this was necessary in terms of initiative by him. We made it clear at the conference table to Mr Sandys that we should like to see him replaced. He could not carry this work.

In July the British Government announced that Mr A. F. Giles would continue in his post.

It remains to be seen how Britain plans to do what is right in the economic sphere. The Basuto took a lot on trust at the conference. It is on the keeping of this trust that Britain's record will finally be judged.

The Basuto are probably sanguine in believing that, short of their doing a political deal with him, Dr Verwoerd would buy the admittedly cheap water and electricity which their Ox-Bow scheme would produce. Certainly Sir John Maud, when he was Commissioner in 1962, met with a blank refusal on all levels of

South African officialdom to even discuss the matter. But the Basuto will never rest easy until they have the dam and sales have at least been tried, and certainly some of the water and electricity from the first stage of the scheme would strengthen their internal economy. At a cost of £2·5 million, Britain could well afford to make a gesture of faith.

It is, of course, true that the Basuto could hitherto have done more to help themselves, and perhaps only part of the reason for failure to do so lies in the enervating effects of colonial rule. In so far as one can generalize about people, the Basuto are possibly more stubborn, conservative and proud than most. Perhaps this is why they have survived. And whilst they are tough and resourceful, they are also, like many people in a tough spot, given to a great deal of wishful thinking.

Thus, when challenged with the problems which an independent Basutoland would have to face, a number of Basuto intellectuals, including a few who have been there for training, like to point to Israel as an example of how the Basuto could survive. The parallel is certainly a very tempting one. Both Basutoland and Israel are tiny, apparently 'non-viable' countries surrounded by hostile territory: both have been said to contain little arable land and no 'payable' or 'worthwhile' mineral deposits; and both are inhabited by a people with an acute sense of national identity.

In both countries Britain has allowed great chunks of territory to go to 'the enemy'; Transjordan and the 'lost lands' of the Free State being equated. Both countries, so the argument continues, have been used by Britain as a pawn in a vastly profitable international game, and both have as a result had their economic development deliberately neglected by Britain; in Israel's case for fear of upsetting vast British investments in Arab oil and in Basutoland's case for fear of upsetting vastly profitable investments in South African gold and industry.

Yet in both Israel, and in Basutoland, Britain made lofty pledges that, be the cost what it may, she would see justice done and in both only moved perceptibly to make her word good when forced by militant local pressure and by world opinion.

Though the parallel obviously cannot be sustained step by step its fundamentals do hold. Basuto intellectuals do not, however, carry it to the penultimate stage, which would be that in Basutoland as in Israel, Britain will never fulfil her promises and will simply throw in her hand.

The Basuto like to believe that, like the Israelis, they will prove the 'experts' wrong and that, overcoming internal political divisions, they will not only survive in independence but will flourish. This, of course, remains to be seen, for aside from lacking the Israeli coastline and an international 'diaspora' which pumps huge sums into the ancient homeland, the Basuto today are in exactly the opposite condition from the Israelis with their abundance of skills and technical know-how.

It is simply not feasible for the underdeveloped Pan-African world, even if it wished to do so, to take the place of international Jewry in financing Basutoland's development. But Basutoland may soon have the unwanted chance of testing at least part of the final stage of the parallel. Basutoland's real human challenge will come at the moment, now rapidly drawing near, when Verwoerd forces tens of thousands of expatriate Basuto to return home.

Given inspired leadership, an alert and proud people can, *in extremis*, approach the impossible. But it is certain that whatever human efforts and sacrifices the Basuto make, they cannot win through without outside help for some years to come. It is equally certain that, whatever the United Nations may do, it is primarily Britain's responsibility to provide this aid.

Speaking at the United Nations in 1962, Ntsu Mokhehle declared:

Britain, with its enormous financial commitments in the Republic of South Africa, which territorially surrounds us and pursues inhuman apartheid policies against us, cannot promote, concurrently, our political independence and Britain's own financial interests in South Africa.

On the purely political plane, Britain is presently proving Mr Mokhehle wrong. But he, together with other Basuto leaders, now realizes that the real question is whether Britain will risk South African displeasure by giving Basutoland the economic underpinning which alone will make its political independence at all meaningful. It is up to Britain to prove that she means this independence to be real and lasting.

THE PREGNANT DESERT

Bechuanaland seems, under its new constitution, to have the best chance among the Territories of establishing successfully a non-racial society, and by allowing her to move, at the urging of black and white legislators alike, to 'one man – one vote' on a single electoral roll, Britain has taken a wise step. Given the small size of its white population, any arrangement for separate racial representation in the Territory would still result in an African majority, as it did in Malawi and Zambia. Token separate representation for the white minority may look like a safeguard, but it can soon enough become an irritant and must, within a short time, in any event, vanish. In Bechuanaland, white and black will now have the chance of learning to work together under British protection, instead of having to try to find a way of doing so only after independence.

As in Basutoland, much will, of course, depend on how Britain exercises the very substantial reserve powers which she has retained, and how quickly she delegates these powers and allows the country to move on to full independence. Here Bechuanaland had one important advantage over the other two Territories, for the Queen's Commissioner, Sir Peter Fawcus, was progressive, able and had an expert knowledge of the country and its needs.

In the political and economic spheres his successor and the Batswana leaders will need these qualities, for more than any other Territory Bechuanaland will be faced with South African pressures over the refugee issue. Bechuanaland alone offers a direct overland escape route to the South African refugee, and with Zambia's independence the tiny meeting point of the two countries on the banks of the Zambesi has taken on an enormous importance.

The threats of local whites against Arthur Goldreich and Harold Wolpe when they sought sanctuary in the Protectorate in 1963; the destruction at Francistown airport of the East African Airways aeroplane which had come to fetch them together with other refugees; the sabotaging since then of the airstrip in the far north of the Protectorate which light aircraft use to fly out refugees; and the near destruction by means of planted bombs in July 1964 of the refugee camp which Amnesty International was building near Francistown; all these show that at least some of Bechuanaland's whites are prepared to put their South African sympathies into practice, almost certainly in collaboration with South African agents.

It remains to be seen whether the more enlightened new white members of the 1965 Legislative Assembly will influence their old constituents; but in any event the British authorities must maintain the rights of political asylum and free transit in Bechuanaland, and make every effort to ensure the physical safety of those who claim such rights.

Bechuanaland could take on an even more crucial international importance if a judgment of the International Court of Justice led to United Nations intervention in the neighbouring and disputed mandate of South West Africa. The same could apply as well to the South African-controlled and militarized Caprivi Strip, which Bechuanaland once administered and to which Zambia may well have a legal claim.

Bechuanaland has great possibilities for economic development, and is fortunate in having far more potentially arable land than its population needs. At present the lives of its people are poor. But water could transform both the country and the lives of its inhabitants, and water is abundantly there in the Okavango swamps. In 1960 the Morse Mission urged the spending of £127,000 over the next three years on the collection of hydrological data, yet by the end of 1963 the British Government had felt able to find only £3,000 [sic] for a survey of the Okavango swamps.

The Morse Mission and a United Nations team of experts have providentially rescued the utilization of the Okavango waters from the dusty pigeon hole into which it had been thrust by bureaucratic scepticism and the – by Bechuanaland standards – large funds which it would require. Yet this would seem to be a project tailor-made for international aid bodies such as the I.D.A., and Britain, if she is not prepared to find the funds herself, must ensure that they are raised elsewhere. Equitably distributed, the Okavango waters, backed by drastically improved roads, a second abbatoir and other marketing facilities, as well as agricultural extension services and rural credit, could dramatically boost the Batswana's standard of living. If steps are taken in time to ensure that the ordinary people participate fully in the profits which will result from the accelerating exploitation of Bechuanaland's mineral resources and if educational and health services are rapidly developed, the country could achieve a much better life not only for its own people, but also for those cousins of the Batswana who, under South African pressure, may be forced to leave Basutoland.

LAST CHANCE FOR DEMOCRACY

It is undoubtedly Swaziland which now faces Britain with the most difficult political decision in the Territories – not, ironically, whether to grant independence, but whether to postpone it until the traditional tribal authorities have been obliged to allow a reasonable degree of genuine internal democracy to function.

It has been noted how in the 1964 elections Sobhuza's party, the Imbokodo, swept the board in coalition with the most conservative group of whites. There can be no doubt that during electioneering time the various African-led political parties were denied access by Sobhuza's chiefs to the tribal lands on which the vast majority of Swazi live, and that independent-minded tribesmen were intimidated into voting for the King's party by threats from the chiefs of fines, loss of land and even physical harm.

In reply to a memorandum in which the political parties, *prior* to the elections, complained of this obstruction and intimidation, Mr Duncan Sandys, Britain's Commonwealth and Colonial Secretary, blandly claimed that he had no jurisdiction over tribal lands unless the public peace was disturbed, and added the gratuitous information that anyone feeling himself wronged under the new constitution could always take his complaint to the courts.

But when the political parties did take flagrant breaches of the electoral regulations by Imbokodo candidates before the courts, Mr Sandys reacted with an action so cynical that it might have been designed to destroy the faith of progressive Swazi in the value of the courts themselves and in all British declarations of principle.

454

The range of symbols by which each candidate was identified in the elections had been limited to inanimate objects, with the express purpose of preventing Sobhuza's men from cashing in on his identification with the picture of a lion. Nevertheless, three subsequently elected Imbokodo candidates used this unauthorized lion symbol in their campaign literature, which also failed to carry the name and address of the printer as required by regulation. The political parties claim that these details were omitted because the literature was printed for the party in South Africa.

When the British Administration failed to take any action to check these abuses, the political parties complained to the police, and so forced court action. But when the case came up, shortly before the elections, it was postponed on a technicality. The three accused Imbokodo candidates were elected to the Legislative Council, and when the case came up again, shortly after the elections, they did not bother to appear in court. It soon enough appeared that they had good reason not to concern themselves, for later on the same day a Government Gazette was published with retrospective amendments to the electoral regulations. Originally it had been proclaimed that anyone convicted of corrupt practice in the elections would, in addition to normal criminal punishment, be automatically disqualified from voting or being elected to the legislature for seven years. The British Administration now announced that it considered these penalties 'excessive . . . if committed in certain circumstances'. It listed these circumstances, and gave the High Court the discretion to relieve a convicted petitioner of the full penalties. As the political parties have rightly commented in a joint statement:

This kind of practice only reduces the respect in which the law and the Administration are held . . . the growing distrust of the politically aware people has been further increased, and the degree of confidence felt in the motives of the protecting power has virtually vanished.

It was, in fact, a political manipulation of the law so barefaced as to be equalled only by Britain's retroactive validation of the recent elections in another tiny Protectorate, the Gambia, after the local courts had ruled them null and void.

Given the illiteracy of most Swazi — there was no broadcasting station in the country — and their political inexperience, it is of course quite possible that Sobhuza's party would have won the 1964 elections even if the political parties had had access to the tribal areas. This possibility must, however, remain hypothetical until elections are held under free conditions, preceded by a substantial period for electioneering and a thorough-going official campaign to persuade tribesmen that, whatever their chiefs might say about Sobhuza's supernatural powers, the ballot is secret and that therefore no one need fear victimization because of the way he or she chooses to vote. None of these conditions was fulfilled in the 1964 elections, and it is particularly difficult to understand why the British Government, after constitutional negotiations lasting three years, limited the electioneering period to only six weeks.

The Joint Council of Swaziland Political Parties planned to challenge in court the validity of the June elections. This challenge materialized and failed; the British authorities must ensure that the next elections do not repeat the failings of the old.

As, however, the 1964 elections are allowed to stand, the next step in the plan prepared for Sobhuza by Mr van Wyk de Vries, the South African Nationalist lawyer and reputed Broederbond member who is now a judge, will be taken, and Sobhuza will demand independence from the British Government, backed by his 'democratically elected' men in the Legislative Council. Mr de Vries, in drawing up the plan which Sobhuza has so far followed to the letter, foresaw with some glee that by the time this demand for independence was made there would probably be a Labour Government in Britain, for, as he observed, it would be particularly hard for the Labour Party to oppose a request for independence from a colonial people. In this Mr de Vries is right.

There is, too, a growing realization amongst thinking people abroad that the Westminster model of government may not be the best one for African countries, that it is Africans themselves who must – and in any case will – decide what is best for them. If they want a one-party State and a personality cult leader, then that, distasteful as Englishmen may find it, is their business.

There will be ample time in the future to reflect on whether Africans might have been more enamoured of democracy if they had been allowed to practise it earlier under colonial rule. Cer-

tainly if the Government of an independent Swaziland or Basutoland wished to restrict the liberty of the subject, it would not have
to pass any fresh legislation. It would suffice to take over the
powers previously held – and exercised by Britain's commissioners. Authoritarianism is no new story in Africa: it applies
wherever the white man has ruled or, to an even greater degree,
where he has settled.

It is here that we come to the nub of the present Swaziland
problem. Whilst it would clearly be an act of gross arrogance for
Britain to insist that the Swazi – or for that matter the Batswana
or Basuto – can only regain the right to run their own lives if
they undertake to run them on lines of which Britain approves,
Britain has a responsibility to ensure that at least independence
is restored under a truly representative form of government.

In Swaziland this means, first of all, that negotiations for independence must include representatives of the political parties
as well as members of the Sobhuza–Todd-dominated Legislative
Council, and, secondly, that before independence can be granted,
genuinely free elections must be held on a single voters' roll, with
universal adult suffrage and no seats reserved for any group, black
or white.

If such elections bring Sobhuza's men to power again, well
and good. The Swazi will have chosen, and their choice will have
to be respected, even if it means that they will become subjects of
one of Verwoerd's Bantustans.

There is, in fact, a real danger of this happening. The connexions between Sobhuza's Swazi National Council and Dr Verwoerd's disciples in South Africa cannot be denied, and those
between Swaziland's whites, led by Mr Carl Todd, and the
Republic's white racialists are patent.

When Dr Verwoerd made his 'offer' to 'guide' the Territories
to 'independence' as black States, with their whites exchanging
their land-holdings for Republican land and their local political
rights for votes in the Republic, Mr Todd accepted with haste on
behalf of Swaziland's whites. The leaders of the United Swaziland
Association have demanded that political refugees from the
Republic be barred from Swaziland, and have announced that they
will introduce measures in the Legislative Council to expel
refugees already in Swaziland and to prevent further ones from

entering. They also want to ensure the prohibition or expulsion of any immigrant who seeks to alter the 'traditional' relationship between white and black in Swaziland.

Quite clearly, the policy of 'racial federation' which the United Swaziland Association and the Imbokodo jointly espouse is a thinly veneered form of apartheid, in which representatives of each race would only meet the other to discuss matters of common interest.

There was, however, reason to think that the political parties, if they had maintained their new-found unity and if they had been assured of access to the electorate, could have greatly improved upon their poor showing in the 1964 elections. Their position would even now, be greatly strengthened if the British Administration did its clear duty in educating the Swazi in the secrecy of the ballot box and the limitations in the powers of their chiefs arbitrarily to dispossess them of land.

When Sobhuza held his so-called referendum on his complicated petition to the British Parliament in 1963, the political parties took no part and he had a completely free hand in organization. Moreover, the choice was presented as one between loyalty to Sobhuza or to Sir Brian Marwick, the then Resident Commissioner. In the event, some 10,000 Swazi predictably voted for Sobhuza and less than 100 against him. But in the 1964 elections, despite all obstacles in their way, the political parties altogether polled 13,471 votes against the Imbokodo's 79,683 on the national or common roll. With almost the same number of votes cast in each, the elections showed a very large advance on the 'referendum', and the Joint Council of Swaziland Political Parties was confident that, given free conditions, they could have done much better yet. On the 'rigged' 1964 showing, they would have had to convince a further 26,400 Swazi to gain a majority of votes next time. What Britain must do is ensure that every political party is given a fair chance to do so, under a non-racial constitution, and then to give Swaziland its independence.

13 The Politics of Independence

In the short time which remains to her in Basutoland, Bechuana-land, and Swaziland, Britain is faced with a number of crucial political and administrative problems which are common to all three Territories.

The greatest of these problems, of course, is the relationship of the Territories to South Africa, and more especially the question of refugees. Here, whilst Britain has commendably stood firm on allowing refugees temporary residence and transit through the Territories, she is making this conditional on absti-nence from local or neighbouring politics. Recent prosecutions by the Swaziland Administration of refugees who have spoken against apartheid show, however, just how restrictively these conditions can be interpreted by over-cautious British officials – or by South Africans acting in that capacity.

Much unease had also been aroused by the Prevention of Violence Abroad Proclamation which Britain introduced in all three Territories in 1963. This makes it an offence for anyone in the Territories to plan, aid, instigate or *incite* [my italics] an act of violence in any outside State which would also be an offence in the British Territory concerned. Indeed, the proclamation seems open to the widest interpretation, so that anyone making a speech calling for the overthrow of white supremacy could become liable to the maximum penalty of three years' imprison-ment or a £500 fine. Fortunately, a Swaziland magistrate has rejected part of this interpretation in a very important judgment, but the same point remains to be established in the other Terri-tories. Meanwhile, it seems clear that the British authorities are going very much further than they need or should in main-taining correct relations with South Africa.

With the exception of Sobhuza's men in Swaziland and the

pro-apartheid white settlers in Bechuanaland, the peoples of the Territories all wish to grant refuge to opponents of Dr Verwoerd's régime. Some of the political and tribal leaders are understandably worried that the more able and sophisticated amongst the South African refugees may present a challenge to their own position, and the British Government is fostering their least generous impulses by barring refugees from local politics. But whilst Britain retains authority over the Territories, it is up to her to provide an example of the widest possible tolerance and freedom. She should, under local law, allow free speech on all subjects to refugees from South Africa, or Moçambique and South West Africa, and she should repeal the Prevention of Violence Abroad Proclamation, replacing it with a simple prohibition on unauthorized armed training in the Territories.

The present restrictions become all the more disquieting when viewed against the close and continuing cooperation between the police in the Republic and those in the Territories, and the apparent failure of the British Government to make any protest against South Africa's arbitrary limitation of free air access to the Territories.

On 25 June 1963, the Lord Privy Seal, Mr Heath, was asked in the House of Commons what guarantees of free access by air to the High Commission Territories had been sought from the South African Government. Mr Heath replied: 'None. We already have satisfactory arrangements for access by air to the High Commission Territories.'

But in September 1963, the South African Government unilaterally issued a list of twenty-seven airfields in the Republic at which all aircraft flying to, from, or *between* the Territories must now land. The names of passengers and the purpose of their flight have to be submitted to the South African authorities. Any pilot disobeying the new regulations will lose his licence to land in South Africa and his company will be banned from operating there. As the charter flight firms operating in the Territories depend completely on South African facilities, the regulations make it practically impossible for refugees to move from Basutoland or Swaziland, and make it possible for Dr Verwoerd, whenever he wishes it, to cut Basutoland off by air from the outside world. Yet no word of protest has emerged from the British Government. It is disturbing, too, to learn* that Britain has given assurances to Dr Verwoerd that the broadcasting stations which are to be set up in each Territory will not broadcast political material considered to be 'hostile' by Dr Verwoerd; will limit their range so as to cover a minimum of South African territory; and will not compete with the Republic's state-owned Springbok Radio commercial network as an advertising medium. There is no need whatever for Britain to impose any such limitations on the Territories. Certainly the South African Government has not hesitated to let an opponent of British policies like Mr Carl Todd broadcast distinctly hostile propaganda over its network into Swaziland.

Britain could hardly permit the Territories to pursue actively hostile policy towards South Africa while she remains in control, and when the Territories are independent they may well, for reasons of self-interest and survival, wish to remain on the friendliest possible terms with their Big Brother, however much they may dislike the Republic's policies. In the meantime, however, there is no reason for Britain to lean over backwards in pandering to Republican susceptibilities.

Where the Territories have legitimate interests to safeguard or promote, Britain must, for as long as she retains control over their foreign relations, speak up on their behalf. If she fails to do so, she may permanently impoverish them. This will happen, for instance, to Basutoland if Britain allows South Africa to carry out its announced intention of using the waters of the Orange River as she pleases. Since almost all the major rivers in the Territories are international ones, permitting South Africa to get away with piracy towards Basutoland could create a precedent for further unilateral action by the Republic, affecting the water supplies of Bechuanaland and Swaziland. Indeed, South Africa had already announced plans for a dam building programme which would flood a considerable area of Swaziland.

While this was being written, the abolition of the High Commission for the three Territories was announced, which means that

* *Sunday Times*, Johannesburg, 11 August 1963.

the duality which bedevilled British representation in South Africa and the government of the Territories has ended at long last.

Her Majesty's Commissioner in each Territory, or the British Government Representative since its new elections, will now have direct authority and access to London, so that the responsibility for standing up to the South Africans on behalf of the Territories is now unmistakably that of the Colonial Office, not of a Foreign Office anxious to maintain good relations with the Republic.

It has been one of the tragedies of Britain's recent colonial history that the post of Colonial Secretary has rarely been given its proper importance. Instead, it has served as a brief station for politicians aspiring to high office, and rarely has this been more marked than in the past decade of Conservative Government in Britain. Colonial Secretaries have come and gone with bewildering speed – between 1961 and 1962 alone there were three – and only one, Mr Iain Macleod, displayed real sympathy for, and understanding of, Africans.

It is particularly unfortunate that the one who finally stuck in the post, Mr Duncan Sandys, has earned a reputation for taking the white man's side in Africa. He also has a record of implacable insistence on colonial 'solutions' which have promptly exploded in his face – and, much more importantly, in the faces of the colonial people on whom he has imposed them.

Coming to colonial affairs fresh from the Blue Streak missile fiasco at the Ministry of Defence, Mr Sandys fought hard to keep South Africa in the Commonwealth. He went on to fight for the continuation of the Federation of Rhodesia and Nyasaland, and effectively surrendered Britain's powers in Southern Rhodesia as a *quid pro quo* for the acceptance by its white minority of the constitution which he and Sir Edgar Whitehead hatched between them – and which today frustrates belated British attempts to prevent the slide of that country into racial violence. So disastrous, in fact, was the effect of Mr Sandys in central Africa that Mr Butler had to be summoned by Mr Macmillan to salvage what he could.

Fresh from this federal triumph in Africa, the Colonial and Commonwealth Secretary went on to create the ill-starred South

Arabian Federation. This is currently exploding, splattering blood and oil on its sands.

Shifting his sphere of operations, he then made history by retroactively validating an illegal election in the Gambia, and went on to impose a constitutional 'solution' on Zanzibar which has led to Communism obtaining its first foothold in Africa and the Commonwealth. British Guiana, Cyprus, Malta – the list can be extended right down to his last days of office, in which he endangered future relations between Zambia and Britain in order to save the British Government £7 million in a compensation deal over mineral rights.

One can hardly disagree with Mr Humphrey Berkley, the Conservative M.P., who recently criticized the Commonwealth Relations Office, which was the *alter ego* of Mr Sandys, for 'amateurism' in its diplomacy, and it is enlightening to be told* that when Mr Berkley spoke to C.R.O. officials about what he termed the 'calamitous' handling of the Zanzibar situation, they had given the 'unbelievable' answer that the Secretary of State liked to deal with one question at a time and had been busy with Cyprus [*sic*].

This answer would not be found so 'unbelievable' by political leaders or administrators in the Territories, whose 'urgent' files have languished for months and even years in the Secretary of State's ante-chamber while he has been busy with other, more immediately explosive, countries.

Mr Sandys has, of course, been asked to bear an enormous load of often intractable problems, but his wards have hardly benefited from his apparent refusal to delegate responsibility, his inability to deal with more than one problem at a time, or from his penchant for forcing through a quick 'solution' when he finally does bring his considerable energies and tough conference technique to bear on a given area.

Thus the Swaziland constitutional crisis, after being allowed to drag on for three years, was followed in a rush by elections under a constitution which, whilst it would inevitably have had to be imposed on one or other Swaziland faction, in fact was opposed by everybody except its creator. Now, having made history by retroactively validating an illegal election in the

* The *Guardian*, 30 July 1964.

Gambia, he has retroactively appeared to condone blatant illegalities in Swaziland's elections. In Basutoland, the goodwill which should result from the restoration of independence is today endangered by the humiliating and short-sighted 'self-government' conditions on which Mr Sandys insisted.

And whilst the Colonial Secretary is, to a very large extent, dependent for his budgets on the Chancellor of the Exchequer, there is no reason to suppose that Mr Sandys had fought very hard, if at all, for development funds for Basutoland, Bechuanaland, or even Swaziland. Thus the Morse Mission, in submitting a sort of top priority economic shopping list in 1960, urgently recommended the expenditure in the three Territories of £9.5 million over the next five years, *over and above* grants-in-aid and development already planned. This extremely modest total, said the mission, would make economic viability 'a near-certainty in the case of Swaziland, a reasonable probability in Bechuanaland and a possibility in Basutoland'.

The need for action was, however, urgent, for the mission felt that 'each Territory is in the position of a patient confronted with the choice between having an expensive operation, which would entail a long period of recuperation but offer a high chance of full recovery, and the alternative of lapsing into a state of chronic illness'.

But despite these warnings in 1960 and the small scale of recommended additional expenditure, the British Government had by the end of 1963 found only £1.2 of the £9.5 million recommended. £751,000 of this has gone to Swaziland, the least needy – but most profitable – of the Territories, and £516,000 of the £1.2 million total has been made available in the form of interest-carrying loans instead of the grants recommended by the mission.

Thus the British Government has not, in fact, found any significant funds at all for the development of the Territories, other than on loan terms with which they can ill afford to be burdened. No doubt, when the time comes to compensate British officials in Basutoland for loss of office or retirement, Britain will also saddle that little country with the repayment of funds generously lent it for that purpose.

It is, perhaps, hardly surprising that nothing has been heard of the £27 million for which Sir John Maud urgently asked by way of grants for the crucial years 1964–6. Yet British officials in the Territories are agreed that this £27 million is the absolute minimum that the three together would need if they were to have any chance of achieving economic survival and the political stability with which it is interwoven.

£27 million to be spent on three countries over three years is surely no excessive sum, representing only £3 million per country per year or less than £3 a year for every inhabitant of the Territories. Though there is a definite, and relatively low, limit to the amount of development capital which underdeveloped and largely pastoral countries can usefully absorb, it seems clear that more would be needed for each Territory if proper long-term economic planning were substituted for the *ad hoc* shopping lists which have hitherto passed for development plans.

Certainly if proper planning is to take place, the planners for each Territory will have to know in advance what funds they can count on for a period of several years. The present system by which the British Treasury doles out grants and loans in annual dollops has made even annual budgeting a guessing game, in which local officials try out an initial budget on London and then have to revise it when the Treasury lets them know how much of their original requests they will have to cut. In such a state of uncertainty, Swaziland has had to revise its next proposed development plan three times in the past year and was still without an approved plan at the time of writing.

As the Basuto so cogently argued in the financial proposals which Mr Sandys refused to discuss at the 1964 London conference, the only way in which financial responsibility can be learned and effective planning promoted is for Britain to commit herself in advance to definite block grants for budgetary and development aid over a period of years.

To this day, despite the urging of the Morse Mission, neither Swaziland nor Basutoland has an independent Development Secretary, and only Basutoland possesses the beginnings of a statistical service. The statistical field is only one example of several expensive and specialized technical services which the three Territories might well share, and the failure to establish one reflects the shoe-string budgets on which the High

Commissioner had to operate in the past. As a result, only the university in Basutoland has been developed as a common facility. If funds were available, the Territories could reduce their dependence on South African technical services by cooperatively developing their own. Such developments would also avoid the present politically dangerous and embarrassing dependence on South Africa's specialized police facilities such as ballistics and forensic medicine.

Aside from money, all three Territories have been starved for years of able and experienced economists, technicians of all sorts, and first-class administrators. Yet today, with the run-down of the former Colonial Service providing an invaluable reservoir of such men, many with a sympathetic understanding of modern Africa, the British Government has seen fit to appoint as its senior representatives several men cast in the old mould of paternalism and aloof pro-consular rule, who have promptly antagonized the progressive elements in the Territories and have given no sign of recognizing, let alone imaginatively tackling, their urgent social and economic problems. It is a sad footnote to over a decade of Tory Government.

When the Labour Party came to power in Britain late in 1964, probably the most imaginative immediate action taken by Mr Harold Wilson as Prime Minister was the creation of a Ministry of Overseas Development. Mrs Barbara Castle as its Minister (with Cabinet rank) was an outstanding choice. While absorbing the staff of the old Department of Technical Cooperation, with Sir Andrew Cohen coming in as top administrator, Mrs Castle's new ministry has attracted an important group of young and undogmatic economists, headed by Mr Dudley Seers, and other 'new frontier' specialists, some of whom are taking a special interest in the Territories. Despite the economic difficulties which it inherited, the Labour Government seems keen to step up aid expenditure.

Mr Wilson also separated again the Commonwealth Relations and Colonies portfolios, with Mr. Anthony Greenwood, able and intelligent, as Colonial Secretary. Under him, Mrs Eirene White, similarly talented, has as Parliamentary Under-Secretary been given special responsibility for the three Territories. That they are being taken seriously was demonstrated by the early tour she made of all three.

14 A Decent Finis

There is a great deal which Britain can still do to put its record right in the Territories, and not all of it centres on grants of British money. Even on the purely financial side, very little has so far been done to seriously interest and involve international bodies such as the International Development Agency in the Territories. On the planning and staffing level, bodies such as the United Nations' Economic Commission for Africa and its Extended Programme for Technical Assistance have yet to be brought properly into play, though there is every sign that they would be keenly interested. It is significant that Mr George Ivan Smith, the extremely able regional representative of U.N.E.P.T.A for southern and central Africa and personal representative of the United Nations Secretary-General, is taking a lively interest in the Territories. He is based on Lusaka, but a regional technical office is to open in Gaberones.

Nor has there been any attempt to involve the Commonwealth in the development of the Territories. A country like India could readily underwrite and absorb expanded production of wool and mohair in Basutoland; other Commonwealth countries could absorb Bechuanaland beef; and all could draw on their own experience in advising on rural development in the Territories. In today's world, there is no queue to distribute largesse to yet more underdeveloped and problematical countries. But the United Nations, its specialized agencies, and the Commonwealth countries would all be favourably disposed to helping Basutoland, Bechuanaland and Swaziland, exposed as they are by geography to the most despised régime in the world. What is needed is for these agencies, British and international, to be enlisted in a planned and large-scale way, instead of in the piecemeal and uncoordinated nibbling which has hitherto characterized British approaches for international aid.

An imaginative effort should also be undertaken by Britain to mobilize private as well as official sources of skilled manpower to help the Territories over the hump of their educational and social problems. One has yet, for instance, to hear of a real drive to recruit large numbers of volunteer teachers in Britain, the Commonwealth or America to help all three Territories tackle their pressing educational needs. It is surely unnecessary to repeat in the Territories the experience of Malawi, where only the advent of an African Government proved that international scholarships were readily available to remedy the lack of university graduates, a lack long cited as an obstacle to the grant of independence.

With approaching independence, the need for localizing all levels of the civil service in the Territories has become urgent, and here again international agencies and Commonwealth countries could help with training facilities. It is even more urgent in the Territories than it has been in east Africa that in each an efficient, contented and highly trained local police force be built up, loyal only to its own Government. In the streets of Mbabane, senior white police officers – there are no commissioned Swazi – can still be heard giving their orders in Afrikaans, and though this may facilitate cooperation with the political police of their South African homeland, it is hardly what Swaziland needs if it is rapidly to develop towards the independence and non-racialism which Britain has named as the twin objectives of her policy.

This is not, of course, to suggest that the many white South Africans who have, for reasons of economy, been recruited by Britain into the civil services of the Territories are automatically suspect. On the contrary, whilst some have brought the racial prejudices of their country with them, many others have rendered devoted and valuable service. But today, when Africanization and localization of the services is so important, it is particularly invidious to have white South Africans promoted to senior positions in services such as the police force. Where, in the event of active hostility between the Territories and the Republic, would their loyalty lie ? Mrs Barbara Castle, the Labour M.P., made a sensible suggestion recently when she urged that Territorial police officers who are South Africans be spared any such conflict by being transferred to some other area.

Similarly, the criticisms which have been made in this book of the colonial administrators in the Territories do not imply that their genuinely well-meant and sometimes arduous efforts to do their best for the Territories have been ignored. On the contrary. But what they have thought best and possible for the Territories has been conditioned by their own backgrounds, by the social apartheid which old-style colonial rule dictated, and by the refusal of the British Government in London to give them either the staff or the money that they needed.

Certainly much more could have been done than has in fact been achieved. But when one considers the continual frustration which has been the lot of the few thrusting and relatively able men who have made their careers in the Territories, it is surprising that any of them should have stuck it out at all. The real blame for past neglect and failure lies with successive British Governments. Not surprisingly, the Africans in the Territories are neither saints nor sinners, but ordinary people whose shortcomings from the viewpoint of a western 'go-getting' administrator would be enhanced by the traditionally valid pattern of their tribal lives.

In the old tribal days and ways, such cultivation as was undertaken was the responsibility of the women, the herding of cattle that of the young boys, and tribal administration, as well as fighting, the role of the men. The Calvinist obsession with work is no part of tribal make-up in Africa, and it would be a bold western executive who, contemplating his ulcers, could firmly say that he knows more about the good life than a tribesman in the Territories.

For many years, however, the tribal patterns have been changing or breaking up under the combined impact of the white man's rule and the modern world, and in many ways this could be of great benefit to those it affects. But the price that has to be paid is almost always a disproportionately large one, and it is time that it was realized more widely in the West how much value there is in the old African ways. Tribalism has become a dirty word to many well-meaning exponents of progress, and usually for excellent reason. But there is much within it, especially its sense of community and the responsibility of the group for the welfare of the individual, which modern societies have lost and sadly miss. The positive aspects of modern ways must be made available to the peoples of the Territories, who have shown clearly that they want them. But if they, or other African peoples, can find a method of fusing the best of our traditions and of theirs, they will have a great deal to teach us about meaningful living.

If there has in this book been more criticism of British than of African failings, it is because it has not lain with the African people of the Territories to decide how their countries should be run. It is the British who have ruled, and it is against their own professions of high principle that their record must be judged.

That record is, fortunately for Britain, not yet quite complete. Basutoland is, it is true, on the verge of independence and Bechuanaland and Swaziland are pushing close behind. No one can doubt any longer that Britain will in the near future restore to all three Territories their independence – or that world opinion would force her to do so if she became reluctant. But the real question is how well equipped she will leave them to stand on their own feet in a modern world which includes a hostile apartheid State on their borders.

Politically and physically, the Territories have little to fear from South Africa, and it is time that Britain in negotiating on their behalf over crucial issues realized that the very proximity of all three countries to South Africa is their strongest, and not their weakest, card. Dr Verwoerd is desperately sincere when he says that he wants them to be good neighbours, for if they decide to be anything else they could cause him a great deal of trouble. Their territorial integrity will certainly find ready guarantors in the Afro-Asian or Communist countries, if not in the United Nations itself, now that Britain has declined to act in this capacity after they become independent. Thus any physical aggression against the Territories by South Africa would at last provide the perfect justification for outside counter-intervention in the heart of South Africa.

Thus, politically, the United Nations, free Africa, or the Communist countries could enable the Territories to turn their weakness into a source of strength. It is Britain's ambivalence which has prevented this from happening so far.

Nor should it be overlooked that Dr Verwoerd is trying to pull off a triple confidence trick over Basutoland, Bechuanaland and Swaziland by boldly asserting that these British-ruled territories would be better off economically and could be independent politically if they became Bantustans. He is, in the first place, trying to obscure his failure to finance substantial development in his own Bantustans. Secondly, he is trying to cover up the sorry sham of the Transkei constitution, which leaves all significant control in his hands. And thirdly, by trying to sell the false idea that the present economic dependence of the Territories on South Africa cannot be significantly eased or broken, he is trying to disguise the fact that full political independence, if backed by continued British aid for development, promises to prove their strongest weapon against him.

Dr Verwoerd has been trying to use the Territories to throw a smoke-screen over his own failures. While he has grandly announced that £57 million would be spent on 250 scattered Bantustans in 1961–6, less than £4 million a year has in fact so far been spent. Against this, even the tragically inadequate British expenditure in the Territories seems handsome.

It would be a sad day, however, if Verwoerd's never-never Bantustans were to be used as the yardstick of British aid to Basutoland, Bechuanaland and Swaziland. The real and final test of British stewardship in these Territories will be whether she henceforth gives them sufficient development aid to enable them to realize whatever potential they have – and for Bechuanaland and Swaziland, at least, this potential is very considerable – to stand on their own feet economically, together with grants to balance their budgets until this development bears fruit. The sums involved are, in all conscience, small enough after the many decades of British neglect.

That all three Territories, and especially Basutoland, will remain vulnerable in some measure to economic warfare by South Africa is undeniable. In the event of international economic sanctions against South Africa, Basutoland in particular could hardly escape their common fate of being apartheid's hostages.

But the choice before them need not be that of becoming either Pan-African Outposts or Bantu Homelands. With every additional million pounds which Britain makes available to the Territories, their position *vis-à-vis* South Africa will be strengthened, and the lives of their people improved.

Professor Chandler Morse rightly stressed that the people of the Territories have 'the invaluable asset of wanting help only to help themselves'. If Britain is now spurred, even at this last hour, to give them that help freely and generously, then Dr Verwoerd will have done them – and Britain – a good turn.

In commenting on Verwoerd's challenge to Britain over the Territories, Sir John Maud, their former High Commissioner, said:

Before long Britain may find herself so placed that she can take an honourable discharge. She cannot do that yet. Until she can, we British taxpayers must insist on paying up at higher rates than we have paid so far – in annual grants to balance budgets and in development and welfare grants and loans. The momentum of recently increased spending *must* be maintained.

After the vexed problem of Southern Rhodesia is settled one way or another, as it must soon be, the Territories will be Britain's last direct responsibility in Africa. Above all, Basutoland, Bechuanaland, and Swaziland offer to Britain the chance, and that at a ludicrously low cost, to write a decent finis to her colonial history in Africa.

U.K. AID TO BASUTOLAND, BECHUANALAND AND SWAZILAND

(in units of £1,000)

	1945–6	1946–7	1947–8	1948–9	1949–50	1950–51	1951–2	1952–3	1953–4
BASUTOLAND									
Grant-in-Aid	–	–	–	–	–	–	–	–	–
D. & W. {Loans	–	2*	13*	23*	30*	2*	–	–	–
Grants	27	58	57	41	63	120	159	179	159
Research Grants	–	–	2	1	1	½	½	1	1
Exchequer Loans	–	–	–	–	–	–	–	–	–
BECHUANALAND									
Bamangwato Chieftainship	–	–	–	–	–	3	9	4	2
Grant-in-Aid	108	–	–	–	–	–	–	–	–
D. & W. {Grants	–	52	48	76	100	118	149	168	126
Research Grants	–	–	–	–	–	–	–	–	–
Exchequer Loans	–	–	–	–	–	–	–	–	–
C.D.C.	–	–	–	–	250	250	850	506	380
SWAZILAND									
Grant-in-Aid	193	–	–	7	70	5	–	–	–
D. & W. {Grants	–	66	85	51	117	158	146	121	125
Research Grants	–	–	1	–	–	–	–	–	–
Exchequer Loans	–	–	–	–	–	–	–	–	–
C.D.C.	–	–	–	–	250	929	769	544	345

	1954-5	1955-6	1956-7	1957-8	1958-9	1959-60 (Coalbrook Relief)	1960-61	1961-2	1962-3	1963-4
BASUTOLAND										
Grant-in-Aid	—	—	—	—	—	10 / 46	390	1,141	1,441	1,534
D. & W. Loans	169	135	228	221	164	219	123	500	454	253
D. & W. Grants	2	1	4	2	2	†	†	—	—	—
Research Grants	—	—	†	—	—	—	—	—	—	—
Exchequer Loans	—	—	—	—	—	—	—	255	115	40
BECHUANALAND										
Bamangwato Chieftainship	1	1	5	1	4	†	—	—	—	—
Grant-in-Aid	145	—	140	480	560	650	970	1,155	1,363	1,592
D. & W. Loans	—	235	472	386	246	266	171	410	497	463
D. & W. Grants	—	—	†	1	19	16	1	†	5	12
Research Grants	—	—	—	—	—	—	277	179	225	—
C.D.C.	75	—	—	—	195	95	95	70	—	—
SWAZILAND										
Grant-in-Aid	162	126	333	269	248	—	—	262	534	855
D. & W. Loans	—	—	6	13	13	414	339	819	454	267
D. & W. Grants	—	—	—	—	—	61	14	48	38	50
Research Grants	—	—	—	—	—	—	—	—	—	—
Exchequer Loans	—	—	—	—	—	200	780	440	276	331
C.D.C.	95	350	100	352	310	1,860	1,825	1,900	1,640	—

† = Under £500   — = Nil

* Converted to Grant 1954-5

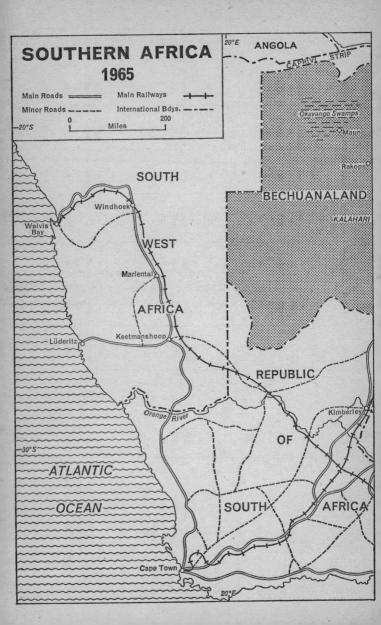

SOUTHERN AFRICA
1965

Main Roads ═══════ Main Railways ┼─┼─┼

Minor Roads ─ ─ ─ ─ International Bdys. ─ · ─ ·

0   Miles   200

20°S

20°E   ANGOLA

CAPRIVI STRIP

Okavango Swamps

Maun

Rakops

BECHUANALAND

KALAHARI

SOUTH

Windhoek

Walvis
Bay

WEST

Marlental

AFRICA

Lüderitz

Keetmanshoop

REPUBLIC

Orange River

Kimberley

30°S

ATLANTIC

OF

OCEAN

SOUTH   AFRICA

Cape Town

20°E

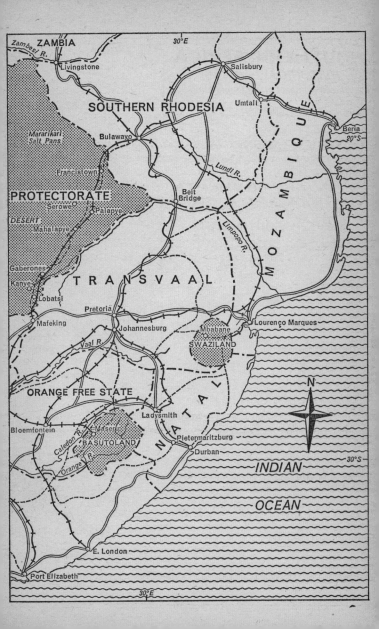

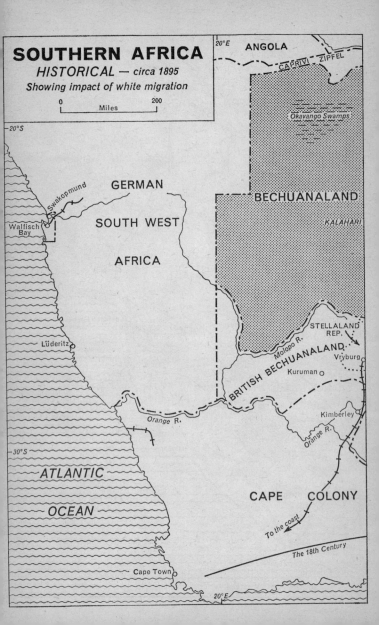

SOUTHERN AFRICA

HISTORICAL — circa 1895
Showing impact of white migration

0 — Miles — 200

20°E ANGOLA

CAPRIVI ZIPFEL

20°S

Okavango Swamps

GERMAN

BECHUANALAND

SOUTH WEST

KALAHARI

AFRICA

Swakopmund

Walfisch
Bay

STELLALAND
REP.

Molopo R.

Vryburg

BRITISH BECHUANALAND

Lüderitz

Kuruman O

Orange R.

Kimberley

Orange R.

30°S

ATLANTIC

CAPE   COLONY

OCEAN

To the coast

The 18th Century

Cape Town

20°E

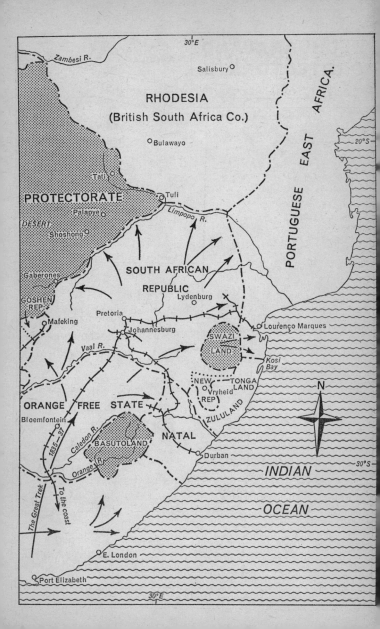

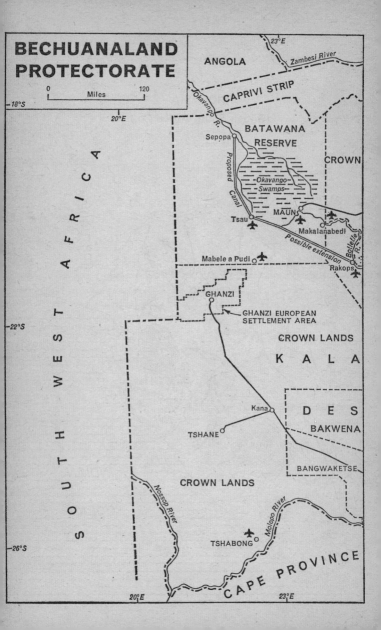

BECHUANALAND PROTECTORATE

Miles 0 — 120

18°S
20°E

ANGOLA

23°E
Zambesi River

CAPRIVI STRIP

Okavango R.

BATAWANA RESERVE

Sepopa

CROWN

Proposed Canal

Okavango Swamps

Tsau

MAUN

Makalanabedi

Possible extension

Bollette R.

Mabele a Pudi

Rakops

GHANZI

GHANZI EUROPEAN SETTLEMENT AREA

22°S

CROWN LANDS

K A L A

S O U T H   W E S T   A F R I C A

D E S

Kana

BAKWENA

TSHANE

BANGWAKETSE

CROWN LANDS

Nossop River

Molopo River

26°S

TSHABONG

C A P E   P R O V I N C E

20°E

23°E

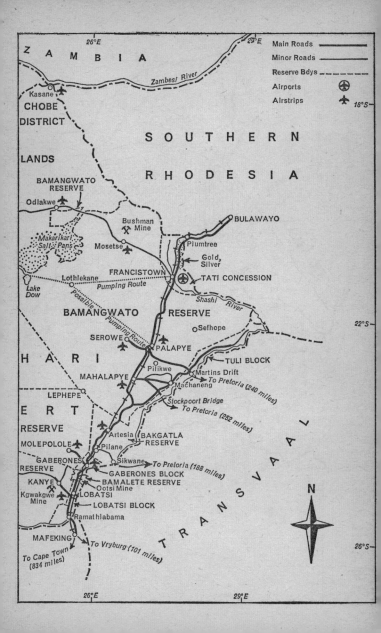

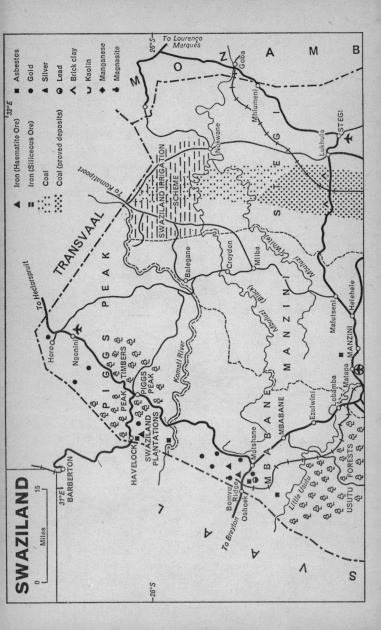

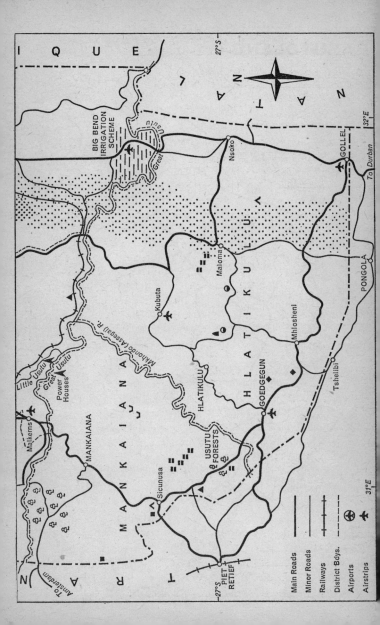

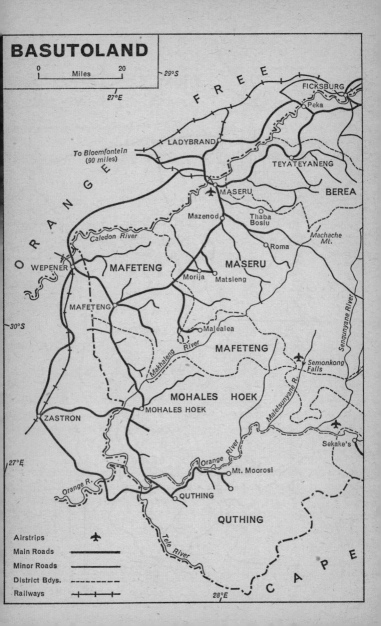

BASUTOLAND

0   Miles   20

29°S
27°E

FREE

FICKSBURG
Peka

To Bloemfontein
(90 miles)

LADYBRAND

TEYATEYANENG

O   R   A   N   G   E

MASERU

BEREA

Mazenod

Thaba
Bosiu

Machache
Mt.

Caledon River

Roma

WEPENER

MAFETENG

MASERU

Morija   Matsieng

MAFETENG

Malealea

MAFETENG

Senqunyane River

Makhaleng   River

Semonkong
Falls

MOHALES   HOEK

Maletsunyane R.

MOHALES HOEK

ZASTRON

27°E

Orange   River

Sekake's

Orange R.

Orange River   Mt. Moorosi

QUTHING

QUTHING

Tele River

30°S

Airstrips   ✈

Main Roads   ——————

Minor Roads   ——————

District Bdys.   - - - - - -

Railways   ┼┼┼┼┼┼

28°E

C   A   P   E

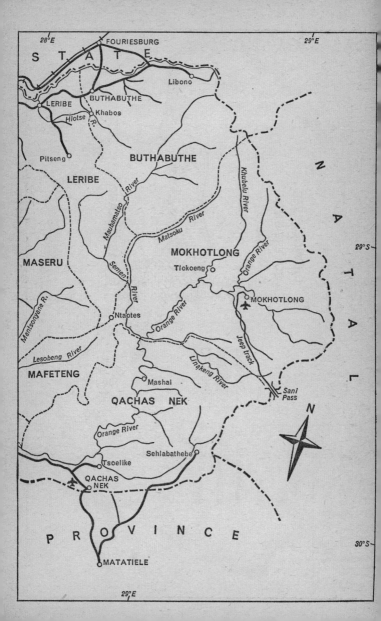

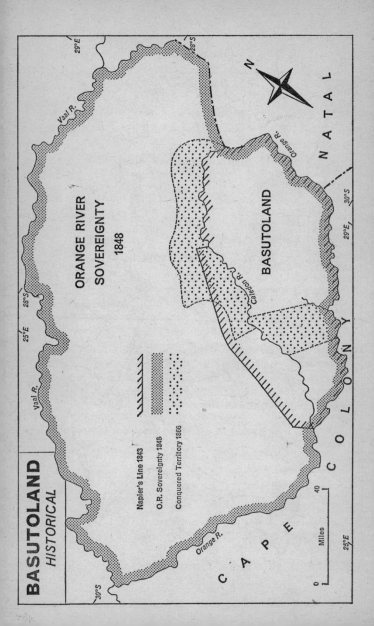

BASUTOLAND
HISTORICAL

ORANGE RIVER SOVEREIGNTY
1848

BASUTOLAND

NATAL

CAPE COLONY

Napier's Line 1843
O.R. Sovereignty 1848
Conquered Territory 1866

Vaal R.

Orange R.

Caledon R.

Miles
0   40

Bibliography

HISTORICAL

A History of South Africa, Social and Economic, C. W. de Kiewiet, O.U.P., 1941.

A History of Southern Africa, Eric A. Walker, Longmans, 1957.

The Fall of Kruger's Republic, J. S. Marais, O.U.P., 1961.

The Protectorates of South Africa; the question of their transfer to the Union, Margery Perham and Lionel Curtis, O.U.P., 1935.

Basutoland, the Bechuanaland Protectorate and Swaziland; History of discussions with the Union of South Africa, 1909–39. H.M.S.O., Cmd 8707, 1952.

The Republic of South Africa and the High Commission Territories, Lord Hailey, O.U.P., 1963.

The Cambridge History of the British Empire, Volume VIII: South Africa, Rhodesia and the Protectorates, C.U.P., 1936.

GENERAL

The New Boer War, Leonard Barnes, Hogarth Press, 1932.

Native Administration in the British African Territories, Part V, Lord Hailey, H.M.S.O., 1953.

An African Survey, revised 1956, Lord Hailey, O.U.P., 1957.

Time Longer Than Rope, Edward Roux, Gollancz, 1948.

Basutoland, Bechuanaland Protectorate and Swaziland: Report of an Economic Survey Mission, chairman: Chandler Morse. H.M.S.O., 1960.

Basutoland, Bechuanaland and Swaziland: An Economic Survey, Barclays Bank, D.C.O., 1962.

The High Commission Territories and the Republic of South Africa, G. V. Doxey. Chatham House Memoranda, Royal Institute of International Affairs, 1963.

Development in Africa: A Study in Regional Analysis with special reference to Southern Africa, L. P. Green and T. J. D. Fair, Witwatersrand University Press, 1962.

Economic and Social Consequences of Racial Discriminatory Practices Economic Commission for Africa, United Nations, 1963.

The High Commission Territories, Central Office of Information, London, 1963.

BIBLIOGRAPHY

Report on the Structure of the Public Services in Basutoland, Bechuana-
land and Swaziland, 1961, Sir Richard Ramage, High Commis-
sioner's Office, Cape Town, 1962.
Problem Territories of Southern Africa: Basutoland, Bechuanaland
Protectorate and Swaziland, Sir Charles Dundas and Hugh Ashton,
South African Institute of International Affairs, Cape Town, 1952.
An Economic Survey of the Colonial Territories, 1951, Vol. I: Central
Africa and the High Commission Territories, H.M.S.O., 1952.
United Nations: Reports of the Special Committee on the Situation
with regard to the Implementation of the Declaration on the Grant-
ing of Independence to Colonial Countries and Peoples; Reports of
the General Assembly; Progress of Non-Self-Governing Territories
under the Charter (April 1963, Volumes 1–5); etc.
Digest of Statistics, Colonial Office.
Sanctions and the High Commission Territories, R. M. Bostock, in
Sanctions against South Africa, ed. Ronald Segal, Penguin Books,
1964.
Proceedings of the Legislative Councils of Swaziland and Bechuanaland and of the Basutoland National Council.

BASUTOLAND

The Basuto, Hugh Ashton, O.U.P., 1952. (Ethnographical.)
The Rise of the Basuto, G. Tylden, Juta, Cape Town, 1950.
Basutoland Enquiry, Isobel Edwards, Africa Bureau, London, 1955.
Basutoland Medicine Murder, G. I. Jones, H.M.S.O., Cmd 8209, 1951.
Report on Constitutional Reform and Chieftainship Affairs, Maseru,
1958.
Report of the Basutoland Constitutional Commission. Maseru, 1963.
Basutoland Constitutional Conference, H.M.S.O., Cmd 2371, 1964.
Annual Reports, H.M.S.O., London; Departmental Reports, Maseru.

BECHUANALAND

The Bechuanaland Protectorate, A. Sillery, O.U.P., 1952.
The Tswana, I. Schapera, International Africa Institute, London, 1953.
Migrant Labour and Tribal Life: A Study of Conditions in the Bechuana-
land Protectorate, I. Schapera, O.U.P., 1947.
Native Land Tenure in the Bechuanaland Protectorate, I. Schapera,
Lovedale Press, South Africa, 1943.
The Harmless People, Elizabeth Marshall Thomas, Secker & Warburg,
1959.
Bechuanaland and South Africa, Tshekedi Khama, Africa Bureau,
London, 1955.
Tshekedi Khama, Mary Benson, Faber and Faber, 1960.
Ruth and Seretse: 'A Very Disreputable Transaction', John Redfern,
Gollancz, 1955.

Report of a mission to the Bechuanaland Protectorate to Investigate the Possibilities of Economic Development in the Western Kalahari, chairman A. Gaitskell, H.M.S.O., 1954.

Factors of Economic Development in the Okavango Delta, Darrell Randall, University of Chicago, 1957.

Report on the Establishment of a Legislative Council and Executive Council for the Bechuanaland Protectorate, Joint Advisory Council, Bechuanaland Government, 1959.

Bechuanaland Protectorate: Constitutional Proposals, H.M.S.O., Cmd 1159, 1960.

Bechuanaland Protectorate (Constitution) Orders 1960 and 1963; Basutoland, Bechuanaland and Swaziland (High Commissioner) Order 1963; Bechuanaland Royal Instructions 1963, H.M.S.O. (These give the pre-1965 Constitution.)

Bechuanaland Constitutional Proposal, H.M.S.O. Cmd 2378, 1964.

SWAZILAND

The Swazi, Brian Allan Marwick, O.U.P., 1940.

An African Aristocracy: Rank among the Swazi, Hilda Kuper, O.U.P., 1947

The Uniform of Colour: A Study of White–Black Relationships in Swaziland, Hilda Kuper, Witwatersrand University Press, 1947.

The Swazi: A South African Kingdom, Hilda Kuper, Holt, Rinehart and Winston, 1963.

Experiment in Swaziland, ed. by J. F. Holleman, Institute for Social Research, University of Natal, 1962.

Swaziland: Report on Constitutional Reform, D. V. Cowen, Swaziland Progressive Party, Mbabane, 1961.

Proposals for a Swaziland Constitution (with Reservations by Official Members). Government of Swaziland, 1962.

Swaziland Constitution. H.M.S.O., Cmd 2052, 1963.

SOME NEWS SOURCES

Press releases, bulletins and magazines published by the respective Information Officers of the Territories, available upon request.

Occasional publications and statements of political parties in the Territories.

The Times of Swaziland. A white-owned weekly newspaper, published in Mbabane.

The Friend. A white-owned and South African orientated daily newspaper, carrying news of Basutoland and published in Bloemfontein.

Africa Digest. A valuable digest of press reports and British parliamentary proceedings, published bi-monthly by The Africa Bureau, Denison House, Vauxhall Bridge Road, London SW1. 25 shillings per annum.

Index